The Letters of St. Paul

Beda Rigaux

The Letters of St. Paul
MODERN STUDIES

Editor and Translator
Stephen Yonick O.F.M., S.S.L.

FRANCISCAN HERALD PRESS
Chicago, Illinois 60609

THE LETTERS OF ST. PAUL: Modern Studies, by Béda Rigaux, translated from *Saint Paul et Ses Lettres*, Paris-Bruges, Desclee de Brouwer, 1962. Translator, Malachy J. Carroll; editor and translator, Stephen Yonick O.F.M., S.S.L. Library of Congress Catalog Card Number: 68-54395. Copyright 1968 by Franciscan Herald Press, 1434 West 51st Street, Chicago, Illinois 60609. Made in the United States of America.

NIHIL OBSTAT: Geron Fournelle O.F.M., *Censor Deputatus;* IMPRIMATUR: Rt. Rev. Msgr. Francis W. Byrne, *Vicar General, Archdiocese of Chicago.* July 30, 1968.

PREFACE
TO THE
ENGLISH EDITION

A diamond has many facets, each of which adds to its brilliance. To isolate one facet from the whole is not to know the diamond; but to encounter the full impact of all facets is to respond breathlessly to sheer beauty. Analogously, Pauline research has many facets, an awareness of which leads us to an even greater appreciation of the man and his message. No single bibliographical study has claimed to be complete, and understandably so; each has its own contribution to make, from A. Schweitzer's *Paul and His Interpreters* (1912) to E. Earle Ellis's *Paul and His Recent Interpreters* (second printing, 1967). Nor does this volume of Rigaux claim to be complete. However, by his concentration on literary and historical research, Rigaux himself contributes to the Pauline bibliographical complex. It is with a feeling of accomplishment that we have been able to play some role in introducing this volume to the English-speaking world.

Concerning the translation, some preliminary observations are in place: First of all, relative to the amount of information at our disposal, we have a few additions to the footnotes by indicating English translations of some European works to which the author refers. The more lengthy additions are indicated as

v

a *Translator's Note*. Only in two instances in the *Epilogue* does this happen in the principal text. Secondly, we have transcribed the Greek and Hebrew citations simply and without sophisticated diacritical marks. Thirdly, the list of abbreviations has been expanded considerably from that appearing in the original French edition. Finally, we are grateful to Geron Fournelle for checking the manuscript and for providing additions to the references.

STEPHEN YONICK
St. Louis, Missouri

CONTENTS

Contents

INTRODUCTION

Professor Rudolf Schnackenburg studied the present stage of research on St. Paul's theology in the first volume of *Studia Neotestamentica*: *Subsidia*. We propose to provide an introduction to the historical and literary problems as they stand today.

First and foremost, we must realize that a variety of opinions exist in the field of contemporary exegesis. The historian who decides to study the thought and work of St. Paul already has his roots in certain philosophical and theological contentions. Such commitments, which he had priorily made because of personal preference, will exert an influence on his judgments. Because of these circumstances, we deem it imperative to present some classification of the various theories. A systematic analysis of the divergent theories will enable us to come to closer grips with the actual problem, to view these theories in their general perspective, and to evaluate their relative truth. From all this, certain important consequences will follow concerning the general nature of the historical method and the task of scientific exegesis.

Secondly, we will present a survey on the biographies of Paul which flowed from the pens of both Catholic authors and the Protestants alike. This survey will provide a working foundation for an examination of two historical problems, which capture the utmost attention of contemporary criticism, namely, the conversion and apostolate of Paul, and the chronology of his activities. The problem of Paul's conversion and apostolate is related to the theological facet of his own existence. Such a relationship cannot possibly be overlooked. For the conversion-event brands the personality of the Apostle in its most authentic depths. Moreover, the problem of the chronology of Paul's apostolate is of no less importance. What decisions are made on this point will determine to a great extent to which dates the Letters are to be assigned, as well as the possible evolution of Paul's thought. Due to the fact that there are so many opinions, together with studies which are important, it is more imperative than ever not only to present the results of such studies, but also to point out those problems which as yet have not been resolved. In that respect we hope to present as adequately as possible the complex of intellectual activity. We shall pay particular attention to the relationship between Acts and Galatians, for once again we encounter here a cardinal point which has repercussions on the career of the Apostle.

Thirdly, we have deliberately avoided an *Introduction* to the Letters when we discuss the problems of literary criticism. There are many studies which cover such questions. We shall merely refer the reader to these books. What concerns us in such studies are the contemporary views and opinions on the authenticity and unity of the Letters. These key positions constitute the foundation for interpretations of the texts. Furthermore, we shall attempt to be original by synthesizing all available data concerning the various "forms" which are present in Paul's writings. Up to the present time, such data has been scattered throughout a veritable mountain of commentaries and monographs. To deal adequately with such an enterprise would require an entire volume. We merely intend to open up new avenues in this regard by means of our initial pursuit. By making available what has been proposed up to the present time, we hope to indicate what method would seem apt as a tool for the contemporary student in further research.

Finally, because of the nature of this collection, we shall have to include the Letter to the Hebrews. This composition is more in tune with Pauline thought than any other document in the entire New Testament. After our studies on St. Paul, a presentation of the problems of this Letter is indeed in place.

The very nature of our work demands that we evaluate the studies to which we refer. Frequently, this aspect of our study is facilitated by the critiques which each author makes of his predecessors. However, each author is expected generally to carry out his work according to his own methodology. Whatever principles we have accepted as accurate are readily recognizable. First of all, we must have an exact knowledge of the nature of the problem through consultation of the more important studies. We would like to observe here that this elementary rule of scientific method has been violated too often. Despite the resources which are easily available to all in basic bibliographies, authors of different surroundings or of different countries are still inadequately acquainted with each other's works. Secondly, we firmly believe in attributing prime value to problems of philosophy and of literary criticism. Especially in the latter case, a purely personal judgment, which has no support in objective reasoning, too often leads to groundless hypothetical constructs or to false a priori pronouncements. Finally, we must insist on this point, namely, that work with historical and literary problems merely constitutes a preliminary step towards a complete reconstruction of Paul's personality, which was influenced by the very movement it embodied. Our judgment on the importance or unimportance of the various studies is relative to the extent to which they helpfully reveal the personality and theology of the Apostle.

We wish to express our deepest gratitude to Canon É. Massaux, Professor at the Catholic University of Louvain, for his most valuable assistance. For us, his comments proved to be highly useful and his help in correcting the proofs invaluable. We offer similar thanks and appreciation to our colleague, Father J.-P. Rézette, Professor of Theology at Chant-d'Oiseau.

ABBREVIATIONS

I. Periodicals, etc.:

AJ	*Acta Jutlandiac* (Copenhagen).
AmiCl	*L'Ami du Clergé* (Langres).
AMNSU	*Arbeiten und Mitteilungen aus d. neuteset. Seminar z. Uppsala.* (Uppsala).
AnglTR	*Anglican Theological Review.* (Evanston, Ill.).
AntJud	*Antiquitates Judaicae,* Flavius Josephus.
AusCR	*Australasian Catholic Record,* (Sydney).
BA	*Biblical Archaeologist,* (New Haven).
BCH	*Bulletin de Correspondence Hellénique* (Paris).
Bell.Jud.	*De Bello Judaico,* Flavius Josephus.
BETS	*Bulletin of the Evangelical Theological Society* (Wheaton, Ill.).
BEvT	*Beiträge zur Evangelischen Theologie* (Munich).
Bib	*Biblica* (Rome).
BiKi	*Bibel und Kirche* (Stuttgart).
BiLit	*Bibel und Liturgie* (Klosterneuburg).
BJRL	*Bulletin of the John Rylands Library* (Manchester).
BL	*Bibel und Leben* (Düsseldorf).
BS	*Bibliotheca sacra* (Dallas, Tex.).
BSt	*Biblische Studien* (Freiburg).
BW	*Biblical Word.*
BZ	*Biblische Zeitschrift* (Paderborn).
CanJT	*Canadian Journal of Theology* (Toronto).
Cath	*Catholica* (Münster).
CB	*Cultura Biblica* (Segovia).
CBQ	*Catholic Biblical Quarterly* (Washington, D.C.).
ChQR	*Church Quarterly Review* (London).
CIL	*Corpus Inscriptorium Latinarum* (Berlin).
ColFrN	*Collectanea Franciscana Neerlandica.*
ColBG	*Collationes Brugenses et Gandavenses* (Bruges).

ColMech	*Collectanea Mechlinensia* (Malines).
ComV	*Communio Viatorum* (Prague).
ConNT	*Coniectanea Neotestamentica* (Uppsala).
ConTM	*Concordia Theological Monthly*, (St. Louis, Mo.).
CQ	*Crozer Quarterly.*
DBS	*Dictionnaire de la Bible, Supplément.*
DTC	*Dictionnaire de la Théologie Catholique.*
DViv	*Dieu Vivant.*
Er	*Eranos* (Göteborg).
EstBib	*Estudios Bíblicos* (Madrid).
EstEc	*Estudios Eclesiásticos* (Madrid).
ETL	*Ephemerides Theologicae Lovanienses* (Louvain).
EvQ	*Evangelical Quarterly* (London).
EvT	*Evangelische Theologie* (Munich).
Exp	*The Expositor* (London)
ExpT	*Expository Times* (Edinburgh).
FrLA	*Studii Biblici Franciscani, Liber Annus* (Jerusalem).
GCS	*Die griechischen christlichen Schriftsteller der ersten drei Jahrhunderte* (Leipzig: 1897 -).
GlD	*Gloria Dei.*
GV	*Glauben und Verstehen* (Tübingen).
Herm	*Hermathena.*
HibJ	*Hibbert Journal* (Liverpool).
Hist.Eccl.	*Historia Ecclesiastica,* Eusebius.
HL	*'t Heilig Land* (Nijmegen).
HomBib	*Homiletica en Biblica* (Hague).
HSS	*Heilige Schrift und Seelsorge.*
HTR	*Harvard Theological Review* (Cambridge, Mass.).
IEJ	*Israel Exploration Journal* (Jerusalem).
Int	*Interpretation* (Richmond, Va.).
ITQ	*Irish Theological Quarterly* (Maynooth).
JBL	*Journal of Biblical Literature* (Philadelphia, Pa.).
JBR	*Journal of Bible and Religion* (Bethlehem, Pa.).
JJS	*Journal of Jewish Studies* (London).
JRel	*Journal of Religion* (Chicago).
JTS	*Journal of Theological Studies* (Oxford).
LQ	*The Lutheran Quarterly* (St. Paul, Minn.).
LTK	*Lexikon für Theologie und Kirche.*
LXX	*The Septuagint Version of the Old Testament.*
MTZ	*Münchener Theologische Zeitschrift* (Munich).
NieuTS	*Nieuwe Theologische Studiën* (Haarlem).
NKZ	*Neue Kirchliche Zeitschrift* (Leipzig).
NRT	*Nouvelle Revue Théologique* (Louvain.)
NT	*Novum Testament* (Leiden).
NIA	*New Testament Abstracts* (Weston, Mass.).
NTD	*Das Neue Testament Deutsch.*
NTS	*New Testament Studies* (Cambridge, England).
NTT	*Norsk Teologisk Tidsskrift* (Oslo).

NuCir	*Numismatic Circular.*
PG	*Patrologia Graeca* (Migne).
PL	*Patrologia Latina* (Migne).
RB	*Revue Biblique* (Jerusalem).
RDT	*Revue Diocésaine de Tournai* (Tournai).
RE	*Review and Expositor* (Louisville, Ky.).
RevQ	*Revue de Qumran* (Paris).
RGG	*Die Religion in Geschichte und Gegenwart* (Tübingen).
RH	*Revue Historique.*
RHE	*Revue d'Histoire Ecclésiastique* (Louvain).
RHPR	*Revue d'Histoire et de Philosophie Religieuses* (Paris).
RHR	*Revue de l'Histoire des Religions* (Paris).
RQ	*Restoration Quarterly* (Houston, Tex.).
RScR	*Revue des Sciences Religieuses* (Strasbourg).
RSPhTh	*Revue des Sciences Philosophiques et Théologiques* (Paris).
RSR	*Recherches de Science Religieuse* (Paris).
RTh	*Revue Thomiste* (Paris).
RTP	*Revue de Theologie et de Philosophie* (Lausanne).
RuchBL	*Ruch Biblijny i Liturgiczny* (Krakow).
SBJ	*La Sainte Bible de Jérusalem* (Paris).
SBN	*Studi Bizantini e Neoellènici* (Rome).
SBT	*Studies in Biblical Theology.*
SC	*Studia Catholica* (Aarhus).
ScotJT	*Scottish Journal of Theology* (Edinburgh).
ScrH	*Scripta Hierosolymita.*
Scrip	*Scripture* (Edinburgh).
ScuolC	*Scuola Cattolica* (Milan).
SEA	*Svenk Exegetisk Arsbok* (Uppsala).
SOr	*Studia Orientalia* (Helsinki).
SP	*Studia Paulina.*
ST	*Studia Theologica* (Lund).
SupplNT	*Supplements to NT* (Leiden).
SymBUp	*Symbolae Biblicae Upsalienses* (Uppsala).
SZ	*Stimmen der Zeit* (Munich).
TBl	*Theologische Blätter* (Leipzig).
TGl	*Theologie und Glaube* (Paderborn).
Th	*Theology* (London).
ThS	*Theologische Studien* (Zollikon).
ThWNT	Kittel, *Theologisches Wörterbuch zum NT.*
TLZ	*Theologische Literaturzeitung* (Leipzig).
TQ	*Theologische Quartalschrift* (Tübingen).
TR	*Theologische Revue* (Münster).
TRu	*Theologische Rundschau* (Tübingen).
TS	*Theological Studies* (Baltimore).
TSK	*Theologische Studien und Kritiken* (Gotha).
TTij	*Theologisch Tijdschrift* (Oslo).
TV	*Theologia Viatorum* (Berlin).
TZ	*Theologische Zeitschrift* (Basel).

VC	*Verbum Caro* (Neuchâtel).
VD	*Verbum Domini* (Rome).
VictI	*The Victorian Institute.*
VSp	*Vie Spirituelle* (Paris).
WW	*Wissenschaft und Weisheit* (Düsseldorf).
ZEvE	*Zeitschrift für Evangelische Ethik* (Gutersloh).
ZKG	*Zeitschrift für Kirchengeschichte* (Stuttgart).
ZKT	*Zeitschrift für Katholische Theologie* (Innsbruck).
ZNW	*Zeitschrift für die Neutestamentliche Wissenschaft* (Berlin).
ZRG	*Zeitschrift für Religions- und Geistesgeschichte* (Marburg).
ZTK	*Zeitschrift für Theologie und Kirche* (Tübingen).
ZWT	*Zeitschrift für Wissenschaftliche Theologie* (Frankfurt).

II. Books of the Bible:

A. Old Testament:

Gn	Jgs	Neh	Prv	Jer	Jl	Hb
Ex	Ru	Tb	Eccl	Lam	Am	Ze
Lv	1-2 Sm	Jdt	Ct	Bar	Ob	Hag
Nm	1-2 Kgs	Est	Wis	Ez	Jon	Zech
Dt	1-2 Chr	Jb	Sir	Dn	Mi	Mal
Jos	Ezr	Ps(s)	Is	Hos	Na	1-2 Mc
		Ps.Sol.(LXX)				

B. New Testament:

Mt	Jn	1-2 Cor	Phil	1-2 Tm	Heb	1-3 Jn
Mk	Acts	Gal	Col	Ti	Jas	Jude
Lk	Rom	Eph	1-2 Thes	Phlm	1-2 Pt	Ap

III. Qumran, Dead Sea Scrolls:

IQS	Rules from Qumran community from the first cave.
1QH	Hymns from 1Q.
IQM	Rules of Sacred Warfare from 1Q.

The Letters of St. Paul

Chapter I

INTERPRETATION OF PAUL
IN
CONTEMPORARY EXEGESIS

A cursory glance at the literary output, whether in book or monograph form, that is devoted to the New Testament, reveals that, in recent years, exegetes, historians, and theologians have concentrated their interest more in the Synoptics and Johannine literature than the Pauline documents. (1) There have certainly been some important works on the Apostle, (2) which we shall encounter shortly. Whoever has delved into this matter would not have a low estimation of it, nor would he consider the topic uninteresting. We believe that the shift of emphasis in scriptural research can be explained by a number of causes. It seems that form-criticism had stirred up a revival in studies concerning Jesus and the primitive community. At the same time, criticism had rediscovered the Gospel of John. Besides, in all of these endeavors, the question arose whether the exegete should become involved in an existentialistic interpretation of the documents. The *Römerbrief* of K. Barth did draw attention to Paul; however, the *Johannes-evangelium* of R. Bultmann was more influential in attracting the concern of the exegetes. On the other hand, the discoveries at Qumran had monopolized most endeavors for almost ten years.

Present interest in Paul should be evident. His Letters, at least the major ones, are universally recognized as authentic. By way of contrast with the anonymous texts assembled in the Synoptics, or even for that matter, in both the Gospel and Apocalypse of John, according to the opinion of some critics, — the Letters of Paul are the expression of a single personality and the products of genuine creativity. These literary productions enable us to probe the thoughts of so personal an author, to perceive the genesis and quality of his thought-patterns, to detect the contours and the course of his speculations, and to comprehend the elaboration and flowering of his synthesis. His is the most conspicuous figure among all the inspired writers — the servant of Christ Jesus, who was called to be an apostle and set apart to announce the Good News (Rom. 1, 1). The Letters which he wrote between 50 and 60 A.D. express an enduring experience, and betray a personal interpretation of facts and of the faith. Such experience and interpretation have their parallels in the lives of others, but those of Paul can at least claim the advantage of having been the first to be set down in written form. On the other hand, would we really do justice to the experience and interpretation of Paul by stating that such happenings are paralleled in the lives of other authors? For they not only already represent a stage of achievement, but additionally offer a well-defined chronological point of departure, namely a period of some twenty years after the death of Christ. Now that New Testament studies are discovering the underlying literary, historical, and doctrinal currents of Christian origins, whose personality and thought could more effectively clarify the continuity and discontinuity of Christianity in relation to Judaism, the elaboration of the kerygma and of the parenesis or moral exhortation, the clash between Judaeo-Christianity and Hellenic-Christianity, the initial features of cult, polemic, and ecclesial organization? Who could better unveil the genuine originality of the new religion and of the new man more effectively than Paul? (3)

In a book entitled *Paulus*, H. J. Schoeps wrote: "The Church was not in any position to understand such a personality in its totality."(4) We do not intend to glamorize the Jewish savant over and above the Church. On the one hand, we can only repeat what is stated in 2 Pt. 3,16, namely, that, in the Letters of St. Paul,

"There are some things in them hard to understand." On the other hand, judgments of this kind provide a tempting invitation for further research into the following questions: Is it impossible to relate one area of the Pauline corpus with others due to peripheral asperities? Or did not the revelation which Paul received, a revelation which he profitably scrutinized and pondered, represent something over and beyond that which his contingently imperfect formulas could not express except as through a glass darkly? Do not such expressions elicit more than what they define — statements which are made with certainty, but which do not expose the reality shackled with words? More than words which are conditioned by history, more than the meeting place of dependencies and influences, more than the sum total of the Jewish and Greek worlds, would it not be the richness of the *reality* itself, as Paul saw, expressed, and exalted it, which still poses the essential question, despite all research: Is the Lord Jesus whom Paul had announced our Lord Jesus? Is He mine?

Art. 1. The Rise of Schools of Exegesis

For more than a century, Ferdinand Christian Baur exerted decisive influence on the interpretation of the Pauline Epistles — an influence whose persistence many authors recognize. (5) Baur's goal was to disengage any study of Paul from the framework of the dogmatic and orthodoxy of the Protestants. In this manner, he inaugurated a new approach by introducing a fresh evaluation. According to his view, Pauline research properly belongs to the historical sphere. From the very first, the Epistles are subject to a twofold scrutiny. Each composition has a purpose and a function; every thought is as it were a tributary of the main stream subjected to the law of evolution. The literary productions of Paul are subject to the very same laws. However, such a judgment on the part of the historian actually appears to be subjected to another and even more categorical law: Baur relinquishing the orthodoxy of the Protestants, only to embrace Hegelian philosophy. History must be functionally dialectic. The principle governing the evolutionist interpretation must be rediscovered, and recourse must be had to the three Hegelian principles of thesis, antithesis, and synthesis. In our case, the terms of the Hegelian dialectic correspond to Judaism, Hellenism, and Catholicism. Whatever contradicts such movement must be thought of as suspect. If any of the writings, traditionally accepted as flowing from Paul's pen, would upset this pattern in any way whatsoever, then one would have to regard such compositions as unauthentic. In Baur's opinion, Paul wrote only the four major Letters. These are the general views of the Tübingen School.

The disciples of Baur quickly modified his philosophical, historical, and literary positions, although his spirit continued to linger. While his successors directly depended on him, but from different viewpoints, they gradually reduced religion to a moral law, and the religious fact to a psychological process. Their positions were now too remote from the general thinking of the Tübingen School to be considered as having any part to play in the latter. Such positions in turn were fundamental to the synthesis of the so-called Liberal School, whose most qualified representatives were E. Reuss, K. Holsten, O. Pfleiderer, and H. J. Holtzmann.

The Hegelian "mind" was diluted in a "synthesis," which simultaneously invoked the influences of historical and psychological factors. Pfleiderer and Holtzmann turned to Greece in order to find an explanation for the origin of Paulinism. They abandoned Baur's attribution of a "system" to Paul since such a conception was too subjective, and hardly in accord with facts and texts. Rather, in order to arrive as closely as possible to the real Apostle, they noted the diverse currents, conflicting concepts, and the various levels of thought. Thus, they deviated from Hegelianism, not to return to orthodoxy, but rather to establish themselves in a positivistic context wherein the enthusiastic admiration of great men and strong personalities is of preponderant value. What characterized the predominant spirit at the turn of the century was a concern for the renewal of history by means of fresh acquisitions. Through the discovery and publications of papyri, ostraca, and inscriptions, philological studies had acquired new dimensions. The usual conception of Biblical Greek had given way to what is now known as the *koine*. E. von Dobschütz (6) and A. Deissmann (7) are two great authorities who attempted to sculpture a new Paul from the sum total of symbols, expressions, events, and sentiments. Because of their efforts, an emphasis on perspective had given these factors proper status within the contemporary religious milieu. According to Deissmann, Paul appears to be primarily the author of a new mystery and a new cult, both of which were strongly influenced by Greece. Generally speaking, he tends to reduce a message primarily supernatural and mystical to a humanism beset with spiritual problems. The latter are merely relegated to the periphery. At the end of his book, *Saint Paul* (8), Renan had already displayed such an attitude. The same position is fundamental to the many volumes of the old editions of the *Meyers-Kommentar* during the first years of the *ZNW*, as well as in the major syntheses of Pauline history and theology, which were published before 1914 and even later. From these works, Goguel gleaned many of the conclusions which characterize his own work. Loisy is much too eclectic for any suitable categorization. However, it would be unfair to judge this epoch only on the basis of its deficiencies. The historical contribution, philosophical research, literary critique, and some aspects of the synthesis of this epoch are still worthy of attention and consideration.

From the beginning of the century, there were two movements known as the School of the History of Religion (*Religionsgeschichtliche Schule*) (9) and the Eschatological School (10), which do not require any detailed presentation here since both are only too familiar. The development of these two Schools was either parallel with the output of the Liberal School, or distinctly antagonistic. Each of the two Schools in its own way contributed much towards the development of a truly new synthesis, without adhering to universally accepted rules or imperatives.

The first School, known as the *Religionsgeschichtliche Schule*, recognized what it considered the centrally important Pauline "mystique." It classified the religion of the Apostle along with the mystery religions. Such a perspective gave rise to important evaluations. Paul and Jesus were compared; in fact, Wrede did not hesitate to place the disciple above the Master. The Incarnation, the Trinity, life, grace, and the Sacraments, became the articulations of Pauline thought. All antiquity was excavated, and Paul's thought was reconstructed with an enthusiasm not lacking in disdain for former positions. Unfortunately, exaggerations compromise the most brilliant pieces of research. One can hardly classify such scholars as W. Wrede, H. Dietrich, G. A. Anrich, W. Bousset, F. Cumont, and R. Reitzenstein, with a single tag simply because of the fact that they differ qualitatively one from the other. (11) For the men of my generation, they were the great teachers of the youth. Even today, their works are indispensable references. (12) Reitzenstein could be accused of extravagance. Nonetheless, his principal work has not been superseded. Moreover, what student does not still use the *Kyrios Christos* of Bousset, or the *Religions Orientales* of Cumont? (13)

The second School is no less *religionsgeschichtlich* than the first; however, it does assume a different form. A. Schweitzer was its founder and teacher. (14) Characterized at times by a harsh criticism of the Liberal School and by an equally positive rejection of any dependence on the mystery religions, the eschatologism of Schweitzer, presented at first in relation to Jesus, was later extended to Paul in two less brilliant works. Schweitzer assumed the positions of W. Wrede, R. Kabisch, and M. Brückner, (15) by emphasizing Paul's dependence on Jewish apocalyptic and eschatology. Paul expected the revelation of the Son of Man and the end of the present era. At the beginning of his career, he entertained the same eschatological illusions as Jesus and the first disciples. In his book on the mystique of Paul, Schweitzer attempted to explain how it was that, since the immediate end of the world had not happened, the eschatological expectation was transformed into a belief in a super-nature-existence. Such new existence *in Christo* and through the Spirit necessitated a sacramental doctrine on Baptism and the Eucharist. Along such lines of thought, Schweitzer felt that he had reinstated Paul into his original milieu, and had opened up to Hellenism a zone of influence which properly belonged to it. (16)

It is hardly possible to characterize the movement of contemporary ideas without reference to these positions, which are already dated and well known. In the course of his book, H. J. Schoeps briefly recalled these positions and included a discussion on more recent opinions. W. G. Kümmel scarcely provided the means whereby one could go beyond the usual state of the question. We should like to present our evaluation as to what

extent recent contributions have profoundly altered the picture. (17)

Art. 2. Reaction to the Schools

By way of introduction, we should like to assemble some
declarations which appear to be basic and axiomatic to contemporary exegetes.

1. Paul can be known and evaluated only on the basis of
his Letters. The Acts, of course, present a problem in itself. It
would be a mistake to interpret the Letters in the light of the
Acts: The contrary would appear to be methodically more pro-
ductive. (18)

2. To continue to speak of Schools is most—difficult. As
always, there are today two basic types of interpretation: The
one involving belief; the other which flows from disbelief. One
could not substantiate whether the scientific method of the one is
superior to that of the other. Everyone involved in research certainly stakes his claims on the historical method, except for
the well-known, but yet remarkable method of K. Barth, and the
no less obvious method of those theologians among the Catholics
and the Protestants, who have wandered into the exegetical
profession. Furthermore, all betray a marked concern for the
history of religions in their philosophical, literary, and historical
research, even though in different degrees. Finally, all agree that
the eschatological problem does constitute one of the nuclei of
Pauline religion, although it remains to specify precisely in
what sense. Therefore, at this point, we must disentangle the
skein of thought.

3. For most authors, a reconstruction of the historical
Paulinism, that is to say, of a history of facts and doctrines, is
partial and deficient. As with Baur, they have recourse to a
principle of interpretation which, in the light of their respective
belief or lack thereof, orientates the direction in their application
of approved methods of historical science, for the contemporary
interest lies in Paul as a theologian. (19) The characteristic knowledge of his message consists in the original deposit concerning
God, man, and the relationships between man and God. There
is no neutral Paul, just as in textual criticism there is no neutral
text. Indeed, there never has been such. Each critic may claim

freedom from prejudice, but not from presuppositions. (20) In his work, he employed hypothesis to attempt a reconstruction. Since Hegelianism is a thing of the past, and since Liberalism is basically unfair, and since the compartmentalized and exclusive reliance on the mystery religions or on the apocalyptic or rabbinic Judaism do not exhaust the gist of the texts, other avenues must be explored. The exegesis of the Epistles has been nourished in many ways: For R. Bultmann and his disciples, it is the dialectic. for K. Barth, it is an interpretation which is characteristically Kantian and Calvinist; as for P. Althaus and W. Lütgert, the Lutheran approach is of importance; for some English authors as well as for a certain number of conservatives, it is a degree of fundamentalism (21); as for the rest, they do not go beyond the framework of a developed systematic theology, where the investigation of *loca probantia* (or the proverbial "proof-texts") supplants history.

But to continue our account, we shall trace in turn the evolution of the Tübingen School, the criticism of the eschatologism of A. Schweitzer and the elaboration of a realized eschatology or a deferred eschatology, and the break-up within the School of the History of Religions.

A. *Anti-Tübingen and Neo-Tübingen Schools*

What is left of Baur's historical interpretation in the liberal historical criticism? I think that the answer was given by M. Dibelius and W. G. Kümmel in their book entitled *Paulus* (1951). No one would question the authority of these scholars, or their admitted affinity: The second is the disciple of the first. Both have an extraordinarily exact knowledge of Christian origins.(22)

According to these authors, Paul is the missionary to the Gentiles. Was he not, indeed, the first to recognize that the preaching of Jesus was not some sort of private affair, but something directed to the well-being of mankind, and therefore also of the pagans? Christianity was no longer the religion of a single people, but that of "all the earth" (Rom. 10, 18). Secondly, Paul promulgated the new religion in many places by establishing communities; but he saw to it that these communities were unified through communion in the same faith, through mutual acts of charity, through an interchange of personalities, and above all through belief in one and the same Lord. Thus, they constituted the new "household of faith" (Gal. 6, 10). Thirdly, Paul's work stems from a theology of divine-human relations. These relations, which take their form from the death and resurrection of Jesus, mark the end of the Law and the beginning of "the Good News." God is a God of salvation, and his essential act, totally out of mercy, rests in the death and resurrection of Jesus. Salvation is present, and reaches us in and through the Church. The latter is independent of Judaism; as the present dispenser of Christ's divine activity, she is not bound to Jerusalem, which can disappear, or to an eschatological expectation, which is already in process of being realized. (23)

J. Munck relegated M. Dibelius and W. G. Kümmel to a current of thought similar to that of H. Lietzmann, M. Goguel, A. D. Nock, and W. Knox — all of whom had plunged as it were into the Tübingen waters. (24) Baur and his heirs had never undergone so systematic a frontal attack as in *Paulus und die Heilsgeschichte* of the Danish scholar. The importance of this work and the exceptional qualities of its author have been generally acknowledged by the critics. He claimed that the majority of exegetes, while having abandoned the extravagant literary positions of the Tübingen School, nevertheless have retained its principles of interpretation, by simply applying to the first century what Baur had claimed for the second century. Paul is the great man who had established the Churches of the Greco-Roman world. Constantly dogging his path were the emissaries from the Jerusalem center. Both faced each other in mutual opposition. Munck constructed his criticism in two stages. At first he took up the criticisms of B. Sundkler (25): (1) The antithesis between particularism and universalism, which is a product of our own modern thought patterns, is a conception which Tübingen had invented. Neither Jesus nor Paul was a universalist as *we* understand the word; (2) contrary to what Baur maintained, the disciples could not possibly have lost almost complete contact with Jesus; (3) the Tübingen School did not explain the readiness with which Jewish Christianity accepted Paul's apostolate among the Gentiles. Munck then added his own remarks, to the effect that the Tübingen portrayal of Paul was composed on the basis of the Acts rather than of the Epistles.

The latter are considered to be anterior in time only in theory. Above all, Paul's enemies are arbitrarily lumped together into a single group, whereas in reality, they had their own local peculiarities and characteristics.

Such destructive criticism is of no avail; the approach must be positive. Paul had encountered enemies wherever he went. Who were they?

In Galatia, the Judaizers were pagans, who had converted and became over-zealous neophytes. They mistakenly regarded Paul as a man who had opposed the Jerusalem Church which they thought of as demanding the circumcision of Gentiles. They were equally mistaken about the very essence of Christianity, which is Spirit and not Law. In Corinth, parties, which rivaled each other, apparently existed. There is no mention of the Judaizers, although they seem to be there from what can be gleaned from the Acts. Paul censured the entire local Church, which writhed in its own wisdom. In 2 Cor. 3,6 and 11, 22, Paul contrasted Judaism with Christianity; the false apostles were Jews and not Christians. The Letters to the Romans, Munck continued to say, was an encyclical, just as T. W. Manson had also maintained; hence, it cannot serve to describe the Church at Rome. (26) Therefore, to claim on the basis of Romans that the Judaizers were everywhere would not be a valid deduction. The Pauline Churches were composed of converted pagans and of converted Jews. Both groups needed proper instruction concerning the nature of the Church, the old and the new Israel, the role of the Law, as well as of the Old Testament. These were the chief problems of the early Church. Later on, the question of relations with Hellenistic philosophy was to arise. At Philippi, Paul's enemies were no longer the Judaizers, but the Christians who thought that the Apostle was transgressing the Law. They reproached him for having compromised the success of the Gospel by dedication to his own cause. He should not have identified his personal cause with that of the Church.

The primitive Church was united and without parties. The *Hellenistai* and the *Hebraioi* were not clannish. Stephen's discourse did not contradict the story of Cornelius. The *Urgemeinde*, or the primitive community, had accepted the admission of Gentiles into its midst. Moreover, the Synoptics confirmed these views. In order to evaluate Paul's position in the primitive Church, we must realize that he had regarded Jerusalem as the place of the decisively redemptive act (2 Thes. 2, 3-4.8-10; Rom. 11, 26-27); that after each missionary journey, he returned there as to a point of departure; that the collection for the Jerusalem community had the nature of an eschatological act which realized the predicted union of pagans and of Jews, since the former gave their contributions "to the saints" in Jerusalem. Upon examination the narrative concerning the hearing before the Emperor, even the arrest of Paul appeared as an eschatological act, in direct relationship to the Hope of Israel (Acts 23, 6; 24,15; 26,6). Moreover, Paul's sufferings paralleled those of Jesus. Hence, according to the Acts, Paul's trial played a role which the Synoptics had attributed to the Passion of Jesus.

The eminent authority, W. D. Davies, had said that this work offered "a provocative and at many points illuminating reinterpretation of Paul." (27) The most important results were: (1) the continuity between Paul and Jesus, whose ministry, while intended principally for the Jews, nevertheless equally envisaged the Gentiles — a conclusion which is comparable to the ideas of J. Jeremias; (2) the basic unity of the Church, a conclusion which the Tübingen School had scorned. Generally speaking, however, the book is acceptable, but with qualifications. Munck presented his views in the form of a counsel's speech in which everything was grist to his mill. Without sufficient control, he accepted some highly questionable opinions, such as those of Cullmann concerning *to katechon* and *ho katechon,* (28) or those of T. W. Manson on the Letter to the Romans. He was particularly adept in abusing texts, especially from Galatians, and from 1 and 2 Corinthians. Finally, how a Judaizing movement arose in the bosom of the Church requires an explanation; moreover, although we do not deny the importance of eschatology, we must remember that it did not constitute the entire Pauline structure. (29) Hence, the anti-Tübingen positions of Munck are much too radical. (30) On the other hand, they have shown at least that the historical interpretation, which seemed to be most certain, could and should be reconsidered. In exegesis, as in any other science, it is often useful to take up the problems again on the basis of original data.

When J. Schoeps portrayed J. Munck as "a man who scorned" (*Verächter*) F. C. Baur, he had to take his views into account. (31) The author was Jewish, and had already expressed his pro-Tübingen views in his previous works on Ebionism. His thesis is well known and is entirely in line with that of the School. Schoeps' book, *Paulus*, stood between the work of A. Deissmann and that of A. Schweitzer. Obviously the author is eclectic. He claimed to belong to the School which concentrated on the history of religions, from which he borrowed more the method than the conclusions. On the other hand, he adhered to Baur's fundamental idea, namely, to localize the birth of the Church within the stream of Ebionism, or rather from Paul's opposition to an Ebionite Christianity. These two currents have their sources in Judaism, but they unite to form Catholicism. Paul's personal contribution lay entirely in the drama of the pharisee of the Diaspora who "saw" the Risen Christ and was sent by him: He was heir to the first formation of character and instruction which he received in the primitive Church, but, at the same time, he was "different" from the rest of the apostles. (32)

Schoeps' brand of "Tübingenism" was modified. At Jerusalem, James, Peter, and Paul were in essential agreement on a compromise. Antioch was simply one episode among many. But the Christian pharisees of Jerusalem had disrupted such unity. Furthermore, the apostolate, as Paul had conceived it, was not of a juridical order; it was pneumatic, as was the Church herself. The Judaizers were active both in Galatia as well as in Corinth; however, it would be a mistake to lump them together as though they all were on the same footing. Originally, Paulinism represented one stream of Christianity among many others, only to triumph in the end. Eventually, Paul had to withdraw from his original Jewish milieu, and Schoeps noted the extent to which he withdrew. His eschatology differed from that of the Jews, since he saw salvation in retrospect, within the factual context of the death and the resurrection of Jesus. Salvation in the present time extended not only to communities but to individuals as well, because it was organized within the framework of the sacraments of Baptism and the Eucharist, both of which provided access to the Spirit. These doctrines, like the soteriological teaching, went

beyond Judaic thinking. The violent death of the Messiah was
an enigma to the Jews, a *skandalon*. For him to give his blood in
order to save the world was a messianic concept that was foreign
to Judaic thought. Such transformations had a common root in
the divine sonship of Jesus, a myth that was radically non-Jewish
(*radikal unjüdisch*). Moreover, other myths were traceable to
Hellenism: The descent from heaven, our dying with Christ, the
valorization of the sacraments in a "realistic" sense. All these conceptions were related to the ideas of the *theoi andres* and the
theoi soteres. Therefore, Paul had abandoned pharisaism. Because
of the inclinations of his own temperament and the particular
needs of each controversy, he was drawn into absurdities. Particularly, the Pauline dialectic on the role of the Law led him to
conclude that the Law was a curse for Israel. Casuistry rendered
him insensible to realities. He even went so far as to maintain that
the Law was responsible for sin; he reduced the Law to a moral
and ritual function, whereas it was essentially a *berith*, a covenant
of salvation.

Such is the general outline of Schoeps' neo-Tübingenism. He
had abridged, qualified, and adjusted the old positions, but
nevertheless had kept them always in view. One cannot but admire
his erudition, his profound knowledge of rabbinic literature, his
sympathy for the hero, his eclectic inspiration to glean what
was useful wherever he found it, his freedom of opinion, and
the clarity in his presentations. Fundamentally, Schoeps claimed
to be a *Religionsgeschichtlicher* and a *jüdischer Geschichtlicher*.
For him, Paul was anti-Jewish in vocation, in preaching, and in
attitude. He had a place among those great Jews who have shaped
the destiny of mankind. Had he remained within the Judaic
framework, he would have become a herald to deliver Judaism
from racial prejudice and from the tragic destinies of
history. (33)

Positing the impossibility of the supernatural as a basic principle, Schoeps could see Paul only from without. The Apostle's
"vision" of Jesus was a psychic and subjective phenomenon; his
faith in Jesus as Savior and Son of God, was part of Greek
legacy; his anti-Judaism was a profound mistake. These were
radical solutions to problems which in reality were far more
complex. The fundamental Tübingen error persisted. In all this,

what became of the message and personal influence of Jesus?
Already in 51 A.D., Paul spoke of Jesus stylistically as the
Son of God (1 Thes. 1,10). Was he already the mouthpiece of
Grecian thought-patterns? The eclecticism of Schoeps enabled
him to speak as a believer, but the formulas and ideas, the rites
and life, were bereft of their meaning. The death and resurrection, the divine affiliation, the Spirit, the mystical life, the
Church, and the Gospel, represented nothing more for the
history of religions than psychological phenomena completely
devoid of truth. Their persistence in men's minds merely represented an outmoded way of thinking and feeling. Schoeps had
sacrificed Hegel, but not idealism. His peremptory judgments
did not solve problems which he had expounded so summarily.

B. *Eschatology and Eschatologies*

Generally speaking, the problem of eschatology in the New
Testament, and particularly in St. Paul has been profoundly
modified since the time of Schweitzer.

In 1933, Hans Windisch, after having drawn up the balance
sheet of studies on primitive Christianity, pointed out the emergence of new facts, forces, and ideas. He deplored a certain lack
of unity. First of all, he demanded an adaptation of the theories
of Baur and of his successors (H.A.W. Meyer, K. Holl, E. Hirsch,
H. Lietzmann) to the effect that Paul was not at odds with Peter,
but with a group. The polemic of 1 Corinthians and Romans was
directed against Jerusalem. Paul's Hellenism had already attacked the *Urgemeinde* to such an extent that it was no stranger
to the Judaism of Jerusalem and of the Diaspora. Over the tri-
logy, "Christology-Ecclesiology-Soteriology," H. Windisch su-
perimposed "Eschatology" as a necessary principle of unity. To
it he added submission to the salvific will of God. (34)

The appeal remained unanswered. Windisch, while caught in
the meshes of his own prodigious erudition, oscillated between
eschatology and recourse to the Hellenistic-oriental sources
which he still favored. What Windisch meant by eschatology was
clearly not the expectation of the imminent end of the world,
as Schweitzer had interpreted the concept. Thus, the term "eschatology" assumed many meanings, and each in turn implied a
different vision of history.

1.   C. H. Dodd made himself the champion of realized eschatology. (35) T. Fr. Glasson (36) and J. A. T. Robinson (37) had extended his theses to the Pauline Epistles. According to Dodd's view, the Kingdom of God has come. The *eschaton* is God's plan, both as revealed and as accomplished; it is the entry into a form of existence wherein time-space coordinates are no longer the containers of a reality which we had come ordinarily to regard as heterogeneous. J. A. T. Robinson's first work, *The Body*, (38) which was very well received, with its wholly speculative and excessively systematic rigor, resorted to criteria governing literary dissection, with the sole purpose of removing anything relative to the Second Coming from the ideas of Jesus and from the apostolic teaching. Such texts and ideas are of Jewish origin and do not represent the true Christian message.

2.   O. Cullmann, (39) W. G. Kümmel, (40) and J. Jeremias (41) insisted on two distinct perspectives in the texts. The eschatology is realized, but the texts also contain a clear provision for a lag between the death-resurrection of Jesus and the parousia. Nevertheless, the presence of the Kingdom of God announced as clearly as the parousia.

3.   In a certain sense, W. G. Kümmel, (42) H. Schuster, (43) and H. A. Babel (44) have shown that Schweitzer's thesis not only did not take into account all the texts, but above all created an enigma concerning the continuity of the Christian movement once it had entered into an apparently blind alley. The Swiss authors, M. Werner, (45) F. Buri, (46) U. Neuenschwander, (47) and Babel to some extent, accepted Schweitzer's ideas favorably. However, they did shift the emphasis, placing it, not on the transformation of eschatology into a mystique, but on the "deeschatologization" of nascent Christianity by delaying the parousia. W. Michaelis (48) followed by Morgenthaler (49) and F. Flückinger, (50) pointed out the positions which the new systematics had taken up. The theses of M. Werner and F. Buri would doubtlessly never have been heard of beyond the Swiss frontiers had they not found a powerful ally in the person and writings of Bultmann. (51)

4.   R. Bultmann reintroduced "deeschatologization" (*Enteschatologisierung*) into "demythologization" (*Entmythologisier-*

ung). The learned professor substituted the *Selbstverständnis*, the
manner in which I understand myself, for the Jewish myth of
the expectation, in such a way that hope yields to the necessity of
present involvement. (52) Erich Grässer, a disciple of Bultmann,
devoted his thesis to the postponement of the parousia. According
to his view, the entire New Testament should be interpreted as
an answer to questions posed by such postponement. However,
he limited himself to the Synoptics and to the Acts of the Apostles,
and did not deal with Paul. (53)

In an article, which appeared in *TLZ*, (54) O. Cullmann gave an
excellent estimate of the entire neo-eschatologistic movement.
One may ask as he did just how the delay of the parousia
could have effected the alleged break between Jesus and the
apostles, without the Church taking it into account. First of all,
the consequent eschatology of Schweitzer must be reexamined.
The method of Werner, Bultmann, and Grässer postulated what
it ought to have proven, and began, so to speak, at a finishing
line instead of taking into account the conditions in which the
particulars of the problem had developed. The postponement of
the parousia could have been painfully felt but eventually
accepted, simply because the eschatology was already realized in
its essential moments.

5. Finally, Schoeps offered a revision of Schweitzer's positions. (55) He agreed with Schweitzer in this that Jesus expected
the end immediately after his death, at the time of his glorification through the resurrection. Paul was the man who had to
re-think the eschatological expectation. Having accepted from
Jewish apocalypticism the doctrine of the two ages, he set the
advent of the new age on retrospect rather than in anticipation.
Therefore, Schoeps attributed to Paul the distinction between
the two advents, but he offered an explanation which properly
described the transformation of this doctrine. It was the death
of some of the faithful, which led Paul to create a belief in
corporal resurrection. By this, he would not mean a revitalization
of cadavers, but simply a rebirth according to the Spirit (*kata
pneuma*), a state identical with that of the Risen Lord himself.
Thus, the intermediate period, the new age, becomes totally spiritual. The sacraments have their true meaning only as eschatological realities: Baptism is the entry into the messianic com-

munity; the Eucharist is the presence of the Lord. Pauline eschatology strongly resembles a rather heteroclite mosaic.

Such diversity of opinions, their similarities and differences,
demand a most fundamental restatement of the question. Clearly,
one should abide with accepted terminology and give to the
term "eschatology" a precise meaning. (56) Literary work
should not be subjected to axioms. One cannot evade the necessity to find realities behind formulas. This does not mean that
such research should be inspired by a Platonizing philosophy, as
Dodd thinks, or by an existentialism, as Bultmann proposes. In
this matter, especially, an excessively strict fundamentalism, from
which O. Cullmann does not seem always to be immune, does
injustice to the profound thought of Paul. (57)

Basically, any system must take into account two facts which
often remain outside the perspective of authors. First of all,
the Old Testament, from Isaiah to Daniel, all of later Jewish
apocalyptic, and the settings of Qumran over a period of two
centuries, had expected the "end" presumably to come immediately
within a time that never exceeded the generation for whom
the writing had been intended. This end did not come. The
prophecy was carried over to a later period, even though it had
ceased to thrive on the first occasion. Such successive delays had
created a credibility-gap, and the author of the *Pesher of Habacuc*
had noted undeceivingly that the end was taking longer to come
than the prophets had imagined. (58) This did not prevent the
author from thinking that, this time, he himself was qualified
to reach a better understanding of the mysteries of God and of
the Scripture. Secondly, to admit that, at the time of 2 Pt., the
problem was definitively raised and resolved, would seem indeed to imply that this delay never had constituted in itself a
problem for John, Paul, the Synoptics, or the Apocalypse. All
express the hope, desire, expectation, and supplication that
Jesus would return in glory. Despite the fact that they had
never wavered from this hope in their parenesis, which too
often reverted to the subject of necessary vigilance, we would
have to say that the Church, far from being scandalized by the
delay of the parousia, had to make greater efforts to keep the
eschatological hope alive and active. History taught them to
expect in *hupomone*, i.e., with perseverance.

Hence, it would seem that the delay of the parousia was peripheral and incidental to the eschatological expectation itself. The latter, while echoing Jewish themes, carried the entire content, and was, as it were, the cornerstone of the New Testament, including Paul. Appearances, however, should not make us oblivious to what is essential. Was Jesus aware of his messiahship? Did he establish his message and his person at the dawn of the new era? Did he regard his death as the new beginning of salvation? Were the apostles aware that Jesus was already in the age of the Spirit, and that they themselves had entered into that age through Pentecost? That the benefits promised by Scripture and by the Master were being realized? That they must labor in the Church in order to secure an ever-increasing holiness, in Christ and through the Spirit? That the present world would finally give way to a future world, through the Judgment and the return of Christ?

C. *The Religionist School*

From the viewpoint of the history of religions, the present discussion can be reduced to the question of influences. (59) We note, that, from a purely rational point of view, there is hardly any way to escape this aspect of the problem. If the theology of Paul is nothing more than an ideology, one could not expect either God, or Christ, or the primitive Church, to explain the Apostle's conversion or the elaboration of his doctrine. (60) However, while completely admitting the reality of the supernatural, it is still possible to raise the question concerning the relations between Pauline thought and his contemporary world. In fact, it is not only possible to do so, but it is a task which exegesis cannot shirk.

Exegesis has not failed in the least in this respect. Paul belonged to two worlds, the Jewish world and the Hellenistic world. We have seen that the School of the history of religions was preoccupied chiefly with the affinities and dependence in relation to the Greek world. It established a foundation especially on the actuality of the Oriental mysteries and on the cult of the *Kyrios*. We have equally indicated that Schoeps himself was convinced that no one could possibly ignore these studies which were not all without relevance once faced with their results. The more clearly archaeology revealed the daily life of those cities where Paul had founded his Churches — Ephesus, Corinth, Philippi, Thessalonica, not to speak of Rome — the less was it possible to accept any notion that Paul and his believers, who, for the most part, belonged to the Greek world, lived in some type of spiritual ghetto. To travel those roads which Paul used in order to reach the four corners of the Empire enabled one to begin to understand why such scholars, as Ramsay and Deissmann, could envisage Paul only as a man who was decidedly marked by the civilization which was constantly before his eyes. (61)

Today, however, the Hellenistic influence is regarded as suspect, in favor of Judaism. Nevertheless, the abandonment of the mysteries has simply led to a considerable pre-occupation with Gnosticism. We shall deal briefly with these two orientations.

1. Paul was a pharisee, the son of a pharisee (.Acts 23,6). According to W. C. van Unnik, he would have received his whole formation at Jerusalem itself rather than at Tarsus. (62) Most authors have accepted Paul as a Jew of the Diaspora. It is very difficult to distinguish this type of Judaism from that of Palestine. The two principal sources which must be used in order to arrive at any knowledge of its nature are the LXX and Philo. (63) Examples are not lacking which show that the alterations of the Hebrew text by the Greek translators are similar to Paul's preoccupations. Schoeps enumerated these: The LXX emphasized the missionary obligation of Israel; they moralized on the concept of the Law, and gave similar treatment to the notion of *dikaiosune;* they reduced the rich Hebrew vocabulary which designated sin to only two words, *adikia* and *anomia.* Paul depended on the LXX in these instances. Before the time of Paul, the LXX had emphasized propitiation, *hilaskesthai,* and had eventually given to the Law and to prophecy a pedagogic role which the Apostle took up later. (64) The very special case in Philo shows that a Jew could stay within his traditional thought-patterns, while at the same time approaching as closely as possible the language and the concepts of his pagan opponents. He became the apologist and the missionary of Alexandria, and he came to regard the Fathers as symbols or type of perfection. (65)

W. D. Davies' *Paul and Rabbinic Judaism* (66) was the work which dealt most methodically with the relations between Paul and rabbinic Judaism. The success of this book was relative to the high quality of its content. Paul's relations with Rabbinism provided a proper understanding of the Apostle himself. He began with the categories of his religion in order to emerge into the realm of new ideas. Paul, the ex-pharisee, retained his understanding of the flesh and of sin; the division of the two humanities, the old and the new, which inspired the doctrine of the first and the second Adam; the Old and the New Israel which posed the question of nationalism; the theme of the old man and of the new man which occasioned Paul to develop his thought about the individual; the old and the new Torah that led to the doctrine on Christ as the wisdom of God; the idea of obedience which found expression in the theme of the Lord who is the Spirit, and in the theme on the death of Christ; finally, the old and the new hope which became relative to the resurrection. Each and every detail which Davies' work provided is certainly not of equal value. Moreover, the reader would not find a complete picture of Paul in the synthesis which the author proposed. It must be admitted, however, that any investigation now undertaken on the rabbinic influence in Paul must begin with this work, the results of original study, that is well documented and of high literary quality. Davies will be especially esteemed for his "sense of limitation" and for the absence of all partisan spirit.

On the other hand, H. J. Schoeps, (67) as J. Klausner (68) before him, could not remain calm when he contemplated Paul, the pharisee and apprentice-rabbi, who gave a false impression of Judaism by making the Law a source of sin. In his opinion, Paul sinned by equating the Law and the Covenant — such living realities as the divine election, the response of the people, the spirit of mercy, and such juridical realities as the observances and their sanctions. Thus, however near as he may have been to Judaism, Paul differed from it, not only by the constitutive elements of his faith, but also by that spirit of opposition which characterized his new life. Here is a thesis which calls for serious reservations, and which is open to immediate refutation. (69)

2. Exegetes are of the opinion that any recourse to Judaism, however indicative and methodical it may be, cannot dispense with a study of Hellenism. We are rather certain that the Greek and Oriental doctrines concerning the mysteries, not to mention with their geographical distribution and their success, cannot be excluded from the perspective of the exegete. Besides, Stoicism had characterized the culture of the first century of our era too profoundly to be committed to obscurity as a museum piece. (70) If it is sufficiently clear that to have a proper method means that we should first of all begin to explain the origin of Pauline formulas and concepts with reference to Judaism, then it would be equally profitable to recall that, even over and beyond these formulas which are attested by the LXX and later Judaism, Paul was able to adapt himself, to adjust to ways of thinking, to make choices, or to take up opinions which Hellenism would have suggested to him. (71) We considered it fitting to make this remark before entering upon the subject of Gnosticism. (72)

Together with H. Schlier and R. M. Wilson, we must distinguish one type of Gnosticism, which is an elaborate system, from another which is a form of diffused thought, more a tendency than a body of doctrine. (73) R. M. Wilson's conclusion appears to be justifiable: "To sum up, Gnosticism arises largely from an imperfect grasp of Christian principles by people brought up in the environment of the Hellenistic world; the Christian heresy is indeed only a part of a wider movement of which the origins are still obscure, although it would appear to be roughly contemporaneous with the rise of Christianity. Even in its earliest stages Gnosticism was a danger to the Church, a danger which Paul and his followers were not slow to observe and to resist. In the New Testament we have as yet only the first murmurs of the storm, which reached its height in the second century, but they are enough to show that the danger had begun to make itself felt. The errors of the Colossians show how people with their background and outlook might react to the presentation of the new faith by a man such as Paul. Similar ideas were widely current, and the very number of the later theories shows the hold which they had upon the popular mind. Not the least of the services rendered by Paul and his fellow-laborers was their exposition of the basic Christian doctrines in the light of contemporary thought, and their resolute rejection of any other Gospel." (74)

How extensively H. Schlier was preoccupied with the subject of Gnosticism is well known. He returned to his favorite topic in the fine commentary on the Letter to the Ephesians. The learned professor from Bonn supposed that the background to the Letters to the Ephesians and Colossians was not an elaborate gnostic system, but "an anteriorly primitive form" (*eine Vor- und Frühform*). He clarified this thought by formulating the hypothesis that a Gnosis was already present in Jewish literature, sapiential as well as apocalyptic, to which the Qumran texts testify. However, the type of Gnosis which Ephesians and Colossians betrayed was not the same as the Judaic brand; it comprised an ontological dualism, a cosmic-soteriological myth of primitive man and finally the revelation of identification of the man who knows with the Savior. The Letter to the Ephesians, whose Pauline authenticity Schlier did accept, was a *Sophiarede,* that is, a wisdom-discourse. (75)

Evidently, the position of Wilson and of Schlier eluded the criticisms of F. Mussner, whose thesis, however remarkable it may have been, was unable to supply a solution to the problems raised which one might have expected from a more profound investigation. Paul took into account the gnostic doctrine as well as the heretical vocabulary and viewpoints; but this did not mean that he became a gnostic, any more than that he became a stoic or a rabbi simply by using their forms of argumentation. Käsemann was not altogether wrong in reproaching Mussner for having added both "sugar and spice" to the problem. (76)

Nevertheless, it is dangerous to be too radical. G. Bornkamm (77) seemed to be rather excessive in his study, *Die Häresie des Kolosserbriefes.* He claimed that the basic religious background to the Colossian heresy was a gnosticizing Judaism in which there was a fusion of Jewish and Irano-Persian elements, as well as of Chaldaic astrology. One could very well admit this, but when he added that these speculations were brought into Christianity itself as if by means of some marked alloy, he seemed to go beyond his premises. Since he depended on the hazardous reconstructions of R. Reitzenstein, he built on quicksand. To

begin with remote ancestors and to enhance them with a long-
dated paternity is to bury oneself into the realm of hypotheses
and to take but a very superficial account of more recent
phenomena.

Similar remarks would apply to E. Käsemann's commentary on
Phil. 2,5-11. (78) Likewise, W. Schmithals' important study on
the Gnosticism at Corinth was just as precarious. (79) The
author analyzed christology, the concept of the Gospel, anthropology, the idea of liberty, the doctrine of the sacraments and
eschatology, and concluded that the unorthodox theology of
Corinth was Gnostic. By the term Gnosis, he meant to include
both the doctrine of the mysteries and the "existential" conscience of Paul. The Gnosis was an interpretation of the world and
of man bedecked with mythological expressions. At Corinth, the
myth of the "God-Savior," the christological dualism, the myth
of "the Savior—the saved," and the passage of souls into heaven,
were the foundations of the Christian Gnosis. If the dualistic
cosmic myth and the radical secularization of the lower world
were not to be found there, the reason was that Paul did not
have to combat dualism, since he himself had accepted it. Besides,
his pessimism was also more accentuated than that of the gnostics.
The latter were Jews who had converted to Christianity. Thus,
Schmithals rallied to the neo-Tübingenism of H. J. Schoeps, but
by way of Hellenism. Such a conception emphatically raises
many doubts. It is insufficient simply to explain the meaning of
the notions of Gnosis or of myth. It is intolerable to ascribe to
Gnosticism the very foundations of Pauline thought, which are
rather Jewish and Christian. Any insertion of themes into the
latter or the emphasis thereon does not necessarily imply any dependence on the heresies which are controverted. So much for
the method. As for the results, Schmithals had compromised them
by relying on the ideas of his master, R. Bultmann. (80)

However, in a more recent article on the Letter to the Galatians, Schmithals continued his investigation, and very para-
doxically reached the same conclusion which he had deduced
from his study on Corinth. (81) Paul's enemies were not Judaizing Christians, but simply Jews. Paul made claim to the divine
origin of his apostolate: This was the first parallel example with
the gnostic doctrine which taught that the apostle was directly

called by God. Similarly, the content of Paul's preaching was gnostic. The Galatians were preoccupied with novel doctrines and were deviating from the patterns of the old teachers; therefore, gnostic Christians were functioning in Galatia. For, whereas the Judaizing heretics were opposed by the Council of Jerusalem, the gnostic Christians, on the contrary, proposed the practice of circumcision so as not to dissatisfy the Jews. They speculated about "days, and months, and seasons, and years" (Gal. 4,10), the service of the *stoicheia tou kosmou*, themes which Paul had resumed in his letter to the Colossians. Furthermore, the laws which he sought to impose on the faithful were not those of Moses, but of the *pneumatikoi* (Gal. 6,1; cfr. 3,2; 5.25; 6.8). The exaltation of the spirit meant the condemnation of the flesh (Gal. 4,12 ff.), which the Christian must shake off, a concept which paralleled the gnostic notion of *eleutheria*. The heretics then would have been gnostic. According to Schmithals, the deep-seated tendency of Luke was anti-gnostic, namely, that authority must govern the *pneuma*. The entire thesis is hardly sound. Already in 1 Thessalonians, Paul declared that he had been found worthy to receive the divine charge to preach the gospel. In the same epistle, the Apostle urged the faithful not to "quench" the Spirit, but to "test everything" and to "hold fast what is good" (5,21). In this case, according to Schmithals, Paul would already have been thinking in categories proper to Gnosticism. Hence, by reason of creating such a context, Schmithals had to date 1 Thessalonians to the period of Paul's third missionary journey. (82)

Art. 3. History, Dialectic, and Theology

The exegetical and historical work which we have described up to this point claimed to be answerable to historical science. The interpretation which F. C. Baur cherished has never been actually absent, although it had established itself specifically in the name of history. Yet, at the conclusion of his very important work, *Das Neue Testament*, W. G. Kümmel echoed the general opinion that historical research cannot be the purpose of exegetical science. The sacred books and their authors, the traditions and the preaching, and, in the final analysis, Jesus himself, can be studied adequately only if the description and reconstruction of the past are coupled with appropriate evaluation. Mere historicism or history can not longer be adequate. There are more than facts and doctrines already in the primary references, which were not composed in order to salvage an event from oblivion. They do not merely record examples or wise sayings any more than they merely record the experience of the authors. They claim to unveil a reality which is inaccessible by human means, in order to confront mankind with a call and a need, and to force a decision. To deny this essential characteristic of the New Testament data would be in effect a disregard for the principal task of exegesis. (83) The great exegetical authori-ties, K. Barth, R. Bultmann, E. Lohmeyer, C. H. Dodd, and and E. C. Hoskyns, agree on that score. (84)

Although there seems to be unanimity here, the avenues of ac-cess are diverse. K. Barth exercised a certain amount of influ-ence on Pauline exegesis. (85) The Swiss theologian thought of literary and historical criticism as no more than a first and quickly-forgotten step. He sought the *Erklärung,* that is the ex-planation beyond the riddle of the text, solved the enigma of the "thing," and substituted the dialectic of reality for historical research. Hence, it was no longer a question of the relation between the book and myself, but between God and myself. The reason is that Barth was not content to elaborate a specula-tive theology of scientific value; he sought to bear witness and to assume the role of a prophet. Thus, his contribution to exege-sis was only indirect. He had destroyed the pretension of Liberal-ism and of Historicism, and had restored interpretation to its true task. However, his method and results should be approached with caution. Barth interpreted with Calvinist ideas as his spring-board, and his own co-religionists did not seem to accept his version of these ideas as correct. He was accused, not without reason, on the one hand, of condemning the human mind as bad and corrupt; and on the other hand, demanding that the same mind ultimately pass judgment on the content of revelation.

At the opposite extreme, it may be said, is R. Bultmann. He claimed to make a distinction between *Historie* and *Geschichte.* Paul belonged preeminently to *Geschichte.* The scholar acquires a knowledge of *Historie* by means of a purely scientific method. However, he cannot attain to *Geschichte* without a new understanding of himself, when he eventually discovers that he must make a commitment. The works of R. Marle and of H. Fries have made these views well known. (86) Paul wrote a real theology. His letters show no trace of influence from the Palestinian tradition concerning the history and the preaching of Jesus. The Apostle knew no more of Jesus than that he was born and lived under the Law, and that he was crucified (Gal. 3,1; 4,4; 1 Cor. 2,2; Phil. 2.5 ff). In some passages, the Apostle refers to the words of the Master. The theology of Paul was therefore the result of a confrontation between the Jesus of history and the Jesus of Hellenistic Christianity, but it taught nothing about God, or about Jesus as Messiah, or as Savior or Son of God. Paul's theology was an anthropology whose constitutive elements were the state of man before *pistis* and the state of man after *pistis*, namely, the justice of God, grace, faith, and liberty. Bultmann chose this viewpoint, which is clearly subjective and partial, in accordance with his own philosophy, in the light of which some of his statements must have their interpretation — statements, by the way, which a Barth or St. Thomas could have written: "The fundamental interest of the exegete is not to ask himself: What do the words signify in their historical setting and in their context? The final question for him is: what is actually involved, to what realities do these discourses lead? — 'von was für Sachen ist die Rede, zu welchen Realitäten führt das Gesagte?'." (87)

E. Lohmeyer arraigned Bultmann for his atheistic interpretation based on Heidegger. He claimed that the Professor from Marburg had confused belief with knowledge, and had reduced theology to a personal experience of faith. As he saw it, Bultmann functioned as a dogmatist, and not as an historian. (88)

However, Lohmeyer himself did not give serious attention to history. He claimed to throw into relief the originality, unicity, and unity of New Testament reality and doctrine, thereby disengaging the lines of force valid for the Christianity of yesterday and of today. Lohmeyer held that the New Testament transcended time to become fixed in a non-temporal present, in such a way that the reality of revelation was released from the temporal moment in order to ensure faith with the value of an absolute. Bultmann retaliated by accusing his colleague of Platonism. (89)

The studies which reflected these tendencies constituted only a segment of the contemporary output. Conservative Protestantism, English, German, and Scandinavian, has maintained an attitude according to which history, while not being pursued for its own sake, became a component of an ever-dynamic *Heilsgeschichte*. (90)

The two British writers, Ch. H. Dodd and E. C. Hoskyns, maintained that history must be re-thought. According to Dodd, the Gospel cannot be reduced to the teaching of the liberal school. Jesus had taught an eschatology that was realized or inaugurated. Paul found his own inspiration in the Hellenistic mysteries. The kerygma bridged the gap between these two. But Hoskyns had clearly seen that the fundamental and inescapable questions must be this: What was the relationship between Jesus of Nazareth and primitive Christianity? He answered this by maintaining that the faith did not precede the actuality; the messianic explanation was merely a consequence of the historical reality itself. This was the answer which the large majority of British scholars had proposed. (91) Among the American authorities, however, J. Knox was the man who approximated the position of R. Bultmann. His books were scarcely known outside America. From the viewpoint of theology, however, he could be classified as a conservative. (92)

Among the German scholars, A. Schlatter, K. L. Schmidt, and J. Schniewind, who pursued the course of the investigations of Th. Zahn, did not sulk at the new religionist method of the *Formgeschichte*. (93) But they all proposed a return to theological interpretation. Examined in the light of historical research, the apostolic witness conserved a real and normative value as regards the foundation and the organization of the Church. Paul was a privileged expression of nascent Christianity, who represented an authority that was authenticated both by tradition and by the Spirit, thus making him the bearer of a word to which the present age is obeisant and obedient in practical life.

Many authors have accepted such an interpretation of Paulinism. Despite the thrust of historical research, they, nevertheless, sacrificed too much to a more remote theology and to the terminology of the Church. The New Testament theology of P. Feine, which was the best reflection of these preoccupations, was not exempt from a rather confirmed formalism. (94) The studies of A. Schlatter went beyond this point, but reflect too much of the Lutheran positions to be regarded as impartial. (95)

To conclude with a word about the situation among the Catholic authorities, we would point out that the theology of F. Prat and of M. Meinertz, however useful and significant they may have been, no longer represented the ideal presentation of Paulinism. (96) Their excessively systematic design, due to the imposition of the general structure of our theological treatises and in accordance with a logic that was foreign to the Pauline synthesis, no longer respond to modern demands. (97) The books by J. Bonsirven are for the most part formal essays. (98) On the other hand, as J. L. McKenzie observed: "The use of the Bible as a mine of proof-texts is dying in Catholic theology and very few will regret it. But there is no organization of material and elaboration of principles to replace it." (99) The studies of Msgr. Cerfaux and his pupils, of P. Benoit, S. Lyonnet, C. Spicq, Professors A. Wikenhauser, S. Schnackenburg, A. Vögtle, and H. Schelkle, by a more rigorous method, have conducted us to a theology which is closer to the reality of revelation. Nevertheless, they are wanting in a common and clear notion of Biblical theology itself. (100)

Even though all attempts have wandered in diverse directions, we feel that a clearer assessment of the total situation is beginning to take shape.

1. With K. Stendahl, we would recognize that the distinction between descriptive work and theological investigation in a proper sense is genuine. The primary task of the exegete will always be to apply to the texts the principles which govern historical interpretation, and to recognize the diversity of ideas, of intellectual currents, and of persons. The proper road leads from diversity to unity. (101)

2. Moreover, when Stendahl left the task of reaching a judgment in the name of faith on the contents of the Biblical assertions to the Church and to her theologians, one could follow him all the more readily since he himself is an *ex professo* exegete and one of those churchmen called upon to give this judgment. Implicitly, he admits that present-day exegesis cannot confine itself to mere descriptive formulations.

3. Biblical theology is beginning to regulate its task and its limitations. It refuses to accept as its sole objective to provide an arsenal of theses and arguments for use in systematic theology. It refuses — although not always with sufficient vigor — to force its interpretation to depend on an ecclesiastical system or on historical preoccupations. It foresees the time when it will be considered abusive to project upon descriptive statements those philosophical opinions that tend to overstep their boundaries. Here, as Stendhal has clearly seen, lies the impasse. Some exegetes speak about tradition, faith, incarnation, miracles, redemption, justification, the Church, eschatology — a vocabulary which would horrify the liberals — and at the same time are farther from the apostolic doctrine than the liberals themselves. They have found a way to speak the language of Paul without being labeled as "noncritical" (*unkritisch*), but they consider the realities which Paul had revealed as nothing more than illusions of a myth-making kerygma. Such Biblical theology is a new type of Gnosticism.

Positively, Biblical theology is becoming aware of its real task. From the experience of the Apostle, reconstructed on the basis of his own testimony and subjected to literary and real criticism, and over and beyond those mere formulas, whose origin, literary type, and milieu have enabled us to grasp their import and their gradual development, it is now possible to measure the word and the reality to which it corresponds in order to establish coefficients of value and of truth. In short, therefore, it is possible to place the apostolic experience at the service of a believing mind. The task cannot be accomplished unless one has been initiated into the exegetical disciplines, and unless, beyond the mere techniques, one would admit and accept the obligation to actualize the word of God in real life.

Chapter II

BIOGRAPHIES OF ST. PAUL

While it is a difficult task to write a "life" of Christ, it might seem apparently simple to compose a biography of St. Paul. The Acts of the Apostles and the Epistles provide ample data. The facts flow within a relatively reliable chronology, and within an historical setting that is sufficiently familiar. The witness of Luke in the Acts, a document amenable to criticism, is unquestionably trustworthy along general lines. In the Epistles, there are many autobiographical passages which, while ranging over a period of more than ten years of activity in many areas, reveal the various facets of a most impressive personage, and accentuate the differentiating range traversed by the Apostle's thinking. The auxiliary sciences, archaeology, studies of the Jewish and Greek religious milieu, and philology, would easily lend assistance to the writer who would undertake to write a "life" of St. Paul.

Nevertheless, there are difficulties. Neither Acts nor the Epistles constitute a dossier sufficient to provide a perfect picture of all events in his life, or, for that matter, to draw up a comprehensive list of all the doctrines of the Apostle. To manipulate both requires a delicate hand. Luke's book must undergo preliminary historical, theological, and literary criticism. The Epistles must be assigned a chronological sequence; however, the chronology of these documents is controversial, since they are occasional writings, and give rise to problems that are very difficult to resolve.

Art. 1. Biographies by Catholic Authors

Among Catholic authorities (1), there is hardly any divergence in the way they use the sources. They rely completely on Acts, which serves as the unifying basis for the reconstruction of Paul's preaching as contained in the Epistles, whose authenticity all accept. The originality of the individual authors is relative to their different points of view. The works of C. Fouard and of E. Le Camus, which were remarkable in their time, are outmoded. Grateful for its smooth style and evocative power, however, Le Camus' work continues to attract readers who find it fruitful. One is even delighted to find there a touch of modernity in his free interpretation of several points; for example, the way he handles eschatology. However, the book of F. Prat, which is more succinct but more substantial, gives a clearer expression to the qualities of Paul's personality. In this small book, the great exegete has condensed all the exegetical knowledge of his time. A. Tricot's book is not outstanding, even though it is more methodical, and more scholarly, but in analysis and in doctrinal reconstruction, it is inferior to its predecessors. Nevertheless, F. Prat's book is still worth reading. Among the contemporaries of these authors, the German writers went their own way. After the probing and meticulous work of F. X. Poelzl, there appeared the *Paulus* of K. Pieper, a valuable work indeed, which deserved greater success than it had actually achieved; however, it was much too erudite and profound for the general public. Because of its great erudition, its concern for linguistic nuances, and its technically involved inquiries, it is more a reference work than a book for leisure or edification. Nevertheless, exegetes will find it replete with much information not readily available elsewhere. It is particularly concerned with Paul as a missionary. Rather than writing a "biography," however, K. Pieper concentrated on the nerve centers of the Apostle's work, as, for example, his vocation, his human genius, the principles of his activity, the purpose and the means of his mission, the organization of the communities, and the foundations of his theology. The book was well received by critics, and still is a work not to be neglected. Together with this book is the very interesting work of A. Steinmann on Paul's development. In 1926, S. Murillo published a volume which is more a course in Latin than a biography. One would suspect that the results of exegetical studies would find prompt expression in the field of popular works; however, the authors have not sated the hunger of those concerned.

For the past thirty years, some books have enjoyed great success with the reading public. The French author, É. Baumann, wrote a vigorous and original book on Paul. After its transient success, the book was buried in oblivion. However, it was far superior to a later but similar work by Daniel-Rops. In Germany, the work of J. Holzner was so widely popular that it appeared in translation into several languages, and seemed to have appealed to the popular taste. Well-written, enchanting, and anxious for a snappy and striking style, it met the needs of the ordinary reader. A Flemish work by Th. van Tichelen, which was the inspiration of Holzner's book, would be worth translating. Even though Holzner was greatly intent upon reconstructing the background, he erred by oversimplifying his explanations of Judaism and Hellenism. His more recent work was a collection of articles and public lectures which did not change the impression that he was lacking in historical and doctrinal perspective. (2) A much better source of information on the Apostle is the work of Msgr. Ricciotti who is known for scientific accuracy and literary skill. The original Italian version was better than the French translation. There are notable gaps, however, in Msgr. Ricciotti's critical treatment. The reputable work of A. Penna, also in Italian, has as its counterpart that of N. Caserta, both of which were written in Italian and which were especially concerned with the doctrine. P. Benoit has praised it deservedly. (3) The general reading public will find suitable to their taste the book of J. Pérez de Urbel. There is no doubt about his talent, but his knowledge is superficial.

To complete this brief survey, we shall select three small volumes from this massive collection, namely, the books of Allo, of Brillet, and of Brunot. Late in life, E. B. Allo condensed into one book some of his ever-personal and brilliant views on Paul:

Contemporary interest in Paul, the conversion, as doctor, Paul and Jesus, and Paul's message to the world. Sketchy though the work may be, it is nevertheless enlightening. The work of G. Brillet, intended for wider circulation, is full of charm, for his impressive piety is matched only by a profound knowledge of the subject. In this small book, A. Brunot, who had published another work of which we shall speak later, combines an historical survey of the periods of Paul's life, together with a presentation of the major doctrinal themes. The divisions are somewhat superficial, but the exposition is clear, striking, and well within the capacity of those readers who are interested in the special series entitled, *"Je sais, Je crois,"* to which it belongs. Noteworthy in all three books is the effort to go beyond a mere enumeration of historical events in order to disengage the doctrine of the Apostle. The distance between the history and the ideas of Paul is blurred, and surely provides an area for investigation.

On this very point we must say that, for a long time, Catholic exegesis has made few attempts towards a new synthesis. We sincerely agree with the wish of L. M. Dewailly: "Ten years from now let us hope that some teacher, who is well versed in the work of his fellow scholars, may give us a small but outstanding book on St. Paul for the generation that is to come." (4) By way of anticipation, the efforts on the part of Catholic scholars on particular points, which we shall take up later, is our assurance that one day such a wish will become a reality.

Art. 2. Biographies by Protestant Authors

Non-Catholic exegesis has produced some works which are truly remarkable. (5) Among the Germans, the influence of the Schools led to a division of the output into various categories. The development of viewpoints created a diversity which was not unattractive. Such diversity compelled the reader to relate fundamental problems to each successive generation. Elsewhere we cover the problems concerning authenticity. Generally speaking, it can be said that scepticism about the authority of Acts has grown incessantly. A recent commentary makes this clearly evident. (6) On the other hand, there is a similar phenomenon, though still more accentuated (as among the Catholic writers), namely, an emphatic interest on Paul as the theologian, to the neglect of the events in the Apostle's life.

The work by A. Hausrath, which was intended for the ordinary reader, comes within the context of the Tübingen School and of the Liberal School. H. Weinel, on the other hand, belongs to the School of the History of Religions. According to his view, Paul became religiously important in word and in deed over the whole world. He carried the reform of Jesus to a higher level. He gave to mankind's aspirations towards purity and eternal life an answer by which the Law was abolished in favor of justification by faith. In him are found the great currents of the ancient religions. Weinel did not intend to write a biography of Paul, but to understand the secret of his personality and of his work in the light of human needs. In his view, Paul is truly the second founder of Christianity. Already in Weinel, we find an unusual concept which appeared in later authors; namely, that Paul is a doctrine, a profoundly complex idea, a master of religion. A. Deissmann removed the Apostle from the University chair to which criticism had elevated him to reestablish him in his proper historical milieu. "An Anatolian and ancient Paul emerged from the lowly masses as a *homo novus,* who, while unnoticed by any educated pagan of the contemporary world, was destined to become a personality that would leave its mark decidely on world history. He was a *homo religiosus,* a classic mystic and, at the same time, an alert moralist, a prophet, a man with tendencies towards speculation, who, crucified to the world in Christ, had immortalized himself as a citizen and a pilgrim of the world, and who, even to our own day, continues to sculpture the image of the world — this is the Paul whom I have attempted to describe."

Deissmann, whose erudition exceeded that of his peers, contributed a knowledge of the places where Paul had worked and lived. His familiarity with archaeology and with papyrology availed him with a new working tool. His goal was to deliver Paul from his "eighth" captivity, namely, that of Pauline scholarship, in order to restore him to the East and to Greece. Did Deissmann succeed? He did so, but only partly. At this time, Hellenism was regarded as the factor which determined the line of Christian development, whereas Judaism was still a closed world. There was a great temptation to align Pauline mysticism with Greek mysticism, to which Deissmann had succumbed. When Deissmann conceived Paul's importance as consisting in the fact that he had added to the new religion the conceptual dimension of "having our being" in Christ, he could do so only in terms of a doctrine concerning the pneuma, the Divine emanation in which the believer was immersed. All Pauline enthusiasts will receive from Deissmann philological precisions, an archaeological awareness, and the need for contact with the East. Even though they will not find him to be a master of theology, nevertheless, this work will long remain their bedside manual. The same must be said of the collection of lectures of E. von Dobschütz, in which the great professor of Halle-Wittenberg presented a synthesis of his studies on Paul. These two thin volumes dealt with the Apostle's importance in world history and with his place in the art of being an apostle. Clearly, the author, obviously a liberal, presented quick, penetrating, and enthusiastic opinions. For him Paul was neither a theologian, nor a doomsday-dreamer, nor a mystic. Rather he was the instrument through whom the unprecedented moral teaching of Jesus had asserted itself.

General works on Paul from Britain are not lacking, the majority of which present the traditional Protestant image of the Apostle Paul, namely, as the preacher of salvation by faith. Written for a large reading public, these books do not ordinarily rise above the popular level. The best one seems to be that of T. R. Glover. Moreover, we are indebted to W. M. Ramsay for his series of studies on the milieu of the Pauline churches. Many things can be gleaned from these studies, but, unfortunately, an increasingly conservative attitude blinded the authors to problems essential to any real penetration on the part of the student of religions. Only with the two volumes of W. L. Knox have we had a highly original contribution on Paul and Jerusalem, and Paul and the Gentiles. Based on a wide range of erudition and an acute critical sense, it was a life of St. Paul in the light of Acts and of the Epistles, with lengthy footnotes to clarify controversial matters. Often highly personal in his approach, Knox was not an infallible guide in all things, but he always deserves attention. The small volume of A.D. Nock, a major authority on the history of religions, merited general appreciation, for it was a clear, balanced, judicious, and brilliant view on the entire subject, in which wide knowledge was matched only with profound wisdom. The author adhered closely to his sources, and his historical reconstruction was untainted by any pre-established theory. Hence, the more scholarly works did not ignore the book. Among the more recently published works we may mention the book of A. N. Williams, which was intended for wide circulation in America. R. S. Kinsey sought the same market for his work which covered Paul's sojourn in Greece, with the aid of the archaeological data for each town which the Apostle visited. H. V. Morton applied the same method to the journeys of Paul.

To reutrn to the German output, P. Feine has written an imposing work from a conservative point of view. In the preface, he presented a detailed review of the previous works, which constituted perhaps the permanent service rendered by the book. He was prompt to indulge in the excesses of the *religionsgeschichtliche Schule*, and was aware of the positions of its opponents, although he had added nothing original to the matter. The interesting and fascinating biography of Paul by Walther von Loewenich used the basic facts merely to awaken the mind to Pauline conceptions and to provide an introduction to the Epistles. The obvious conclusion to be drawn on the basis of what Von Loewenich wrote is that, without the Apostle, Christianity would have remained a Jewish sect or a pagan religious brotherhood (*thiasos*). A highly indicative study was the *Paulus* of M. Dibelius and W. G. Kümmel in the small Goeschen volumes, which was similar to that of Nock. In a few pages, the co-authors defined and evaluated the essential aspects of timely problems. The approach was liberalistic, as is usual in the studies on the history of religions, with emphasis on the theology of Paul. The evident calm in the process of evaluation did not however conceal the fact that the authors had already made up their minds on certain issues. We have in other publications by these same men materials complementary to their more recent work, in which the Jewish elements of the Apostle's ideas have not been sufficiently stressed. Without doubt, this work is comparable with the methodical study of E. Fascher in the *Pauly-Wissowa Encyclopedia*, which, indeed, is of great service, but is no more than an outline.

In conclusion, we would like to mention two other works of special interest. First, there is the important work by Klausner, a Jewish author, who recounted the biography of the Apostle in the light of the contemporary attitude of Israel towards the man who had opposed the Law. The learned professor was cautious of the excesses of criticism, and sketched a portrait of Paul which on the whole was very sympathetic. He was extensively acquainted with the problems, and did all the justice he could to the great Apostle. The ideas of R. Bultmann on Paul did not appear in his already dated article entitled *Paulus*, as they did in his study on the theology of the New Testament. Secondly, in an interesting American work, J. Knox assembled some highly personal studies which did not constitute as much a biography as a collection of consistently original views on a number of questions, which are our concern as we shall point out later.

Such an abundance of literary output constitutes an irrefutable reply to the words of Renan in the brilliant conclusion to his *Saint Paul*: "After having been grateful for three hundred years to orthodox Protestantism, our own day is seeing the end of the reign of the greatest doctor of Christianity, Paul." (7) On the contrary, Paul was never so much alive as he is today.

Chapter III

CONVERSION AND APOSTOLATE

Art. 1. Status of the Problem

One of the most characteristic features of contemporary studies on St. Paul is that they veer from the standard pattern of biography towards a synthesis of facts and of doctrines. History and theology so merge that Paul is not someone apart from his message.

The tendency will become increasingly marked as long as the sources themselves are kept in their proper perspective.

Neither the author of Acts nor the Apostle ever had intended to perpetuate the memory of men, of their actions, of their doctrines, or of their lives. Acts is not a history in the modern sense of the term. Were one to demand that Acts give a complete picture of Christianity from the years 30 to 62 A.D., he would encounter some rather inexplicable lacunas. In Luke's case, it is not astonishing that he is silent on the question concerning the foundation of the Church of Rome or about the deaths of Peter and Paul. Such lack of concern about the lives of those personalities who are so conspicuous in his account, is most revealing. However prominently Luke presented the two Princes of the nascent Church in Acts, he was not writing a biography such as we today would want; rather, he confined their activity to the perspective of his history of salvation. He intended to give more than a mere record of their words and deed, because he called on them to be witnesses to the facts as he recounted them, and to this end he ascribed certain discourses to them. Hence, he made each function as a witness (*martyr*) rather than simply accept each as an eyewitness (*autoptes*). More than the simple case of "I have seen" and "I have heard," both Luke and his heroes are swept into and absorbed in the very truth which they are proclaimed, truth that is of revelation and of theology. The life and the words of the witnesses were reported in terms of their missionary function, which was a continuation of the mission of Christ. They appeared under the dynamic movement of the Spirit. The solemn moments of their existence as well as their profound meaning were portrayed in terms of their relation to salvation-history. (1)

The same is true of Paul's Epistles. They contain abundant detail which serves to describe the man, the Jew, the Greek, the thinker, and the writer; however, their lasting value lay in the existential significance of their theology. The autobiographical references, so frequent in Paul's correspondence, are not valuable merely for the reconstruction of events, which invariably appear after all in doctrinal robes.

When Paul speaks about himself, he gives snatches of his reasoning, of his polemic, and of his popular preaching. Just as the revelation of Jesus simultaneously included his words and his deeds, and led to a knowledge of his person, so, accordingly, the Apostle attentively regarded his own existence, works, letters, and plans, within the perspective of the unfolding of the work of God in Christ Jesus. At this level, he should no longer be judged simply as a great man of the past, or as the founder and Doctor of the Gentile churches, or as the initiator of Christian theology. His person and his life are concerned with the same fundamental questions which are directed to each and every man, and which exact an unconditional "yes" or "no", thus engaging a man's total existence. (2)

The cardinal moments in the Apostle's life were his conversion and mission. Through these acts of God, Paul gained his real transcendence, because they constituted the beginning of his thought and work. (3) It is necessarily incumbent on every exegete to study their real nature and their repercussions on the apostolic life and message. We shall attempt to assess them as they have been dealt with in modern studies.

Art. 2. The Happening at Damascus

Unquestionably Paul was the only man who experienced a religious transformation on the road from Jerusalem to Damascus. Some regard this experience as a natural phenomenon, whereas others believe that it was supernatural. The skeptic explains the phenomenon by alleging that Paul passed through some crisis of either an intellectual or a moral nature, for in the process of opposing Jesus the Messiah, Paul could have been interiorly vanquished by his own conscience. On the other hand, he was experiencing more and more frustration in complying with pharisaic prescriptions to such a point that he sought a new message of God, grace, and mercy as a solution to his moral crisis. Does chapter seven of the letter to the Romans provide the key to the problem by disclosing Paul's state of soul to us? The religionists have refused to face the problem on the psychological level. Paul was influenced by Hellenism, by the pre-Christian Jewish sects, by the traditions of the Hellenistic Christian communities, and finally by Jewish piety. Even the psychiatrists entered into the debate. They sought to explain in their own terms the reasons for and the form assumed by what they regarded as an irruption of Paul's subconscious into the conscious mind. For the believer, on the other hand, Paul's conversion has its explanation in a direct intervention on the part of the glorified Christ. The persecutor became a believer and an apostle by means of a vision, whose nature and importance are to be assessed by reference to the accounts in Acts and to the Epistles.

A. *Nature and Value of the Accounts*

E. Pfaff's book, published in 1942, summarized the discussions up to the year 1940. The book is well structured, though perhaps, on occasion, the subtle shades of opinions presented are sacrificed for rigidity of form. Nevertheless, the study is an indispensable source for anyone who would want general information on the different currents of thought. (4)

It can be said that, up to 1940, apologetic concerns had

predominantly captured the attention of the critics. The skeptics felt bound, in the name of history and of literary criticism, to deny any value to Paul's autobiographical passages and to Luke's testimony. The scholars, who had the faith, entrenched themselves in the defensive position of apologetics and honorably acquitted themselves. As a result, few authors who claimed to be critical did not betray a "bad" conscience about this extraordinary fact. In 1948, E. Stauffer asked why the allegedly independent researchers were subjecting authentic texts to such ruthless treatment. In answer to this question, he wrote: "Because any trace of transcendence which overshadowed the happening on the way to Damascus must be eliminated." (5)

The Catholic author, J. L. Lilly, wrote a good article, but still in terms of the old way of presentation. With his analysis of the narratives in the Acts of the Apostles, he upheld their historical authority by comparing the three accounts of the conversion. He emphasized the similarities and the differences according to the ordinary methods, and then proceeded to deal with the various hypotheses which resorted to physiology or psychology in order to provide a purely natural explanation of the conversion. (6)

In the same review, another Catholic, D. M. Stanley, subjected the three accounts (Acts 9, 1-19; 22, 6-16; 26, 12-18) to a thorough examination. (7) He restated, first of all, the various explanations which had been given to the triple repetition of the conversion account in Luke: (a) Some regarded the repetitions as indicative of different sources, as, for example, F. Spitta, H. H. Wendt, and E. Hirsch; (8) (b) E. von Dobschütz interpreted the literary phenomenon as an instance of fidelity to the stylistic devices governing ancient historiography (9); (c) W. L. Knox preferred rather to see the problem in the light of a semitic mode of composition, namely, the tendency towards parallel repetitions (10); (d) finally, others read into the recitation Luke's deliberate intention to emphasize the importance of the conversion and its significance for the channeling of the Gospel to the pagans. (11) In turn, Stanley interpreted the triple account as a literary device which Luke used to secure the legitimacy of Paul's apostolate. Each of the accounts focuses attention on a parrticular facet of the conversion. The account which Luke himself drafted was intended to show that Paul, like the other Apostles, had actually seen Jesus. Paul's Aramaic discourse to the Jews accentuated his encounter with the glorified Lord. Paul's crisis consisted in the impossibility for natural man to reach the supernatural. Finally, the apologia before Agrippa emphasized that the vision of Christ marked the official beginning of Paul's prophetic function under the symbol of the Ebed Yahweh.

In his well-conducted study, A. Wikenhauser was also interested in the differences between the three accounts. (12) First of all, he presented some general considerations on the similarities between the narratives, and then took up two points: 1) That Paul "saw" and "heard" has its parallel in the fact that "the men who journeyed with him" did not "see" and did not "hear"; 2) the "fall to the ground". These two points appear in the descriptions of the vision as they were presented in very different contexts — Biblical, Jewish, Greek, and Christian. In his new commentary, Wilkenhauser evaluated the special qualities, the influences, and the originality of each of the visions. His account is succinct but enlightening. (13)

The most original work on this question is that of J. Munck, which first appeared in French as *La vocation de l'Apôtre Paul* (1947), and republished in the author's major work: *Paulus und die Heilsgeschichte*. (14) The work has two parts, the second of which analyzed the accounts of the conversion. He concluded that the passages in Acts and Gal. 1, 15-16 have traits which essentially concur. The novelty of his contribution consists in his conclusion, that, on the basis of his study in terms of a literary criticism, Luke's attestations had their origin in Paul himself, as well as the very literary forms of the accounts. In the first part of this important study, the author had shown that the happening at Damascus had no pyschological preconditioning, a problem to which we shall return later. Furthermore, Munck relocated the Pauline experience within the province of ecstatic phenomena, for instance, being "caught up to the third heaven" (2 Cor. 12, 2-4), or, speaking in tongues (1 Cor. 14, 6-7). Here we have a new orientation in research which we shall specify later.

The way was open for E. Benz's study, which we mention at this point because he sought to reconcile the three accounts in

Acts. He was principally concerned with the nature of Paul's vision. (15)

According to the regressive type article of W. Prentice, all that we know about the jounrey to Damascus is contained in Gal. 1, 15-17, while the rest is nothing but popular legend. The conversion is a purely psychological affair. Apart from some remarks about the methodology of ancient historiographers, no special attention need be paid to an essay such as this, so thoroughly a priori. (16)

These works clearly indicate how research has been orientated. Before any real criticism can be undertaken, however, the accounts of Luke and of Paul must be strongly subjected to literary criticism, in which process the Epistles should precede the Acts. In such a manner, the Epistles must be studied in the light of the vertical and thematic interrelationships of each factor, and functionally in terms of Paul's perspective on the occasion of each letter. Luke's accounts, on the other hand, have their own proper outlook. In this connection, none of these can escape the critical examination of the sources of the Acts as also of the composition of the discourses which Luke ascribed to Paul. The relationship of these discourses to the actual events constitutes the crucial point in an assessment of the evidence. Too great insistence should not be placed, therefore, on those details which seem contradictory. In the case of Luke's discourse to Theophilus, it is easily recognizable that the reason why the author left various loose ends in his texts is that in the process of editing his work, he adhered to certain criteria and observed laws of composition which allowed or entailed variety within unity.

The sources therefore must be questioned as witnesses and not as defendants. The avenue to follow is that which leads towards a study of their significance.

B. *Psychology of Conversion*

With the deliberate intention to discredit Luke's accounts, some authors were determined from the very beginning to discover factors which must have been influential in setting the stage for Paul's conversion, whether proximately or remotely.

J. Weiss regarded the conversion as the final result of an interior crisis. (17) Similarly, M. Goguel wrote: "The vision was the externalization of a conviction which had sunken deep roots into Paul's soul. Hence, the gradual growth of this certitude constituted the whole problem of the apparition of Christ and the conversion of Paul." (18)

How is the crisis to be imagined? Each author who attempted to do so analyzed it on the basis of his own personal suggestion. For each one, the crisis was nothing but a piece of psychological fiction with one basic postulate, namely, that there must be a natural explanation; therefore, the crisis was psychologically preconditioned.

The vast majority of sceptical historians spoke of an inner restlessness which Paul had experienced and of which Rom. 7 must surely be a description. Life under the Law had become a burden to him. The Law produced sin. The absence of true justice in Israel hindered the inauguration of the messianic era.

This basic position, with appreciable differences, was maintained by C. Weizsäcker, C. Clemen, H. Weinel, R. Knopf, H. H. Wendt, and H. A. A. Kennedy. Those who read into Rom. 7 that Paul had suffered from deep guilt-feelings belong to the same category. Following R. Seeberg, W. Olschewski, and E. Weber, A. Deissmann had accepted and developed the thesis. To this negative factor, Deissmann added a positive preconditioning. (19)

Similar to the explanation of the crisis because of a feeling of restlessness is another argument, based on the Christian influences from which Paul could not have disengaged himself. The journey across the desert gave Paul the opportunity to question the legitimacy of his actions. Of a lively but disquiet mind, fiery but unstable, idealistic but scrupulous, he had experienced the shock of "revelation" which, for him, could have been nothing less than total and decisive. This is the opinion of O. Pfleiderer, which M. Goguel had taken up only to make it satisfactorily presentable. (20)

On the one hand, Goguel seemed to have rejected all psychological preconditioning and had abandoned the description of the restlessness as caused by a non-observance of the Law. On the other hand, he maintained that Paul was influenced by: 1) the ideal of the nascent Christianity which was substituting a morality of the human person for the cult of the Law; and 2) the Christian claim concerning the Resurrection which had occasioned an epidemic of apparitions: "What Paul knew about the group of Christians, the sayings of Jesus which were current in that group, and perhaps also the serenity with which Stephen and others were prepared to suffer for their faith, all exerted on him an attraction that was temporarily repressed by two strong forces — the religious pride of the Pharisee, and the authority of the Law which proclaimed that every crucified person was cursed. Repressed in his subconscious, the forces which were pushing Paul towards the new religion were suddenly released and given new strength." (21) In 1933, nearly twenty years earlier, M. Goguel had already written: "Paul's conversion was not preceded by any crisis of which the Apostle could have been aware. The conversion was preconditioned by a deep anterior ferment in his sublimial *ego*, wherein the Christian claims concerning the resurrection of the Master and the new moral ideal proclaimed by Jesus had made slow headway, while, at the same time, in his conscious mind, they were repressed by the axiom of the curse uttered against the cross and by attachment to the traditional religious forms." (22)

The Christian element in the preconditioning of Paul's conversion was stressed particularly by J. Weiss. He did not admit that a vision of Jesus could have occurred without previous acquaintance with Jesus. Paul, therefore, had known Jesus, and it is in this sense that 2 Cor. 5, 16 is to be understood. (23) Both K. L. Schmidt and O. Michel followed the same line of thought. (24)

Finally, the Judaism and the pharisaism of the Apostle could have prepared him for his vision: As a pharisee, Paul believed in the resurrection of the dead, and the ancient accounts of the "seeing" and the "hearing" of the Prophets paved the way for a new idea concerning the visual and aural experiences of the Son of Man in glory. These suggestions were made by E. Meyer, and perfected by F. Büchsel. (25)

The numerous studies devoted to the problem contributed nothing more, since they merely repeated what had already been said only to coagulate into a subjectivism of the most blatant kind.

However, these works did influence a number of believing Protestants as well as some Catholics. Without denying the supernatural nature of the vision, they accepted the view that Paul underwent some kind of prior psychological conditioning.

Protestant exegetes may be conveniently classified into two groups. The first included the religionists, who were of the opinion that the accounts themselves must be explained in the light of Jewish and Hellenistic parallels, apart from any consideration of the truth of the facts, which cannot be established anyway. (26) The second group belonged with the Catholic authors who did not find in the text any crisis of conscience prior to the happening at Damascus, caused by the inadequacy of the Law, or any proof for the after-effects of Christian events on Paul, or, above all, any trace of the morbid qualities in the Apostle's psychological condition. This attitude predominates even at the present time. (27)

If we would abstract from such arbitrary, psychological reconstructions, then we could concentrate on the following texts, 2 Cor. 5, 16; Acts 26. 14; and Rom. 7, 7-25.

In 2 Cor. 5, 16, Paul writes: "From now on, therefore, we regard no one from a human point of view; even though we once regarded Christ from a human point of view, we regard him thus no longer." (28) It is possible to interpret this verse in two ways. According to the first interpretation, Paul knew Jesus of Nazareth during his public ministry. Hence, in this passage, Paul contrasted his former knowledge with the knowledge he now had. The second interpretation regarded the first as false. The expression, *ei kai egnokamen* could imply an *unfulfilled condition,* so that it could read: "Even had we regarded Christ from a human point of view." However, it is not necessary to go to such lengths as to make the Apostle affirm that he knew only a heavenly Jesus, whereas the earthly Jesus was imperceptible to him. In any event, there does not seem to be any question here of an historical meeting: The expression *egnokenai* signifies more than just a mere external acquaintance; the phrase *kata sarka,* which occurs twice, should have the same meaning in both instances. Now, we cannot force Paul to say that he no longer knew anyone except in the Spirit. The personal pronoun *hemais* is not a synonym for the pronoun "I." *We* now live in a more excellent economy; for we live *kata pneuma.* Those who had known the terrestrial Jesus should not pride themselves in this, since what is important now is to possess the true knowledge which is in the Spirit, for "now the Lord is the Spirit" (2 Cor. 3, 17). Such an exegesis of the text shows that it cannot contain an allusion to any psychological preconditioning for the conversion.

In Acts 26, 14 — "And when we had all fallen to the ground, I heard a voice saying to me in the Hebrew language, 'Saul, Saul, why do you persecute me? It hurts you to kick against the goads'," (29) — the very last phrase cannot be understood as a description of Paul's psychological condition. It is simply a proverb, for which there are parallels in Greek literature, (30) meaning: what can man do against divinity? In itself, the expression in 14b could refer to Paul's resistance to God's advances before his conversion, or it might equally refer to those which he could posit to the present and future summons of the Risen Christ. J. Munck had emphasized clearly that Paul always felt the *anagke* of his apostolic condition. He cited two texts in this connection: 1 Cor. 9, 16, "For if I preach the Gospel, that gives me no ground for boasting. For necessity is laid upon me"; and Phil. 3, 12, "but I press on to make it my own, because Christ Jesus has made me his own." There is no trace of interior struggle before the conversion. Everywhere in Acts and in the Epistles, Paul appears as a zealot for the Law, unhesitatingly sure of himself, for as he himself wrote: "As to the law a Pharisee, as to zeal a persecutor of the church, as to righteousness under the law blameless" (Phil. 3, 6) — in fact, a man who numbered among his glories in Judaism that he was "a persecutor of the church of God." (31)

The final passage, which has taken up the attention of the greatest exegetical scholars for a long time, is Rom. 7, 7-25. (32) This passage is written in the first person and has been interpreted as a summary of Paul's experience under the Law, in which we are made to share his inability, his discouragement, and his revolt against a religious system whose emptiness was all the more bitterly felt for having been previously embraced with such enthusiasm. It could perhaps be regarded as the description of his sentiments as a Jewish child. (33)

It may be said that such an explanation today is almost universally discarded. "The trauma arising from Paul's painful failure in the observance of the Law, which some have sought to read into Rom. 7, is now relegated to the museum of exegetical misinterpretations," wrote P. Démann, whose staunch supporter was F. J. Leenhardt. (34) In fact, the commentators refer only briefly to this so-called autobiography of Paul the Jew.

However, O. Kuss, who strongly emphasized the difficulty and obscurity of Rom. 7, 7-25, offered some new material by sifting out certain arguments against the autobiographical character of the passage, without returning to the former positions. The following was his line of reasoning: (a) In no other reference to Paul's conversion is there any allusion to a psychological preconditioning by means of doubts and an emotional or intellectual crisis. *Kuss replied*: This would not necessarily exclude the possibility of such an allusion in Rom. 7; (b) Our pericope is not intended to be biographical but clearly theological. It is not a slice of Paul's life, but a reflection expressed in dramatic depth (Huby). *Kuss Replied*: Nevertheless, parallel passages in Jewish literature are not lacking, where the difficulty and even the impossibility of observing the Law are described; (c) The conversion is described as a miracle due to the unexpected initiative of God. *Kuss replied*: This does not rule out a preconditioning process; (d) Paul never felt that he was leading a life of unhappiness and strain under the Law, since he gloried in pharisaic conduct before his conversion (Gal. 1, 14; Phil. 3, 5-6). *Kuss replied*: In these passages, Paul argued against the Judaizers and took another approach. Consequently, Kuss concluded that it cannot be denied that the debate involved much more than Paul's individuality; but equally it cannot be denied that there may be indications of traits from his life as a Jew in Rom. 7, 7-25.(35)

We regard O. Kuss' answers as no more than partly valid. There is one point we would like to make. Even if Paul did use reminiscenses and experiences from his life as a Jew in order to paint a theological picture of man's status before the coming of Christ, there is no indication that the Apostle related these thoughts to his conversion. Account must be taken of two series of texts, namely, Rom. 7, 7-25, and Gal. 1, 14 together with Phil. 3, 5-6. The two lines never converge in the event of the conversion, or even, for that matter, in any preconditioning process for that conversion. It is necessary to take into account the very nature of the conversion, which, according to Luke and Paul, is not a psychological fact, but a vision caused by a positive act of God in which Paul saw and heard the Risen Christ. Finally — and I regard this an essential factor — it is one thing to include oneself in a perspective where the type is sought for its own sake, and another thing to present oneself as an exemplar in the form of an autobiography. In the first case, the author would not be a total stranger to the states as described, but, at the same time, the general perspective would not necessarily apply to him in each and every detail; in fact, it may very well contain traits which he did not possess at all. A disclosure of autobiographical data would have an entirely different significance.

By way of conclusion, we would maintain that the reasoning, underlying any attempt to establish a psychological preconditioning process towards conversion in the case of Paul, is not sound.

C. *Conversion and Mysticism*

Recourse to hysteria or to epilepsy as the key to explain Paul's vision is such a thing of the past that it is surprising to find the thesis of Pauline epilepsy resurrected by J. Klausner, whose works are otherwise so outstanding. (36) Wilthout going so far, Dibelius and Kümmel asked whether Paul's health did not predispose him to such a visionary state. (37) As we have already observed, M. Goguel understood the term "vision" as a release of the subconscious, a deliverance from complexes and the projection into the conscious mind of elements hitherto repressed. (38) E. Hirsch spoke of a spiritual experience, a visionary stare, mental hypertension, a state in which what is normally imperceptible presents itself to the mind. (39)

The Catholic, W. Prokulski, held that Paul's conversion was an event due to the direct and manifest intervention of God. (40) Jesus of Nazareth, risen and glorified, appeared personally to Paul on the road to Damascus. (41) While most authors contentedly accepted the fact as it stands, W. Prokulski related the phenomenon to mysticism, which he understands as the sum total of those supernatural experiences accorded by God to certain beneficiaries.

According to Paul, God is the author of the Law, which is the manifestation of his love and of his wisdom, and which should bring light and life. Saul was completely dedicated to the Law, and, at the end of his life, Paul looked back with pride to his pharisaic youth. Furthermore, he was a man of prayer, and prayer of course leads to contemplation: When he reached Damascus, the sign given to Ananias was: "For behold, he is praying" (Acts 9, 11). Finally, his messianic ideal consisted in the expectation of a glorious Messiah. For him, it was a religious duty to persecute the Christians, because One who had died on the cross could not have been the true Messiah. It was not a man with a tormented mind and soul who made his way purposively towards Damascus, but a fanatic concerning the things of God, of His people, of His Law, always ready to deliver himself up entirely to the Divine Will.

In the three accounts as we find them in Acts (9, 1-29; 22, 3-21; 26, 9-20), there are some minor differences to which criticism no longer attaches any great importance. What were the obvious signs of the "conversion"? First of all, there was "a light from heaven" which caused Paul's blindness. Then, there was "a voice." St. Augustine had already remarked that, since Paul had been blinded by the light, he could have seen Christ only as a mental picture. Equally, was not the voice also internal? We know that the minor differences concern the visual and aural experiences of his companions. (42)

If from the Acts we proceed to the Epistles, we note the following: (a) Gal. 1, 14-17 speaks of revelations and of revelation *en emoi,* that is, *"in me."* The phrase may mean nothing more than "to me." J. Dupont (43), in line with A. Oepka (44) and W. G. Kümmel (45), claimed that there is no trace here of a psychological experience; (b) In 1 Cor. 15, 3-8, Paul numbered himself among those to whom the Risen Christ had appeared; 1 Cor. 9, 1 ("Have I not seen Jesus our Lord?") says the same thing. But this does not imply an exterior vision, any more than does the apparition in the Temple as recorded in Acts 22, 17-21, which was very real, but not external: *ophthe* can be used in this sense; (c) Similarly, 1 Cor. 5, 8 and 9, 1; Phil. 3, 6-8, and 2 Cor. 4, 6, are all to be understood in terms of an interior revelation.

The expression "interior revelation" does not signify that the phenomenon was entirely subjective. We know about mystical experiences of such Christians as St. Francis of Assisi, St. Thomas Aquinas, and St. Ignatius Loyola. The science of Christian Mysticism recognizes three kinds of visions: the corporal, the imaginative, and the purely spiritual. In the case of the purely spiritual vision, the subject is conscious of the presence of God or of Christ in his soul and receives indubitable experimental knowledge in which the senses and the imagination play no part. It is in this category that Paul's vision must be placed. For him this was his first mystical experience. The instruction and the mission of the Apostle are subsequent phenomena. It is only in terms of a totally profound vision can there be an explanation for the change in the life, thought, and action of the Apostle. Such are the broad outlines of W. Prokulski's study.

For our purposes, a recapitulation of this study is pertinent, but we feel that it is necessary to point out the limitations. In the first place, Prokulski's study does not sufficiently emphasize the difference which Paul himself notes between his Christophany on the road to Damascus and his other visions. Secondly, the parallels he suggests with the phenomena of visions and of auditions experienced by the great mystics call for more careful scrutiny. The difference between a grace given by God as the crowning point of a life of contemplation on the one hand, and a sudden intervention into a life so diametrically opposed to the reception of the divine favor on the other is considerable. Finally, Paul himself placed the vision of the Risen Christ on the same level with the post-resurrection apparitions (1 Cor. 15, 2-8), and ascribed to his vision the characteristics and the originality of the other apparitions. The fact that Paul, as we shall see later on, telescoped his vocation and his apostolic mission into the single moment of his visionary experience (Acts 9, 22-26), shows that the latter was of a special kind and should be considered apart from the post-resurrection apparitions.

However, it is not only among Catholics that an appeal is made to mysticism in order to explain the Pauline Christophany. H. G. Wood upheld the authority of Acts. According to his view, Luke did not invent the accounts, and the traditions on which he based his work are worthy of credence. We cannot reject as fictitious that Paul studied under Gamaliel, that he took part in the martyrdom of Stephen, and that he received letters from the

Sanhedrin authorizing him to persecute the Christians in Damascus. To be completely skeptical about these matters would necessitate the invention of another history. Before his conversion, Paul felt affronted by the anomaly of a crucified Messiah (Dt. 21, 23), and, as J. Klausner has clearly shown (49), by the condemnation of Jesus who endangered the national existence of Israel. Wood claimed that Rom. 7 does not express Paul's interior sentiments. His attitude towards Christ was typically that of the Pharisees; however, the criticisms which Christ had leveled against the Pharisees must have made their mark on Paul. Was the observance of the Law sufficient to ensure salvation? Paul must have had at least some vague notions concerning the claims of the disciples to the resurrection of their Master, and he himself had witnessed the faith of the martyrs. But all this does not explain the fact of his conversion. "Contrary to the opinions of Sadhu and Ratisbonne the Jew, he (Paul) was not converted to a system of Christian thought or to a completely organized tradition. His conversion did not signify any assent to any anterior formulation of the faith, whether of the Judaeo-Christian Church, or of the nascent Hellenistic Church which Stephen represented. Paul was converted to Christ rather than to a Christianity." (50)

Wood's position is similar to the one found in the fine book on Paul by W. von Loewenich. (51) The experience on the road to Damascus must have been an interior phenomenon. But it was a new creation. Spiritual things are no less real than material things. The facts defy all materialistic analysis. How are we to explain the change in Paul's life? We cannot ascribe it simply to imagination, for a disease of the imagination never engendered a spiritual recuperation. Paul was not afflicted with a morbid fanaticism. He was a man of action, with both feet on the ground. Are we to reduce everything to the suggestion that Paul simply lied? His whole life refutes such a suggestion. Can the disciple of Christ be a prevaricator? Of course, in the eyes of those who regard the supernatural as utterly unreal, Paul, Luke, and the Church were simply the victims of self-deception. Paul's vision on the way to Damascus had a twofold effect on him: The Crucified was the Messiah, and Christ's preaching of the love of God had suppressed the Law. In his conversion, Paul discovered the two main themes in his teaching: the Passover and justification. For Paul, to experience Christ was Damascus. His mystical encounter became the Christian mystery.

An analysis of the mystical phenomenon in the conversion of Paul merits further pursuit. Should we not however emphasize all that the phenomenon contains of the original, the singular, and the unique? To enter into the highest level of the supernatural is not accorded to all men; but is not *mysticism* the only name to be given to such privileged experiences which God can and does accord to certain chosen individuals?

Art. 3. Apostle to the Gentiles (52)

What connections are there between the christophany on the way to Damascus and the mission of the Apostle Paul? It is unlikely that anyone can grasp the complexity of the situation by a quick and superficial reading of Acts 9, 15-16; 22, 14-15; 26, 16-18, or of Gal. 1, 11-23. One might say that the vision and the mission are coincident; however, there are several difficulties involved in accepting such a conclusion. As a preliminary step, the accounts must be restudied within the literary context of the scriptural narratives concerning the prophetic vocation. Then, after a re-examination of the status quo of the problem concerning the coincidence or the sequence of the vision and the mission, it would be necessary to call attention to two problems essentially related to the principal question. First of all, what was the theological function of the Damascus vision? Did Paul receive a knowledge of the Christian kerygma at that time, or did he have to rely on a prior ecclesiastical tradition for such knowledge? Secondly, whatever influence the vision may have exerted on the relations between Paul and the Church, there is no doubt that the christophany played an important role in Paul's life and message.

Therefore, our procedure will be as follows: 1) The literary and doctrinal dependences in the accounts within the context of the vocation of the prophets; 2) The relations between vision and mission; 3) revelation and tradition; 4) the vision in the life of Paul. Our intention is not to solve these problems, but simply to point out their principal factors and to indicate the results.

A. *Literary and Doctrinal Dependence in the Accounts.*

Two interrelated problems arise. In the first place, there is no better source from which we can understand Paul than Paul himself. However, his sporadic declarations, as they occur in such occasional compositions within clearly defined circumstances and with well determined goals, must be interpreted in the light of the corpus of Pauline literature. This point is emphasized by the fact that the passages concerning the apostolate and the mission are contextually polemic. As far as Luke is concerned, it would be necessary to decide the nature of the literary composition of the conversion accounts and to compare them with each other, in order to be able to get some picture of the apostolate at this stage of the redaction. G. Klein attempted this in a very informative book, but whose conclusions seem to rest on weak foundations with regard to certain matters. (53) The author assumed that many problems had been critically resolved which in reality required a more thorough investigation. (54) At times he attempted to reconstruct Luke's propensities on the basis of some quite tenuous indications, or by adopting an interpretation, often peremptory, other than his own. In any case, the study of Luke must be taken up again on the basis of the *Redaktionsgeschichte.*

The second problem is less a question of comparison than of an understanding of the texts themselves. E. Lohmeyer, K. H. Rengstorf, and H. Windisch, among others, have directed their attention to the dependence of the Pauline and Lucan accounts of Paul's conversion on the descriptions of the vocations of the prophets as given in the Old Testament. (55)

Msgr. Cerfaux made a special study of the problem, and directed our attention particularly to the influence of the theme of the "Servant of Yahweh" in the accounts of Paul's vocation. (56) However, it fell to the lot of A. Bertrangs, a disciple of Msgr. Cerfaux, to tackle the problem again, and to develop it more completely. He transferred the problem to the level of literary criticism, and asked how Paul had related his vocation and his mission to the happening on the way to Damascus and to the Old Testament. (57)

The vocation as presented in Gal. 1, 15-16 has its parallel in Is. 49, 1 and Jer. 1, 5. Both texts and ideas correspond with

those of Paul. However, instead of God, it was Christ who took
the initiative and who was the object of the visions. Furthermore,
Paul characterized his vision as apocalyptic. Bertrangs interpreted
the preposition *en* in the phrase *en emoi* as indicative of the
place where the phenomenon occurred as well as of the means
whereby the revelation was effected. Paul however depended
more on Isaiah. His realization of the vocation is described in
the Epistles in terms of the image of the *Ebed Yahweh*, in harmony with Is. 49. Not only does Gal. 1, 15-16 bear similar dependence, but 2 Cor. 6, 12 explicitly quotes Is. 49.8. Paul claimed
that he was sent to the Corinthians in the place of Christ, and
thereby he applied to himself the text from Isaiah. Furthermore,
Rom. 14, 11; Gal. 2, 2; Phil. 2, 16; and 1 Thes. 3, 5, either by
quoting Is. 49, 18 and 45, 24, or by allusion to Is. 49, 9, all
presuppose that Paul had resorted to the same thought complex.

Acts 26, 16-18 contains allusions to Is. 52, 6, 7-16, as also to
Ez. 2, 1 and Jer. 1, 7-8; Acts 9, 15 recalls Jer. 1, 10; Acts 13, 47
= Is. 49, 6; Acts 18, 9-10 = Is. 41, 10 and Jer. 1, 8; Rom. 14,
11 = Is. 45, 23; 2 Cor. 6, 1 = Is. 49, 4; 2 Cor. 6, 2 = Is. 49,
8; Phil. 2, 16 + Gal. 2, 2 + 1 Thes. 3, 5 = Is. 49, 4; 2 Cor. 4,
6 = Is. 41 + 49, 6:9; Rom. 15, 20-21 = Is. 52, 15; 2 Cor.
10, 8 + 13, 10 =. Jer. 1, 10. Paul however did not identify himself with the *Ebed Yahweh*, but claimed only to have continued
his work. Luke applied Is. 49, 6 and 42, 6 only to Christ (Lk. 2,
32), for it was Christ who alone fulfilled the mission in accord
with the Isaian passage (Acts 13, 7 and Is. 49, 6; Acts 18, 9-10
and Is. 41, 10). In conclusion, if Christ was the realization of
the *Ebed Yahweh*, then Christ's vocation was the model for Paul's
vocation, for it is not improbable that the Apostle understood that
Christ entrusted him with a task in accord with the prophecies of
Isaiah. Among the Catholics, A. M. Denis accepted and used
the same cross references (58) ; J. Munck carried out the research for the Protestants. (59)

The dependence is more actual than merely literary. Thus, the
settings for the apostolic vocation in Is. 6, Jer. 1, and Ez. 2, 1-3,
11 evidence the immediate intervention of Yahweh, and praise the
authoritative initiative of God. It is, in effect, a mark of these
visions that the recipient felt the grasping power of Yahweh,
which he could not counteract.

It is advisable not to follow this line of thought to such an extent that one would go beyond the normal limits of the texts themselves. A distinction must be made between the fact and how Paul and Luke made use of Old Testament texts theologically. A keen interest in these studies is not out of place. The underlying currents of a text fixate it in its literary genre and highlight its originality. However, are we to conclude that any use of Old Testament texts implies a resumption of a doctrine in the exact perspective of the texts which are borrowed? Some may think that the real link between the Servant of Yahweh and Paul is distinctly weak, and they would feel secure in their opinion by the fact that Paul makes no explicit reference to it.

On the basis of these analyses, one conclusion clearly stands out, namely, that Paul had described his vision and his vocation in the light of the Old Testament — not only in the light of Deutero-Isaiah, but, of Ezechiel as well, and, above all, of Jeremiah. Paul's literary interpretation goes hand in hand with the vision and the vocation by virtue of his subsequent theological study. It is quite clear that the Apostle did not begin with the texts and the facts of the Old Testament to describe the event. He began with the vision and the vocation, and proceeded to adapt the prophetic texts from which he derived the significance of the facts. Such recourse to Old Testament texts made him apostolically aware that he was an integral part of the prophetic line. It is possible to pursue the matter any further?

B. *Vision and Mission*

Concerning the problem of the connection of the Christophany with the mission of Paul as the Apostle to the Gentiles, there are many opinions which are diametrically opposed.

For a great number of authors, Paul's vocation coincided with the time of his conversion. To cite only the principal studies in recent years, there are E. Pfaff (60), J. Munck (61), L. Cerfaux (62), E. Stauffer (63), and H. Schlier (64). For example, according to Msgr. Cerfaux, "what we call his conversion is simply his vocation to the apostolate to the Gentiles." (65) E. Stauffer wrote: "The happening at Damascus is therefore an act of vocation," (66) to which H. Schlier added, "a conversion which, on the basis of the texts, we should call a vocation." (67) E. Barnikol (68) and A. Oepke (69) also had this opinion.

In support of this opinion, E. Pfaff proposed some traditional considerations. (70) With the exception of Phil. 3, 12, Paul, in his Epistles, always speaks of vocation and not of "conversion." Acts does the same. In Acts 9, Ananias gave Paul a revelation from the Lord which included a universal apostolate. The account occurs in a literary context which develops the motif on the spread of the Church of Jerusalem to the Gentiles. Chapters 22 and 26 are missionary discourses wherein the primary element is the vocation to the apostolate of the Jews and of the Gentiles.

However, F. Benz (71), E. Fascher (72), and A. Fridrichsen (73) believed that the vision and the vocation were two acts which were chronologically distinct. The words of Ananias to Paul are not clear. The words ascribed by Luke to Jesus (26, 16-18), the only words which explicitly state the coincidence in time of the vision and of the vocation, are a summary reconstruction of the facts. The vocation is telescoped here with the vision, and there is no question of a denial that, after his sojourn to Arabia and his return to Damascus, Paul received an additional call concerning a mission to the Gentiles. We do not know when this happened. According to Fridrichsen, Paul's vocation was confided to him in a later mission — the one recorded in Acts 22, 17-21. Paul never was the Apostle to the Gentiles exclusively. Greeks and Jews were never placed on the same footing, except in Eph. 2, 19, which Paul did not write. The "Gospel" preached by the Apostle was an interpretation of the common data. Fridrichsen derived proof for this conclusion from his interpretation of 2 Cor. 4, 3. For him, the expression "veiled" meant that the knowledge came only through "apocalypse," and the latter was distinct from the vision. (74)

A. Bertrangs attempted to refute A. Fridrichsen. (75) He admitted two developmental phases in the Pauline vocation. In the first phase, it would not have occurred to the Apostle to establish Christian communities which would have been ethnically separated. It was at Antioch in Pisidia that he had this new idea. Once the Jews proved to have been recalcitrant, Paul turned to the Gentiles (Acts 14, 15-17). Another change of attitude is shown by the fact that, at Antioch, the discourse was properly intended for the Judaeo-Christian type, whereas, at Lystra, it was properly universal in tone. But, he added, one cannot deny that at the time of the Damascus vision, Paul received his vocation as Apostle to the Gentiles. Luke understood this clearly and intended that it be understood in such a way as is evident from Acts 9, 29.

Paul Gächter returned to the question explicitly and in greater detail. (76) The eminent professor examined the Epistles and the Acts to establish the relationship between vision and vocation. Of the Epistles, he examined the following passages: Gal. 1, 15 f; 2 Cor. 4, 6; Phil. 3, 12; 1 Cor. 9, 1; 1 Cor. 15, 7-10. From these passages he concluded that the Pauline writings do not enable us to reach a final decision as to the time, place, and manner of the mission with which Christ had entrusted Paul. However, such information can be deduced from I Cor. 1, 17; Gal. 1, 1 and 1, 16. (77) Von Campenhausen reached the same conclusion. (78)

As far as the Acts is concerned, it is necessary to distinguish between the simple narration of the facts as reported in the three accounts, and the subsequent reflection on and presentation of those facts such as we have in Acts 26, 16b-18. Having based his argument on the accommodation of passages from Jer. 1, 5-8 and Is. 49, 1, Gächter found evidence here of a subsequent rumination on the facts. Even if these accommodations are to be traced back to Paul (cfr. Gal. 1, 15), they may still be the fruit of a theological reflection on the past events. Besides, a comparison of Acts 9, 10-19 with 22, 12-16 clearly evidences a conscious literary occupation and a co-ordination of traditions at the period of redaction. Thus, Gächter concluded positively: "In his Damascus vision, Paul did not receive a mission and at that time did not become the Apostle to the Gentiles." (79) Damascus represented nothing more than one point in the development which was to follow, but whose precise line is difficult to trace. The awareness of being set aside for a mission to the Gentiles came to him during his missions among the Jews between the years 46 and 48. Thus, Gächter, seemingly without knowing it, fell in line with Fridrichsen's opinions.

The professor from Innsbruck finally raised a second question: In his Damascus vision, did Paul perceive any mission whatever to the apostolate? He answered in the negative. However, there is a subjective element to be taken into account. Previously, Paul had been entirely dedicated to Judaism, but now as a Christian, he felt that it was imperative that he devote himself to Christ as ardently as he had opposed him. It is in this way that the *anagke* of 1 Cor. 9, 16 and the *katelemphthen* of Phil. 3, 12 must be interpreted.

Undoubtedly, somewhere between these two opinions is the truth. At the very moment of the Christophany, Paul had no clear conception of his election as Apostle to the Gentiles; however, he was delegated by the Church to carry out his mission. His understanding of salvation was radically changed by the fact that he had seen the Risen Christ; hence, fervor for the Law was transformed into zeal for Christ (Rom. 10, 4). Now he was completely at the disposal of Christ, although his temperament had not changed in any way. When Christ took hold of Paul, he became his servant first, and then he became his witness and Apostle. On the other hand, Paul never betrayed an awareness of ecclesial or authoritative intermediation. He remained faithful to his race and to his early conception of Israel's privileged election (Rom. 9-11), but at the same time, he became aware of new factors. Jesus was the Christ, and had been raised from the dead by the God whose Son he is. (80) Paul realized thereby that religion was for the good of all and that salvation was for all since it was no longer bound up with the observance of the Law (2 Cor. 5, 17). The message was to be carried to the Gentiles as well as to the Jews. Those who believed were united, and this unity demanded solidarity with those who had the following credentials: First of all, as witnesses to the acts and the words of Jesus; as witnesses to the Christ who had shown himself in his glorified state, before Paul had the experience; as witnesses in their own lives to the truth of the events. The Twelve were the Twelve Apostles. (81) But it was the Risen Christ who had made Paul an "apostle" by a unique privilege equivalent to the mission of the other apostles. He regarded the Church in Jerusalem as the first realization of the economy of salvation, (82) and those who labored there as the first persons to be inheritors of the messianic promises. Independently, in view of his own vision, he regarded himself as having been appointed immediately by Christ (Gal. 1, 1; cfr.

Rom. 1, 1), as they had been, to proclaim what he had seen. The vision did not per se create Paul an Apostle, although he did know that the Damascus vision was not to be considered to be on the same footing with his other visions. It was not only unique, but it also represented more than an individual experience, for it contained the germ of a vocation that was to be revealed later. (83) The growth of the Church at Antioch (Gal. 2, 1-10) as well as of the first missionary endeavors took care of the rest. Subsequent reflection upon God's actions, in which the light of the Old Testament (Gal. 1, 12-16) and the mounting polemics gave depth to the initial data (1 Cor. 11, 23; 15, 2:11), enriched the event. Luke carried this development over into his accounts of the conversion: While he reported the original facts, he also presented a version which included both the event and its subsequent interpretation. Since there was only one Risen Christ, there could be but one salvation and one Church; and the *koinonia* in doctrine and in charity was the ideal for all. The alternative Peter *or* Paul evinced a false perspective; it is necessary to adhere to the combination of Peter *and* Paul, both apostles of the same Christ, and founders of the same Church. (84)

C. *Revelation and Tradition*

That Paul was chosen by God to proclaim the Gospel to the world is a fact which emphatically stands out in his correspondence. That he received direct communications from God was something which the Apostle incessantly maintained. Once this twofold presupposition is admitted, there immediately arises the question concerning the relations between the direct revelation and the ecclesiastical tradition. But, as P. Gächter remarked, it would be a mistake to envisage Paul as if he were, so to speak, a parachutist with complete equipment in infallibly working condition. (85) When H. Dieckmann (86), and Y. Zapelena (87) saw Paul as one who possessed all necessary knowledge to begin immediately to conquer the entire world, they demonstrated their evident lack of respect for history and for the texts. And as Gächter clearly pointed out, such a position incurs the risk of positing a twofold foundation of Christianity: An institutional foundation by the Twelve, and a charismatic foundation by Paul. A position such as E. B. Allo had assumed, namely, that from the very day of his conversion, Paul already had in his mind explicitly all those propositions which were essential to his teaching, must therefore be categorically rejected. (88)

An article of Ph. H. Menoud contains the most penetrating study we have on Paul's relations with tradition. (89) In his usual lucid style, the author studied the influence Paul's conversion had on his theology. For Paul, the conversion constituted a revelation, for it entailed a transformation of his faith and of his Jewish hope in the Messiah. His conversion was not the final outcome of a moral crisis; rather, it was a theological fact. The error in the Jewish conception of the Messiah became clear to him. The Christians were the ones who were right after all. On the basis of these ideas, the author made two deductions: First, if God has revealed himself through the Son, then theology must be a revelation (Gal. 1, 11 f.); and secondly, Paul could not have been the founder of a new religion, for Paul had to take his proper place among those who had been constituted apostles before he was (Gal. 1, 17). The implication is that his new faith was deeply rooted in tradition. Such a theology was based on the conversion along the following lines: 1) There is unity between the Old Testament and the New Testament because of God's action. Hence, the Christians are the continuants of Israel, but constitute the Israel of God (Gal. 6, 16). They differed from the Jews because their Messiah had already come: He died and rose from the dead. Justification is an event that is both past and present (Rom. 4, 25). 2) The cross was much more than a scandal; it was not simply a fact in the life of Jesus, but the affirmation of the value of redemption, namely, a transformation of the wisdom of the wise (1 Cor. 1, 18-25). 3) Eschatology was not of two types, present eschatology and future eschatology. As for tradition, Paul thought of it: (a) as a communion of the saints in love and in unity; he sought the approval of "the men in authority" (at Jerusalem) lest he "should be running or had run in vain" (Gal. 2, 1-10); (b) Paul appealed to the traditions (1 Cor. 11, 2; 11, 23; 15, 18); (c) he was completely aware of the unity among the believers — everything that came from Jerusalem returned to Jerusalem.

Beginning with the concept of tradition, Msgr. Cerfaux likewise reached an identical conclusion. The apparent contradiction between the direct communication from God (Gal. 1, 12:16) and the reliance on the apostolic tradition (1 Cor. 15, 3 ff) was resolved in the unity of the Risen Christ, since Christ was the object of two syntheses — the one evangelical and the other apostolic — both of which merged into the same faith and in the same notion of a living and teaching community. (90)

In dealing with Gal. 1, 16, Msgr. Cerfaux and A. M. Denis correlated the revelation given to Paul with eschatology. As they saw it, the apparition of the Risen Christ should belong in the category of eschatological events. (91) This revelation (*apokalupsai*) is the brand on salvation-history, which now has entered into the fullness of time. Thus, the conversion is no longer a personal event, but belongs to salvation-history. It is the presentation of the glorified Christ through his Apostle, and it represents an important theological moment in the revelation of the mystery of God.

W. Michaelis reached the same conclusion. For him, the term *ophthe* (1 Cor. 15, 8) has a dynamic meaning: The word includes not only the meaning of a "visual perception," but also the meaning of a "revelatory happening" (*Erscheinungen und Offenbarungsgeschehen*). It is just another way of expressing what Paul himself said in Gal. 1, 16. (92)

D. *The Vision in the Life of Paul*

The vision on the way to Damascus made a deep impression on Paul's life. This is not the place to deal with the entire problem of the apostolate, which was the subject of an exhaustive bibliographical study by E. M. Kredel. (93) We shall only consider three titles which the great Apostle applied to himself, in order that we may more clearly determine the originality of his personality within these categories.

1). *APOSTLE.* In his work, *L'Institution et l'événement*, Professor Leuba proposed some profound views. (94) He made a distinction between the charismatic apostolate and the institutional apostolate, and showed that such a distinction does not constitute an opposition. Both are founded on the same initiative and on a command of the Risen Christ. Paul's apostolate was real and was recognized by the Church as such. Leuba's book was enthusiastically received by Catholic scholars, among others, by J.

Hamer and R. Aubert. (95)

Msgr. Cerfaux dealt with the same point in his study on the unity of the apostolic community in the New Testament, in the Church and the churches. (96) We are also indebted to the same scholar from Louvain for his profound study on the Pauline antinomy of the apostolic life. (97) An original element in Paul's description of the apostolic life is the systematically recurrent motif of his awareness of the divine call, which is simultaneously linked with the avowal of his weakness according to the flesh. The theme has its origin in the Prophets, but in Paul, it predominates as much by the exaltation of his apostolic awareness, of his certainty, of the necessity to obey the command, of the *parresia*, (98) as by the description of the weakness of the "chosen vessel." In accordance with the natural patterns of his temperament, however, Paul passed from the confession of his limitations to the exaltation of his merits. He does not shrink from sounding his own praises and glorifying himself in the Lord (1 Cor. 1, 3; 2 Cor. 10, 17; 11, 1; 12, 11; 12, 19), but here again he was simply following the example of the prophets (Jer. 9, 22-23). Finally, as if from the depths of his own being, Msgr. Cerfaux subtly analyzed the Apostle in the presence of God, advancing from obedience to prayer, from oblation to mystical union. (99) In a most enlightening article, M. Sabbe summarized well the studies of his master. (100)

2). *PROPHET*. Two other students of Msgr. Cerfaux, namely, A. M. Denis (101) and J. Giblet, (102) have taken as their subject the prophetic function of Paul. A. M. Denis paid special attention to the themes, whereas J. Giblet penetrated into the very heart of the matter. Msgr. Descamps (103) dealt summarily with the same material, but at the same time, placed it in its true light.

3). *SERVANT*. G. Sass emphasized the idea of the *doulos* in Paul. (104) The semantics of the word indicate that it has lost its original meaning as designating a "slave," to take on the meaning "to be at the service of" and, in particular, "to be at the service of God." In the New Testament, it is predicated of only a few persons. Paul reserved it for himself, Timothy, and Epaphras. Above all, he gave it a meaning that was social and religious. The *doulos* was the delegate at the service of the community. This function came from God, and was not due to "the favor of men" (Phil. 1, 1; Gal. 1, 10; Rom. 1, 1). The meaning of "service" persisted, so that the *doulos* of Christ should be a servant to all men (2 Cor. 4, 5). This term included the ideas of belonging to Christ, of fulfilling a community function, and of being at the disposal of others, — not independently of each other, but all three meanings combined into one unified thought. What more suitable word could be found to characterize the personality of the Apostle? (105)

E. *Conclusion*

It is extremely difficult to formulate a comprehensive judgment on the personality of Paul. If interest lies in something more than some broad generalizations, then it would be necessary to glean the characteristics of the Apostle from a meticulous analysis of all the Epistles, and to cull from Luke the impress which the Master left on the disciple. In the introduction to the translation of the Epistles in the *Jerusalem Bible*, P. Benoit condensed the essential elements of these two sources of information.

What we would like to emphasize by way of conclusion is the profound union of the man with his message. One may well attempt to distinguish in Paul the Jew from the Greek, the preacher from the theologian, the mystic from the apostle; one might even wish to highlight his doctrine of Christ as dead and risen, his soteriology and his christology, his ecclesiological teaching and his moral system, his attitudes towards the Law, and his breadth of vision with respect to the Gentiles; however, one invariably is compelled to return, not to a melange of ideas, but to the vision of Jesus Christ, not to a myth, but to a reality, not to an object of worship, but to worship itself, not to an aggregate of people who believed, but to the very soul of the Church, which is the extension of the Risen Christ through the action of the Spirit. Of course, it will be recalled that Paul was an ardent lover of God and of Christ, a warmhearted man, a violent polemicist, a mystic who was also at times an intellectual, a Jew, and a Greek.

Paul's work cannot be separated from his person, and both are inscribed in an experience which began at Damascus and was to end only with his martyrdom. Jesus of Nazareth was the Messiah and the Lord, and his Gospel became not only the Gospel of Paul, but also Paul's work, life, and very being. Whether Paul resounded with an ardent hope in the Lord's Return, or superseded all worldly wisdom with that of the Cross, or substituted salvation by faith in Jesus Christ for salvation through the Law, or organized the mores and cult of the communities, or polemicized against embryonal errors, what was always of importance to him and to the faithful was the dynamic presence of this Jesus in the New Age. Jesus was present by the freshness and the strength of the Messianic promise that was fulfilled in his person; he enacted self-realization through the outpouring of his Spirit and the demands of his Love, through the promise and the expectation, in the totality of his limitless Body. This same Jesus so inspired the *prophet*, so mastered the *servant*, and so powerfully communicated his action to the *apostle*, that Paul's personality appears as a transparent realization and the literal translation in terms of real-life of those words: "It is no longer I who live, but Christ who lives in me" (Gal. 2, 20).

Chapter IV

PAULINE CHRONOLOGY

The problem in studies on the history of St. Paul which has commanded considerable attention is certainly the chronological sequence of his journeys. It is a problem which cannot be ignored, because what decisions are made in these matters directly relate to the question concerning the chronology of the Epistles, as well as to the time-intervals which separate one letter from another chronologically. Moreover, the resolution of the problem has a direct bearing on another question which has provoked considerable thought, namely, St. Paul's development.

In connection with chronology, two problems arise, which are distinct, but related. The first problem is whether there are events in the life of Paul which can be synchronized with events in the general history of the times. Once these dates are fixed, the second problem is whether it is possible to determine the relationship of the different points of the chronology. The first problem is a question of absolute chronology; the second, of relative chronology. We shall deal with each in turn. (1)

Art. 1. An Absolute Chronology

Our primary sources here, as before, are the Pauline Epistles and the Acts of the Apostles. Moreover, as we have already

pointed out, a host of literary and historical problems condition
the relative value of the Acts, and determine to what extent the
Acts can be used. A lack of space and the nature of our present
work do not warrant an engagement with the details of the discussions, which the reader can find elsewhere. (2)

Neither the date of the birth of the Apostle nor of his conversion can be known by means of some relationship with fixed
dates. The first event which can be evoked is Paul's escape from
Damascus; the second is Paul's journey to Jerusalem at the time
of the famine; the third is his trip to Corinth; and the fourth
is the deposition of Felix, the Roman procurator. There is no
system which would enable a historian to fix the points of the
Pauline chronology on the basis of the Acts. (3) In fact, we shall
not even follow the chronological sequence of those events. But
even here, one date more than any other deserves investigation,
namely, Paul's first sojourn to Corinth and his encounter with
Gallio. This date is the most reliable in the entire chronology
and, in fact, helps to determine other points in the sequence.
Therefore, it surely deserves primary consideration.

A. *Gallio at Corinth*

Apparently, everything has been said that could be said about
the fragmentary inscription discovered at Delphi, which has made
it possible to date the sojourn of Gallio at Achaia, and to determine with certainty a definite point in Pauline chronology.
We shall merely present a brief summary of the facts. (4)

Border disputes between Delphi and neighboring villages were
brought to the attention of Claudius for resolution. In his response
in the form of an imperial rescript, which was discovered at
Delphi, he cited the name of a certain Lucius Junius Gallio, son
of the rhetorician Annaeus Seneca, and elder brother of the
philosopher Seneca. Since the year 27 A.D., Achaia was a sena-
torial province governed by a Proconsul. The office was ordinarily determined by lot, and lasted for one year. Even though
Claudius had returned the province of Achaia to the hands of the
Roman Senate in the year 44 A.D., it was still possible for him
to directly nominate the Proconsul.

The inscription has been dated to the twenty-sixth acclamation,
which was the honor accorded to an Emperor after a victory. (5)

The date of the twenty-seventh acclamation has been determined, since it is recorded on the dedicatory arch of the Aqua Claudia (the Porta Maggiore in Rome), and in an inscription published by H. Dessau. (6) According to Frontinus, the date for the dedication of the Aqua Claudia was August 1st, 52 A.D. This would mean that the dedication occurred in the twelfth year of the tribunate of Claudius, which extended from January 25th, 52 A.D. to January 24th, 53 A.D. In the course of the preceding year January 25, 51 A.D. to January 24, 52 A.D. there were three acclamations: The twenty-second, for which we have a date, (8) the twenty-third, whose date we do not know, and the twenty-fourth, whose date we do know. Hence, should the twenty-fifth acclamation be then assigned to the same year as the other three, the eleventh year? (9) If so, then the twenty-fifth acclamation would have occurred in the Autumn of 51 A.D., since the winter months would not have been well suited for military operations. However, in that case, this would have been the only year in which there were more than three acclamations. More likely, it should be dated therefore to the twelfth year of Claudius, after January 25th, 52 A.D. Consequently, the twenty-sixth acclamation, in which we are interested, should be placed between January and August of 52 A.D., since the twenty-seventh acclamation occurred in August of the same year. (10) The Proconsuls elect would have left Rome in April, and the one assigned to Achaia could have arrived there in the month of May. Since the rescript of Claudius, dated on the basis of the twenty-sixth acclamation, was issued during the beginning of the year 52 A.D., then Gallio could have occupied his post either from June 1st, 51 A.D. to June 1st, 52 A.D., or from June 1st, 52 A.D. to June 1st, 53 A.D. Since the letter of Claudius was issued before August 1st, 52 A.D., if we opt for the second date, then the case of the Delphic border dispute was heard, judged, and reported to the Proconsul on his arrival. Therefore, we would accept the first date as the more probable, and that Gallio was Proconsul from 51 to 52 A.D.

It is equally probable that Paul's appearance in Gallio's court should be dated towards the end of Gallio's stay in Achaia. We know that the Apostle spent a year and a half at Corinth, (11) and that after the judicial process, he stayed there only "for some time" — *hemeras hikanas.* The phrase in itself can be used to indicate either a long period of time or a short period of time; but since by way of analogy the case is quite similar to what had taken place at Philippi, Thessalonica, and Ephesus, (12) it would be more probable to say that Paul stayed on for only a short while. Since the interval of "a year and a half" is almost a certainty, we would date Paul's stay at Corinth from the end of the year 50 A.D. to July-September of 52 A.D.

Even though these conclusions may appear to be unquestionable their accuracy depends on several presuppositions: 1) We are not certain whether Gallio was the Proconsul for a period of one or two years; 2) we have calculated Gallio's visit to Corinth towards the end of his mandate; 3) we have estimated that Paul left almost immediately after the case had been settled; and 4) we have assumed that a nomination and an accession to power had occurred in accordance with the usual laws which governed such affairs.

B. *Escape from Damascus*

Acts 9, 23-26 recounts Paul's flight from the city of Damascus. From 2 Cor. 11, 32-33, we know that the result that Paul had Aretas put guards around the city, with the result that Paul had to be let down over the wall in a hamper, through a window, in order to escape. Aretas, king of the Nabataeans, is known in the annals of history as Arithat IV, who ascended the throne about the year 9 B.C. and died in 40 A.D. or a short time thereafter. (13) Apparently, he was not king over Damascus, but the ethnarch would have had the power to control the gates. He must have been the chief of the Arabs who were camped round Damascus, and whom the Jews had charged to get rid of Paul at the time of the escape. The first date, before the year 40 A.D., is of little use for our purposes. Evidently Paul's first journey to Jerusalem should be dated before the year 40 A.D., as we shall see presently.

C. *Journeys to Jerusalem*

Gal. 1, 15-2, 10 records two journeys which Paul made to Jerusalem, the one "after three years," and the other "not till fourteen years had passed." On the other hand, Acts mentions

three, if not four, journeys: In 9, 26, from Damascus on the
occasion of his escape; in 11, 30-12, 24, from Antioch, when
Barnabas and Paul delivered the money of the collection to the
Elders in Jerusalem at the time of a famine; and in 15, 2, from
Antioch, when Paul, Barnabas, and others departed for the Coun-
cil of Jerusalem.

The problem of the relations between these two traditions has
been discussed at considerable length, and perhaps is insoluble.
We shall merely trace the results of the numerous studies by
attempting to assign to the various opinions their relative worth.

Msgr. Cerfaux drew up a program and outlined a method for
those who would tackle such a difficult problem. (14) The
accounts of Luke and Paul are presented from different viewpoints. Only after the details have been studied and interpreted
in the light of these viewpoints, would we be in a position to
handle the entire passage in each case. However, the problem
involves much more than just the details of the journeys to Jerusalem. The best course perhaps would be to content ourselves with
a general concordance. The letter to the Galatians and the Acts
of the Apostles both recount, but with very different interests at
heart, Paul's relations with the apostles at Jerusalem. Paul presents an apologia in behalf of his apostolate; Luke simply
highlights the fact of harmony which existed between the two
parties. When Paul spoke, he did so on the basis of his memories,
and the details which he pretends are of the greatest value; Luke,
on the other hand, had to combine patches of information from
different sources, in which case the resulting combination
partly depended on his own personal suppositions. The best
method would be to interpret Galatians first of all, and then
to enrich the facts thus gleaned with the supplementary information from the accounts in the book of the Acts. However, there
is no real reason to set up Luke's perspective in opposition to
that of Paul. J. Dupont justifiably protested against a tendency
among many exegetes, (15) — who, by the way, are important
men in their field — to give free reign to their creative imagina-
tions. Certainly, the literary processes of Luke in the Acts should
be the starting point of such study, for any ignorance thereof
could only result in reconstructions replete with fantasy. However, an exaggerated pessimism, as found, for example, in the

studies of H. Sahlin and K. Thieme, is quite another matter. As they see it, there is absolutely no chronology at all in Acts 9, 15. (16) With the preliminary remarks taken care of, our principal task at hand is to examine the journeys of Paul in detail.

1. *Famine under Claudius*: An important question arises immediately at the outset of any discussion. In Acts 11, 30-12, 24, Luke states that Barnabas and Paul went up to Jerusalem to deliver the collection, and that they handed the mony over to the Elders there. The collection had been taken up as a result of the prophecy of Agabus, who predicted that a famine would spread over the whole empire. Apart from the Sacred Scriptures, there are extant documents which state that, between the years 40 and 60 A.D., a critical shortage of food spread throughout the empire. Is it possible to synchronize the data from secular history with the text of Acts? If we could fix with certainty the date of the journey of these two companions, one important result would thereby be secured.

Problems of food control are known to have occurred during the reign of Claudius (41-54 A.D.). (17) Suetonius mentioned years in which the crops and harvests were poor. (18) Cassius Dio (60, 11) spoke of a famine which occurred at the beginning of the reign. (19) Tacitus recorded a great famine during the winter of 51-52 A.D. (*Ann.* XII, 43). If one could rely on the testimony of Orosius (20) and of Eusebius in his chronicle (21), the date could be fixed as the year 50 A.D. The chronicle also speaks of a famine in Greece in the year 48 A.D. In order to establish the date for the famine in Palestine, we have to rely on two texts from Josephus. (22)

The first passage states that there was a famine in the Holy Land during the reign of Claudius and the pontificate of Ismael (*Ant.* III, 15, 5). The High Priest is otherwise unknown, and to try to include him in the established list of pontificates between the years 41 and 54 A.D. is for all practical purposes impossible. The second passage is more meaningful, but also more difficult to interpret (*Ant.* XX, 5, 2). As we understand it, the text of Josephus should be read as dating the famine "during the procuratorships of Fadus and Tiberius Alexander." Fadus must have been procurator in the year 45 A.D., and Tiberius Alexander must have taken over the office in 46 A.D. to be dismissed in 48 A.D. When the regime of Fadus ended and that of Tiberius began is uncertain. However, the year 45 A.D. which marks the beginning of the procuratorship of Fadus, and the year 48 A.D. which marks the end of the procuratorship of Tiberius seem to be established.

J. Jeremias had attempted to bring out more precise details on the entire question. He pointed out that the year 47-48 A.D. was a sabbatical year. Consequently, all arable land in Israel would have been left untilled. The high-point of the calamitous famine would have occurred after that year, and therefore in 48-49 A.D., if there had been no harvest until the year 49 A.D. However, such a line of reasoning leaves much to be desired. If the famine had lasted for several years, would the Jews have observed the sabbatical year in the face of such a disaster? Surely, not all Palestinians were Chassidim who would have preferred to die rather than observe sabbatical prescriptions. (25) A famine of such geographical distribution, which would have included Rome, Greece, and the Orient, must have lasted for a long time.

2. *Data from Acts 11-12:* Even though the results are meager and admittedly we cannot establish with certainty the date of the famine, nevertheless, the situation is not so serious. Had we succeeded in so doing, we could not have deduced any certain synchronism with the events which Luke relates in Acts. Luke states that Barnabas left for Tarsus to look for Paul, and when he found him, he brought him to Antioch, where they stayed and worked a whole year (Acts 11, 25-26). In the following verses (Acts 11, 27-30), Luke says that "while they were there some prophets came down to Antioch from Jerusalem, and one of them whose name was Agabus, seized by the Spirit, stood up and predicted that a famine would spread over the whole empire." Luke immediately added as if by way of parenthesis, "this in fact happened before the reign of Claudius came to an end." The next verse records the decision to organize a collection and to place the contributions in the care of Barnabas and Paul to deliver the money to the Elders in Jerusalem. In these texts, there are two principal points which are distinct but related: a) the prophecy and its fulfillment; and b) the collection and the mission of the delegates. If Agabus had really prognosticated, then

the event clearly had not as yet occurred. By adding immediately that the prophecy was fulfilled, Luke really introduces an element of uncertainty. Actually, we do not know whether the collection was begun before the onset of the famine or how long it lasted, or at what time Barnabas and Paul were sent as envoys. Another difficulty arises from the fact that Agabus had announced a famine for the entire *oikoumene,* which, of course, could be reduced to include simply the Mediterranean basin. That the collection was taken up in Antioch and its district for the sake of those who were living in Jerusalem would surely indicate that the famine had not as yet spread to that area.

Even in the chapter that follows, Luke is of little help in clearing up our difficulties. A superficial reading of these texts from Acts would suggest that Barnabas and Paul were in Jerusalem at the time Herod Agrippa (26) put James, a relative of the Lord, to death, imprisoned Peter, and died (Acts 12, 1-23). Actually, these accounts are placed between the report concerning the mission of the delegates (Acts 11, 30) and another report (Acts 12, 24-25) in which Luke begins to point out the growth and spread of the Church (v. 24). Then he immediately adds in verse 25: "Barnabas and Saul completed their task and came back from Jerusalem, bringing John Mark with them." (27) Such a situation would of course place us in the year 44 A.D., the date of the death of Herod Agrippa I.

Such a conclusion is fundamentally premature, because it would imply that we are providing solutions to problems not as yet analyzed. We stated previously that Acts 12 actually is placed between two references to the Journey of Barnabas and Paul to Jerusalem (Acts 11, 30; 12.25). For the passage in Acts 12, 25, we would follow the translation of J. Dupont: "Barnabas and Saul completed their task and came back from Jerusalem, bringing John Mark with them" ("Quant à Barnabé et Saul, après avoir accompli leur ministere à Jérusalem, ils revinrent ramenant avec eux Jean surnommè Marc . . . ") (28). This translation retains the more probable reading *eis Ierousalem,* without, however, reading into the verse a fourth journey of Paul to Jerusalem. Is it possible to separate these two references from the other facts stated in chapter 12 of Acts, — the death of James, the imprisonment of Peter, and the death of Herod? Many authors thought along these lines. First of all, no one would affirm that all these events had taken place during the sojourn of Barnabas and Paul to Jerusalem. Secondly, Acts 12, unlike Acts 16-28, is not based on a diary of Luke, but on traditions which could have originated only from among the inhabitants of Jerusalem. This, as far as Luke would be concerned, would render the traditions more removed, and therefore more incapable of being assimilated and attested. Thirdly, the pericope in Acts 12, 1-23 is a well-defined unit of composition and style, which recalls events from the lives of Mark and Peter, and which undoubtedly can be traced to Luke's Palestinian source. (29) Fourthly, one could easily explain just why Luke had not organized Acts 9, 32-11, 18 and 12, 1-23 in an immediate sequence, but rather had inserted a passage of Antiochian origin (Acts 11, 19-30) between the two Palestinian traditions. Such a sequence would have entailed the inconvenience of placing two large fragments of Palestinian origin end to end. Moreover, since Luke had intended to place the conference after the first missionary juorney, he had to introduce both the conference and the journey. To set the stage for the journey, he had to bring Mark to Antioch with Barnabas and Paul; to fix a proper setting for the conference, he had to emphasize the important role which Antioch played in the birth of the Church. After Luke had pointed out that the collection had been taken up as a result of the prophecy of Agabus, he then proceeded to insert the Palestinian events between Acts 11, 19-26 and Acts 23-14. Since the famine came during the reign of Claudius, "the prophecy which announced the famine had to be properly placed before the reign and hence before the episode describing Herod's death in 44 A.D." (30) The use of the term "hence" does not seem very justifiable as far as evidence is concerned. Suffice it to say with H. W. Beyer (31), that, faced with a tradition which described the events at Jerusalem, Luke sought to point out the sequence of events from the prediction of Agabus to the service rendered by Barnabas and Paul, without much concern for a chronological perspective. Finally, we believe that there has not been sufficient emphasis into a unified context are not very substantial: Acts 12, 1 begins with the phrase *kat' ekeinon de ton kairon*, which, by way of comparison with Acts 19, 23, is understandably vague as far as chronology is concerned (32); moreover, the passage in Acts 12, 25 is separated from the narratives of Palestinian origin by verse 24, with no other result perhaps than that verses 24-25 could have simply served as an appropriate introduction to Chapters 13 and 14.

Therefore, the literary analysis clearly seems to confirm the fact that the events of the collection and of the journey are connected with the death of Herod by links which are very weak. By way of summary, we would like to make the following points: First of all, reference to a famine during the reign of Claudius does not serve as a very likely established point of reference in an absolute chronology. Secondly, the journey of Barnabas and Paul need not necessarily coincide with the reign of Herod Agrippa. The latter point, however, deserves further clarification which we shall present later. For the present, we shall continue our discussion on the question of Paul's journeys.

3. *The First Journey*: *Gal.* 1, 18-19 *and Acts* 9, 26-29: According to text in Gal. 1, 18-19, Paul states that he did not go up to Jerusalem until three years after his conversion. There are no solid reasons why we should doubt the accuracy of the memories of the Apostle. Luke's account of the first journey to Jerusalem in Acts 9, 26-29 establishes the temporal relationship of the event with the escape from Damascus by using the expression *hikanai hemerai*. Moreover, Paul reported that he remained in the Holy City for only fifteen days. Luke's account of the events, on the other hand, would seem to require a much longer period of time. The great majority of exegetes, however, claim that both Acts and Galatians refer to one and the same journey. Paul himself is very explicit on this point, and any suggestion to the effect that he went up to Jerusalem immediately after his conversion would definitely falsify his remarks. (33) On the other hand, there are some dissident voices among exegetes. For example, H. Schlier and D. F. Robinson have identified Gal. 1, 18-19 with Acts 11, 30, namely, the journey involving the collection. Such an opinion has not been favorably accepted, and, as presented by Robinson, definitely causes havoc in Luke's entire arrangement. (34)

4. *Two or Three Journeys?* a) To begin once again with a question of an interpretation of Gal. 2, 1, Paul states that "It

was not till fourteen years (*dia dekatessaron eton*) had passed
that I went up to Jerusalem again. I went with Barnabas . . . "
It is hopeless to substitute the number 4 for the number 14, as
some writers have suggested. (35) Nor is the solution, which S.
Giet proposed, any better, namely, to translate the term *dia* in
the sense of "in the course of." (36) J. Dupont subjected the
reasoning of the professor from Strassburg to a penetrating
critique. (37) Briefly, it is certainly true that the preposition *dia*
has the meaning of "during" rather than of "after." However,
Paul uses the preposition in the sense of "during" only twice,
namely, in Rom. 11, 10 in a citation, and in 2 Thes. 3, 16 where
the expression *dia pantos* means "all the time." However, in Acts
24, 17, the preposition *dia* signifies "after." Therefore, the passage from Galatians should retain the reading "not till fourteen
years" or "after fourteen years."

b) What would be the starting point in time in reckoning the
period of fourteen years? Some authors, who claimed that the
conversion of Paul always loomed large in his thoughts, had
decided to accept the happening on the road to Damascus as the
terminus a quo. (38) Others, who regard highly the expression
epeita of Gal. 2, 1, thought that the point of reference was a
period of fourteen years after the first journey. (39) Since for
the ancients a year begun was a year completed, we could be
justified in reducing the three to two and a half, and the fourteen to twelve and a half or to thirteen, which would come out
to about fifteen and a half years between the time of the conversion and the time of the first journey. We feel that the conclusion of M. Goguel seems to be generally correct: "Neither of
these two arguments is really decisive, and it must be acknowledged that, theoretically at least, the passage from the letter
to the Galatians would warrant the dating of the Council of
Jerusalem some seventeen years after Paul's conversion, and
therefore as closely as some fourteen years after the latter
event." (40)

c) It seems important to decide the question concerning the
identification of the second journey as related in the letter to
the Galatians with the Council of Jerusalem as recorded in Acts
15. We believe that there is far greater probability in favor of
such identity. J. B. Lightfoot and H. Schlier established the

identity of Gal. 2, 1-10 with Acts 15, which, formerly, had been
the general opinion. The geography is the same, the time is the
same, the persons involved are the same, the topic under discussion is the same, the nature of the conference is the same, and
the results are the same. (41)

Such an opinion would not prejudice the value and the significance of Luke's accounts in Acts 11. Few authors, as, for
example, M. Dibelius and his disciple and successor W. G. Kümmel, defended the thesis that those accounts lack all authority.
As they see it, Luke's intention was purely theological, namely,
to show that the call of the Gentiles was due to a direct intervention on the part of God. Whatever facts he may have used in
order to support his thesis were simply fictional. The only reliable sources on this particular point is a statement in Paul's
letter to the Galatians. The only fact with which Luke had been
acquainted was that there was trouble at Antioch and that an
agreement had been reached. All else is pure invention, and Luke's
worth as far as real history is concerned is of no account.

To go to such an extreme does violence to the texts and also
jeopardize Luke's authority in chapter 15. Nevertheless, J. Porter
did not hesitate to do exactly that. (43) According to his
opinion, the Apostolic Council should not be dated after the
first missionary journey. The letter which Luke records in chapter 15 of the Acts is nothing more than an act of intervention on the part of the Church of Jerusalem, and Luke simply
errs by bringing Barnabas and Paul on the scene. The journey
mentioned in Gal. 2, 1 coincides with the affair of the collection,
and should be dated in connection with the latter event.

Ch. H. Buck did not hesitate to go even further. (44) For him,
the chronological data of Acts 11 and 15 should be drastically
rearranged. The collections referred to in Rom. 1 and 2. Cor.
and Gal. represent one and the same undertaking. Twice Paul
brought alms to Jerusalem (Acts 11, 27-30 and Acts 12, 25).
The latter, which must be distinguished from the one mentioned in Acts 11, 27-30, should be dated to a period after the
second missionary journey through Asia and Greece. The Council of Jerusalem took place afterwards, and the other letters mentioned (Rom. 1-2 Cor. and Gal.) belong to the period prior to
the Council. To disturb the chronological relations between the

Council of Jerusalem and the Epistles in such a manner is much too violent. The implication would be a forced exegesis of the expression "fourteen years" in the letter to the Galatians. Moreover, what is reconstructed is a sequence of events which is contrary to Luke's thought without having at one's disposal the factors which Luke did have. And as far as a choice between Buck and Luke is concerned, it would be impossible even to hesitate.

d) This, of course, raises a question which we would consider to be of the greatest importance, namely, whether it is necessary to claim that there were three journeys. An important group of exegetes maintain that there were three, but from two different points of view. The first group held that Paul did not have to mention the journey which involved the collection. (45) Luke, they stated, affirmed that Paul was content to hand over the alms from Antioch to the Elders. In Galatians, therefore, Paul had no real reason to mention the journey. Besides, in this letter Paul had no intention to give a list of his journeys to Jerusalem. When he does refer to his first journey, he merely intended to show that the Gospel, which he had, came from God. In Chapter 2, however, the topic under discussion is entirely different; it is no longer a question of his authority, but of the approbation of his conduct, since he refers to the fact that the authorities recognized his right not to circumcize the Gentiles. (46) Such an acknowledgment was not granted to him when he had delivered the collection to the Elders in Jerusalem, but at the time of the Council in the same city. The journey which involved the collection could have taken place in the year 44 A.D., before the death of Herod Agrippa I, or between the years 46-49 A.D., at the time of the famine.

The authors usually prefer the year 44 A.D. as the date so that the time of the second journey may be reconciled with Luke's statement which apparently affirms the fact that Paul's journey with the collection antedated the death of Herod.

In that case, the passages in Acts 11, 30 and 12, 24 are not necessarily tied up with the event of the Council of Jerusalem. However, the second group of exegetes avoids the apparent contradiction between the statements of Paul and of Luke by maintaining that the passage in Gal. 2, 1-10 does refer to the second journey, and that Paul must have made a third journey during the time of the Council of Jerusalem. These authors adhere to an identification of the passages in Acts 11, 30 and 12, 24 with what Paul states in Gal. 2, 1-10, by accepting as a fact that Luke, a good historian, records three journeys, and that his record cannot be sacrificed for the sake of theories, which, even though based on principles of literary criticm, are nevertheless diversifying and inevitably subjective. In their opinion the statements of Luke and of Paul do not conflict. Hence, the journey which Paul makes after a fourteen year period is the one involving the collection affair. Such a conclusion has dire consequences as far as Paul's letter to the Galatians is concerned; it would mean that we would have to maintain that Paul wrote his letter to the Galatians of the south before the time of the Council of Jerusalem. Therefore, his letter to these Galatians would have to be the first in the line of his correspondence. (47)

The consequences of such thinking encumbers a reconstruction of the given facts with a rather awkward hypothesis. We have emphatically pointed out that the identification of Gal. 2, 1-10 with Acts 15 cannot be rejected. Moreover, that the letter to the Galatians was composed before the year 50 A.D. is highly improbable. Furthermore, to claim that the time interval between the compositions of the letters to the Galatians and the Romans was a period of eight years would be at best a guess. We propose that the most probable recipients of the letter to the Galatians were the Galatians of the north.

Even if one wished to retain the concept of three journeys, the simplest plan would be to date the unquestionable journey Barnabas and Paul made to take the collection to Jerusalem to the year 44 A.D., and to consider this particular journey as one to which Paul makes no reference when he does enumerate those trips involving only official contacts with the Mother Church in Jerusalem. Such a solution would safeguard the authority of Luke, but only at the expense of Paul's. But, after all, the Apostle is the most direct witness to the facts, and with the Galatians he argued in such a fashion that any error would have militated against his whole case, since it would impugn his own authority. On the other hand, Luke's statements are admittedly not exempt from difficulty and lack of precision. Not only is the entire first section of Acts lacking in clear points of reference as far as the succession of facts is concerned, but we have also shown that, on the basis of literary criticism of chapters 11 and 12, there are no absolute affirmations concerning the sequence of events.

e) We realize very well why it is that many historians regard the collection-journey and the journey to the Council of Jerusalem as coincident. It is their opinion that Acts 11, 25-30 describes the event recorded also in Acts 12, 24, and the latter is to be identified with the journey recorded in Acts 15. However, when they attempt to reconstruct the facts, they do so in different ways.

(1) In the first place there is the position of T. W. Manson. He claimed that Gal. 2, 1-10 refers neither to the journey that invloved the collection nor the trip to the Council. Rather, there were two Councils, one before and one after the first missionary journey. The Council which occurred before the journey is the one corresponding to the account in Gal. 2, 1-10. (48)

(2) For some of the critics, the Council of Jerusalem took place before the first missionary journey in the year 44 A.D. In their analysis, the dates for events as well as for the Council are based on Acts 11, 25-30. In the chronological sequence, they also incorporate the death of Agrippa as sychronous. Hence, the fourteen year period stated in Gal. 2, 1 must include the three year period given in Gal. 1. Since the period of fourteen years can be easily reduced to thirteen, the conversion of Paul can be dated to the years 31-32 A.D. In this case, one would have to push the date for the death of Jesus back to the year 28 A.D., or simply retain the year 30 A.D. as the date which would allow only a very short interval of time between the death of Jesus and the conversion of Paul. (49)

(3) As far as other exegetes are concerned, the prophecy of Agabus in the year 44 should be separated from the journey of Barnabas and Paul to Jerusalem to deliver the collection. This particular journey would have taken place only after the first missionary trip of Barnabas and Paul to Cyprus, Pisidia, and Iconium as recorded in Acts 13-14, and would thereby coincide with the time of the famine under Claudius. The year 49 would be the more preferable date. Hence, Paul's conversion would have taken place in the year 35 or 36 A.D. according to the

short chronology, or in the year 33 or 34 A.D. according to the extended chronology. (50)

Exegetes who hold either one or the other of these opinions usually add various theories concerning the literary composition of Acts 15. (51) Generally speaking, some of them consider the chapter to be homogeneous, belonging to the Palestinian source which supplements the ordinary Antiochian strain. (52) Other exegetes see two sources in Acts 15, only one of which would have been originally relative to the Council of Jerusalem and which would have been a continuation of Chapter 11. The other source would have been concerned about facts of an entirely different nature. (53) How the one source is to be distinguished from the other and to what extent each source is present in the narrative are not points on which authors agree. However, discussions of this type are only relatively important as far as Pauline chronology is concerned. We would like to point out that W. G. Kümmel reacted vigorously against such dissections of the text. He stated that the opinion that would claim the presence of interpolation or editorial attempts to unify materials from different sources in Acts 15 rests on rather weak foundations. (54)

(4) John Knox has taken the same general direction, but with some decided differences. (55) Along with many other authors, he identified Gal. 2, 1 with Acts 15. On the basis of these texts, the Council of Jerusalem did not occur, as Luke would have it, between the times of the first and the second missionary journeys, but after the second and before the third, namely, in the year 51 A.D. Furthermore, Knox did not admit that the journey involving the collection could be dated to the years 44 or 49 A.D.; rather, Paul made only one trip to Jerusalem with a collection in the year 53, the date for his last visit to the city. This would mean that the imprisonment at Caesarea should be dated to the years 53-55 A.D., and the Roman captivity to the years 55-57 A.D. Thus, Knox partially follows the thinking of Buck. The result of course is a truncated chronology which changes generally recognized data and which would require a review of the chronology of the Pauline epistles.

Even though such an approach is not impossible, it does entail serious difficulties: (56)

(a) Is it possible that the Council was not held after the

second missionary journey? Knox proposed three arguments: 1) when Paul composed the two letters to the Corinthians, the problem of the Judaizers was still foremost in his mind. G. Ogg made the observation that the misunderstandings between the two camps of the Christian community could have originated at an earlier date, and that it was not because the echoes of the controversy had reverberated during the time of the second journey that the Council could not have predated that journey. 2) Knox identified the mystical experience described in 2 Cor. 12, 3-15 with the conversion, so that the time-interval of fourteen years in Acts would synchronize with the period of fourteen years mentioned in 2 Cor. This of course is pure conjecture with no supporting evidence. At the time of his conversion, Paul was really and truly "in the body." The experience described in 2 Cor is a Christian experience. 3) Even, if at the time of the Council, the "leaders . . . insisted . . . that" Paul "should remember to help the poor" (Gal. 2, 10), nevertheless, he was not required to take up a collection immediately through the evangelized world. However, there is nothing in the text that would exclude collecting the money before the time of the Council.

(b) More positively, the groundwork towards a new chronology would entail serious improbabilities: 1) One of the most important time-references in Pauline chronology is the occasion when Paul appeared in the court of Gallio at Corinth. Knox surely must admit that the decision of the court did not occur during Paul's first visit to Corinth, but must be dated to a subsequent journey. 2) Knox dated Paul's arrest in Jerusalem to the year 53 A.D., because Festus would have been Procurator in the year 55. We shall return to this particular point; however, for the moment, Knox's point of view is highly improbable. 3) Knox is wrong in presenting a truncated chronology as more in accord with the events in Paul's life. According to his opinion, there is scarcely any time not taken up with journeys and activities, from the time of his conversion in the year 37 to his arrest in 53 A.D. There is no certainty about this at all. Our knowledge is much too fragmentary and sporadic to warrant an appeal to a general argument *e silentio*.

5) *Conclusion*: *First of all*, there is no system or approach that would give us absolutely certain results. That the solu-

tions to the problems proposed are only probable is rather discouraging, but an important point to keep in mind.

Second, the writings of both Paul and Luke must be examined from the viewpoint of their literary forms. Questions concerning the agreement or disagreement of data gleaned from the respective texts should be taken care of as corollaries, since neither Paul nor Luke had intentions of setting up a chronology for its own sake. To handle Acts is a delicate matter because of the literary questions. As far as the choice is concerned between the concrete memories of Paul and the narratives of Luke, it is fitting to grant priority to the former.

Third, on the basis of the previous principle, in spite of the slight differences, it is fitting to identify the first journey described in Gal. 1 with the journey recorded in Acts 9.

Fourth, the framework of the entire chronology of the visits is given in the account of the second journey in the Acts: (a) We believe that the coincidence of the second journey with the death of Herod Agrippa I is not clearly and indubitably attested by Luke; (b) on the other hand, we feel that a synchronism with the famine in Palestine should be retained.

Fifth, we think that there is something to be said for the opinion of those who regard the second visit in the year 44 as authentic, and who feel that there was no reason for Paul to speak about it.

Sixth, the literary composition of Acts does not seem to be of such a nature as to exclude the possibility that Acts 11, 30 together with 12, 24 constitute the doublet of Acts 15. We admit that Gal. 2, 1-10 should be identified with Acts 15, and we believe that Paul's second visit occurred after his first missionary journey. The year 49 A.D. would seem to be the probable date coincident with the famine in Palestine and with Paul's presence in Corinth in the years 50-51 A.D.

Seventh, this solution does not seem to be excluded by the assertions made in Acts 11, 30 and 12, 24, nor does it depend on a method of literary criticism that is tarnished by the precarious and the subjective.

Eighth, we are additionally convinced that, because of the recurrence of the expression *epeita* in Gal. 1, 18 and 2, 1, which should have the same meaning in each case, that the three year period should be added to the fourteen year period.

As a result, we would obtain the following sequence of events:

34 A.D. — the conversion of Paul

36 A.D. — the first visit to Jerusalem

47-48 A.D. — the first missionary journey

49 A.D. — the second visit to Jerusalem and the Council

D. *Sergius Paulus in Cyprus*

There is little to gain from any preoccupation with Sergius Paulus. (57) It is certain that the Proconsul carried out his functions in Cyprus; however, it is impossible to date the exact years in which he held office.

One of the inscriptions discovered at Soli, published by Louis Palma de Cesnola (58) and by D. G. Hogarth (59), contains the name Paulus, but without the gentilic name Sergius. It has been inferred that this name must refer to the Sergius Paulus mentioned in Acts (13, 6-13). However, the last two lines of the inscription in which the name occurs had been added to an original inscription. According to K. Lake, these lines were added because, at the time of the first cutting of the original inscription by Co, a certain Apollonius mentioned in the inscription had not as yet received his office of Censor. Hogarth was of the opinion that these lines were added merely to supply for an involuntary omission. The inscription has the expression, "the thirteenth year." If we would follow Lake's explanation of the additional lines, then Apollonius took the office of Censor only after that date; but if we would agree with Hogart, then the lines would have been added at any point within a thirteen year period. Zahn claimed that the thirteen year period began with the accession of Claudius to the throne in the year 41 and therefore would have ended in the year 53 A.D. From such calculations, he concluded that Sergius Paulus was confirmed in office in the year 51-52 A.D. Th. Mommsen and Dessau, however, date the inscription to the year 14 B.C. (61) In any event, the year 53 as the date would have been impossible for Paul's sojourn in Cyprus. Hogarth gave several suggestions on other ways to correct the number "thirteen", but as things stand, the matter is uncertain, since none of the computations successfully identified the Paulus of the inscription with the Sergius Paulus of the

Acts. (62)

A Roman inscription lists the name of a certain Lucius Sergius Paulus among the names of the *curatores riparum*. However, there is no date for the inscription. (63) Pliny mentions among the sources of his Second Book a certain Sergius Plautus, but not a Sergius Paulus as has been supposed. (64)

E. *Banishment of the Jews from Rome*

The banishment of the Jews by Claudius is mentioned in Acts 18, 2. (65) When Paul arrived in Corinth, he met a Jew called Aquila whose family came from Pontus, and whose wife was called Priscilla. Recently they left Italy because an edict of Claudius had expelled all the Jews from Rome.

What was the nature of the edict of Claudius, and when was it issued? It is the usual procedure to refer to the famous statement of Suetonius in connection with Luke's text: "He expelled the Jews from Rome who were incessantly rioting under the instigation of Chrestus" ("Iudaeos impulsore Chresto adsidue tumultuantes Roma expulit".) (66) It is generally admitted that the name *Chrestus* is the equivalent of the name *Christus* (Christ), rather than the name of some emancipated slave. Tacitus confirms the equivalence when he wrote: "Those who were hated because of their shameful deeds were commonly called '*Christians*'" ("quos per flagitia invisos vulgus '*Chrestianos*' appellabat"), to which he immediately adds as a good historian: "The origin of this name is to be traced to a man called Christ, who was punished by order of Tiberius at the request of Pontius Pilate, the Procurator" ("Auctor nominis eius Christus Tiberio imperitante per procuratorem Pontium Pilatum supplicio affectus erat."). (67) However, this is of little consequence for the purposes of our chronology.

Nevertheless, Cassius Dio seems to contradict the statement of Suetonius: "Since it was difficult to banish them from the City without any concomitant trouble, he did not expel them, but merely forbade them to band together." (68) The explanation of this passage presents difficulties. According to some commentators, Cassius Dio, who had in mind the year 41 A.D. when he wrote the statement, was alluding to a decree of expulsion promulgated by Tiberius, which Cassius mentioned earlier in his work, and which Claudius did not execute. (69) We know from the earlier part of his reign that the Emperor was disposed rather favorably towards the Jews. As E. Haenchen suggested, Cassius intended to portray the overall attitude of Claudius towards the Jews. (70) He would have allowed them to retain their rights to practice their religion in separate communities, but not *sunathroizesthai*, that is, to band together on a wider scale. Other authors, including K. Lake, claimed that Dio does not deny the existence of a decree of Claudius, but simply presupposes it. (71) M. J. Lagrange proposed that there were two decrees: The first, issued in the early part of Claudius' reign, would have been liberal in nature, and this would have been the one to which Cassius Dio alluded; the second, issued in the year 49 A.D., was more severe in nature, and this would have been the one to which Suetonius and Luke referred. (72) It is well known that Claudius was as much a fecund legislator as he was a heavy eater. There is no doubt that Suetonius and Acts are right. (73)

Orosius knew the passage from Suetonius and related it to a piece of evidence provided by Josephus. (74) He proceeded to date the decree of expulsion to the year 49 A.D., a decree which we unfortunately cannot find mentioned in Josephus. A. von Harnack pointed out that wherever Orosius used the expression *anno eius* ("in his year") in the account to indicate the chronological sequence, he borrowed texts from the *Chronicon* of Eusebius-Jerome. Furthermore, this is the only instance in which Orosius refers to Josephus, indicating a direct quote from the original source, which could have been either Julius Africanus or Justus of Tiberias. In any case, the ninth year of Claudius, 49 A.D., would suit the general chronology of Paul, and if perchance Orosius had deduced this date from the text of Acts, he should be complimented. (75) Hence, Aquila and Priscilla must have left Rome towards the end of the year 49 A.D. to arrive at Corinth in the early part of 50 A.D., the time when Paul met them.

F. *Deposition of Felix*

The date for the deposition of Felix and the succession by Porcius Festus is most important for the chronology of the letters of St. Paul, and for an appreciation of the development of his thought. (76) There seem to be two opinions: Some date the change of office of Procuratorship to the year 55 or 56 A.D., (77) while others prefer the year 60 A.D. (78) To follow the first opinions would mean that the letters to the Thessalonians, the Corinthians, the Galatians, the Romans, and even to the Philippians would have to be dated to the period between 51 and 53-54 A.D. On the supposition that Paul was imprisoned for two years in Caesarea, all of these letters, except for Philippians, would have had to be written before the time of his imprisonment. Even if we were to suppose that the mention of a two year period would have been a reference to the duration of the procuratorship of Felix, the ordinary time-chart for the composition of the Epistles would be entirely upset.

Without becoming over-concerned with studies which have simply confused the issue, the best place to begin is with the sources. First of all, according to the Acts, Paul was escorted to Caesarea a few days after his arrest in Jerusalem. He remained at the disposition of the Procurator Felix for two years (Acts 24, 27). The new Procurator Festus immediately took up the case, and in the Autumn of that year, sent Paul to Rome. We would agree, therefore, that the expression on "when the two years came to an end" (Acts 24, 27) refers to the maximum duration of protective custody for Paul, and not to the length of time during which Felix held his office. There is no implication at all that a two-year term was the established period for the duration of the Procurator's office, and Luke would have had no reason to mention that Felix had terminated his career in Palestine after a two-year period. (79)

Besides the Acts, we have three other sources of information on the chronology of Cumanus, Felix, and Festus, namely, Eusebius, Tacitus, and Josephus.

Eusebius presents his testimony in his work *The Chronicle,* (80) which has come down to us in an Armenian translation, and in a Latin translation by St. Jerome. The Armenian version dates the accession of Festus to office in the year 54 A.D. (81) According to C. Erbes and D. Plooij (82), Eusebius would have obtained his information from some source, perhaps from a work of Justus of Tiberias. The latter had reckoned the reign of Agrippa II, not from the date of the death of Agrippa I in the year

44, but from his accession to the throne as king in the year 50 when he succeeded Herod of Chalcis. Eusebius, on the other hand, would have begun his calculations with the year 44, which would mean that in order to correct his dates, one would have to add five more years to his calculations in order to date the transference of office from Felix to Festus in the year 59. Luke, however, pointed out certain difficulties in this procedure (83): 1) There is no definite proof that Eusebius had used a source composed by Justus of Tiberias; 2) Eusebius actually uses information gleaned from Josephus, who dated the nomination of Festus to office during the reign of Nero (54-68 A.D.), before the disgrace of the freedman Pallas, the brother of Felix; (84) 3) If the *Chronicle* of Eusebius is correct, then the same principle would be applicable as much to Felix as it is to Festus, which would mean that the former's career had to begin in the year 56 — a date that is clearly much too late, since Claudius was the person who certainly sent Felix to Palestine. According to Jerome's translation of the *Chronicle* of Eusebius, Festus succeeded Felix in the year 56 A.D., and Paul appeared in the court of Felix in the year 53. Since the Armenian version is wrong about the date for the famine as the year 42, and also erroneous about the date of the arrival of Festus in the year 54, many authors prefer to follow Jerome.

It is very difficult to establish what Eusebius had exactly written. Furthermore, his authority is no stronger than the sources which he used — or perhaps source, if he depended only on Josephus. Hence, it is better not to accept his testimony. (85)

The bit of evidence which Tacitus provided is confused to say the least. (86) The date he provided is the year 52 A.D. After mentioning Pallas whom he lauded for desiring to persist in his initial poverty, he proceeds to describe Felix as a man who did not imitate the example of his brother. According to his description, Felix was in charge of Judea "for a long time," and did not hesitate to satisfy his every excessive desire. Side by side with Felix, to whom the Samaritans were subject. Tacitus places Ventidius Cumanus, who ruled over the Galileans. The two peoples plundered each other and brought their booty to the two Procurators. The practice was at first tolerated, but then it got out of hand. Both Procurators attempted to intervene and sent soldiers to restore public order. The detachment, however, was slaughtered. The Governor of Syria intervened to exercise strict justice against the Jews. As for the Procurators, Cumanus and Felix, Claudius had delivered them into the hands of Quadratus to be taken care of as the latter saw fit. Quadratus condemned Cumanus, but protected Felix, whom he could not judge since Felix had been allotted a position in Quadratus' tribunal.

That Tacitus' account is filled with several improbabilities has been well established. Moreover, it gives us no information concerning the succession of Felix (87), and of Festus. However, the reference had to be noted before we could present what evidence we have from the testimony of Josephus.

The Jewish author covers the events in two different places. (88) He never alludes to a division of authority between Felix and Cumanus as far as Galilee and Samaria are concerned. According to his account, Cumanus was succeeded by Tiberius Alexander in the year 48 A.D. Three years later in 51, trouble broke out between the Samaritans and the Galileans, which occasioned the latter to appeal to their fellow Jews in Jerusalem. Their extortions in Samaria forced Cumanus to intervene to subdue them and to take prisoners. Then, both Samaritans and Jews had appealed to Quadratus, Legate of Syria. In his first intervention at Caesarea, Quadratus made a decision against the Jews and issued the order to crucify the prisoners. In his second intervention at Lydda, Quadratus again ordered the crucifixion of some eighteen Jews, and dispatched to Rome as prisoners the High Priest Ananias and his sons, together with the strategist Ananus and others. On the other hand, Cumanus, a leader of the Samaritans and the tribune Celer had to leave for Rome to plead their case.

The intrigues of the Imperial Court decided the outcome of the case. Agrippa II secured the good graces of Agrippina. Claudius had three Samaritans executed, banished Cumanus, and delivered Celer into the hands of the Jews for extermination. Jonathan, the High Priest, sent a petition to the Emperor to give control over Judea, Samaria, Galilee, and Perea to the brother of the very influential freedman, Pallas. Felix was the man.

From the viewpoint of chronology with which we are solely

interested here, we would conclude that Quadratus would have dispatched the captives to Rome during the Passover of the year 52 A.D. Since it must have taken some time to carry out the negotiations, Felix could not have replaced Cumanus until at least the year 53 A.D.

Claudius died in 54. Pallas had helped Agrippina to become Empress, and had persuaded Claudius to adopt her son, Nero, who eventually had succeeded to the Imperial throne. Hence, the freedman did not fall into disgrace immediately. According to Josephus, the Jews in Caesarea laid charges against Felix, and he would have had to expiate his defects had not Pallas been able to save him. (89)

Some historians, including E. Haenchen, have deduced from this text that Felix must have been deposed as soon as Pallas had been disgraced. According to Tacitus, Pallas lost his office as minister of finances, which Claudius had entrusted to him, shortly before the poisoning of Britannicus. (90) It has been established almost with certainty that Britannicus died at the end of the year 55. The authors then claim that Pallas could not have been in any position to protect his brother any longer after that time. Hence, they concluded that Felix must have left Caesarea in the year 55. Such a line of reasoning is hardly convincing, since there are many factors which the authors have not taken into account.

> (1) It is difficult to establish with certainty the
>   date and the scope of Pallas' disgrace. Some authors
>   have connected the event with the death of Britannicus.

According to Suetonius (91), Britannicus was born "on the twentieth day of the sovereignty and in the second year of the consulship" ("vicesimo emperii die inque secundo anno consulatus") of Claudius. These indications are contradictory. The twentieth day of the sovereignty of Claudius must be calculated from the day after the death of Caligula and his burial on February 13th, 41 A.D. The second consulship of Claudius is dated to the year 42. According to Tacitus, Nero was two years older than Britannicus. (92) Since Nero was born on December 15th, 37 A.D., Britannicus would have been born on February 13th, 40 A.D. This is impossible, since Nero had his rival assassinated before his fourteenth birthday, and on February 13th, 54 A.D.,

Nero was not yet the Emperor. Together with Mommsen and Haenchen, therefore, the first time-reference of Suetonius would indicate the day, and the second time-reference would indicate the year, that is, the twentieth day of the second year of the consulship of Claudius. Claudius would have begun his role on January 25th, most probably in the year 42. Hence, Britannicus would have died in December of 55 A.D.

However, there is no certainty at all that Felix was deposed in 55. Even though Pallas was deprived of his official post, he was still highly influential. Nero was indebted to him for having been adopted by Claudius, and Agrippina could not cease showering him with her favors. Pallas became a very wealthy man, and did not die until the year 62 A.D. Envious of Pallas' wealth, the Emperor saw to his destruction. Pallas, therefore, could have given considerable aid to his brother even though he had suffered relative banishment from the imperial Court. Haenchen was wrong in trying to argue to the contrary.

(2) Nero ascended the throne on October 13th, 54 A.D. Pallas lost his power in December of 55.

Within this short period of time there would have occurred the events of the denunciation of the Jews at Caesarea, their journey to Rome, their court intrigues, and the appearance of Felix in court. Since voyages were not made during the winter months, Felix would have gone to Rome in the spring of 65.

So many events had occurred during Felix's Proconsulship in Judea that it would be difficult to crowd them into a two-year period. He married three queens, (93), and in 54 A.D. was espoused to Drusilla, the sister of Agrippa II and the divorced wife of King Azizus of Emesa. (94) Moreover, he suppressed troublesome bands of robbers who were pillaging the area. (95) He also used hired assassins to kill Jonathan the High Priest, the very one who had petitioned the Emperor that Felix be given the commission to Judea; however, Jonathan was the leader of a group of rebels who were terrorizing the countryside. (96) Furthermore, he tangled with an Egyptian who proclaimed himself a prophet and had established himself on the Mount of Olives with numerous followers. (97) Of these followers, Felix had four hundred killed, and two hundred imprisoned. Under pretext of resistance to Rome, civil disorders were multiplying.

In Caesarea itself, Jews and Syrians were at each other's throats; Felix intervened and dispatched a delegation from each party to Rome. (98) Only with great difficulty could so many happenings be squeezed into a short period of two years in public office.

        (3) Josephus went to Rome in the year 64 A.D. to negotiate the release of priests whom Felix had sent there in chains. If Felix had been deposed in the year 55, then what explanation would there be for the prolonged detention of the priests? (99) Moreover, the case of the quarrel between the Syrians and the Jews in Caesarea had not been taken to court until the year 66, and Nero's decision, which was unfavorable to the Jews, was one of the causes of the war. (100)

        (4) The date for the accession of Porcius Festus to public office is confirmatory evidence for the year 66 A.D. as the time which marks the end of Felix's term of office. Festus' successor was Albinus, who was in Palestine during the Feast of the Tabernacles in the year 62. Between the reigns of Albinus and Festus, there was an interregnum of several months. (101) What information Josephus supplies concerning the career of Festus would not necessarily imply a long period in office. It is possible to imagine that Festus arrived in Palestine only as late as 61, but there is no reason not to restrict the duration of his sojourn to just a one year period. While the year 61 is possible, the year 60 is equally so. In that case, since the term of office would commence on the 1st of May, then Felix could have been deposed in the year 59 or 60 A.D. To give critical reasons why the one date should be preferred to the other is impossible.

Art. 2. A Relative Chronology

On the basis of the results which have been gleaned from the analysis of the absolute chronology, it is possible to try to determine some dates in the biography of Paul. (102) It is an incontestable fact that we rarely achieve a state of certitude, for "there are as many opinions as there are minds" ("Tot capita, tot senteniae").

First of all, the actual number of fixed dates in the chronological scale are few and far between, for example, the death of Herod Agrippa, the Proconsulship of Gallio, and we may add the succession of Festus to Felix. The date for the crucifixion of Jesus is relevant in the attempt to establish the date for the conversion of Paul. We simply accept the year 30 as the date for the crucifixion, since we are not able at this point to justify our choice. (103) With these dates as our starting point, we can hazard some conclusions.

The date for the *birth of Paul* is uncertain. When Paul wrote to Philemon sometimes between the years 61 and 63, he referred to himself as an "old man," *presbytes*, which would ordinarily mean that he was about 60 years old. On the other hand, in his account concerning the stoning of Stephen, Luke portrays Saul as a young man, *neanias* (Acts 7, 58), the meaning of which is rather loose in Greek. The term could be used just as well to describe a young man of twenty as a man thirty years of age. Therefore, we would date Paul's birth to about 10 A.D.

A text from the Talmud (104), compiled long after Paul's time and which probably had established only a very flexible norm, can be of some help in an attempt to date the event when *Paul came to Jerusalem* to study at the feet of Gamaliel. The norm reads as follows: "At the age of five, the reading (of the Bible); at the age of ten, the Mishnah; at the age of thirteen, the commandments; at the age of fifteen, the Talmud; at the age of eighteen, marriage; at the age of twenty, pursuit (of a vocation); at the age of thirty, a grown man; at the age of fifty, for the council; at the age of sixty, an old man, etc."

The events of the *stoning of Stephen* and the *conversion of Paul* are related. The nature of the church in Jerusalem at that time would indicate strongly a state of withdrawal in comparison with the boldness so manifest at the events of Pentecost.

The community was large (Acts 4, 4; 5, 14; 6, 7), progress was made as far as its internal organization was concerned (Acts 4, 32; 6, 1), and it had expanded beyond the boundaries of the city of Jerusalem (Acts 8, 5; 9, 2.19). Moreover, the rivalries between the Christians of Palestinian origin and the Christian Hellenists presupposes some lapse of time. All of these events could have required at least a period of some four years, which would then point to the year 34 A.D. as the approximate date for Paul's conversion.

We would seem to have similar results by considering the status of the Church as it was outside of Jerusalem, and particularly in Damascus. This famous city was the center of a Christianity whose reputation was sufficiently widespread to reach the ears of Jews in Jerusalem, to disturb the Sanhedrin, and to warrant an official dispatch in the hands of a delegated persecutor. Furthermore, the community was well organized and active in an expansion program under the leadership of Ananias.

A. von Harnack tried a different approach. He began with the death of Jesus in the year 30, and noted that the period for the apparitions of Jesus before his ascension was computed long ago in three different ways: First of all, a forty-day period on the basis of Acts 1, 3; secondly, a period of eighteen months, according to the calculations of the Gnostics, Ophites, and Valentinians, as well as by the author of the *Ascension of Isaiah;* and thirdly, a twelve-year period, according to the computations of third-century Gnostics. Harnack rejected the first and the third hypotheses, and chose the second, in which he would include all of the apparitions, the last of which Paul had been the recipient. Therefore, the date for Paul's conversion would have been in the year 32 A.D.: " . . . and last of all he appeared to me too . . . " (*eskaton de panton . . . ophthe kamoi*: 1 Cor. 15, 1-11). But who would sacrifice Lukes' authority to that of gnostic speculations? (105)

At times a different approach is taken by authors. They say that the Roman Procurator did not intervene on the occasion when Stephen was condemned to death. He alone possessed the *jus gladii,* and during the trial of Jesus, those who were involved had to refer the case to him. Could not this have been the situation because, at the time of the stoning of the first martyr, there was an interregnum? Pilate was relieved of his office in the year 36. Since the Sanhedrin alone had intervened in the case, perhaps the reason was that Pilate's successor had not as yet arrived. This would date Stephen's martyrdom to the year 36, that is, after the departure of Pontius Pilate. A parallel case could have been the death of James, a relative of the Lord, in the year 62, for since Festus was dead, the Sanhedrin would have assumed the rights over life and death. (106)

Such a line of reasoning seems to be extremely hypothetical. An ordinary trial, such as that of Jesus, must be distinguished from a type of disturbance in the course of which a man would be put to death by a frenzied mob. In the latter case, the Sanhedrin could have misused its powers. (107)

Paul was converted shortly thereafter, and remained in *Damascus* "only a few days" (Acts 9, 19). (108) From there he went to Arabia (Gal. 1, 17), and then returned to Damascus. We have no idea how long he stayed there, since the only time-reference in the Acts is "some time passed" (*hemerai hikanai*: 9, 23). (109) The time interval, according to Gal. 1, 18, could have extended over more than a two-year period, which would bring us to the year 36 or 37 A.D., *when Paul made his first trip to Jerusalem.*

After his first visit to Jerusalem, Paul went to Tarsus by way of Caesarea which was on the way (Gal. 1, 21; Acts 9, 30). Barnabas joined him in order to take him to Antioch where he was to remain for a whole year (Acts 11, 26). (110)

If the journey involving the collection (Acts 11, 27-30) is to be identified with the journey to the Council of Jerusalem (Acts 15), then the *first missionary journey* would have to belong here. But since it is impossible to calculate the exact amount of time Paul spent in Damascus, it is not easy to even conjecture at what time he began his first journey. To travel through all of Cyprus, on to Pamphilia, Pisidia, and Iconium, (111) and to return along the same route to establish flourishing communities at those places would require a rather long period of time, *chronon ouk oligon.* Fourteen years after the first missionary journey, Paul went to the *Council of Jerusalem* in the year 49 (Gal. 2, 1), and his conference with Peter in Antioch would have been held in that same year.

Paul spent some time in Antioch (Acts 15, 33), and "on a later occasion" (*meta de tinas hemeras*) (Acts 15, 36), began the *second journey*. He set out sometime at the end of the year 49 or at the beginning of the year 50 A.D., and traveled through Syria, Cilicia, Iconium, and Phrygia, arrived in Galatia where he spent considerable time due to an illness, and finally went to Troas. After he evangelized Philippi, Thessalonica, and Beroea, he arrived at Corinth after some delay at Athens. (112) At Corinth, he met Priscilla and Aquila and, towards the end of his stay there, he was summoned before Gallio in the year 52 rather than in 51. (113) Paul then had to leave Corinth in the year 52 after spending eighteen months there (Acts 18, 18).

The Apostle went to *Ephesus*, (114) passed through Caesarea (Acts 18, 22), and went up to Jerusalem, after which he returned to Antioch (Acts 18, 23), where he spent some time.

From Antioch, Paul began his *third missionary journey*, which again included the territories of Galatia and Phrygia (Acts 18, 23). Either at the end of the year 53, or in the spring of 54, Paul reached Ephesus, where he remained for about three years (Acts 19, 8.10.22; 20, 31), that is, until the year 57. He reached Macedonia and during this period he had to spend some time in Illyricum (Rom. 15, 19). From Macedonia, he proceeded to Corinth, where he spent three months during the winter of 57-58 A.D. (Acts 20, 3). From Corinth, the Apostle returned to Macedonia, (115) where he celebrated the Passover at Philippi in the year 58 (Acts 20, 3-6). He set out again for *Jerusalem*, touched at Samos and Miletus, but passed wide of Ephesus, "so as to avoid spending time in Asia, since he was anxious to be in Jerusalem, if possible, for the day of Pentecost" (Acts 20, 16). Paul was in Jerusalem in May of the year 58, where he was imprisoned. Hence, the voyage had taken less than fifteen days (Acts 20, 6.13-15; 21, 1-4.7-10.15-16).

Paul was taken from Jerusalem to Caesarea, where he was a prisoner for two years, and, in the autumn of 60, he embarked for Rome (116) which he reached in the spring of 61 A.D. After a period of one month, he reached the Island of Crete (Acts 27, 2-8) in the second half of September (Acts 27, 9). Fifteen days later, he was shipwrecked at Malta (Acts 28, 1). Three months later in January (Acts 28, 11), he set out for Rome, where he arrived after a three-week period (Acts 28, 12-16), probably in the month of February. (117)

From this point on, the Acts no longer is our guide. According to Rom. 15, 25, Paul expressed a wish to go to *Spain*. In the year 95 A.D., Clement of Rome wrote that Paul went to the very edge of the western world (*eis to terma tes dyseos*: 5, 7), a geographical expression which could refer to Spain. Lines 38-39 of the Muratorian Canon confirms this; "the departure of Paul who traveled from the City to Spain" ("profectio Pauli ab urbe ad Spaniam proficiscentis"). According to the Pastoral Letters, Paul returned to the East, where he met Titus in Crete, and Timothy at Ephesus (Ti. 1, 3; 1 Tm. 1, 3). (118) Once again he was imprisoned and sent to Rome, where he suffered martyrdom (2 Tm. 1, 17; 4, 6-8). *Paul's death* occurred during the reign of Nero, whose persecution of the Christians extended from the year 64 to his death on June 9th, 68 A.D. The time of Paul's death is frequently dated as the year 67 A.D., but the date is not certain.

Chapter V

THE CRITICS AND THE LETTERS

Art. 1. Authenticity

F. Ch. Baur accepted Gal, Rom 1 and 2 Cor as authentic. Contemporary criticism now adds 1 Thes, Phil, and Phlm to the line-up of these four major epistles. Since all reputable critics agree on this matter, there is no reason for us to deal with them here. On the other hand, such is not the case concerning 2 Thes, Col, Eph, and the so-called Pastoral Letters.

A. 2 *Thessalonians*

At the beginning of the century, there supposedly would have been no reason to doubt that Paul was the author of 2 Thes. (1) However, since that time, things have changed. Wrede had made the most of the subordination of 2 Thes to 1 Thes with such skill of which he alone was capable to show that the former is unauthentic. (2) According to A. Wikenhauser (3) and to our own way of thinking, such an approach does seem to put the problem in its true light. However, actual opposition to such an approach is nothing more than a relinquishment of a course of action which has the advantage of offering reliable groundwork in the texts as a suitable beginning for discussion. Today, arguments, which lack originality and which have repeatedly been refuted in the past, are being resurrected. R. Bultmann and H. J.

Schoeps (4) have been outspoken advocates against the authenticity of 2 Thes, but without a reasonable explanation. H. Braun
based his reasoning against authenticity on the theological differences between 1 and 2 Thes. Ch. Masson emphasized the
differences in matters eschatological. (5) It is sufficiently clear
that none of these authors can place this allegedly apocryphal
letter within the context of the development of primitive Christianity, particularly in the obvious case of Masson. For after he
had unequivocally opposed Pauline authenticity, he proceeded
to interpret 2 Thes as if Paul had written the letter immediately
after the composition of 1 Thes. (6) There must be an explanation for the existence of a mistake or an error. As long as the
doctrinal and literary nature and status of this epistle has not
been determined, more insoluble problems arise from failing to
ascribe the letter to its supposedly real author than by attributing
it to him. The resultant impression is that whatever could be
said about the matter seems to have been said already. (7)

B. *Colossians*

The case of the letters to the Colossians and Ephesians is of
greater complexity. The most detailed study of both epistles is
that of E. Percy. (8)

Some recent authors refuse to accept complete authenticity of
the letter to the Colossians. Percy cited P. Wendland (9), R.
Bultmann (10), R. Reitzenstein (11), H. Schlier, and E. Käsemann. (12) Actually, Bornkamm (13) should be added to the
list. Ch. Masson (14), P. N. Harrison (15), and J. Schoeps
(16) would admit some degree of authenticity, since they believed that the letter had been padded with interpolations of
greater or lesser importance. For Percy to mention H. Schlier in
the line-up was a mistake, (17) an error which was repeated by
C.F.D. Moule, (18) who gave an excellent presentation of the
traditional argument.

1) From the viewpoint of internal criticism, Moule did not
consider it possible to doubt either that Paul actually wrote the
letter to Philemon, or that there was a very close connection between the two letters. In both epistles, Paul alludes to his imprisonment. To try to read the expression *désmios* in a metaphor-
ical sense, as E. R. Goodenough proposed, (19) is nothing but

a subterfuge. Furthermore, in both letters, Timothy is associated with Paul as the author. Aristarchus, Epaphras, Mark, Demas, and Luke are all with the Apostle. Archippus is greeted, and Onesimus is mentioned. The question of interpolation is the only one which could possibly be raised. Masson distinguished between an original Pauline composition and a later revision composed by the author of the letter to the Ephesians. The thesis, of course, is not new, for it had already been proposed and defended by such men as H. J. Holtzmann (20), F. Hitzig, and H. von Soden, (21) and subjected to the profound critical examination of W. Bieder. (22)

2) Present-day discussions on the problem are less concerned about literary arguments than on the possibility that, during Paul's lifetime, Gnostic-type errors had crept into the community at Colossae to which he refers in the letter. In this connection, C.F.D. Moule made some pertinent observations. The ideas, vocabulary, and sophisticated style of the letter can be explained by the circumstances which occasioned the letter. A person could easily imagine very well what errors had affected the Colossians at the time of Paul's imprisonment, for the tone of his letter is one emanating from an Apostle-martyr, who addresses himself to Christians who hardly could be identified with the term.

H. Chadwick was concerned with the doctrinal nature of the letter and its relevance to the question of authenticity. It had been claimed that a Gnostic heresy was inconceivable at the time of St. Paul. Moreover, Paul would have been most incompetent in attempting to refute the error with the masterful touch that so characterizes the letter to the Colossians, for Paul was much too Jewish to understand Gnostic subtleties, or to speak to a Gnostic as a Gnostic would understand. H. Chadwick rejected such an interpretation. The purpose of his study was to show what role a "given situation" could play in the development of the Pauline argument, for, after examining the technique of the Apostle as seen in his first letter to the Corinthians, he showed that Paul was sufficiently flexible to be able to adopt an understanding attitude when he had encountered his inquisitors. The same could be equally true as far as the Colossians are concerned. (23)

To say that the letter to the Colossians depended on the letter to the Ephesians is a mistake. Nevertheless, F. C. Synge presented and promulgated such a thesis. The criteria on which he based his judgments were purely artistic, for, as he saw it, the structure of Col was of poorer quality than that of Eph. Such a purely subjective hypothesis (24) was given more serious investigation by J. Coutts. (25)

C. *Ephesians*

The authenticity of the letter to the Ephesians is still highly contested. (26) H. J. Holtzmann, J. Moffatt, and M. Dibelius (27) had rejected the letter as unauthentic, and found many disciples among recent critics, the most significant of which would be E. J. Goodspeed, W. L. Knox, C. L. Mitton, Ch. Masson, along with R. Bultmann, and E. Käsemann. M. Goguel claimed to have discovered two different strata in the letter; the first stratum would originally have been Pauline, but the second was the work of a disciple of Paul, who wrote some ten or twenty years later. (28) E. J. Goodspeed had concocted a theory that was hardly relevant to a critical investigation, According to his theory, the slave Onesimus not only composed the letter to the Ephesians, but, at the same time, was the real author of the entire Pauline collection. (29) Onesimus' intent would have been to salvage the waning authority of Paul. W. L. Knox contented himself with the classical line of argumentation (30): a style characterized by lengthy, involved, and obscure periods; a purpose that is not apparently evident; texts borrowed from other letters. Moreover, the general atmosphere is no longer the same as that of the authentic letters, for, with the exception of two passages (2, 5 and 2, 8), there is no question of controversy; rather, the Church is simply being tempted into idolatry. Finally, the nature of the "mystery" in 5, 32 is different from the one in the first letter to the Corinthians. That the letter may well be the work of Tychius is an archaic concept already proposed by Schleiermacher and Renan, and revived by E. Meyer, M. Goguel, and M. Albertz. (31) In an important work, (32) C. L. Mitton developed further the entire classical argument against the authenticity of the letter. D. E. Nineham presented a brief summary of the same arguments in a collection of studies on the letter to the Ephesians; in the same collection, H. A. Sanders developed a thesis for the authenticity. (33) Sanders received good support in the works of J. Schmid and E. Percy, (34) whose position fell in line with that of many exegetes, both Catholic and Protestant. (35) H. Schlier was also very explicit in his commentary in defense of the authorship of the Apostle. (36) The hypotheses of Goodspeed and of Knox were nothing more than an "absurd notion" (*absurde Vorstellung*). There seems to be a revival of the criticism to some extent in an article by G. Schille, who was convinced that a re-examination of the question was imperative. (37) According to his judgment, Paul could have been the author of the epistle, since form-criticism (*Formgeschichte*) has shown that the epistolary composition contains liturgical and didactic passages. Furthermore, the Gnostic elements which are contained therein are not far removed from Jewish mentality, since even the Qumran sect was not exempt from such influences. H. J. Cadbury made the same point but from a more objective point of view. (38) He concluded that 95% of the epistle did not present any difficulty as far as Pauline authenticity was concerned; 5% of the letter definitely pointed to a different author. Must we not hold that someone imitated Paul in composing the letter, 95% of which represents the thoughts and vocabulary of the Apostle as assimilated by the writer, and the remaining 5% of which was proper to the disciple himself? In his recent *Introduction*, D. Guthrie defended the thesis of strict authenticity.

Between those scholars who upheld the thesis of unauthenticity and those scholars who defended the thesis of authenticity are others who could not make up their minds. They simply examined the pros and cons for both theses, and embarrassingly concluded with the declaration, "it is not clear" (*non liquet*). (39)

It is common knowledge that the question of authenticity depends strongly on the question concerning the relationship between the letter to the Colossians and the one to the Ephesians. W. Ochel (40) had already chosen this question as the specific topic for his dissertation in 1934. All commentaries dealt with the question. Recently, it was taken up by J. Coutts, who examined the four passages which are usually cited as evidence to the effect that the letter to the Ephesians depends on the letter to the Colossians. He concluded his study by claiming that the proper role of each letter must be reversed, namely, that the letter to the Colossians presupposes the existence of the epistle to the Ephesians. However, his arguments are not convincing. (41)

Much more refined and worthy of special citation is the hypothesis of P. Benoit. (42) The general line of argument is based on the listing of the literary affinities between the two epistles. Benoit would admit that, more than in any other epistle, the disciple who drafted the letter was granted more liberty. (43) Paul could have dictated a certain amount of development in his own thought, and then proceeded to commission his disciple to draw up the final draft of Ephesians, with the letter to the Colossians as an auxiliary source of information. The epistle to the Ephesians clearly expresses the ideas of Paul, and owes its origin to the Apostle's influence. These views were revived in the *Jerusalem Bible*, in a review of Schlier's commentary, and in that article which occurs in *DBS*, (44) all of which deserve careful consideration. In effect, there seems to be more than a similarity in vocabulary between Colossians and Ephesians. It can also be maintained that there are themes common to both, as well as a similar pattern in literary usages. If it would be accepted as a fact that certain literary expressions were borrowed from one letter to be used in another, then it would certainly be a situation in which the letter to the Colossians had directly influenced the drafting of the epistle to the Ephesians. The following citations are noteworthy: Eph. 3,2 = Col. 1,25; Eph. 4, 16 = Col. 2, 19; Eph. 4, 22-24 = Col. 3, 9-10; Eph. 6, 21-22 = Col. 3, 7-8. Moreover, there are conflations of two passages from Colossians into a single passage in Ephesians: Col. 1, 14 + 1, 20 = Eph. 1, 7; Col. 1, 25 + 1, 20 + 1, 12 = Eph. 1, 10-11. Furthermore, the pericope in Eph. 3, 2-13 takes up once again themes already considered in Col. 1, 24-29, together with other passages which are their parallel in Pauline literature. The development by way of reduplication of Col. 1, 24-29 is obvious; however, at the same time, it must be noted that the Colossian passage is autobiographical in nature! These facts require an explanation. (45) H. Schlier and Msgr. Cerfaux (46) have pointed out that the repetition of words and of themes from the epistle to the Colossians in the letter to the Ephesians goes hand in hand with the fact that the author exercised great freedom in using the words and themes without given proper consideration to the close bond that exists between them. The supposition is that, in this case, there is evidence for "an astounding pentration into Paul's ideas together with an extraordinary command of his vocabulary." Furthermore, it seems that the letter plausibly opposes a Judaeo-Christian Gnosis that is both syncretic as well as cosmic. What anonymous disciple of Paul could have tapped the theology of the epistles so effectively and at the same time imbibed so powerful an inspiration together with the many variations "without making any egregious errors?" Such defense for the case of strict authenticity by an appeal to the homogeneous development of doctrine does not, however, take into account the question of literary dependence, in addition to the differences in vocabulary and style. If the disciple had been in intimate contact with Paul, then it would be understandable that, not only with the help of the letters, but also because of daily contact with Paul and perhaps under the actual supervision of the Apostle, he could have created such an extraordinarily rich synthesis of the apostolic teaching. There is no doubt concerning the difficulties in attempting an assessment of the literary potentialities of Paul; but if there actually is both a literary and a doctrinal dependence between Ephesians and the Pauline corpus, particularly Colossians, could we not rightly suppose that the Master left this work for the disciple rather than do it himself? (47)

D. *The Pastoral Letters*

A. Médebielle covered these documents in a rather lengthy article in the *Dictionnarie de la Théologie Catholique,* (48) in which he dealt with the question of their authenticity, and particularly with the opinions of both classical and modern critics. M. Metzner has recently taken up the question again. (49) The studies of R. Falconer (50) and of P. N. Harrison (51) continue to serve as the basis for at least partial unauthenticity. Both authors claimed that it is possible to find authentic notes or fragments in these letters, as, for example, in 2 Tm. 4, 6-8. Two German scholars, Ch. Maurer (52) and H. von Campenhausen made emphatic declarations against Pauline authorship. (53)

The last edition of the Dibelius commentary (54) by H. Conzelmann was much more cautious than the previous editions, and left the door open for a constructive criticism. W. Michaelis was a strong defender of the authenticity of these epistles, (55) as well as O. Michel (56), B. E. Easton, J. Behm, J. Jeremias, J. de Zwaan, D. Guthrie, and B. M. Metzger. (57) The type of partial unauthenticity as had been proposed by Henry A. Sanders (58) and accepted by M. Goguel (59) and R. Bultmann (60) is hardly encountered. On the basis of the approximate measurements of Papyrus no. 46, Sanders concluded that an abridged form of the Pastoral Letters was probably included in the Beatty Papyrus. (61)

Harrison evaluated the argument on a statistical basis; however, today, such an approach is considered amateurish, for even the professional statisticians have tried to define the possibilities and limitation of their method. G. Udny Yule made pioneering efforts in his very remarkable book. (62) K. Grayson, in collaboration with G. Herdan (63), who is a professional statistician, took up the question from this particular angle. In their opinion, statistics weigh against an identification of the author of the Pastoral Letters as compared with the other epistles. However, Grayson carefully pointed out that vocabulary was only one element involved in style. It should also be added that, if the style is to be identified with the man, it does not constitute the whole man, especially a man like Paul. Other factors which must be added to stylistic considerations are: The organization of the Church, the theological thought in its many different forms and formulations, the nature of the errors that are opposed, as well as the history of the Apostle. In this connection, the learned professor from Berne, W. Michaelis, made some useful observations, in an important article in which he studied the question of statistics. (64) While a too ready appeal must not be made to changes of mood or to circumstances as proof that these causes validly account for profound differences of style, there is always a subjective element in the handling of figures, even with the use of logarithms. Be that as it may, the great differences in vocabulary remain a puzzle, and it would be in place to subscribe readily to the wise and modest advice of Msgr. Cerfaux: "There is good reason not to use the Pastoral letters in truly erudite studies without due prudence, whether there is a question of defining the theology of the Apostle, or an attempt to reconstruct the history of primitive Christianity." (65)

Art. 2. Unity or Compilation

The techniques of literary criticism have been used to discover traces of compilation or successive redactions in the Pauline letters. Very few of the epistles have totally escaped such treatment. We can deal only with recent attempts, which periodically deserve more careful examination.

We note in passing that if the scissors would be used according to the method which we shall describe below, then the letters to the Thessalonians should not be spared. The first letter to the Thessalonians can be divided into two parts, with a dividing line between chapters three and four. In the passage 3, 11-13, Paul seems to end with an invocation. The expression *loipòn oûn* ("finally") of 4, 1, which introduces a section that presents the only new teaching in the epistle, is peculiar. Beginning with 4, 13, a new instructive section, which cannot be a "left-over," is actually the most important part of the epistle for which the Thessalonians had waited with bated breath. (66)

The instance of the second letter to the Thessalonians is even more characteristic. Verses 1 to 5 of chapter 3 constitute a conclusion — after the introductory *tò loipón*, there follow a request for prayers, a brief congratulatory note, and finally a prayer. Naturally, one would expect the letter to end at this point. However, verses 6-16 address a serious admonition to the rebels in the community! According to our present knowledge, no one has proposed that four letters were sent to the Thessalonians — but this is intended as a word to the wise.

A. *Letters to the Corinthians* (67)

The same is not true concerning the letters to the Corinthians, for it is known that Paul wrote four letters to the Corinthians. Chronologically, our two canonical epistles occupied the second and fourth places. P. Cleary, a Catholic, tried to discover traces of the two missing letters in the two letters that we have. He claimed that the present form of the canonical epistles was the

work of a redactor. (68) W. Schmithals went even further. (69)
According to his opinion, the two passages in 2 Cor. 5, 16 and
2 Cor. 3, 16-18 are glosses. Moreover, both letters can be divided
into six epistles:

        A = 2 Cor. 6, 14 - 7, 1; 1 Cor. 9, 24 - 10, 22;
             6, 12-20; 11, 2-34; 15; 16, 13-24.
        B = 1 Cor. 1, 1 - 6, 11; 7, 1 - 9, 23; 10, 23 - 11, 1;
             12, 1-14, 40; 16, 1-12.
        C = 2 Cor. 2, 14- 6,13; 7, 2-4.
        D = 2 Cor. 10, 1-13, 13.
        E = 2 Cor. 9, 1-15.
        F = 2 Cor. 1, 1-2, 3; 7, 5 - 8, 24.

Therefore, letter A is made up almost entirely of 1 Cor, except
for the section of 2 Cor 6, 14 - 7, 1, which contains three and
a half verses of texts, and two and a half verses of citations.
The second letter to the Corinthians is distributed among four
of the letters, C, D, E, and F.

The dissections of W. Schmithals represent nothing more than
an attempt to add to a long history of literary criticism. Before
his time, there were Hagge (1876), C. Clemen (1894), L. Hal-
mel (1894 and 1904), H. Lisco (1896), J. Weiss, A. Loisy, P. L.
Couchoud, H. Windisch, M. Goguel, (70) and not very long ago,
J. Héring (71), who gives the impression of someone succumbing
to a disagreeable task.

The very existence of so many and so diverse attempts is a
sufficient witness to the deficiency of the necessary information
required to determine the existence of a plurality of letters in
1 Cor. Because of these circumstances, we could do no more
than refer the reader to the studies mentioned above for a more
detailed examination.

On the other hand, to lay open the nature of the problem as far
as the second letter to the Corinthians is concerned is more bene-
ficial. A. Wikenhauser has carefully gleaned those considerations
on which the exegetes had depended in order to effect a dissection of the epistle. (72)

1. The short section in 6, 14 - 7, 1 interrupts the flow of the
narrative to warn the Corinthians against idolatry. Such an inter-
ruption comes as a surprise, and hardly has any particular
context. Moreover, the passage in 7, 2 naturally continues what

was stated in 6, 13. Is the passage authentic? It could be a section of the first letter to the Corinthians which has been lost (1 Cor. 5, 9), or else has been displaced from its original position after 5, 14 to 6, 2. Against these suggestions it must be pointed out that consideration of language and subject matter do not rule out a Pauline origin (73), and there are sharp transitions also in 5, 11; 6, 1; and 6, 11.

2. J. S. Semler (1776) described chapter 9 as a doublet of chapter 8. Windisch (74), followed by É. Osty (75), regarded chapter 9 as a document intended for the churches of all Achaia. There are three arguments for this theory: first, chapter 8 is a literary unit; secondly, chapter 9 has the appearance of a doublet, for it presents a self-contained treatment of the same theme, and to some extent expresses the same ideas and thoughts as chapter 8; finally, there is a certain inconsistency between the two chapters: in 8, 1-5, Paul exhorts the Corinthians to follow the example of the Macedonian communities in their eagerness for the collection, while according to 9, 1-6, he commends to the Macedonians the generosity of the Corinthians in this matter. Compare also 8, 7-15 with 9, 6-14, where the motives for generosity are dealt with twice but in different ways. There is no objection on principle to this theory, but the two chapters can be reconciled without undue difficulty, as was pointed out by H. Lietzmann, H. D. Wendland, and E. B. Allo. Indeed, a man like Paul cannot be shackled with a set of rules.

3. The most popular theory has been to partition chapters 10-13 as a separate epistle. A Hausrath in 1870, and others since, wished to identify it with the "intermediate epistle." (76) M. Krenkel (1890), H. Windisch and É. Osty (77) thought it to be a fifth epistle to the Corinthians. The reason for partitioning these chapters is the sharp change of tone between chapters 1-9 and 10-13. It is pointed out that in 10-13 Paul treats his opponents with the greatest sharpness and with biting irony, while chapters 1-9 are devoted to reconciling his dispute with the community. Yet both forms of this theory are open to serious objections. These four chapters cannot be identical with the "intermediate epistle," for there is no reference in these chapters to the "offender" of 2, 5-6 and 7, 12. Moreover, chapters 1-9 pass over in silence the confrontation of his adversaries which is the

substance of chapters 10-13. The second form of this theory presupposes that, when he had already sent off chapters 1-9, Paul learned that since the departure of Titus, his opponents in Corinth were using every means at their disposal to undermine his authority and were not without success in this and in their attack on the legitimacy of his apostolate; a further epistle, namely chapters 10-13, would be the answer to this. Against this theory it must be pointed out that the difference in tone should not be exaggerated; chapters 1-9 are addressed to the whole community, while in chapters 10-13, he deals with the intruders and the contingent of the community that gave them a hearing; this fact provides a fairly easy explanation for the difference in tone between the two parts. Moreover, as Wikenhauser noted, the Apostle does defend himself against bigoted attacks in chapters 1-9, and chapters 10-13 are not without expressions of affection and reconciliation (10, 8; 11, 2; 12, 14; 13, 7).

One final observation is that such divisions are compatible with Pauline authenticity. The great difficulty attendant on such arrangements is that they must have come into existence very quickly, prior to any circulation of copies of the original, and before they had been accepted by the church at Corinth. The purpose of such work was not to offer a cover up for the vices of the Corinthians. What is the real reason for such scissors-and-scotch tape-procedure is impossible to determine. Without denying the differences, the inequalities, and the abrupt changes of subject matter, we would be better off in the long run just to recognize them as such and to admit that we simply cannot find an explanation for their presence. To demand that Paul must follow the logical patterns of a university professor is an *a priori* state of mind that is hardly critical. The differences between the various reconstructions that the critics proposed, except for the case itself, emphasize the fact that decisive arguments in favor of the proposed systems are lacking. (78)

B. *Letter to the Philippians*

A similar problem arises concerning the letter to the Philippians. An analysis of this letter has shown that it does not follow the usual pattern of parenesis with the subsequent dogmatic exposition. In the case of the letter to the Philippians, the two elements intermingle. Furthermore, there are certainly abrupt changes in the subject matter: 2, 14; 3,2; 4, 2-10. Hence, it is possible that we could have here an amalgam of several documents:

> A = 4, 10-23, thanksgivings after the arrival of Epaphroditus.
>
> B = 1, 1-2, 18; 3, 1-4, 1; 4, 8-9, news about Paul, and exhortations to remain strong and united in the faith.
>
> C = 2, 19-30; 4, 2-7, a letter of recommendation in favor of Timothy and Epaphroditus. (79)

With good reason, P. Benoit wrote: "Such speculations are plausible, but they cannot be proven; one can take an interest in them, while recognizing that they throw no great light on the interpretation of the epistle." (80)

C. *Letter to the Romans*

Concerning the letter to the Romans, the problem is not so much that of division as addition. The problem has a very long history behind it, but we shall limit ourselves just to its more recent repercussions. The data of the problem have been summarized very well by A. Wikenhauser. (81)

The Tübingen School regarded chapters 15 and 16 as a second century addition, but nowadays, no one questions their authenticity. (82) It is a matter of dispute whether chapter 16 originally belonged to it. Many exegetes have adopted the theory that chapter 16, or more specifically 16, 3-20, is an epistle of Paul to the community at Ephesus, which later became attached to Romans. Michaelis said that 16, 3-24 is the conclusion of an epistle which Paul wrote in Philippi or Troas, instructing the presbyters of Ephesus to come to Miletus (cfr. Acts 20, 17). (83)

The authenticity of the doxology in 16, 25-27 is disputed, and the reasons for questioning its authenticity are its alleged unpauline character. Besides the authors cited previously, mention should be made of two important contributions by J. Dupont. (84)

Finally, the proposals of F. Müller (85) are always apropos to any discussion on Romans. He proposed to resolve the difficulties surrounding the continuity of ideas between 7, 22-28 and

10, 13-18 by regarding 7, 24-25a; 8, 2; and 10, 15a-17 as glosses. R. Bultmann (86) took up the question and also regarded the presence of glosses in 7, 25a; 8, 1; and 10, 17, to which he added 2, 1; 13, 5; 2, 16; and 6, 17b. According to his opinion the editor of the epistle added 2, 16; 6, 17b, as well as 16, 25-27. H. Sahlin (87) believed that the text in 2, 15f.-2,18f.; 5, 5-10; 6, 16-20; and 13, 4 were corrupt, and proposed as the solution some reconstructions which were highly subjective. These attempts frequently reveal a type of criticism wherein the authors content themselves with hypotheses that are rather questionable.

Finally, we should note that the structure of the epistle has been the subject of some penetrating studies, and again some writers are doubtful about the date of composition. (88)

Conclusion

Since this completes our examination of the literary questions concerning the Pauline epistles, we shall now line up some pertinent conclusions.

1. No one can really study a text without becoming involved in questions concerning its author, purpose, and unity. Such necessity is even more pressing when the Pauline epistles are involved. When it comes to Pauline criticism, one point that does stand out above all others is that the old division among exegetes resulting from such endeavors continues to persist. The members of the ranks of F. Ch. Baur staunchly remain arm in arm with their founder by a relentless defense of his positions. Apart from the major epistles, they would accept only the first letter to the Thessalonians and the letter to the Philippians. As far as they are concerned, Second Thessalonians, Colossians, Ephesians, Philemon, and the Pastoral Epistles are deutero-Pauline. It is remarkable how such rejections are very often formulated without prior justification. But here again we stand face to face with the age old problem of the ever-surging fear of being considered "uncritical" (*unkritisch*). The *Formgeschichte*, on the other hand, as well as the more intensive study of Jewish and Hellenistic background have forced many authors to see in the deutero-Pauline dossier elements that are much older. This is definitely a step in the right direction; however, a word of caution is in place. Contemporary interest is focused on the de-

velopments in the field of biblical theology; but to labor in the realm of theological concepts requires a more delicate hand than in the handling of vocabulary, grammar, and style. Obviously, the appraisals will be tinted with subjective elements, since the philosophical and theological suppositions of the individual author play a more determinant role. For this reason, we would insist that any examination of questions concerning authenticity and unity should be undertaken in the light of all available means, philological, historical, and doctrinal.

2. It is quite clear that the unity of the letters to the Corinthians and to the Philippians presents difficulties. In this case, literary criticism has to work on the basis of hypotheses. That such studies should necessarily abstain from an unending multiplication of attempts toward a solution should be recognized. We believe that propositions which go beyond the mere stage of "it could be that" are definitely admissible, as long as they do not become certainties on the very next page or become the starting points of a chain of hypotheses. But here again, the byzantinistic quality of the discussions run the risk of throwing a discreditable pall over critical studies, which, as is already well known, has happened not too long ago.

Chapter VI

FORM-CRITICISM AND THE LETTERS

Introduction

There is no longer a reference book in any language which presents a complete and up-to-date collection of scientific commentaries on all the Epistles of St. Paul. The volumes of the English *International Critical Commentary* have become obsolete. Other publications are incomplete, and do not offer the same scientific standard. The great German *Meyers-Kommentar* has not revised its commentaries on Thessalonians, Corinthians, Ephesians, and the Pastoral Epistles. Lohmeyer's commentaries are fragmentary and highly subjective. The French series *Études Bibliques* is lacking in a commentary on the Captivity Epistles, and several volumes of this famous collection are outdated. On the other hand, less scientific commentaries abound. Moreover, there are isolated essays of some value in all languages.

With the entire collection of such literary production in mind, some general observations would be in place. First of all, a re-examination of the textual criticism of each epistle under consideration is necessary, for it is impossible to explain a given text whose value has not been weighed and whose history has not been assessed. Secondly, philosophical groundwork still is the indispensable foundation for every elucidation of the text. Semantics makes it possible to fix the particular nuance of a word as it is used by the various writers. Consequently, recourse to the papyri as well as to non-literary texts is essential. Therefore, it is regrettable that such groundwork is missing in such a valuable commentary as that of O. Kuss. (1) To be regretted also is the lack of a decent grammar on the Greek of the LXX. Thirdly, studies on the part of scholars in the field of Jewish and Greek religion is progressing. It could be said that emphasis has shifted to the role of the Jewish religious background and its influence in preference to the Greek. But even on this particular point, there is some fear that such a factor has been exaggerated. However, what is certain is that Paul's dependence on the Old Testament, Targum, Qumran, and the Rabbinical texts, will, if controlled by means of a proper method and procedure, throw new light on some points. Finally, the commentaries have been more attentive to the thought of the Apostle than anything else. In this type of work, however, a well-determined methodology is lacking. The preconceived notions of the individual exegetes often come into play, to exercise an influence that is more or less successful on the results of their work.

The scientific monographs and articles on the Pauline epistles for the most part have been concerned with individual points. Because of this situation, we could really say that we have an atomization of research, and for that matter, as far as the entire New Testament is concerned. To offer even a resume of all the results would require volumes. In connection with the distinction that was clearly brought out by R. Asting, (2) we also would make a distinction between the object of the kerygma and the many forms it has taken to itself. The object of the kerygma involves the study of the theology of Paul. In this chapter, we shall restrict ourselves to a study of the forms.

In 1931, M. Dibelius raised the question of form-criticism in connection with books of the New Testament other than the Gospels. He emphasized certain literary characteristics which had been recognized for a long time, but brought into special prominence by the *Handbuch* of H. Lietzmann, whose work was more sensitive to this aspect of literary criticism than any of the other commentaries, as, for example, rhythm and hymn-type prose, the use of personal rhetoric, popular preaching, confessions, and stylized formulas. These first indications were to receive important developments. (3)

Recently, A. Descamps could write: "In the case of a writer as personal as Paul, some attention must be given to Form-Criticism, which simply means an investigation of the influences of tradition and of the milieu. Even geniuses themselves remain to be to some extent children of their age and the beneficiaries of past heritage. We must recognize that at the very heart of a composition that is stamped with the personality of the writer there is already a stereotyped formula which takes us back to the influences and life-situations of the community." (4) To this very day, there does not exist for the Pauline literature a work which would correspond to one which covers the Gospels in the light of Form-Criticism. For this reason, the pages that follow will attempt no more than a synthesis with no intention or pretense to exhaust the subject. Such a synthesis has been inspired by those studies which have been carried out on particular details in recent years. Methodologically, we shall cover the following points: 1) the literary form of the epistle; 2) the thanksgiving; 3) autobiographical passages; 4) expression of the kerygma; 5) recourse to Sacred Scripture; 6) rhetoric; 7) apocalyptic form; 8) blessings and doxologies; 9) rhythmic prose and hymns; and 10) parenesis or popular preachings.

Art. 1. The Literary Form of the Epistle

We have abundant information concerning the form of a letter in ancient times. (5) The availability of such information is due largely to the works of O. Gerhardt, A. Deissmann, J. Sykutris, but especially of O. Roller. It is in reference to such works that the new studies have been orientated. The Finn, H. Koskenniemi (6) has drawn attention particularly to the peculiar characteristics of the Greek letter from the times of its origin until 400 A.D.

Michaelis, Percy, and Lyonnet (7) have shown that they were skeptical about the conclusions of Roller concerning the *dictation* and the time necessary for the writing of the epistles. Deissmann was the man responsible for the distinction between *epistles* on the one hand, and *letters* on the other. An epistle is a literary product that uses the form of a letter, but is basically a treatise. The Pauline letters are real letters since they have a well-determined circumstantial character and since they are addressed to individuals who are known. Even the letter to the Ephesians belongs to this category. Of course, this does not mean that the Pauline letters should be regarded as ephemeral compositions intended to be read once to the community and subsequently to be forgotten. Such letters are also apostolic acts, and, like preaching, are truly the words of God (1 Thes. 2, 13).

J. A. Eschlimann (8) did well by comparing the Pauline epistles with *profane letters*. However, he concentrated on the addresses that were in the body of the composition, whereas the addresses outside the main body were either written on the reverse side of the papyrus or on a separate sheet. While E. Lohmeyer emphasized particularly the dependence of the Pauline formulas on Semitic and liturgical parallels, G. Friedrich modified these exaggerated positions to their proper limits, and distinguished the twofold influence that the concepts of "grace" and "peace" demand. (9) Essentially, Paul divided his introductions into an address and a greeting, whose liturgical nature as a blessing is admitted by many. As the letter-form of the ancient world, Paul's epistles end with a conclusion (*apographé, clausula, subscriptio*), which includes a final salutation, the authentification of the letter by Paul's own handwriting, and a final blessing (1 Thes. 5, 26-28: the formula of 5, 28 recurs in all the letters, 2 Thes. 3, 11; 1 Cor. 16, 21; Col. 4, 18; Gal. 6, 11). Paul wrote only the letter to Philemon with his own hand (10), and, contrary to what Roller claimed, we must also admit the activity of a secretary. Just what the extent of Paul's influence was is a much debated question. It is not difficult to find a pagan letter that is authenticated with the use of autographic expressions. (11)

The ancient form of letters enables us to find in the Pauline literature the basic structure, the use of conventionalized expressions, as well as some aspects of composition-techniques. What is of importance to us is the fact that in the process of education, the Christian teachers had recourse to this literary form as a means of propaganda, instruction, and polemic. It is in the book of the Apocalypse where such a technique reaches the literary stage wherein the letters to the Churches of Asia are classed in the genre of imaginary letters. Such a development or evolution of a form is highly significant.

Our principal concern about the Pauline letters themselves is to point out their originality.

First of all, among these letters there is diversity, but such diversity should be evaluated within the context of the same genre so that the individuality of each letter could be more appreciated. Philemon is the only letter that comes closest to the nature of a private letter. The first and second letters to the Thessalonians clearly have a letter-form intended for the instruction of and exhortation for the community. The two letters to the Corinthians are really consultations and apostolic interventions into the affairs of the Church. The general tone and dominant effect as well as the content are more elevated and more solemn. Not only is the public reading of the letters ordered, but the letters themselves are so composed with communal organization and parenesis in view. The letter to the Galatians differs from the one to the Romans because of its polemic nature, its spontaneity, and its violence. Romans resembles a treatise more than anything else, a mature reflection of indisputable unity, with only slightly marked shifts of thought in some instances. Since it was not a response to a definite situation or to specific questions, it moves to a higher level of thought, of exegesis, and of speculation. Nevertheless, Romans still is a letter because of the highly personal character of its developments. The letter to the Philippians belongs to the same genre as the letters to the Thessalonians; the only marked difference is the more superior level on which the topics are discussed. The letter to the Colossians, that is addressed to recipients who are not known and that is related to a new problem, is both a liturgical work and a theological thought-piece. The letter to the Ephesians belongs to the same category. Eevn though the Pastoral Letters are addressed to the leaders of the Church, they are nevertheless not private letters. Timothy and Titus are directly the recipients of these compositions; however, the Pastoral Letters are destined for the Churches and are greatly characterized by an emotion which is intensely paternal.

Secondly, all of the letters of Paul are official acts in his capacity of being an Apostle. Such a characteristic that is common to them all does not rule out notations and opinions that are entirely personal, as well as emotional effusions, concrete directives, and individual greetings. Nevertheless, they are documents of the Church and for the Church. The following distinctions are in place: 1) the voice of the Gospel witness and the proclamation of the kerygma, the reminders concerning the content of oral preaching, and the insistence on tradition and faithfulness to the word of the Savior; 2) the word of the theologian who handled the Sacred Scriptures according to the manners of the rabbis or according to his own personal method. In adapting himself to the objection that was raised, he argued by taking up the statement of his adversary, by giving an exact and precise description of the doctrines and ecclesial positions, and by speculating on data known and accepted in order to add new light; 3) the exaltation of the prophet and the effusion of the mystic who demanded from the new revelation the flowering of the mystery and the fulfillment of the new cult in praise of the perfect economy of salvation.

It is to such a character, at once occasional and universal, that we are grateful. For the Pauline letters taken together represent slices of actual life and treatises; they are both historical documents and sources of faith; they have shaped the past and still confront mankind with a decisive choice and engagement.

Art. 2. Thanksgiving

Despite the stereotyped nature of the thanksgiving, Paul nevertheless enjoys considerable freedom of choice. Hence, the exegete can rightfully search for the personal thought of the Apostle in these patterns as well as those changes which influence the development of his religious attitude.

The letters of Paul, with the exception of Galatians, the first to Timothy, and the one to Titus, begin with an expression of thanksgiving. (12)

The expression of thanksgiving has a structure proper to itself: a) there is a link between it and the mention of prayers for those for whom the letter had been destined (1 Thes. 1, 2-3; Phil. 1, 4; Col. 1, 3; Eph. 1, 16; Phlm. 4, 2 Tm. 1, 3); b) the formula of thanksgiving then proceeds to develop into two directions. First of all, congratulations are extended because of the possession of certain virtues: for example, 1 Thes. 1, 3, faith, love, and perseverance; Rom. 1, 8: faith; 1 Cor. 1, 4: graces of knowing and keeping the word; Phil. 1, 5: helping to spread the good news, cfr. 1, 9; Col. 1, 4: faith, love, and hope; Eph. 1, 15: faith and love; 2 Tm. 1, 5: faith. The second direction in which the formula of thanksgiving develops occurs only in 2 Cor. 1, 3, where Paul blesses the God and Father of the Lord for the comfort which he received from on high. In this case, the expression of thanksgiving actually assumes the form of a blessing. Therefore, the formula of thanksgiving almost always involves the thematic sequence of faith, hope, and charity; c) the stylized quality of the expression of thanksgiving is highlighted with the addition of the term *pántote* ("always"; e.g., 1 Thes. 1, 2; 2 Thes. 1, 3; 1 Cor. 1, 4; Phil. 1, 3; Col. 1, 3; Col. 1, 3; and Phlm. 4) to the expression *eucharistéo*. The expression *eulogetós* in 2 Cor. 1, 3 and Eph. 1, 3 is a literary allusion to the Hebrew equivalent *baruk Yahweh* of Ps. 144, 1 (in the Vulgate 143.1) and of Ps. Sol. 2, 37, which is also the initial phrase of the Jewish morning and evening prayer; d) the formula of thanksgiving is also often cloaked with an eschatological perspective, such that the present is united with the "final days" (1 Cor. 1, 4-9; Phil. 1, 3-11; Col. 1, 3-23; 1 Thes. 1, 2-4; 2 Thes. 1, 2-10).

Some have maintained that such a practice can be traced to Oriental or Greek usage; in fact, the dependence seems to be hypothetical. Greek letters of the third and second centuries B.C. did express a wish for good health, but apart from the opening address. In the first century, the formulation of a wish tended to disappear and to be absorbed into the term *chairein kaì errôsthai, hugíainon dè kaì autós*. Added to such a wish for good health was a prayer, to which form some authorities have traced the Pauline expression of thanksgiving. However, many of the ancient letters lack this prayer, and the custom seems to be more Egyptian than Greek. Only in the second century A.D. does the prayer-form appear, and independently of the formula expressing the wish for good health. But even here, the instances are rare, although in the third century A.D., the custom became more frequent. (13) In the light of these facts, the Pauline use of the thanksgiving form in his letters does not seem to owe its origin to some external inlfuence. According to a Jewish custom, Paul most likely simply used to begin his preaching with an expression of thanksgiving, a pattern which he later incorporated into his correspondence.

Whatever the actual case may have been, what is certain is is that the expression of thanksgiving was part of his standard pattern. The fact, moreover, that he used the formula frequently is indicative of certain consequences in the analysis of his epistles. Many authors do indicate the opening statements of the various epistles by inserting the title: Thanksgiving. However, as we see it, emphasis should be placed more on the content of the statement of thanksgiving than on the mere external form.

Art. 3. Autobiography

The profane letter usually began with some news concerning the correspondent or the addressee. The procedure of course is so natural a phenomenon that we still find it in use today among unsophisticated people, whose letters usually begin with the words: "I am well, and I do hope that you are the same." For Paul, it was most difficult to separate himself from what he was saying. Therefore, his correspondence is impregnated with personalistic expressions. We recall what St. Jerome once wrote: "The only thing to do is to make those who are absent, present" ("Sola res est quae absentes praesentes faciat" (Ep. 8, *CSEL* 54).

The autobiographical passages are literary units which assume different forms. (14) We shall attempt to establish some kind of classification:

1.   Simple autobiography, in which the Apostle has news about himself: 1 Cor. 16, 5-9; 2 Cor. 7, 5; Rom. 1, 11-14; Phil. 1, 12-26.

2.   Apostolic autobiography, which is an expression of the zeal of the Apostle: 1 Thes. 2, 1-12. 18; 3, 1-2, 6; 1 Cor. 1, 12-14; 2 Cor. 1, 8-6, 10; Rom. 15, 17-21; Col. 2, 1-3; 3, 7-9; as an example to be imitated: 2 Thes. 3, 7-9; 1 Cor. 3, 9-13; 7, 9; essence of his mission: 1 Cor. 1, 14-16; 2, 1-5; 2, 1-4.10.11.23.

3.   Apologetic and polemic autobiography: 1 Cor. 9, 1-27; 15, 9; 2 Cor. 10, 1-12, 21; Gal. 1, 11-2, 14.

4.   Mystical autobiography: 2 Cor. 12, 1-10; Eph. 3, 1-13.

5.   The occurrence of the "I", so frequent in Paul's letters, at times assumes the value of a type: Rom. 7, 14-25. The bond be-

tween the individuality and person of Paul and his function is subordinate, but can scarcely be denied. (15)

It is on the basis of such evidence that we are in a position to evaluate the temperament and the character of the Apostle; however, we can also make an assessment of him as a preacher, polemicist, and mystic. By emphasizing his personal experiences, his interior states, the repercussion of eevnts on his spirit, and all of these as having a value for example and doctrine, Paul goes beyond mere concern with events, to become deeply involved in a religion of existence and in categories of value and of action. (16)

Art. 4. Expression of the Kerygma

Paul does not undertake in his letters a Christian catechesis of the facts and the words of Jesus. However, this is not the place to analyze such a phenomenon. But no one denies that Paul's first Christian formation occurred in the context of an already organized pattern of preaching. At the time of his conversion, certain expressions, such as the term "Gospel," existed, and standard Christian formulas were already in vogue. In the light of his first letter to the Thessalonians, which was his first piece of epistolary correspondence, we attempted to trace some of the expressions which were available to Paul, and to construct a doctrinal synthesis which such vocabulary implied. (17) That some Hebrew or Aramaic expressions such as *amen, abba,* and *maranatha,* had been taken over into the Epistles from existing cult. It is more difficult to decide at what precise stage of development are to be ascribed the nomenclature concerning God, Jesus, and the Spirit. (18) Nevertheless, it is an essential problem that is basic for a reconstruction of Pauline theology. We must therefore realize that the very vocabulary which the Apostle uses raises the question of the *Sitz im Leben* as is the case with any highly-developed literary collections. Just as the use of the word *logos* in Johannine compositions evokes a whole world of cultural background, so equally, such terms as "gospel," "body," "head," "fulness," as well as the words "justice," "law," "grace," and "spirit," must lead exegesis to an intellectual substructure, which must be thoroughly investigated if we are to reach any understanding of Paul at all. The initial data of this type of work are given in the *Theological Dictionary of the New Testament* and in a series of monographs. These attempts, however, represent only the preliminary stages of a task which is constantly being made more complicated by the publication of the Qumran texts. Nor is vocabulary the only factor involved. (19) In preaching as well as in writing, Paul resorted to schemes and patterns which were already existing and had been given their respective formulations. We have attempted to show this in the case of 1 Thes. 1, 9-10. (20) The most celebrated instance is that of 1 Cor. 15, 3b-7a, but we must not overlook such a passage as Rom. 1, 2-5.

Art. 5. Recourse to Scripture

Paul's attitude towards the Old Testament has been the subject of study for a very long time. (21) As far as Form-Criticism is concerned, we can distinguish between the following factors: A) the citation properly so-called; B) the use of citations; and C) the Pauline exegesis.

A. *Citations in the Strict Sense*

Paul cites the Old Testament fifty-three times, a number which represents about one-third of all citations from the Old Testament in the New Testament. With the exception of the four instances in the letter to the Ephesians and the single instance in the first and second letters to Timothy, these citations all occur in the four major epistles. Besides such explicit references, there are also allusions to passages in the Old Testament as well as a rich incorporation of verbatim techniques. The implicit citations are taken from sixteen books of the Old Testament — particularly, thirty-three are from the Pentateuch, twenty-five from Isaiah, and nineteen from the book of Psalms.

Such frequent use of the Old Testament in the Pauline epistles has provoked many problems, which have been subjected to very intensive study. From what *text* is Paul quoting? Paul certainly was acquainted with the Hebrew text (Rom. 10, 15; 1 Cor. 14, 21; 15, 24). But in general, he depends on the LXX; for, of the ninety-three citations, fifty-one are from the LXX. In four passages, he follows the Hebrew text. But in thirty-eight instances, he deviates from both the Hebrew and the LXX. As far as his dependence on the text of the LXX is concerned, Paul goes beyond the mere level of citation to the actual use of its vocabulary. The Greek of the LXX becomes the most natural means of the apostolic expression.

Moreover, when Paul cites a passage, he is not always a slave to a mechanical sequence of words, since whether he quotes them from memory or whether he makes some deliberate change in the verbal sequences, he continues to exercise great liberty in the matter. Whether Paul was acquainted with translations other than the LXX is a question that has been raised, but a difficult one to answer. The problem is further complicated if considered in the light of the history of the text of the LXX itself. (22)

B. *Use of Citations*

In the Pauline epistles, the citations from the Old Testament occur within a literary and doctrinal framework. (23) The use of the term *graphe* and of such introductory lemmata as *gegraptai, he graphe legei, kathos gegraptai, ho nomos elegen* or *legei,* (24) "David said," "Isaiah said," "God said," shows that Paul accepted the Scriptures as the word of God and as an incontestable authoritative unit. Such formulas however do not in any exclude from the Sacred Scriptures the presence of the human character. What value the lemmata have as far as the insistence on the personality of the writer is concerned is a debated question.

From the doctrinal point of view, the use of the expressions *graphe* and of *gramma* is part of the Pauline theology on the relations between the two covenants.

The antitheses "letter and law" (Rom. 2, 27), "letter and spirit" (Rom. 2, 29), and "law and spirit" (Rom. 7, 67; 2 Cor. 3, 6-7) do not just constitute some literary device, for they express the total novelty of the new preaching. Thus, the expression *graphe* assumes its total meaning which comprises the movement of the Spirit and the eschatological function.

Basing his argument on the fact that the Old Testament had assumed too great and important a role in the major epistles than in the rest of the Pauline corpus, Harnack claimed that this usage did not include the imposition of the Old Testament on the Christian as an *Erbauungsbuch,* that is, as a book for edification. When apostolic thought is not dominated by the Law-Gospel polemic, it appeals only to "the word of the Lord," to the Gospel, to apostolic authority, revelation, and example, and to teachings which had been previously delivered. Lohmeyer had already weakened Harnack's thesis. Michel had resolutely opposed it. (25)

Finally, we would like to merely point out the problem concerning the use of the ordinary lemmata and the impossibility of tracing the alleged quotation from the Old Testament, certainly in connection with 1 Cor. 2, 9; Eph. 4, 18; 5, 14, and probably with 1 Tm. 5, 18b.

C. *Pauline Exegesis*

As far as Pauline exegesis of scriptural texts is concerned, research efforts have fanned out in three different directions. The first line of investigation offered a comparison between the methods of Jewish exegesis and the techniques of Pauline exegesis. (26) As far as the methods of Jewish exegesis are concerned, the Targums, the Talmud and the Midrash for the Palestinian Jews, and the Jewish works of the Alexandrian community for Hellenistic Jews are no longer the only sources, because the writings from Qumran are now available. (27)

The second line of research merely situates Pauline exegesis with the exegesis of the other books of the New Testament. (28)

The third line traced the contours of Pauline exegesis itself. In this case, the following distinctions are readily upheld: 1) recourse to exegesis in order to illustrate certain themes, such as Jew-Gentile, faith-good works, popular preaching, wisdom, and eschatology; b) messianic typology; and c) the midrashic form of *pesher*. A presentation of details on these matters lies beyond the purpose of the present work.

Art. 6. Rhetoric

Paul is not a rhetorician in the classical sense. When such terminology is used to describe him, it is nothing more than a reference to his recourse to certain forms of discourse which were imposed on him, either through his own literary formation, or because of the oratorical tendencies of his own personality. Exegetes take this into account, not only to discover the quality of the ideas of the Apostle and of their formulation, but also to establish precisely the import of what he has to say. While the study of vocabulary is very important, the individual word bears its true meaning only within a given context. The context itself in turn is dependent on the larger complex, namely, the discourse. We make a distinction between the stylistic devices and the style itself.

A. *Stylistic Devices*

1. Since Paul was a Semite whose daily nourishment was the Bible, he often has recourse to a stylistic technique known as *parallelism*, (30) a fact which is so well established that there is no particular need to deal with it any further here.

2. One form of parallelism is known as *antithetic parallelism*. Paul uses it to such an extent that it seems to respond to a deep need in his own temperament. The technique of antithesis is used not only as regards words, ideas, and phrases but even to the very structure of pericopes and sections of the epistles, as, for example, in the letter to the Romans with its dual fresco composed of the wrath of God and of the grace of God. The most celebrated of the Pauline antitheses have inspired some well-documented studies: death and resurrection (31); faith and works (32); letter and spirit (33); knowledge and wisdom (34); flesh and spirit. (35)

3. The stylistic development which inverts the sequence of words when repeated is called *chiasmus* (A - B - B - A). Formerly, the device was very much in vogue, but research has shown that the practice had become obsolete, only to be noticed intermittently as a stylistic curiosity. J. Jeremias has recently revived our interest on this point by showing how frequently *chiasmus* occurs in Paul's letters, not only at the very heart of a phrase, but also in more extended developments. (36)

4. Other stylistic devices have been pointed out. For example, Paul like to use *paradox*. V. Heylen has emphasized his use of *metaphor* and *metonymy*. (37)

5. We think that the binary and ternary groupings are of equal importance. (38) Together with antithesis, these enumerations follow one another forming pleonasm or gradation. The one word reacts upon another, for greater precision, clarification, or

orientation. By means of these devices, the orator reveals that at times he simply reaches for a dramatic effect, a pause, or a shock-term. The exegete must always be suspicious of himself, since he must take into account all types of liaison in order to evaluate the truth conveyed by the word. Every orator seeks an effect. To interpret a discourse as rigorously as one would analyze a law-code is an error into which many have often fallen.

B. *Oratorical Style*

1. While all authors agree in this, that they do not think of Paul as a professional rhetorician, they nevertheless acknowledge the influence of rhetoric on the composition of the letters. (39) In many instances, the letters seem to be nothing more than a literary prolongation of a previous sermon text which had been delivered orally. This is true of all epistles, but especially of those epistles that are most remote from the nature and quality of a private letter or from the type of letter whose purpose was to answer certain questions which had been raised. The letters to the Romans and to the Ephesians could be pointed out as examples. The former letter, particularly, seems to be much more concerned with Paul's preoccupations of the moment than with the problems of the Church at Rome. (40) The developments that constitute its structure must have passed through a prior stage of oral teaching. But whether in the type of letter that is official in tone or in the more intimate type letter such as the first letter to the Thessalonians or the letter to the Philippians, there is the recurrence of formulas which give the impression of having already been used with such frequency that they have become fossilized.

2. For a long time, authors have been cognizant of the fact that Paul uses rather lengthy phrases, both at the beginning of the letters and in the body of the composition (Rom. 15; 2 Cor. 8 and 9). (41)

3. Furthermore, it is in the style of oral communication where one will find an explanation for instances of *meiosis* (1 Thes. 2, 15; 2 Thes. 3, 2-7) and of certain deliberate *anacolutha* (2 Thes. 2, 2). (42)

4. In the final statements of the development-sections, the action of the orator becomes more evident, with the use of recita-

tive formulas (1 Thes. 1, 9-10), cumulative formulas which synthesize the circumstances of the situations (1 Thes. 2, 14-15), or apocalyptic descriptions (1 Thes. 4, 16-17, 2 Thes. 2, 3-4; 8, 12). (43)

5. The same is true of parenetic passages (1 Thes. 5, 14-22). (44)

6. It is also the orator who uses *rhythm* that characterizes certain passages. The same device also appears in the autobiographical texts (2 Cor. 11, 22-32). The cases which we have referred to are nothing more than examples.

7. R. Bultmann has shown the close relationship between Romans and the *diatribe*. The passage in this letter which approaches this form of discussion most of all is Rom. 2, 1-20. (45)

8. There is one final aspect of the stylistic phenomenon peculiar to the Semitic orator and the Jew. A perfect bilinguist does not exist. Paul thought in Aramaic. His dependence on the Greek text of the LXX offers abundant proof concerning the nature of his formation. He is a Jew, whose second language was Greek. Only with difficulty does a Greek word materialize a Hebrew concept, not only in the translation of a text, but also as the expression of thought. Many examples to this effect are available; but for our purposes, one will be sufficient. The Greek word *eirene* is not the same as the Hebrew term *shalom*. Moreover, vocabulary is a function of precise thinking. The Greek genius was moulded in term of exact terminology and in nuances which its language alone could express in many different ways. The movement and the regulatory aspects of the Greek tongue were products of Hellenistic intellectualism. The Semite and the Jew, on the other hand, are verbally propelled, since for them, the word is a gesture, a sound, a note in a melodic line. To attribute to a Semitic word a fixed and a clearly defined content is to betray its profound meaning. There is of course a centrally determined signification, but such nucleate meaning is encompassed by emanating concentric circles, analogous to those set into action and multiplied by a stone thrown into a lake. It is at this level where exegesis is transformed from a science to an art. It abandons geometric rigidity for delicacy of spirit. At this juncture, "many are called, but few are chosen." (46)

Art. 7. Apocalyptic Form

In 1 Thes. 4, 13-5, 11; 2 Thes. 2, 1-12; and 1 Cor. 15, 12-53, Paul took his inspiration from the apocalyptic genre to describe the end of time. Throughout his entire life, the parousia remained the terminal point in his vision of time. The eschatological era began with the death and the resurrection of Jesus, which constituted the foundation for his belief in the resurrection of the dead. These doctrines, received as they were from the primitive kergyma, were dubbed into the descriptions of the Second Coming. Paul traced his tableaus artistically by using ancient components, texts, and themes, from the Old Testament apocalypses or from current traditions. Thus, the "man of iniquity" assumes the contours of the enemies of God as described by Daniel (11, 16), Ezekiel (28, 2), and Isaiah (11, 4 14, 23;). To these texts, Paul injects the cry of command, the trumpet, the voice of the archangel, the clouds, the fire, the signs in the heavens, the apostasy, the throne in God's sanctuary, the conflict, and the slaughter with the breath of Christ's mouth, whose anti-Christ is both anti-God and anti-Christian.

In accordance with the laws of the apocalyptic genre, these various elements which constitute the stage for the Second Coming are functional only in terms of the profound concepts that are expressed, and not in themselves. It is difficult to attribute equal value to them. In any case, what Paul borrowed from traditional imagery is not graced with the prerogative of possessing the quality of being absoluely true. It is difficult to establish their reality-quotient, since there is no clear equation between image and reality. Paul does not seem to append a supplementary guarantee to the truth-value of the genre which would enable the themes of the genre to enter the category of truths to be simply accepted. Once a literary device is acknowledged, then one could say that, at least as far as some elements are concerned, we would have a situation in which ancient traditions, the value of which is impossible to determine, simply linger on in usage without any specific value-judgment. As far as other factors are concerned, such as the themes of the anit-Christ, the apostasy, and the obstacle that is to be removed, we are merely in the realm of conjecture. The teachings of the Johannine epistles and of the

Apocalypse are on guard against any unity of doctrine whatsoever, and thereby leave themselves open to a development of
their implications, an operation which should not be disdained.
(47) The essential elements are the return and final victory of
the Lord, the resurrection of the dead, and eternal life with him.
The concept of the augmentation of evil at the end of time seems
to derive from a constant Biblical tradition.

Art. 8. Blessings and Doxologies

Blessings, which can be conveniently accepted as distinct from
doxologies, properly belong to a liturgical context as expressive
of an apostolic function. We believe that the salutational expressions "grace and peace" possess greater value than that of a simple wish. To show this, we have only to point out the phrase,
"from God the Father and the Lord Jesus Christ," which is added
to the initial salutation in the text of the second letter to the Thessalonians and on through the other epistles. The final blessing,
"the grace of our Lord Jesus Christ (be) with you (all),", seems
to be equally ritualistic, occurring as it does in all the letters in
an almost identical form. In 2 Cor. 13, 13, the trinitarian aspect
is emphasized; in Gal. 6, 18 and Phil. 4, 23, and in a slightly altered form in Phlm. 25, " with your spirit;" in Col. 4, 18; 1 Tm.
6, 21; 2 Tm. 4, 22; and Tm. 3, 15, "Grace be with you all," an
expression which is paraphrased to some extent in Eph. 6, 24.

Doxologies (48) are short phrases expressive of praise to God
or of blessing. There are two types of doxology.

TYPE A is introduced by the expression *eulogetos*, and instances occur in Rom. 1, 25; 9, 6; 2 Cor. 1, 3; 11, 31; Eph. 1,
3; and 1 Pt. 1, 3. The formulas of 2 Cor. 1, 3; Eph. 1, 3; and
1 Pt. 1, 3 are identical in the reading: "Blessed be God the
Father of our Lord Jesus Christ," although the emphasis in
each case differs. All three passages, in the very form which
they have, have once again the value of a current expression from
the times. The formulations in the other three passages are sim-
pler, and terminate with the *Amen*.

The expression *eulogeîn* evidently points to the Hebrew substratum *baruk*, which in Old Testament passages was apposi-
tionally related to the Divine Name functionally as a participial
phrase. It is the *berakah* (49) of the prayers which were recited

in both synagogue and home. Both morning and evening prayers are of this type, as also are the prayers before and after meals. The documents from Qumran furnish abundant material. Not only is the benediction frequently addressed to God or to his Name (1QS 9, 26; 1 QH 2, 30; 11, 6; 11, 25), but the same theme flourishes also in the hymns (1 QS 10, 13-17). Either the "God of Israel" (1 QH 11, 15; 1 QM 13, 2; 14, 4; 1 QH 11, 29), or *Adonai* (1 QH 11, 32; 16, 8; etc.), or the "God of mercy" (1 QH 10, 14) is praised. In the passage from 1 QH 5, 20, there is a twofold entry, "I will give thanks," and immediately above this phrase there are written the words "May you be blessed." Furthermore, the conjunction of the benediction and the wish for peace is noteworthy in 1 QM 1, 9; 1, 7. That such expressions in Rom. 1, 25; 11, 32-36 (cfr. 1 Cor. 14, 16-17) is of Jewish origin is assured by the addition of the Jewish *Amen*, which the people repeated after the benedictions or the maledictions, a custom that has been well confirmed by the Qumran texts (1 QS 1, 20; 2, 10; 2, 18). The Greek of the LXX rendered the expression *baruk* of the Old Testament benedictions with the term *eulogetós*. These Jewish benedictions formed part of the liturgy of the ancient people of Israel.

TYPE B doxology is less formal in structure but more current in usage. Its simplest form occurs in Rom. 11, 36, "To him be glory for ever! Amen." Other instances occur in Rom. 16, 27; Gal. 1, 5; Eph. 3, 20-21; Phil. 4, 20; 1 Tm. 1, 17; 2 Tm. 4, 18. Such expressions are addressed to God, although the instance in Rom. 9, 5 transfers the benediction to Jesus (cfr. Heb. 13, 21), while 2 Tm. 4, 18 is directed to both God and Jesus in one breath.

It is possible to determine the position of the Christian doxology. It occurs at the level of the preaching activity (Rom. 15, 6; 2 Cor. 9, 12), but quickly passes into the Christian assemblies and into the liturgy. According to 1 Cor. 14, 16, "Any uninitiated person will never be able to say Amen to your thanksgiving, if you only bless God with the spirit, for he will have no idea what you are saying." A final stage in the evolution of the usage of the expression occurs in literary activities. Jesus becomes the instrument, *dià lesoû, en Christô*, or simply *en onómati*. There is ready recourse to the solemn title, "Lord Jesus Christ"

(Rom. 5, 11-21; 1 Cor. 1, 2:10; 9, 1; cfr. Rom. 1, 8; 16, 27;
1 Cor. 1, 4; Eph. 1, 3; 3, 21).

Art. 9. Rhythmic Prose and Hymns

We shall consider rhythmic prose and hymns together, since
Paul moves imperceptibly from the one to the other. The reason
why we would link these two types with the doxologies and the
blessings is that the hymns belong to the common *Sitz im Leben,*
namely, the liturgy.

First of all, we have already referred to the *rhythm* of certain
passages as the expression of the oral style. However, in other
passages, the rhythmic phenomenon is maintained for a longer
period, and, from all appearances, represents a stylistic effect as
well as a form of expression. F. Blass had attempted to trace
such rhythm throughout a complete composition, as, for instance,
the first letter to the Thessalonians. (50) He did not win a following on this matter, but it is quite clear that even a passage
like Rom. 1, 1-7 has this type of modal structure. The classic
example is the parenesis on love in 1 Cor. 13, 1-13. (51) Other
parenetic passages and paratactic phrases also register the
same rhythmic pattern (e.g. 1 Thes. 5, 14-22).

These rhythmic passages are helpful in circumscribing certain
norms for exegetical operations, since they are constituted as units
which stand independently of the overall structure of the epistle.
For example, we think that it is certain that the parenesis of 1
Thes. 5, 14-22 does not describe the needs of the Church at
Thessalonica, just as the pericope on the fruits of the flesh and
the fruits of the spirit in Gal. 5, 16-26 is part of an oratorical
flow, independent of the question concerning the conditions of
the Churches in Galatia. We could say the same for the passage
concerning the love of God in Rom. 8, 31-39, and the final pericope in Rom. 16, 25-27, which approaches the nature of the
hymns of which we shall consider shortly.

As a stylistic effect in oral presentation, the factor of rhythm
gives us an indication of the living principles which inspired
Paul to move. Oftentimes, his accents soar to the realms of
great literary beauty. On the other hand, the form and matter
are as one — it is the spiritual being of the Apostle that finds
expression, and since his being is charged with the richness of

the ancient heritage and is engaged in the actual living of his time, it is capable of blending the one with the other with a new glow. At the same time, the expression is controlled, ruled, and unified by his own genius. Words are never used to detract from the reasoning and the thought. On the contrary, it is frequently in such passages that the substructure of the Pauline edifice is firmly established, in such a way that the very words which he uses reveal a substratum rich in meaning. A convincing instance is the passage in Rom. 1, 1b-7. Perhaps, in such autobiographical passages with their polemic qualities, the rhythm reaches its acme of strength and its highest density. In this respect, no other letter is on a par with Second Corinthians (4, 7-10:16-17; 6, 3-10; 11, 23-31), in which all stylistic devices blend to the delight of the reader.

Secondly, is it possible to speak of hymns? That depends on how one understands the term. If a hymn is a prayer in strophic form conforming to regulated prosody and designed to be chanted in the religious assembly, then we could say that there are no such types in Pauline literature. (52) F. R. M. Hitchcock exaggerated (53) when he claimed that Paul had composed the first letter to the Corinthians in metric form, under the inspiration of the lyricism and strophic qualities of the ancient chorus, particularly of Euripides and Pindar. It is only in a broad sense, which must be determined and justified in each instance, that one could speak of hymns and strophes in Paul's letters. We shall single out the principal examples:

1) 1 Cor. 12, 31 - 14, 1 - IN PRAISE OF CHARITY. (54) In his excellent study on this most important passage concerning charity in the entire New Testament, C. Spicq correctly observes that the passage is not a psalm or hymn, properly speaking, but rather an exhortation to virtue. "Commentators have noted the literary beauty of this chapter: its rhythm, the musical effect of its pleasant sounding words; the choice of images; the balance and parallelism of its propositions; the use of antithesis, chiasmis, hyperbole, and anaphora; and above all its lyric tone and the exact correspondence between its form and its fervent, elevated thought." (55)

Critics usually divided this didactic presentation into three "strophes" which are scanned on the basis of repetitions: the first strophe with its threefold repetition of the phrase "but have no love;" the second strophe with its presentation of the effects of charity on Christian conduct in three groups — what charity does in two positive descriptions, what charity does not in eight negative descriptions, and what charity does in four positive descriptions (with four repetitions of the term "always") ; and the third strophe with several antitheses ("now-then;" "imperfection-perfection;" "infancy-maturity;" "ephemeral-eternal"). The structure is very elaborate, and the development of St. Paul's thought and the expression he uses are reminiscent of many Jewish and profane parallels. A. von Harnack (56) had insisted on a Jewish milieu, whereas E. Hoffman (57) and G. Rudberg (58) had pointed to the influence of Plato's description of *eros*. Others resorted to Stoic parallels, especially of Maximus of Tyre. (59) Thus, the praise of the greatest virtue reappeared as a frequent topic of discussion among wise men and in popular philosophical preaching at the Hellenistic period. The development of the topic (*topos*) followed a traditional form: a series of comparisons, complementary images, and positive and negative characteristics. (60) G. von Rad had called attention to a passage in the *Testament of Issachar, 4* and in the *Testament of Benjamin, 6.* Already an author like Plutarch used six negative and asyndetic propositions which culminate antithetically in a positive proposition. (61) Even though such studies do not firmly establish a literary dependence, nevertheless, they do link the Pauline eulogy with the usage in classical rhetoric.

    2) Phil. 2, 6-11 - A HYMN TO CHRIST-SAVIOR OF GOD. For a long time, the rhythmic pattern of this passage had attracted attention. In 1928, E. Lohmeyer (62) proposed that this passage was a hymn, a veritable "Carmen Christi." In his commentary of 1953, he continued to maintain his position with even greater precision: the hymn is divided into two equal parts, vv. 6-8 and vv. 9-11. Each part in turn is further divided into nine small phrases, having three verbs with six afferent determinations, two determinants per verb. Hence, the two periods are divided into six strophes of three lines each. The two parts are harmonious and are formally and really constructed according to the

same mode. The first and fourth strophes are syntactically distinct. These characteristics are highly significant. We must add that the position of the words is not in accord with the epistolary genre. The genitive constructive are separated from the substantives which they qualify, and the predicates stand independently of their verbs. There are even words which occur nowhere else in Paul's correspondences. Lohmeyer critically attributed the hymn to an earlier tradition with a subsequent denial of its authenticity. Paul did not write the hymn, but simply used it since it was available. With these views in mind, P. Benoit wrote in the *Jerusalem Bible*: "Verses 6-11 constitute a hymn, whose very delicate arrangement has a rhythmic quality. The various stages of the mystery of Christ numerically correspond to as many strophes (6.7.8:9.10.11)." (63) P. Bonnard followed the views of Lohmeyer. (64) Dibelius (65) and W. Michaelis (66) were more cautious. Msgr. Cerfaux proposed his own opinion. (67) With reason he rejected Lohmeyer's omission of the phrase "yes, death by the Cross" from verse 8. Hence, Cerfaux proposed that there were three "strophes": the first four lines constitute the first strophes, the next five lines constitute the second strophe, and the last six lines constitute the third strophe. J. Jeremias independently proposed a tripartite division. He criticized Lohmeyer's division of the hymn into six strophes for terminating only the third and sixth strophes with a complete phrase, whereas in the other four strophes, the phrase continues to run beyond the alleged limits of the strophe. He, on the other hand, based his division on *parallelismus membrorum*: from vv. 9-11, there is a double parallelism. Lohmeyer violently separated 7c from 7d. Jeremias accepted as additions, not only the phrase "yes, death by the Cross," but also the readings" those in heaven, on earth, in the infernal regions" and "thus glorifying God his Father." Thus, Jeremias arrived at three strophes: Strophe I = 6-7a, b; Strophe II = 7c, d-8; and Strophe III = 9-11. (68) Finally, we would like to note the very interesting study of W. K. L. Clarke, (69) who scanned the hymn according to the Greek metric-pattern 3:3:3, which he claimed to have discovered also in Eph. 5, 14; 1 Tm. 3, 16; and Lk. 2, 29-32. Furthermore, he said that the hymn may have been composed in Aramaic, but was soon translated into Greek for the sake of the Hellenistic communities. The theory concerning the second translation of the Greek back into the Aramaic, which P. P. Levertoff had added to Clarke's study, would show that the first to the fourth strophes of Lohmeyer constitute the hymn, whereas strophes five and six would be Pauline additions.

As for the source of the hymn, Lohmeyer pointed to a Judaeo-Christian milieu. P. Bonnard (70) denied Pauline authenticity completely. O Cullmann claimed that the composition was a confession of faith for use in the primitive liturgy. (71) E. Barnikol attributed its origin to Marcionism. (72) J. Héring saw it as a Judaeo-Christian hymn that was composed either at Damascus or at Antioch. (73) According to Cerfaux, it is a hymn which Paul had composed, and later inserted into his letter to the Philippians, a position also held by Stauffer. (74) V. Taylor, on the other hand, was rather cautious about the latter opinion. (75) J. M. Furness (76) made an objective and well-documented survey of the entire question. After an examination of the vocabulary, the context, the poetic form, and the theology, he concluded that, apart from the theological nature of the passage which should be restudied, there is no reason why there should be any other author except Paul. R. P. Martin re-examined the whole question in a well-documented monograph. (77)

3) Col. 1, 13-20 - A LITURGICAL HYMN ON SALVA-TION: The character of this passage as a hymn is much less accentuated than that of Phil. 2, 6-11. Msgr. Cerfaux nevertheless called it a hymn. (78) Most authors point out its rather studied literary structure. Lohmeyer himself considered it a period composed of four members with three sub-divisions. (79)

In each, there are a verb and a central theme. The style is rhetorical, and its origin is Aramaic. The entire passage possesses a rhythm and a poetic form which isolates the pericope from the current language and gives it a quality inspired by liturgical compositions. It has the appearance of being a prolonged "eucharist or thanksgiving," an action which properly belonged to the office of the community leader.

J. Weiss, (80) E. Norden, (81) M. Dibelius, (82) Eth. Stauffer, (83) E. Percy, (84) and J. Héring (85) emphasized the liturgical nature of the style or treated the passage as a hymn. Ch.

Masson went even further in his analysis than his predecessors. (86) "As we see it, the law governing this type of poetry
which is more Semitic than Greek in character is parallelism in
the actual number of syllables, and the assonance or alliteration
of the initial or final syllables of the members of the phrase,
which we ordinarily call verses are grouped in strophes, which
represent as many units of sound and which are linked together
according to the same law of parallelism." In order to reconstruct the desired balance, Masson deleted the phrase "Now the
Church in his body, he is its head" in verse 18a. Moreover, he
postulated an introduction which had been lost. Then he confined the language of the hymn to verses of no greater length
than fourteen syllables so as not to disrupt the rhythm, but con-
ceded to four lines of thirteen syllables each. The *hapaxlegomena*
are explained as instances of texts borrowed from some pre-
existing composition from the liturgy of the primitive Church.
Finally, it was the author of the letter to the Ephesians who inserted the hymn into the letter to the Colossians.

Ch. Masson was not acquainted with the study of E. Käsemann,
(87) and the latter was not aware of the article or the commentary of Ch. Masson. Therefore, the fact that they had agreed on
certain points in their independent studies is all the more significant. The critical accuracy of the Swiss scholar is surpassed
by Käsemann's analysis.

Ernst Käsemann accepted as a fact that Col. 1, 13-20 was a
hymn. Lohmeyer had proposed a division of the hymn into
two strophes, seven lines in length, each strophe introduced by
three lines of text. Hence, vv. 13-14 introduces vv. 15-16a, b, c,
d, e, f, and vv. 16g-17 introduces vv. 17-20. Käsemann rejected
Lohmeyer's division because it violated the content due to the
fact that v. 16g cannot be separated from the rest of the verse.
Consequently, any division of verse 17 could no longer be guar-
anteed. Therefore, the second strophe must begin only with verse
18. The expression *ta panta* of verse 17 corresponds to *ta panta*
of verse 16. On the other hand, verse 18 could also belong to
the first strophe, because the relative clause in 18b, which is
parallel to the relative clause in 15a, a characteristic of the
oriental-style hymn, takes up the idea of exaltation with the term
prototokos. Besides, it is impossible to set up a formal division

at verse 18 since the idea of cosmic mediation in verse 16 is linked with the idea of the mediation of the Church in verse 18 — the first-born of creation now becoming the first-born from among the dead. Hence, there is no real discontinuity between the two strophes. The question now is: What happens from this point on? The actual difficulty arises from the addition to verse 18 of the epexigetic genetive, *tes ekklesias,* which should be considered a gloss. Such a gloss is indicative of editorial work on a pre-Christian hymn in order to produce the present text. In verse 20, the words, "by his death on the Cross," should be deleted. If such editorial work is admissible, then verses 13-14 could be considered as a pre-existing unit that originated in the liturgy. These verses would not have the work of the final editor who confined himself merely to additions to verses 18 and 20 in the hymn; he found verses 13-14 already united to the previous verse 12. Verse 12 itself could have belonged to the same source. The connection between verse 12 and the subsequent verses becomes clear if the meaning for *eucharistountes* as the articulation of a eucharistic confession, which G. Bornkamm (88) ascribed to it, is accepted. As a result of such analysis, verses 15-20 must be regarded as a pre-Christian hymn. If eight of the words are deleted from the 112 words of the pericope, then every bit of Christian flavor would disappear. In that case, we would actually have a Gnostic hymn. In opposition to verses 12-14, verses 15-20 take up some themes concerning the Gnosis. As far as the rest of his argument is concerned, Käsemann relies on the *Sachkritik* rather than on literary criticism. He sought to establish that Col. 1, 15-20 was originally a Gnostic composition, which passed into the baptismal liturgy after some Christian interpolation, and was incorporated by the author of the letter to the Colossians, who was not Paul. The study of E. Schweizer follows the same line of thought. The learned Swiss divided the hymn into two strophes: 15-18a and 18b-20a. He assumed that the post-Pauline author had accepted a Jewish hymn and had given the hymn a Christian slant, for 16b, 18c, and 20c are additions, and the expression *tes ekklesias* is a gloss. Moreover, he distinguished between the Hellenistic-Jewish elements of the first strophe, and the Christian elements in the second strophe. The latter were particularly apparent in those additions which reflect a theology of a different nature and quality. The redactor had transformed a cosmic theology into ecclesial speculation. Such transformations which were common in the post-apostolic epistles gave Schweizer the opportunity to attempt a reconstruction of the articulations. (89)

I have lingered on this particular brand of literary argumentation simply to show that when the process of atomization of a text goes to such limits, it really goes beyond the real realm of criticism into that of the sorcerer's apprentice. First, a theory is created, and then, by means of a purely subjective microscopic analysis, whatever is incompatible with the theory is easily removed from the text. Surely, one or the other observation is of value, but the entire composite breaks down due to lack of evidence. Procedures of this type simply do not exceed the limits of groundless hypothesis. In a well thought-out article, N. A. Dahl showed that the opening verses of the hymn were an integral part of the letter, namely, to combat nascent heresy from the very first line, and at the same time, to promote the glorification of Christ. (90) W. Bieder was in complete agreement with the thoughts of Dahl. (91)

After all has been said and done, we have to admit that the difficulty consists in trying to repair the caesura in such a lengthy phrase. P. Benoit connected verses 13 and 14 with the thanksgiving and prayer in verses 3-14. We believe that verses 13-14 must be united to verses 15-20, for the mention of the "Son that he loves" is the factor which elicits the praise that follows. Furthermore, Benoit ends the first strophe at 18a, although others prefer to begin the second period at verse 18. The difficulty actually lies in the tension which arises between literary criticism and the theological concerns. In any case, the structure of the hymn is rather loose.

J. M. Robinson (92) tackled the problem. He felt that the text had suffered from the agonies of a procrustean bed, and that we should return to the analysis of Norden. On the basis of his own analysis, he concluded that the style is definitely liturgical and that its structure consists in two strophes, verses 15, 16a, e, 18b, 19, and 20a on the one hand, and verses 17, 18a, c, on the other, both of which had been reworked with different adjunctions. In his attempts to reconstruct the hymn, he would be easily criticized for its definite lack of rhythm. The first strophe, which begins with a relative pronoun continues with the conjunction *hoti*, followed by the threefold recurrence of the particle *kai*. The second strophe, which also begins with a relative pronoun, continues formally with the instance of the conjunction *hoti*, a double instance of the particle *kai*, and finally an instance of the conjunction *hina*. For a hymn, such a sequence is excessively labored, but, after all, any textual dissection of this type is always unpleasant.

> 4) Eph. 1, 3-14: HYMN CONCERNING GOD'S PLAN OF SALVATION:
>
> Upon encountering this pericope from Ephesians, one would be tempted to quote, along with Charles Masson, (93), the following comment of Edouard Norden: "The most outrageous phraseological conglomeration which I have encountered in the Greek lan-

guage." (94) To this comment, we may also add Masson's own judgment: "What is striking is its verbal plenitude, its liturgical majesty, and its perceptible rhythm from beginning to end." (95)

The history of the literary analysis of Eph. 1, 3-14 can be divided into two periods. The article of E. Lohmeyer in 1926 marks the turning point in this history.

Up to the time of Lohmeyer's work, the commentaries and studies tried to find a logical division. In this spirit, Th. Innitzer resumed the ideas of J. Knabenbauer (97), and F. Prat (98) followed the very exhaustive views of H. Coppieters. (99) In 1921, M. Bover did not go any further. (100) H. Coppieters' observations retained their value.

After Lohmeyer's study, attention was given to the character of the pericope as a hymn. M. Dibelius hesitate to accept the strophic division proposed by Lohmeyer, (101) but did agree in acknowledging its liturgical character. W. Ochel, (102) Ch. Maurer, (103), and Ch. Masson (104) had no doubts about the nature of the passage as a hymn. In the Jerusalem Bible, P. Benoit arranged the text in such a way that it seems to allow for strophic divisions. (105) On the other hand, H. Schlier did not favor such division. (106)

Once again, divergent opinions originate because of different perspectives. Some attribute the greatest importance to doctrinal

development, whereas others place maximum weight on elements of form. Thus, a division of the pericope into two parts
(3-6; 7-14) is maintained by J. Vosté, F. C. Ceuppens, J. M.
Bover, M. Meinertz, A. Médebielle, A. Lemonnyer, J. Knabenbauer, J. Huby, M. Dibelius, L. Cerfaux, and H. von Soden.
(107) What these authors see in the first part is an eternal divine
decree, and in the second, the execution of that decree in time.
Innitzer introduced a trinitarian division: In vv. 4-6, the election by the Father; in vv. 7-12, salvation by the Son; and in
vv. 13-14, sanctification by the Spirit. Lohmeyer, on the other
hand, distinguished four parts: 3-4, 5-8, 9-12, and 13-14. N. A.
Dahl (108) linked verse 3 with vv. 4-6a, wherein the latter verses
present the reason for the former verse; as far as vv. 6b-12 are
concerned, a distinction must be made between verses 6b-7 on the
remission of sins, verses 8-9a on revelation, verses 9b-10 on
the universality of salvation, and verses 11-12 on the participation of the faithful. Masson maintained that the structure of the
hymn was regulated by parallelism between the number of syllables, and the assonance of the initial and final syllables. He
distinguished six strophes, grouped two by two, each of which
has the same theme and form, with each stanza ending with
the sound *o* or *ou*. Periodically, the text must be altered, especially in verse 13 which requires the third person, and not the
second person.

H. Schlier's basic principle (109) was to find a division that
would take into account the tenor of the composition as well as its
literary form. Verses 4-10 explain the eulogy in verse 3; verses
11-14, which constitute the conclusion, begins another line of
thought with its emphatic expression, *en auto*. The phrase, *en
christo* is the pivotal point of the entire passage. (110) Struc-
turally, verses 11-14 develop according to two relative clauses
which contain a verbal clause and a relative clause in inverted
order: *en ho . . . eklerothemen prooristhentes*, and, *en ho . . .
akousantes . . . kai pisteusantes . . . esphragisthete*. The first
relative clause is expanded by means of a final clause (v. 11);
the second relative clause is developed by means of a nominal
abridgment without the verb. Both clauses refer back to *eis
epainon tes doxes autou* of verse 6 (cfr. Phil. 1, 11). The tenor
of the eulogy is clearly indicated by the expression *en auto* of

verse 11, namely, Christ effected the union of Jews and Christians. This pericope is a composition in the form of a hymn, but it is not a cultic hymn, whose tenor is functionally qualified by the overall design of the author. There is no reason to postulate a pre-existing hymn.

The phrases of the pericope do have a decided rhythm, the repetitions serve as a refrain, and elements of the vocabulary suggest the idea of the liturgy. However, these factors do not constitute sufficient evidence to isolate the pericope as if it were some type of hymn that had been reworked by the writer of the letter to the Ephesians and then inserted into the epistolary context. Even though the perspective may be highly sophisticated and broad, nevertheless, the accumulation of clauses and of prepositional additions betray a heavy and turgid style, which is not very conducive to vocal renditions. Moreover, the heavy thought-content does not lend itself readily to be moulded into a perfcet form. Together with Ch. Masson, we sincerely hope that subsequent research will unravel this difficult problem. (111)

Art. 10. Parenesis, Moral Exhortation

In his thesis of 1936, A. Vögtle, presently professor of the New Testament at Freiburg, raised the problem of the literary form, relative to the catalogues of virtues and vices in New Testament texts. (112) Previously, in 1928, K. Weidinger composed an essay on the subject of *Haustafeln* or home-baptisms, which showed a certain amount of originality. Vögtle's work, on the other hand, contains a great deal of information written with precision and clarity, and is the model of its kind. (113)

Catalogues of vices occur in: Rom. 1, 29-30; 13, 13; 1 Cor. 5, 10-11; 6, 9-10; 2 Cor. 12, 20-20; Gal. 5, 19-21; Eph. 4, 31; 5, 3-5; Col. 3, 5-8; 1 Tm. 1, 9-10; 6, 4-5; 2 Tm. 3, 2-5; and Ti. 3, 3.

Catalogues of virtues are presented in: 2 Cor. 6, 6; Gal. 5, 22-23; Eph. 4, 2-3; 4, 32 - 5, 2 (5, 9); Phil. 4, 8; Col. 3, 12; 1 Tm. 4, 12; 6, 11; 2 Tm. 2, 29; 3, 10.

The duties of the various vocations in life are described in the Pastoral Letters: 1 Tm. 2, 9; 3, 2-6; 3, 11; 2 Tm. 2, 24; Ti. 1, 7-8; 2, 2-5.

Such lists have caught the attention of exegetes and were subjected to investigation. Vögtle's merit lies in establishing a method and in deriving positive results from his analysis. His first objective was to pursue an analysis of the vocabulary, separately, in pairs, and in series, in order to group them, to situate them in the context, and to determine their specific function. His second objective was to locate the role of such lists in apostolic preaching, directed either to the Christian communities or to the pagans of the Hellenistic world. His third objective was to determine their function in the epistolary contexts. The fourth objective was to raise the problem concerning apostolic catechesis. To all such initial tasks, a further objective would be to localize such lists in the general background of the Greco-Roman world, as well as in the worlds of the Old Testament and of the Jewish people. Finally, there must be an evaluation of the Christian mentality and a specification of the importance of such lists within the larger framework of morality. Thus, the pattern would be to move from the literary and historical analysis to the theological realm.

Vögtle's thesis must be supplemented with those materials that were made available by the discoveries at Qumran. We know that the *Manual of Discipline* (1 QS or DSD) contains several lists, and that other manuscripts provide parallels which are extraordinarily similar to the Pauline groups. S. Wibbing made a comparative study in his scholarly work. (114) Finally, these parenetic formulas have raised the problem of early Christian catechesis. (115) The opinions of Ph. Carrington and of E. G. Selwyn are certainly exaggerated because they are based on very weak foundations. The problem would have to be encountered with more rigid control.

Conclusion

In our study of Paul's literary techniques, we have restricted ourselves essentially to a study of the literary forms. In order to make our study complete, we would have to draw up the balance sheet of all historical and doctrinal studies, so that the *Sachkritik*, or the study of the content, would complement the results gained through literary criticism. In this connection, we would have encountered scholars whom we would have gladly honored. There are representatives from all schools of thought, and it was our pleasure to realize that the Catholics are also well represented. To have taken up such a task would have involved the writing of a comprehensive study on Pauline theology. Since it is to this method that the best works on Paul owed their inspiration, we consider it fitting to at least point out some of their principles.

First of all, we acknowledge that the study of literary techniques is not an end in itself. Of course, the archaeology of a text is a curiosity, but the exegete is not an archaeologist. The exegete notes the relation between words, the forms of expression, the literary genres, and the nature of the thoughts which are expressed. There is an evolution of thought, but this does not mean that there is a concomitant development of literary forms according to the rhythms of life and thought. Therefore, it is necessary to study such factors as literary dependence, the citations and the use of words and themes, as well as their adaptation to entirely new surroundings. Only in such a way can we reach the personality of the author and his modes of thought and formulation, so as to be able to reconstruct his doctrine in its total reality. The proper way to move is from *Formgeschichte* to *Traditionsgeschichte*; not to separate the two is a necessary object-lesson for our own age.

Secondly, that the study of thought patterns must begin with a study of the vocabulary has gradually become an accepted fact. In this connection, the *Theological Dictionary of the New Testament* of G. Kittel and of G. Fraedrich had a decisive role to play. A Greek work has its own personal history before it enters into the religious language of the New Testament. It not only renders the Hebrew substratum of the LXX, but was also used by the Hellenistic world with a well-determined content of its own. It had a meaning, and, at times, a significance which went beyond its usual limits to the point of becoming a "slogan." However, with words and beyond words there is the idea, and it is at this point where the difficulty begins. An idea is expressed by several words with the result that semantic studies cannot portray a complete picture of the reality unless such studies are synthesized. (115)

Thirdly, studies in the *Formgeschichte* must have recourse to research in the history of religions. Each concept gives rise to serious problems of comparison, dependence, and transcendence, all of which no one can avoid or side-step. When we are in a situation wherein it is most difficult to arrive at an objective evaluation, then we do have the right to demand greater rigor methodologically. New information is readily available, since the worlds of Judaism, Gnosticism, and Hellenism have been opened to an even greater amount of knowledge. We look forward to the day when the first volumes of the new Wettstein will appear, and we are just as grateful to those who have recently made a concordance of the Qumran materials a reality.

On the whole, the balance-sheet is propitious, and for this reason, we have every right to be optimistic.

Chapter VII

THE LETTER TO THE HEBREWS

The Problems

There is no commentary on the letter to the Hebrews that is more complete than the commentary of C. Spicq, (1) which was praised highly by the German exegete, O. Michel, who had published an important volume on the same subject in the *Meyerskommentar*. (2) Such a monumental work should be the starting point in any attempt to describe the actual orientation on this important composition of the New Testament.

According to Spicq, the letter to the Hebrews is an apologetic, parenetic, and doctrinal treatise, which resorts to the art of rhetoric and is developed in the form of a homily. The carrier of the letter communicated to the addressees information about the author and the circumstances that called for his intervention. Apollos, a converted Alexandrian Jew, who betrays certain affinities with Philo, wrote the letter in the year 67 at the time of the first critical threat of the Jewish War. The place of origin was Italy. The addressees were certain converted Jewish priests who were in exile in a town on the Palestinian coast (perhaps Caesarea) or at Antioch. The purpose of the letter was to prepare these priests for the imminent catastrophe. The connections of the author with Paul are very vague. The Apostle did not commission the author to write the letter, nor did Paul inspect and approve the composition in its final form. The author was a spiritual disciple of Paul who made use of the Apostle's writings. Moreover, the originality in thought is most striking. The letter to the Hebrews is the composition in the New Testament which was influenced by Judaism to a high degree. Four major sections constitute its basic structure: The Incarnate Son of God is the king of the universe; Jesus is the faithful and compassionate High Priest; the nature of the true priesthood of Jesus Christ; and persevering faith. In accordance with our usual procedure, we note the exhaustive bibliography on the subject which C. Spicq supplies. (3)

Almost all the points which Spicq covered still remain matters for discussion: 1) the author; 2) the date; 3) the addressees; 4) the literary form and structure; and 5) the literary and doctrinal dependences.

Art. 1. Author

That Paul himself was the author of the letter to the Hebrews was still maintained by A. Médebielle, A. Vitti, and W. Leonard, (4) but this opinion is no longer defended even by such Catholic exegetes as J. Bonsirven (5), O. Kuss (6), C. Spicq (7), A. Wikenhauser (8), and J. Cambier. (9)

Various people have been proposed as candidates for the authorship of this letter, for example, Barnabas, Luke, Clement of Rome, Apollos, Silvanus, Philip the deacon, Aquila and Priscilla, Jude "the brother of the Lord," and Aristion. (10) However, it is an impossible task to justify any choice with certainty. From among these many candidates, two names have gained prominence: Barnabas (E. Riggenbach, K. Bornhäuser, H. Strathmann, F. Prat, A. Merk, and K. Pieper), (11) and Apollos (M. Luther, F. Bleek, Th. Zahn, R. Ch. A. Lenski, J. Belser, I. Rohr, H. J. Vogels, W. Manson, P. Ketter, and C. Spicq). (12)

Whatever decision one makes depends primarily on the greater or lesser dependence one would recognize between Paul and the letter to the Hebrews.

The similarities between Hebrews and the Pauline epistles are considerable: (a) The conclusion of the letter is reminiscent of those of the Pauline letters: Heb. 13, 18-19 = 2 Cor. 1, 11-12;

Heb. 13, 19:23 = Phlm. 22; Phil. 2, 19: 23-24; Heb. 13, 16 = Phil. 4, 18; Heb. 13, 24 = Phil. 4, 21-22; (b) there is a reference to Timothy's release in Heb. 13, 23; (c) there are coincidences of doctrine: Christ, through whom the world was created and is sustained by his power, is the mediator in the universe - Heb. 1, 2-3, 6 = Col. 1, 15-17; 1 Cor. 8, 6; 2 Cor. 4, 4; Phil. 2, 5-6; the incarnation and abasement - Heb. 2, 14-17 = Rom. 8, 3; Gal. 4, 4; Phil. 2, 7; immeasurable exaltation above the angels at the right hand of God - Heb. 1, 3-4 = Eph. 1, 20-21; Col. 2, 10; 3, 1; Rom. 8, 34; Phil. 2, 9; suffering and redemptive death - Heb. 2, 18; 5, 7-8; 9, 14-18; 10, 14; the substitution of the new economy of salvation for the old - Heb. 7, 19; 8, 6 = 2 Cor. 3, 9. (13)

The differences are of such a nature that they can be explained only by postulating an author other than Paul: (a) the vocabulary is proper to this letter; (b) the style is not the style of Paul; (c) citations from the Old Testament always follow the LXX reading and are introduced in a different way; (d) the priesthood of Christ is different, and speculations on the Law are based on a cultic viewpoint, rather than on moral exigencies; and (e) the letter appears to be a composition of the second generation of Christianity, cfr. Heb. 2, 3. (14)

Therefore, the author seems to be someone who depends on Paul doctrinally, but who at the same time conserves his own personality in the composition. His knowledge of the Old Testament, his fondness for frequent citations, and his exegesis which is typological, requires over-familiarity with the Jewish world. Hence, the author's point of origin must be sought after in the Judaeo-Christian world. On the other hand, he is also a Hellenized Jew, as we shall see later on.

Some reputable authors even refuse to identify the author with a name, for instance, H. von Soden, G. Milligan, J. M. Moffatt, J. Nikel, J. Behm, H. Windisch, J. Schneider, W. Michaelis, E. F. Scott, O. Michel, E. Mangenot, L. Pirot, and A. Oepke. (15)

Those authors who put in their bids for a man like Barnabas base their opinion on such arguments as the levitival origin of this disciple of Paul (Acts 4, 36) and on his relations with Paul (Acts 11, 25-26). However, we also know that Barnabas broke off his relations with Paul (Acts 15, 36-40). Furthermore, the passage in Heb. 9, 4 contains an inaccuracy, for the text tells us that the golden censer stands in the Holy of Holies. Finally, would Barnabas have had the literary background that is proper to the author of this letter?

The authors who choose a man like Apollos have much more on their side. (16) For Apollos was "an eloquent man" (Acts 18, 24), a close friend of Paul (1 Cor. 3, 4 ff.; cfr. 1 Cor. 1, 12; 16, 12; Ti. 3, 13), and he was a Jew. As a skillful apologist, "mighty in the Scriptures," he loved to speak about Jesus. Moreover, he had lived at Ephesus in a community that was preoccupied with questions on cult and the priesthood — a veritable Johannine milieu which could have inspired certain developments in the letter to the Hebrews. Also the tact and finesse which won him Paul's affection are recognizable in the text. The poverty in the contents of the letter to the Hebrews concerning the role of the Spirit would be due to the deficiency on this particular point in the early formation of Apollos.

However, it could be asked just how tradition had lost the name of the author of so important a document in the New Testament? The Church in Alexandria, which was so proud of its tradition, was the first to attribute the composition to Paul through Pantaenus (around 180 A.D.; cfr. Eusebius, *Hist. Eccl.* VI, 14, 4). Origen was more cautious on the matter (cfr. Eusebius, *Hist. Eccl.* VI, 25, 11-14), for, according to his opinion, the author of the letter to the Hebrews was an unknown person, who was nourished on Pauline doctrine, but who was not commissioned to compose the letter. Tertullian attributed the letter to Barnabas (*De Pudicitia* 20, in *PL* 2, 1021). (17)

Art. 2. Date

As far as the date for the composition is concerned, we at least have a point in time that is *post quem*. The letter was cited by the *First Letter of Clement to the Corinthians* 36, 2-5 (95-96 A.D.), which could point to the year 90 A.D. as the date. E. J. Goodspeed (18) favored the year 90 as the date, but the majority of the authors claim that the letter was composed between the years 85 to 90 A.D. (19), which is also the opinion of W. Strathmann, H. Michaelis, F. V. Filson, and V. Taylor. (20) Some of the Protestants, like W. Manson, recognize in the letter to the Hebrews such a degree of affinity with the writings of St. Paul that they would prefer to date it to a period prior to the death of the Apostle; some of these even go back to the years 58-60 A.D., or shortly thereafter. (21) Again, the indications are meager. Whatever historical and theological synthesis of the first Christian century the critics tried to reconstruct had influenced their relative positions on the question of the date of the composition. No decisive argument can be derived on the basis that the letter emerged as a composition of the second generation of Christianity, or that the Temple in Jerusalem must have existed at the time of composition (Heb. 8, 13; 9, 2-5). The allusion to the Temple in Hebrews is actually a reference to the Tabernacle of the Pentateuch, and not to the Temple of Herod. To base an opinion on the author's positions concerning matters eschatological is tenuous since such positions are highly debatable. (22)

Art. 3. Addresses

To whom the letter to the Hebrews is addressed is a question that has brought into existence an abundance of very divergent opinions, and the many arguments pro and con have not produced anything that could be considered as certain.

a) According to some authors, the composition is not a letter but a homily or a theological treatise. (23) Therefore, the author of Hebrews would not have intended the letter for any particular community, rather for a situation which every young Christian foundation had to encounter. (24)

b) The title, "to the Hebrews", has no authoritative basis. It would imply that the corpus of New Testament documents was already set, and therefore would date only from the second century.

c) Since the time of E. M. Roeth (1836) and especially of the work of H. von Soden, (25) many exegetes see the addresses as Christians of pagan origin: A. Jülicher, A. von Harnack, W. Wrede, F. Barth, A. Seeberg, H. Windisch, J. Moffatt, M. S. Enslin, W. Michaelis, A. Oepke, including the two Catholic authors, A. M. Dubarle and F. J. Schierse. (26) Their arguments deserve some consideration: (1) Heb. 3, 12; 6, 1-2; and 9, 14 can be understood only with an eye open to paganism; (2) the use of Old Testament texts proves nothing, since the letters to the Romans and Galatians do the same thing. Moreover, recourse to the LXX version is natural: (3) The Judaeo-Christians could not have returned to the Jewish cult, since they had never given it up, cfr. Acts 21, 20 ff.; (4) the moral exhortations are directed to former pagans, who could not be permitted to return to some condemned moral practices, "all sorts of strange doctrines" (Heb. 13, 9). This latter expression would suggest syncretic activities involving Jewish and pagan tendencies, rather than just Jewish practices. If the addressees had formerly been Jews, then the letter would have clearly indicated this situation. As far as a determination of the ethnic origin of these Christians, the authors do not agree. A. M. Dubarle suggested Galatia, on the basis of the letter to the Galatians. (27) W. Manson thought more in terms of Christians of the Lycus Valley, Colossae, and Laodicia. (28) Most authors prefer to think more in terms of Rome, where the letter soon became known (*The First Letter of Clement to the Corinthians* and *The Shepherd of Hermas*); they infer from Heb. 13, 24, "The saints of Italy send you greetings," that the author was writing outside of Italy, and that the Christians of Italian origin were sending their greetings. The leaders are called *hegoumenoi* (Heb. 13, 7-24, as also in *The First Letter of Clement to the Corinthians*, 1, 3; *The Shepherd of Hermas*, Second Vision II, 6; Third Vision, IX, 7); moreover, Timothy, who was well known to the Roman community, is mentioned in Heb. 13, 23 (Col. 1, 1; Phlm. 1). If the addressees were Romans then such a circumstance could imply that the letter was addressed to a section of the community or to a domestic church. (29)

Among those who claimed that Judaeo-Christians were the addressees of the letter are: Th. Zahn, E. Riggenbach, Fr. Büchsel, K. Bornhaüser, H. Strathmann, C. Spicq, and F. V. Filson. (30) They argued from the fact that the author of the letter was apprehensive of an apostasy (Heb. 2, 1: 3; 3, 12; 4, 1; 6, 4-6; 10, 23-29; 12, 3-17). If the addressees had been pagans formerly, then the argument of the letter to the effect that Christianity was superior to Judaism would be entirely out of place. Furthermore, every argument that is used derives from Jewish dialectic. Whatever the letter contains is structured out of Jewish elements that were well known to the recipients of the letter and accepted by them. This epistle is one of the writings in the New Testament which offers many contacts with the texts from Qumran. This could be a point of reference.

Who were these Judaeo-Christians? They constitute a community whom the author hopes to visit soon (Heb. 13, 23). Jerusalem is the place suggested by many; (31) others look to the Judaeo-Christian community in Rome (Th. Zahn, H. Strathmann), (32) at Cyprus (E. Riggenbach), (33) of Palestine in general, and in Caesarea in particular. Recently, F. Lo Bue tried to identify the community in question as the Judaeo-Christian segment of the Church at Corinth (Acts 18, 1-17). (34) H. Appel had already made this suggestion. Spain, Ravenna, Thessalonica, and Beroea also have their advocates. (35) Others reject any determination of place whatsoever. Of all these suggestions, the least probable seems to be the opinion which identified the addressees as the Christians in Jerusalem. If Paul was the author of the letter, how could he even think of returning there after the events of 58-60 A.D. (Heb. 13, 23)? If the author was not Paul, but someone who knew the community, then why did he even use the expression *hegoumenoi* (Heb. 13, 7), when he knew that this was not the proper title for the leaders of the Jerusalem Church? Furthermore, the persecutions of which the letter speaks in 10, 32-39 are not of the type with which the early community would have been afflicted only once. Moreover, the community was sufficiently wealthy to be able to assist the brethren, a situation that would be rather astonishing for a Church for which alms were being constantly sought (Heb. 6, 10; cfr. Gal. 2, 10; 2 Cor. 8). Finally, the author, so concerned about style, so careful in his exegetical techniques, would have been completely discredited for having placed the golden censer in the Holy of Holies. The effect would be analogous in the reaction to a modern preacher who would speak of the baptistry as being in the center of the Cathedral choir. (36)

F. V. Filson (37) already tried to show that the recipients of the letter were some Jewish priests who had converted to Christianity (Acts 13, 23), a view to which K. Pieper had subscribed. (38) C. Spicq (39) revived the idea together with some personal nuances, which in the long run do not affect the hypothesis.

What should be kept of this opinion is that the letter does give the impression of being addressed to a rather restricted group of individuals, who would be capable of such sophisticated reasoning and who would be more responsive to such highly developed doctrine than to those basic elements of Christianity relative to the mentality, background, and interest of people who could not take much more. That these individuals would have been converted Jewish priests seems to be ruled out by the fact that the author certainly was not himself a priest, and that his moral exhortations would have taken an entirely different slant had these converts been sons of Levi or of Sadok. (40)

In short, the problem concerning the addressees regrettably remains an open question, despite the present tendency to situate the composition in a strongly Hellenized Judaeo-Christian milieu.

Art. 4. Literary Form and Structure

Particularly in former times, the letter to the Hebrews was considered to be a *treatise* on the priesthood of Christ, addressed to the Church. More recently, such an opinion has been modified, so that the composition is now regarded as an epistle characterized by an attenuated external form of a letter. The author would have chosen the letter-form only from literary considerations. Deissmann considered this composition as the first artistic document (*Kunstliteratur*) of Christianity. (41)

This opinion has not been completely abandoned. O. Michel (42) still regarded the letter to the Hebrews as "the first completely preserved primitive Christian preaching." F. J. Schierse also claimed that the letter is a sermon put into written form, a homily of a liturgical nature. O. Kuss revived the idea with complete approval in his review of Schierse's opinion. (43) H. Windisch and H. Strathmann almost follow the same opinion. (44) Such an orientation in exegesis can be justified only partially. In its present form, the composition is presented as a *letter*, whose author, geographically far removed from the addressees, is stepping into a concrete situation. Form and content must not be confused. Within the epistolary genre, many variations do exist.

a) As O. Roller had pointed out very clearly, the absence of the internal address and salutation should not mislead us, since the first letter of John lacks both the address and the final salutations. Nor can one suppose that a mutilation of the text is a case in question.

b) The letter-form of Heb is closest to that of Rom, but also to that of Eph. In an effort to sidestep such a conclusion, some have rejected chapter 13 as an interpolation. However, there is nothing to support such a conclusion, as C. Spicq had demonstrated very well. (45) The many moral exhortations that are scattered throughout the entire letter witness to a concrete situation and an immediate concern (Heb. 2, 1 ff; 3, 7 ff; 5, 11 ff; 10, 19 ff; 12, 1 ff; 13, 1 ff). The author himself characterized his own composition as a *logos parakleseos,* "words of advice" (13, 22). Hence, the exposition of doctrine is presented with a practical purpose in mind.

c) The author knew his addressees very well because he had lived among them (Heb. 13, 19); he also builds up their hopes of seeing him soon (Heb. 13, 19: 23).

This letter had some particularly characteristic traits, and the observations which have been proposed to classify it formally as a homily are not entirely irrelevant. First of all, this letter is the most learned composition of the New Testament. The style is highly polished and highlighted by several devices borrowed from Greek rhetoric. A literary analysis of the introduction shows this clearly. The divisions are balanced and well arranged. The author evidently manifests great literary skill, for, without being eccentric or affected, he is consistently affluent in manipulating antithesis, verbal wit, alliteration, and a controlled rhythm in language that is lavishly pertinent. The entire composition radiates with a perfect finish with its use of longs and shorts to achieve the desired harmony. Stylistically, we are far removed from the thunder of Paul. (46) Secondly, some of the passages are constructed with forms that are easily recognizable today. Thus, O. Michel drew attention to Heb. 3, 7-4, 10 as a midrash on Ps. 95, and to Heb. 7, which is another midrash on Ps. 110 and Gn. 14. H. Windisch had previously proposed the same explanation. E. Käsemann saw in chapter 7 a tradition that pointed to an early Judaeo-Christian composition. (47) Much work remains to be done along these lines. The question becomes even more complicated when the indisputable connections of the epistle with Philo are injected into the inquiry. But to what extent are the two related?

The structure of the epistle has been the object of several interesting studies. The question is very important for an understanding of the content of the epistle and for an overall evaluation. The old-fashioned division of the letter into two parts, dogmatic and moral, with the turning point at 10, 19, (48) has been superseded by three attempts to unravel the basic structure of the epistle. Some authors rejected all systematic dissections since they were satisfied with empirical divisions: F. Blak, J. Moffatt, and W. Michaelis. (49) O. Holtzmann calculated ten divisions, and H. Windisch fourteen. (50) Others, including E. Riggenbach, (51) indulged in systematization to the extreme. A third group of authors preferred to seek a golden mean. G. Hollmann (52) divided the first section into small units, but recognized in the second section only two large units; 7, 1-10 and 10, 14-13, 19. O. Michel, (53) following the suggestions of others, identified three parts: 1, 1-43; 4, 14-10, 18; and 10, 19-13, 20. The expressions *archegos* and *archiereus* command each proper section of the moral exhortations, 3, 1-4, 16 and 10, 19-29, which exert a reciprocal influence on each other. H. Strathmann proposed that the letter be divided into four sections: 1, 1-6, 20; 7, 1-10, 18; 10, 19-12, 29; and 13, 1-25. (54) F. J. Schierse pointed out that the moral exhortations are scattered throughout the letter, and therefore proposed a threefold division: (1) The community and the word of the promise (1, 1-4, 13); (2) the community and the work of the promise, the *diatheke* (4, 14 - 10, 31); and (3) the community and the purpose of the promise (10, 32-13, 25). (55)

L. Vaganay made some advances concerning the structural aspects of the letter. He resorted to the compositional techniques in the poetic and prophetic books of the Old Testament in order to trace two principles: First of all, the principle of inclusion, namely, the repetition of certain words, either at the beginning or at the end of a strophe, or again in transition from one strophe to the next; secondly, the principle of concatenation, strophes linked together by means of words which are identical or of the same nature. By means of this method, Vaganay obtained a theory of interlocking-words (*Mots crochets*), and applied it to the letter to the Hebrews. C. Spicq (57) accepted Vaganay's conclusion but did not honor all his deductions.

A. Vanhoye concentrated on the central section (Heb. 8, 1-9, 28), and developed the theory of Vaganay. This pericope has two parts: A negative part concerning the end of the ancient sacrificial worship, and a positive part concerning Christ as the Eternal High Priest. Each of these parts has three paragraphs, which are mutually contrasted in the form of a chiasmus: (58) c (8, 3-5) - b (8, 6-13) - a (9, 1-10) = A (9, 11-14) - B (9, 15-23) - C (9, 24-28) A. Descamps, (59) took up the problem and refined it. The key words not only have an interlocking function, but actually constitute themes. Furthermore, Descamps emphasized the alteration between the dogmatic and exhortatory passages. Finally, he rejected a binary division. In his thesis, P. Gillis (60) analyzed Heb. 1-10, 18. He dealt precisely with what L. Vaganay and A. Descamps had advanced. The division between interlocking-words and thematic-words was correct, but there is no overlap. In Heb. 1, 1-4; 4, 14-16; 8, 1-2; and 9, 19-25, he discovered summaries (*kephalaia*), which were markers for the different parts of the epistle. The construction of small units seems to have been accomplished in accordance with the rules governing Greek rhetoric (Heb. 3, 1-4, 13; 8, 1-10, 18). It is also possible to find compositions of the nature of a hymn (Heb. 1, 1-4; 4, 12-13; 7, 3-26), lengthy sentences based on the agglutination of participles (Heb. 1, 1-4; 7, 1-3) or of relatives (Heb. 5 7-10; 6, 14-20; 7, 27). Furthermore, the author proposed a method of development in terms of concentric circles from Heb. 1, 1 to 10, 18.

Finally, R. Gyllenberg (61) dealt with the problem. He seems not to have been acquainted with Catholic studies, in relation to which, his own work is developmentally regressive. He set out to investigate the articulations in the form of the epistle, but confined himself to the alteration between doctrinal and exhortatory passages. The combinations which A. Descamps had proposed had escaped him. He noted that the alteration was not constant, but that the thought followed a logical pattern which broadened the subject. The letter to the Hebrews is a treatise that is logically developed and carefully structured: The thesis of the priesthood, already announced in 1, 3 and specifically stated in 2, 17, is developed in the last three dogmatic sections (3, 1-4, 16; 5, 1-10, 18; 10, 19-12, 29) with its practical applications in the sections of moral exhortation. In the light of its content, the letter can be divided into two parts: 1, 1-4, 16 and 5, 1-12, 29, both of which deal with Christ.

In conclusion, what we need today is a more developed generalized study which would take into account the interlocking-words, the thematic-words, the alternation between doctrine and moral exhortation, and finally, the general evolution of the epistle. However, such an investigation belongs only to the more important question of the undercurrents in the epistle.

Art. 5. Literary and Doctrinal Sources

The author who composed the letter to the Hebrews produced a work that was both personal and original. The sources which had inspired him had been carefully studied by the commentators as well as in numerous particularized monographs. These sources can be systematically arranged on the basis of the following three titles: A) Christianity; B) the Old Testament and Judaism; and C) Hellenism. (62)

A. *Christianity*

C. Spicq devoted two entire chapters to the study of the relations of the epistle to the Hebrews with the evangelical catechesis, St. John's Gospel, the first epistle of St. Peter, and with St. Paul. His treatment of St. John's Gospel was especially original. He covered the question in sixteen points, and concluded that "in the majority of instances, Heb must depend on Johannine catechesis, which will become fixed later on in the Gospel and the epistles. They represent, therefore, a current of religious thought that is identical with evangelical date." (63) We should also not forget that Paul reserved the more sophisticated doctrine (64) for the more perfect Christians, just as the letter to the Hebrews, and that, from the first letter to the Corinthians to Colossians and Ephesians, there is a development in the presentation of the fundamental concept of the Apostle. While in the first letter to the Corinthians Paul seems to reserve the more substantial food for a group of Christians who had more wisdom, in the later epistles he calls on all Christians to come to the superior wisdom and to a full knowledge of the mystery. The letter to the Hebrews knows no better way to retain the threatened community in the faith than to lead it beyond the fundamentals (*stoicheia*) to the desired quarantee of fidelity (*teleiosis*). The similarities and the differences between the letter to the Hebrews and other New Testament compositions underline the originality of the former and localize it within the framework of a spiritual movement. These studies are most enlightening and deserve further pursuit with increasing thoroughness.

B. *Old Testament-Judaism*

The use of the Old Testament in the letter to the Hebrews has been studied from many angles.

a. *The Text*: (65) Ordinarily, the letter to the Hebrews cites the reading of the LXX. However, there are some variant readings whose study has revealed the decree of freedom which the author allowed himself to take. We also know that the terminology of Hebrews is not that of Paul. For the author of this letter, the Scriptures are the Word of the Holy Spirit (3, 7; 9, 8; 10, 15), of Christ (2, 12; 5, 5-16; 10, 5), and very often of God.

b. *The Exegesis*: The literal sense often yields to a midrashic exegesis or to allegory. Traces of Alexandrian influence have been seen here; however, such phenomena should be compared with the exegesis of the monks at Qumran. In both cases, the materiality of the text is outstripped by application which derive their doctrinal and moral value only from the authority to which the author himself lays claim. What is involved here is the entire problem concerning the *pesher*, which means that a problem which had been regarded as definitevly resolved must be reconsidered. (66)

c. *The Judaism of Philo*: C. Spicq covered this relationship with unprecedented completeness. Referring to a statement made by F. Ménégoz, the scholar concluded that "the author of the epistle is a disciple of Philo who had converted to Christianity." (67) The conclusion of course is not universally accepted, because some criticize it for being based on insufficient grounds.

C. *Hellenism*

Hellenism could have filtered down into the letter to the He-

brews through the influences from the Alexandrian milieu. Does
this really provide an adequate explanation? Some time ago,
E. Käsemann had proposed that Gnosticism had influenced the
letter to the Hebrews in a thesis that has recently been republished. (68) Now that the question of Gnosticism is so much to
the fore, Käsemann's position can only gain more ground. It
would be a waste of time to press such ideas that we know Gnosticism only from its later sources, that Gnosticism, as Jonas described it, (69) is a vague doctrine, and that the term "gnostic"
is attributed to many concepts which properly do not belong to
that system. The facts are that Qumran itself must now enter into
the picture as far as gnostic data are concerned, and that the
disputes among the exegetes about Pauline Gnosticism have not
as yet been definitively settled. Once again we are faced with
an open question. The thesis of F. J. Schierse joined the movement begun by E. Käsemann, He saw in the central section of
the epistle the march of the people towards repose. Moreover, he
directed attention to the fundamental substructure underlying
the doctrinal exposition. F. J. Schierse developed a thesis which
would mean that the imposition of an antithesis between the old
and new covenant and between the terrestrial and celestial must
be abandoned. Christ, the High Priest, leads the people of the
Christian God into the heavenly sanctuary to come to the impreg-
nable kingdom. The author of the letter pursued a practical and
religious goal: He sought to free the community from its in-
feriority complex and to set up his moral exhortations within
a liturgical scenario that was basically soteriological. The thesis
has received severe criticism, since it is unilateral and depends
more on a priori suppositions than on the totality of data available. (70) At this point, we cannot proceed further into an exposé
of doctrine, since the problem is more theological than literary.

EPILOGUE

St. Paul and Modern Study: 1962-1968

The American edition of *Saint Paul et ses Lettres* offers an opportunity to present a brief survey of more recent publications on Pauline research since 1962. The survey will be conducted according to the sequence of chapters in the book. An exhaustive bibliography is not intended.

Art. 1. Interpretation of Paul in Contemporary Exegesis

That the literary output on St. Paul and his letters has not abated in recent years is evident from the following observations. Different areas of the question were given special treatment. However there is no evidence for any fresh approach to the problems or of new orientations. (1) We shall attempt to highlight some of these tendencies.

1. That exegetes are trying to discover a pre-Pauline stage on the basis of the Pauline compositions themselves is not new. We have already discussed this question in our brief study on the first letter to the Thessalonians. (2) Two important studies have substantially improved the methodology. The first work is that of G. Braumann concerning the question of pre-Pauline preaching on Christian baptism. (3) The second study on the titulature for Christ as "Lord" and "Son of God" by W.

161

Kramer is even more decisive and rigorously controlled. Kramer presented his investigations on the use and significance of christological designations in Paul's compositions and within the pre-Pauline communities. The work is timely since it clarifies a problem that came to the fore recently in profoundly exhaustive studies. (4)

2.   There is another series of studies that are being published concerning the relations between Jesus and Paul. The problem concerning the Jesus of history and the Jesus of faith should lead only to a resumption of a theme already sufficiently strained. (5) The dissertation of E. Jüngel, a disciple of E. Fuchs, on the subject of Paul and Jesus (6) has encouraged W.G. Kümmel to give greater focus to the matter by broadening the lines of the problem and by examining contemporary solutions of both Christian and Jewish scholars. Kümmel's study is so well documented that no serious scholar can afford to ignore it. (7) Despite such efforts, the problem obviously is still open to possibilities. An investigation of the *Sitz im Leben* of the Synoptic Gospels concerning Jesus, the Christian community, and the redactional formation of the documents can lead to a fruitful comparison of nuances peculiar to Paul and the evangelists.

3.   The central question in some new works and recent discussions is still eschatology. In a work referred to previously, E. Earle Ellis sees in Paul's eschatology "the meaning of his theology." (8) There are several bibliographical presentations which cover part of the area on Pauline eschatology, two presentations by Catholic authors, (9) and two by Protestant exegetes. (10) Neither of these cover the entire area of Pauline eschatology.

Generally speaking, research is conducted on two levels. Some scholars limit themselves to the task of determining the exact tenor of Pauline thought. These exegetes parenthesize their own theology to effectively "suspend" their own doctrinal suppositions. They analyze the vocabulary, forms, and themes, and investigate the purpose, object, and originality of the developments. Philosophers and historians refer to this operation as *epokhe*. (11) The conclusions flowing from such analyses are important: Are we to accept the existence of one Pauline eschatology or several? (12) How do the Apostle's ideas relate to the

Old Testament, to Judaism, but especially to Qumran? What position does Paul hold in relation to Jesus and in the context of the nascent Church? At this level of investigation, both the exegete and the historian distinguish between the peripheral adventitious factors imposed by literary or real dependences on the one hand, and the profundity of thought, the source and measure of the teaching properly so-called, on the otheer. (13)

Such a horizontally descriptive plan did not satisfy a great number of critics, who regarded themselves as theologians or as philosophers, presenting an *interpretation* of the Pauline texts. (14) At the present time, diverse tendencies are most vigorously evidenced in this area.

A. Schweitzer's proposal that Paul "de-eschatologized" the message of Jesus to inaugurate what might be called an interim ethic is refuted in a study by H.P. Owen. (15) Schweitzer's views are too absolutely partial to constitute an acceptable solution. Elsewhere, W. Sachs summarized Schweitzer's interpretation of Pauline thought. (16)

Another method of "de-eschatologization" is that of Dodd and his disciples. However, these studies offer nothing that would be considered original. (17)

Bultmann's position has aroused various reactions. O. Cullmann (18) attacked the very basis of Bultmann's position in an important work. At the same time the author had an opportunity to crystallize his conception of salvation-history. In his opinion, the concept of the *heilsgeschichte* needs of a definition that would be generally acceptable. At the 1965 congress of the Seminar on New Testament Studies in Heidelberg, at which L. Goppelt presided, emphasis was given to the difficulty of the question. It would be useless to take into consideration all the different opinions of each New Testament scholar. If those involved in such endeavors would refrain from imposing on the New Testament texts a systematization that is excessively rigid, then it would be possible to show greater respect to the texts in the long run. Both components of the concept must be defined, namely, *Heils*, "salvation," and *Geschichte*, "history." The definitions must be formulated in accordance with the individual context of each of the sacred writers, rather than on the basis of relations that are always somewhat arbitrary.

The question concerning the delay of the parousia is still the point of many discussions. Moreover, even though the Bultmannian system is being questioned, the problem continues to be of the essence of that system. (19) It is no longer acceptable to reduce Pauline theology to an anthropology in which the singular gnosis of the new faith transforms human existence. U. Wickert leads the opposition to the Bultmannian system. He has the support of E. Käsemann, who rejects the existentialist system in two reverberating studies. (20) J.M. Robinson has clearly shown that the philosophical foundations of the Marburg professor was itself shaken by the later development of Heidegger's ideas. (21) Even in the *Festschrift* volume dedicated to Bultmann, N.A. Dahl drew up a resume of the ideas which actually turns out to be very remote from the masterplan of the Jubilarian. (22)

Briefly, the points on which there seems to be a certain consensus of opinion are the following: (1) Eschatology cannot be restricted to a study of statements concerning the end of the world, but must be extended to the question concerning the fulfillment of the promise; (2) Pauline eschatology does not enjoy an existence independent of the eschatology of Jesus. This fact has its roots in the historical Jesus and in the existing set of circumstances in which the new Messianiam does not correspond to some prefabricated image. The end of time is considered in its own fundamental existence, seen in itself, having a new value proper only to itself. The Christian expectation of such an end is a waiting process for a person who is coming and who has already come; (3) the delay of the parousia is merely a peripheral phenomenon. The death and resurrection of Christ have effected a strengthening of the eschatological anticipation. He who is to come is identified with him who has already come.

Worthy of note is the fact that most prominent exegetes still study Pauline eschatology independently of any established system. They are of the opinion that, on the basis of the texts themselves, Paul appears to take his position within the context of a present and a future eschatology, both of which are nothing more than two aspects of the same fundamental concept. Paul would not necessarily assume an individual position distinct from that of Jesus on the eschatological question. The man who continued to be the protagonist of such an interpretation is W.

G. Kümmel, with whom are associated O. Cullmann, G. Delling, R. Schnackenburg, A. Vögtle, B. Rigaux, and others. (23) The distinction between present eschatology and future eschatology is sitll present in the works of Bultmann and his followers. (24) Little by little, by being directed towards the future, the expectation changes to an actual fulfillment of hopes, of realized salvation, of the new creation, of existing "in Christ."

Those who propose a distinction between present and future eschatology together with their interdependence are in a position to do justice to the various aspects of the Apostle's doctrine. Today, emphasis is most appropriately placed on the way in which the present and future eschatology colors the apostolate and the preaching of the Gospel, (25) salvation and justification, (26) having existence in Christ, (27) community life in Baptism, Eucharist, and prayer, (28) the status of Israel and of the mission to the Genitles, (29) but above all, the parenesis (30) and the Church. (31)

Such a perspective makes it possible to relate the Pauline conceptual corpus to its true origin, and to confer on that synthesis the depth and originality which are proper to it. Furthermore, such perspective gives expression to a vital movement that is in danger of disappearing in an excessively conceptualizing presentation.

4. An interpretation of Paulinism cannot be complete without an investigation of the religious background. The reason is that the Apostle must be seen in the Jewish and pagan milieu in which he did his work.

Comparison of the Apostle's writings with Jewish ideas are conducted along several lines: the Old Testament, Jewish apocalyptic writings, and the documents from Qumran. Details of such studies are out of the question here. However, we would like to note the warning of S. Sandmel and of J. Barr against what might be called "parallelomania." (32) Comparisons with Jewish apocalyptic writings have led L. Goppelt to review the important question of Pauline typology. (33) The results of the studies of the Essene documents have been reviewed and evaluated at great length by H. Braun and others. (34) Much remains to be done. However, some permanent results have been secured. Furthermore, tools necessary for such research are

being made available with the publication of editions and translations of texts.

The Hellenistic contacts have been studied particularly in
relation to Paul's encounter with Gnosticism. W. Schmithals'
theses have forced exegesis to rethink its former conclusions,
as well as to qualify either the acceptance of the positions that
are advanced, or the rejection of any notions that would postulate contact with Hellenism. The works of R. Mc L. Wilson are
important contributions and in many instances are sure guides
in such endeavors. (36)

Under the impetus of the studies just listed, and thanks to
the influence of the work that is in progress in New Testament
research, attempts at any synthesis on Saint Paul register a distinct advance. The most recent volume of Msgr. L. Cerfaux, which
dealt with the Christian in the theology of Saint Paul, clearly
confirms this. Mastery of the sources, intuitive penetration of
the materials, clarity of exposition, and unerring synthetic thinking endows this work with an authority it justly deserves. The reprint of his book, *The Theology of the Church according to
Saint Paul* (*Théologie de l'Eglise suivant saint Paul*), an enlarged
and up-dated edition, equally deserves special mention. Together with his volume on *Christ in the Theology of Saint Paul*
(*Le Christ dans le théologie de Saint Paul*), these two works
offer an approach to Pauline thought that has more value than
any other comparable work in contemporary biblical literature.
(37) With due allowance, we recommend D.E.H. Whiteley's work
on the theology of St. Paul since it is a worthwhile introduction
that is succinct and lucid, even though at times it tends to be
too systematically condensed. (38) G. Delling's booklet on the
message of Paul is rather interesting. (39)

Art. 2. Chronology

There is a dearth of recent studies concerning the biography
of Paul, (40) his conversion and apostolate, (41) as well as
chronology. What efforts have been made could either alter the
perspective of the problems, or improve it perceptibly.

The problem of chronology has been touched in several instances. G. Strecker studied the problem of Paul's second journey
to Jerusalem. For this author, Luke wrote Acts 11, 27-30. The pur-

pose of the second journey was to integrate the Antiochian Church into the plan of salvation-history, a topic of which Luke was so fond. Hence, Strecker would actually agree with our conclusions. (42) F. Hahn sketchily considered the problem of chronology. (43) He dated the Council of Jerusalem to 43-44; Paul's conversion to the year 28; Christ's death to 27; Paul's sojourn at Corinth to 49-50; his return to the East in 61; his stay at Ephesus to the year 52-55, and at Corinth in 55, a date which he attached to the journey to Jerusalem. Moreover, he agreed that Festus succeeded Felix in 55-56 and that the trip to Rome occurred in the year 58 A.D. Hence, Peter and Paul would have ben martyred in Rome in the early part of the year 60 A.D.

B. Reicke offered a different chronology: conversion in 36; The collection journey in 46; the first journey in 47-48; the Council of Jerusalem in 49; the second missionary journey in 50-53; the third missionary journey in 54-58; the succession of Festus in 60; Paul's stay at Rome in 60-62; and the martyrdom of Peter and Paul in 65 A.D. (44)

The topic of V. Mancebo's study was the relation between the epistle to the Galatians and Acts in connection with Paul's journeys. In his opinion, the exactitude of the Pauline data in Acts could be easily sacrificed to retain the Lucan chronology for the three journeys. (45) The article is worthwhile inasmuch as it gives an exact summary of the present state of the question. What reasons he gave for his preferences are of no account as far as exegesis is concerned.

For H. Conzelmann, there never was a journey that involved a collection. The Council of Jerusalem, to be dated most probably to the year 48 A.D., was convened after the first missionary journey. Moreover, preference should be given to the letter to the Galatians rather than the literary constructs of Luke. Gallio was proconsul either in the year 51-52 or 52-53, although the former would be the more probable hypothesis. The author tended to be very hasty in arriving at decisions concerning these questions, and he really had nothing original to add. (46)

On the occasion of ceremonies and a congress commemorating Paul's arrival at Rome or his plans to visit Spain, a series of studies of an archaeological and doctrinal nature were published.

Most of them are popularizations, although some of the studies are of interest. (47)

Art. 3. Literary Criticism

Literary criticism of the Pauline epistles have been in the front-lines of scientific research. In connection with the Epistle to the Thessalonians, W.G. Kümmel published a definitively hopeful refutation of K.G. Eckart's thesis. (48) We would like to point out that the anti-Judaic text in 1 Thes.2,15-16, whose authenticity was also doubted by S. Sundmel, is correctly regarded by Kümmel as Pauline. (49)

The purpose of K. Thieme's interesting study was to indicate a recurrence of certain words and phrases in the First Letter to the Thessalonians which enable us to rediscover the actual concern of the author. In the following passages, 2,13; 4,8; 5,16-18, the addressees are instructed to continue to regard the apostolic word as of divine origin, and to receive the word as the norm of their faith and of their conduct. (50)

W. Schmithals applied his well-known methodology in his dissections of the letters to the Corinthians to the Thessalonian Epistles. (51) Without presenting new proofs or fresh approaches he began with the supposition that the second letter to the Thessalonians is an imitation of the first letter, and therefore, is unauthentic. Moreover, he was incorrect when he made the statement to the effect that, from the time of E. von Dobschütz to W.G. Kümmel, many authors, who were not convinced by the arguments of W. Wrede against the authenticity of 1 Thessalonians, have really ignored or minimized the valid reasons which had been proposed. That he does hastily condemn so many outstanding exegetes is amazing, since he himself had claimed that the existence of numerous literary and doctrinal parallels in the two Thessalonian letters proves nothing. What seems to be decisive for him is that 1 Thes.1,2 and 2,13 are both Thanksgivings, which Schmithals had regarded as two protocols. Furthermore, 1 Thes.3,11 and 4,1 indicate that the letter had ended at this point. As far as the second letter to the Thessalonians is concerned, he claimed that it naturally ended at 2,16, which would mean that we have here a case parallel to 1 Thessalonians. Therefore, Schmithals concluded that we have definite proof that the second letter is actually an imitation of the first: both end, only to begin again! He declared: "No man would normally compose a letter in this fashion, nor would any theologian. And if Paul is not a normal theologian, at least he is a normal man." However, he failed to indicate the source of so objective and historical definition of normality! Meanwhile, he proposed that 1 Thessalonians should be dissected into two letters:

A Thes 1,1-2, 12+4,3-5,28

B Thes 2,13-4,2

Moreover, 2 Thessalonians should also be divided into two letters:

A Thes 1,1-12+3,6-16

B Thes 2,13-14+2,1-12+2,15- 3,5+3,17-18.

Furthermore, the chronology for these letters has been completely transformed: IIA Thes is prior to IA Thes; IIB Thes is prior to IB Thes.

Such hypothetical proposals are analogous to his dissections of the two Corinthian letters, and will similarly not fail to arouse many objections.

According to W. Marxsen, the difficulties in connection with 2 Thessalonians are of gnostic origin. (52) The letter could have been written approximately in the year 70 A.D. Many critics would agree that the gnostic indications on which the author based his case are very meagre indeed. The best antidote to Marxsen's work is supplied by the conclusions of W.G. Kümmel. His *Introduction to the New Testament* excels Marxsen's study on two accounts, namely, wealth of information and the sure touch of a master. Finally, there is also the fine work of L. M. Dewailly which offers an excellent introduction to the reading of these letters. (53)

As far as the Corinthian Epistles are concerned, there is the position of Neuenzeit's book on the Lord's Supper, against the theses of Schmithals. (54) An article by A.M.G. Stephenson does not even refer to this problem. (55)

John Coolidge Hurd Jr. has published an important and penetrating study on the first letter to the Corinthians. (56) In the light of a very profound investigation into the matter, he intended to show that attempts to establish a chronology of Paul's activities results in anything but certitude. As he sees it, it would be just as well to rely only on the data of the letters to retrace the different stages of the Pauline apostolate. In the case of 1 Corinthians, it is possible to reconstruct the phases of the evangelizing process of the Corinthian Church. First of all, Hurd attempted to reconstruct a letter that some Corinthians had written to Paul, to which Paul in turn had replied. On the basis of the final reconstruction, he then endeavored to go back even further to a first letter from Paul which was lost. Hurd proceeded to compare these initial instructions with the Apostolic Decree. The final stage of the investigation led the author all the way back to Paul's actual preaching activities in Corinth. Hurd's study is well organized and is replete with highly interesting suggestions. However, what has resulted from the investigation is hypothetical; but happily, the author himself is aware of the situation. Because of the title of the book, *The Origin of 1 Corinthians,* Hurd should have examined a number of important points concering doctrinal aspects and parenetic instructions. By the fact that Hurd limited his subject of investigation, he narrowed down the scope of his work. His conclusions do not seem to weaken the chronology of Luke at all. Our remarks are not intended to belittle the important contribution that Hurd has made; rather, we intend our criticism merely as an aid to a proper appreciation of Hurd's study. Because of the extensive bibliography, Hurd's study constitutes an excellent starting point for further research.

It is important to establish who the adversaries were against whom Paul had directed his polemic in 2 Corinthians. If this were possible, then a slice of the history of the primitive Church would fall into place. If the circumstances of the addressees of the letter were known more clearly, then our knowledge of the letter would be substantially increased. The question, which F. C. Braun had raised and which had been periodically taken into reconsideration, has been subjected to re-examination in an important work by D. Georgi. The basis for his study is 2 Cor.2, 14-7,4, together with chapters 10-13. These passages do not belong to one and the same context: 2,14-7,4 indicates that the danger of falling is not an absolute, since there is some hope in averting the fall; in chapter 10-13, on the other hand, the community has succumbed to a tolerant attitude as far as Paul's adversaries are concerned. These fragments belong to different letters. During the interval of time that elapsed between the writing of the two compositions, Georgi supposes that Paul paid a brief visit to Corinth. The first letter would have been sent during the Spring of 54, and the second in the Autumn of that same year. In the year 55, Paul would have dispatched two other letters, namely, a letter of reconciliation, and a document concerning the collection. On this basis, then, Georgi attempted to identify Paul's adversaries as itinerant Judeo-Christian preachers, who arrived on the scene after Paul had sent his first letter to the Corinthian Church. The substance of the novel preaching of these itinerants would have consisted chiefly in Hellenistic-Jewish apologetic themes, in which gnostic elements played a preponderant role. Georgi's analysis merits considerable attention, even if we would not be tempted to accept his literary and historical reconstruction of 2 Cor, the hypothetical character of which would be obvious to anyone. (57)

Gerhard Friedrich was generally acquainted with Georgi's conclusions when he took up the question. His lengthy article presents a calm but critical evaluation of the opinions of Schmithals, Bornkamm, and Georgi. His opinion is that Paul's adversaries should be found among the Judeo-Christians in the entourage of Stephen and of Philip, that is, in the powerful Christian movement of Hellenistic origin. One could possibly see traces of their influence in Acts 6-7; Mt. 5-7; Phil.1; and 2 Cor. 3ff. Friedrich's study is very rich in the suggestions offered, and demonstrates just how little we know about the vitally complex milieu of the first Christian centuries, despite the abundant data from the New Testament documents. (58)

While the historical and literary problems concerning the letter to the Galatians have received scant attention in recent years, (59) many critical studies have concentrated on the literary structure of the letter to the Romans. In a scholarly publication, R.C.M. Ruys presented, summarized, and classified their contents. (60) Some Catholic authors, A. Feuillet, S. Lyonnet, J. Dupont, A. Descamps, and others, have paid particular attention to this question. (61) It is impossible to write about Romans without taking a stand. Ruys covered comprehensively all that has been published. His review of the individual investigations led him to a conclusion that would be the principle of all analysis from this point on, namely, that it is necessary to take into account both the literary criteria and the doctrinal themes. Furthermore, Ruys established that the themes of the epistle are moulded in literary schemas which form interconnected units. He also took into account both the style and the history of the forms and of the themes. He limited the extent of his investigation to Rom.1,16-3, 23, wherein he discovered two dominant principles: chiasmus as the formal element, and the law of retaliation as the doctrinal element. By means of such a technique, Paul conformed his presentation to the general antithesis which runs through the entire letter. One cannot but agree with the overall drift of Ruys' study. However, it is also of the greatest importance to realize the limitations of investigations of this type. Once such studies become entangled in minutiae, they are no longer based on literary processes deliberately chosen by the author. They would reveal dependences and general lines of thought and work, but they would not be able to plumb the depths of latent intent. Structure is constructive only when it unveils that which lies behind the obvious affirmations, so that the thought is understood more clearly than from a first reading. Positive results of analysis of the structure of Romans reveals the following: (1) chapters 9-11 should not be regarded as an excrescence or an appendix; (2) from chapter 5 to chapter 8 there is the resumption of an idea in terms of concentric circles which develops the constituents of the justice of God in two interrelated themes: the recapitulation of the history of mankind, and the new creation — themes essential to the revelation of the mystery of God in Jesus Christ.

Concerning Rom. 16 as a possible fragment of a letter to the Ephesian community, consult the excellent discussion by W.G. Kümmel. (62)

[*Translator's Editorial Note*: The study of J. Kinoshita may be of some interest to the reader. In the prologue and epilogue, Romans is addressed to Gentiles (1,5:13; 15,16:18), whereas the letter speaks to the mixed congregation of Jews and Gentiles. Chapter 16 and other sections of our letter should be separated from the rest. Paul wrote only to the Gentiles. Abrupt transitions, changes in tone and the evidence of a Cynic-Stoic diatribe (ch. 2) lead to the conclusion that our Romans is a conflation. Paul wrote, in addition to the letter to the Gentiles, a manual of in-

struction on Jewish problems which was added to the Gentile letter. The manual discussed (a) the salvation of the Jews, in 2,1-5:
17 - 3,20; 3,27-4,25; 5,12-7,25; 9,1-11,36, which was sermon
material but also included materials from debates Paul had with
opponents in Ephesus; (b) the problem of vegetarianism, in 14,
1-15, 3, which was against the "weak," i.e., Jews and those under
their influences such as Gentile converts, "God-fearers" and
proselytes, who constituted a splinter group in Ephesus; and
(c) contained a postscript, in 15,4-13, appended when the letter
was sent to a Church, probably at Ephesus. Parts (a) and (b)
were written in Ephesus, and part (c) was written in Corinth.
The manual and the original Romans (to a Gentile group) were
entrusted to Phoebe to be read at Ephesus. Chapter 16 is an introductory letter for Phoebe. The original Romans (to the Gentiles) was written during the three-months stay in Greece,
probably in Corinth (Acts 20,2). In both documents, there are
different emphases and slightly different approaches to faith,
Christology, and the Holy Spirit.]

The next problems for consideration are the so-called Captivity Letters. The unity of the letter to the Philippians is still
questioned. Besides the studies to which we have referred in the
earlier part of the book, there are those of J. Müller-Bardorff,
G. Bornkamm, and H. Koester. (63) A new element has been
added concerning Phil. 3-4,9 (Bornkamm and Schmithals: 3,
2-4,3; 4-8-9; Müller-Bardorff: 3,2,21; 4,8-9), namely, that
this section constitutes a separate letter and the very last one
which Paul had addressed to the Philippian community. This
section of the epistle manifests differences in tone and in content as compared with the rest of the composition. G. Bornkamm
thought that the passage constituted a separate letter, which he
dated to Paul's stay at Ephesus in 54-57 A.D. There is no reference at all here to the Apostle's captivity. Rightly Bornkamm
pointed out that the passage must have been added in a short time,
since the apocryphal letter to the Laodicians, already cited in
the Muratorian Canon, actually depended on the complete letter
to the Philippians. Moreover, the christological hymn in 2,6-11
could be a pre-Pauline liturgical chant which the Apostle simply
polished for his own use. However, it is necessary to repeat that,
in such matters as these, the exegete is treading on the quicksands

of hypothesis. (64) V. Furnish continued to favor the integrity of the epistle, which actually ended with chapters 2-3,1a, although Paul would have added a post-script. This of course is a new conjecture that should be added to the present list. (65)

In his *Introduction*, W. Marxsen placed the letter to the Colossians at the head of the deutero-Pauline compositions, since Paul simply cannot be considered its author due to the style, the relation between ministries and the concept of tradition, and the long list of greetings. W.G. Kümmel has already directed a substantial refutation of such claims. Progress on this question has not been made, nor are the various positions clarified. Whatever can be said seems to have been said, and the same is also almost true of the hymn in 2,15-20. (66)

Some critical work on the letter to the Ephesians has been done. The positions of a number of authors, including the Catholics, are well known. The letter was composed by one of Paul's collaborators who synthesized the Apostle's teaching, depending strictly on the ideas of the master with the help of previous letters, particularly, the one to the Colossians. P. Benoit has investigated the literary and doctrinal bonds between Colossians and Ephesians. (67) But one question is still open: Is Ephesians a treatise or a letter? The answer to this question will considerably modify any approach to the composition. A compromise is possible: Ephesians is a letter by reason of its form, its occasional nature, and its carefully defined subject; on the other hand, it is also a treatise by reason of its attempt to synthesize. Another consideration of equal importance is the determination of the *Sitz im Leben* of the epistle. Those who regard the Apostle merely as marginally involved with the letter must account for the doctrinal differences between the letters to the Colossians and the Ephesians. Their arguments are not pertinent. Scholars who considered the letter spurious and anonymous look for a post-Pauline milieu that would account for the twofold movement of Gnosticism and Early Catholicism (*Frühkatholizismus*). There is no reason to reject on principle the possibility of an anonymous composition in the Pauline corpus. After all, this is the case as far as the letter to the Hebrews is concerned. Moreover, who really knows the author of Greek Matthew? However, it seems that the problem of the date for Ephesians and of its doc-

trinal relations with the Pauline epistles is still open. Far too
many studies are based on arguments *e silentio,* and fail to take
into account the literary genre of the composition. The genre is
a synthesis that depends on earlier compositions and is adapted
to a situation in which a group of churches are involved. Moreover, it is the creation of a keen and powerful mind, characterized
by its determination to be faithful to the ideas of the Apostle, and
by its reuse of externalized structures of thought, while, at the
same time, there is introduced thematic modifications to some
extent. To measure the distance which separates the disciple from
the master or the proximity of the one to the other would be a
task so subtle that only with difficulty would the conclusions
arise above the hypothetical level. (68)

Some important contributions have been made in the area of
the Pastoral Letters. W.G. Kümmel has reenforced his position
for inauthenticity, on the basis of language and style, of the
historical setting, of the conflict with heretics, of the ecclesial
situation, and of the theology. Much emphasis has been placed
on the linguistic and stylistic peculiarities, while the other arguments have no greater weight than the "it is not clear" affirmations. (69) The American scholar, E. Earle Ellis published a
work on the entire problem in which he favors authenticity for
the Pastorals, a view, which he thinks, will gain considerable
ground in the future. (70) J. Jeremias and C. Spicq also defended
the same conservative position. Other authors, on the other hand,
would claim that these letters are nothing more than a revamping
of Pauline materials. (71) C.F.D. Moule proposed an original
hypothesis in which he claimed that the Pastoral Epistles, especially 1 Timothy, are the free renderings on the part of an
emanuensis during the life-time of the Apostle. Such a suggestion
on the part of the Cambridge scholar is rather surprising: the
letters could have been written by Luke, who also could have
collated Paul's letters after his death. (72)

P.N. Harrison published a second edition of his book, *The
Problem of the Pastoral Epistles* (Oxford: 1921). He did not re-
cast his book completely, but simply modified it with many additions and corrections, without changing his methodology. In
order to retain his position for the inauthenticity of these letters,
he continued to give priority to linguistic arguments. Moreover, he

accepted the opinion of J. Knox and of E.J. Goodspeed that Ephesians was written in Colossae around the year 90 A.D. by Onesimus, who also interpolated the letter to the Colossians. A similar literary activity towards the end of the first century produced the Pastoral Epistles. In 1921, Harrison admitted only four passages which he considered to be authentically Pauline. Now, he claims that there are only three, namely, Tit.3,12-15; 2 Tm. 4,9-15: 20:21a:22b; and 2 Tm.1,16-18; 3,10-11; 4,1:2a:5b-8:16-19:21b:22a. "Bonum est cribare modium sabuli ut quis inveniat unam margaritam," i.e., it is good to sift a measure of sand, and find one pearl. Harrison claims that Averroes made this statement; however, the likely impression would be that the griddle let the pearls through and retained some of the sand. The Professor Emeritus must, however, be credited for an uncommon ardor for work and a notable perseverance in the defense of his notions. The study bears several traces of the bonhomie of the aged scholar, and deserves the attention of young scholars who take up the subject. Harrison himself, who has devoted so much effort to the Pastoral Epistles, would be the first to admit that their authenticity is still an open question. (73)

Finally, there is the opinion of Msgr. L. Cerfaux who claimed that the solidarity of the subject-matter presents a good case for the authenticity of the Pastoral Epistles. The resemblances to the *First Letter of Clement* are striking, which would suggest an hypothesis sufficiently respectful for tradition: "Paul's authentic letters were probably edited in Rome after his death; a good Roman writer . . . may have arranged an earlier, more hasty draft, and even added a few memories of Paul's activity preserved by his two disciples." (74)

Art. 4. The Literary Form

Judging from the reviews of the French and German editions of our present work, the chapter on literary forms in Paul's epistles has accomplished its task, namely, to collate the results of studies scattered throughout a veritable mountain of literature, and to draw up a provisional balance-sheet concerning a basic hermeneutical principle. We would be the first to admit that each paragraph could have been developed in monographic form. Furthermore, we are acutely aware of the many lacunae in our exposition. Even at this point we regret that we can do no more than supply additional bibliography.

1. There is a worthwhile article by J.N. Sanders concerning the transition from the address-salutation to the thanksgiving in Paul's epistles. (75)

2. The problems of epistolography have been presented in different ways with pertinent remarks, in the *Introductions* of W.G. Kümmel and W. Marxsen. (76)

3. In particular, there are some supplementary notes which we should add to our discussion concerning citations from the Scriptures in the Pauline corpus.

The problem of the relationship of Paul to the LXX should be reconsidered in the light of the more advanced knowledge we have concerning Greek translations during apostolic times, as well as the condition of the LXX prior to the work of Origen. However, this is a larger problem involving the enitre New Testament.

On the basis of recent studies, investigation can be classified under three points: the original nature of recourse to the Old Testament; the use of allegory; and typology. Increasingly intensive study of rabbinical compositions and of the Qumranic documents throws new light on Paul's methods in using Old Testament literature. Obviously, the scholar actually and necessarily ends up in a domain far beyond the mere literary problem, since the Pauline conceptual structure and the implications of the entire mystery of salvation are involved. The Old Testament is not a reservoir of texts or of doctrines, for it is integrated into the very proclamation and consideration of the Christian reality as an expression of the new revelation, and not by reason of an allegedly fuller sense. On this level, the problem is no longer one of forms, but of content, not of *Literaturkritik*, but of *Sachkritik*. (77) Exegesis has every reason to keep this distinction clearly in mind.

4. Exegetes still manifest interest in studies of the lists of vices and of virtues. Wolfgang Schrage composed a most practical book on the particular concrete moral injunctions in the Pauline parenesis. Schrage's interest is specifically doctrinal; as is indicated in the very title of the book which poses four ques-

tions: Are the Pauline moral injunctions the result of a deeschatologizing process? Do they represent a compromise between ideology and reality? Are they only provisionally necessary and valid, but superfluous at a later date? Are they exclusively concrete and relevant to a specific situation? Even though Schrage's study is orientated towards content, he spends most of his time on forms. (78) Due to its organization and clarity, this study, whose erudition is not the least of its merits, is really the work of a master.

By way of contrast to Schrage's concern for content, Ehlrhard Kamlah's study deals explicit with the formal aspects of the parenetic lists in the New Testament, with particular attention to Pauline compositions. He distinguished two types of lists: descriptive, that leads up to a threat or a condemnation, or to the bestowal of salvation; and parenetic, that leads up to the exclusion of sins and the entry into new life. These two forms have a common *Sitz im Leben*, namely, the baptismal parenesis, or at least the basic parenesis in close connection with baptism. He directed his efforts particularly to the study of the motifs of these catalogues, and the study of texts and doctrines in the light of the Judeo-hellenistic milieu. Once again, we have a substantial contribution to resolve the pertinent problems, in which balanced judgment and extensive erudition go hand in hand. (79)

5. Vernon H. Neufeld's excellent monograph on the formulas of the early Christian confessions completes and revivifies the previous studies on the origin and nature of the *homologia*, as well as their development within the early Church, their functional qualities in the intimate life of the communities, not to underestimate their relationship with the world at large. Generally speaking, the confession should be regarded as an integral part of cult as a threshold to the *Credo*, as an apologetic motif, as a norm for the moral existence in the faith, and finally, as a proclamation of fidelity in times of persecution. Delicate judgment and lucidity demand only praise. (80)

Art. 5. Letter to the Hebrews

Witht genuine pleasure we refer the reader to a bibliographical panorama which cover all publications on this letter from 1938-

1963. Erich Grässer is the author responsible for such splendid work in line with the best traditions of the celebrated periodical in which it appeared. (81) Eight pages of bibliography precede a compact expose. The question concerning authorship led him to conclude that the age-old speculation on the identity of the author of Hebrews has not carried us beyond Origen's declaration that God alone knows who wrote that letter (Eusebius, *Hist.Eccl.*, VI, 25, 11f). Similarly, we are not certain of the addressees, the date, and the place of composition. Some progress, however, has been made on the question of original sources. The influence of synagogal preaching is recognized; but once we try to go any further, certainty begins to diminish. It cannot be denied that a common body of traditions relates Philo to the letter to the Hebrews. (82) Besides Michel and Spicq, some scholars in recent years have studied the text of Hebrews. (83) As far as the literary genre of the letter is concerned, it must be identified as a *zugesandte Predigt*, i.e. preaching transmitted in written form. The question of composition and of structure is essential. Grässer attached great importance to the studies of such men as Synge, Vaganay, Vanhoye, and Gyllenberg. (84) Synge identified three sections: (1) WITNESS: 1,1-14; 2,5-18; 3,1-6; 4,14-5,10; 6,13 -10,25 (a document addressed to a Jewish group before the year 70 A.D.); (2) EXHORTATION: 2,1-4; 3,7-4, 13; 5,11-6,12; 10,26-31; 12,18 ff. (also addressed to a Jewish group that had contacts with the Christian community, *circa* 55 A.D.); and (3) 10,32 - 12,27, of the same nature of the preceding. Grässer rightly rejected this thesis on the grounds that the systematic quality of the letter rules out such an interpretation. Against Vaganay and Gyllenberg, Grässer pointed out that the alternation between dogmatic and parenetic sections cannot constitute a fundamental principle of interpretation; furthermore, he regarded as untenable both the connecting phrases (*mots crochets*) and the sequences on supposedly regularly disposed levels. Grässer thought highly of Vanhoye's contribution, (85) which emphasized three points: first, that the literary composition is deliberately powerful; second, that the structure is concentric, whose individual parts are solidly geared to the basic theme; third, the thought structure is intense. On the basis of these three points, Vanhoye suggested a new division of the letter.

However, Grässer seems to concur more with the proposals of Nauck: 1,1-4,13; 4,14 - 10,31; 10,32 - 13,17. The rest of Grässer's study dealt with the question of the religious background (Judaism, paganism, and Christianity), and with the theological problem (the central theme, the use of Scripture, christology, eschatology, and the Christian life). Besides gleaning these important and instructive results, Grässer also published an equally remarkable monograph on the motif of faith in the letter to the Hebrews. Clarity, method, and erudition mark this study as a model of scientific precision. Even though it properly pertains to the theological realm, we refer to it here because of its exhaustive bibliography on the epistle. (86)

[*Translator's Editorial Note*: A very recent structural analysis of the Letter to the Hebrews is that of John Bligh. (87) The epistle is divided into thirty-five sections, each of which is made up of chiastically ordered verses. No indication, however, is given of the relationship of these thirty-five sections among themselves. The size of the sections varies considerably, from the two verses of 4,12-13 to the twenty-seven of 11,1-27. In his review of this work, (88) James Sweetnam stated that upon waiting for a division of the epistle that he would find completely convincing, he remains in the same situation after studying Bligh's presentation: "It is not that I see that Bligh's arrangement (or other arrangements) is false; it is just that I fail to see that it is true." Finally, the review ended with this general evaluation of the study: "No one would be more pleased than the present reviewer if the Epistle to the Hebrews could be divided according to the formal literary criteria which could be upheld by a detailed commentary of the material so divided. Form can be considered apart from content, but the dissociation is a perilous one; and the resulting analysis is of necessity incomplete (and hence of necessity not really convincing) until the material element is brought in. Bligh has given the formal elements of a structure of the epistle. It is to be hoped that the necessary complement — a consideration of the subject matter in the form of a commentary — will not be too long delayed."]

Conclusion

Even though this additional material to *St. Paul and Modern*

Study has been offered in so skeletal a form, nevertheless, it is indicative to the fact that exegesis is increasingly becoming interested in the Apostle Paul. The fact would be even more obvious had we covered the studies on Pauline doctrine. Interest in the latter can be traced to the contemporary efforts in investigating the essence and value of the Christian reality. It is generally accepted that any scientific study of Christianity must begin with a return to the sources, before any attempts at synthesis or speculation. In other words, theology must make up its mind to listen first of all to the voice of revelation. Only by beginning with a critical analysis of the language of revelation will revelation become comprehensible, in which case the historical word finally takes on its true significance. In this way the scholar is prepared to carry out his essential task in rendering judgment on matters of truth and of value. Relative to the horizontal plane is the vertical in which the data secured from analysis can be related to the scholar and to the Church of which he is a member. In the past it may have been understandably possible to relate Pauline literature only to the "in-crowd." Today, no exegete can in good conscience dispense with the need for intercommunication among the various groups and denominations. The Second Vatican Council was but one stage of this movement in which ecumenism finds its most powerful factor of unity. The actuality and the influence of Christianity in and upon the contemporary world now and in the future depend on such fundamental awareness. Paul of Tarsus still is the Apostle of the Nations. A more thorough knowledge of his ideas and of his message emerges as a necessity and a sign of our age!

Notes to Chapter I

1. This chapter was originally published in *Littérature et théologie pauliniennes* (*Recherches bibliques*, V) (Bruges-Paris: 1959), pp. 17-46, to which we are extremely indebted.
2. The state of the problems has been published in the book of A. Schweitzer, *Geschichte der Paulinischen Forschung von der Reformation bis auf die Gegenwart* (Tübingen: 1911) English translation, *Paul and his Interpreters* (London: 1912), paperback edition, Schocken Book, SB 79 (New York: 1964); confer also the lengthy exposition in the studies on St. Paul by P. Feine, *Der Apostel Paulus* (*Beiträge zur Förderung christlicher Theologie*, s. 2, 12) (Gutersloh 1927), pp. 11-206. Some additional works are: R. Bultmann, *Zur Geschichte der Paulusforschung*, in *TRu*, I (new series: 1929), pp. 26-59; 6 (1934), pp. 229-246; 8 (1936), pp. 1-22; W. G. Kümmel, *Das Urchristentum*, in *TRu*, 14 (new series: 1942), pp. 81-95; 155-173; 17 (1948), pp. 3-50, 103-142; 18 (1950), pp. 1-53; 22 (1954), pp. 138-170; H. R. Willoughby (ed.), *The Study of the Bible Today and Tomorrow* (Chicago: 1947); A. M. Denis, *Saint Paul dans la littérature récente*, in *ETL* 26 (1950), pp. 383-408; S. Lyonnet, *Bulletin d'exégèse paulinienne*, in *Bib* 32 (1951), pp. 104-113, 281-297, 432-439, 569-586; 33 (1952), pp. 240-257; J. J. Collins, *Bulletin of the N. T. - The Pauline Epistles*, in *TS* 17 (1956), pp. 531-548; J. Delorme, *Paul et le Paulinism*, in *AmiCl* 67 (1957), pp. 625-638; D. Mollat, in *RSR* 45 (1957), pp. 240-261; W. G. Kümmel, *Das Neue Testament. Geschichte der Erforschung seiner Probleme* (*Orbis-Band*, III, 3) (Munich: 1958), a teacher's manual. For scientific studies in English, confer the interesting book of W. F. Howard, *The Romance of New Testament Scholarship*, (London: 1949), pp. 33-54; G. Delling, *Zum neueren Paulusverständnis*, in *NT* 4 (1960), pp. 95-121.
3. On the theology of St. Paul, see R. Schnackenburg, *La Théologie du*

182

Nouveau Testament. État de la question (*Studia Neotestamentica, Subsidia* 1) (Paris-Bruges: 1961), pp. 63-78.

4. H. J. Schoeps, *Paulus - Die Theologie des Apostels im Lichte der jüdischen Religionsgeschichte* (Tübingen: 1959), p. 291: English translation, *Paul: The Theology of the Apostle in the Light of Jewish Thought* (Westminster: 1961).

5. Cfr. F. C. Baur (1792-1860), *Paulus, der Apostel Jesu Christi. Sein Leben und Wirken, seine Briefe und seine Lehre. Ein Beitrag zu einer kritischen Geschichte des Urchristenthums* (Stuttgart: 1845), 2nd ed. after his death by Zeller, 2 vols. (Leipzig: 1866-1867); concerning Baur, cfr. the monograph of G. Fraedrich, *Ferdinand Christian Baur, der Begründer der Tübingen Schule, als Theologe, Schriftsteller, und Charakter* (Gotha: 1909), pp. 171-195; E. Hirsch, *Geschichte der neuern evangelischen Theologie in Zusammenhang mit den allgemeinen Bewegungen des europäischen Denkens* 5, (Gutersloh: 1954), pp. 518-553; K. Barth, *Die protestantische Theologie im 19. Jh. - Ihre Vorgeschichte und ihre Geschichte* (Zollikon: 1947), pp. 450-458; Chr. Senft, *Wahrhaftigkeit und Wahrheit* (*Beiträge z. hist. Theol.* 22) (Tübingen: 1956); W. G. Kümmel, *Das Neue Testament*, 156-176, offers the following evaluation: "Only when one follows the basic propositions of Baur which he had methodically demonstrated, and replaced or improved his general view of history, would the scientific study of the New Testament be subsequently feasible"; K. Barth, *op. cit.*, 451, wrote: "Baur has asked a basic theological question: No matter how you may evaluate it, it cannot in any case, be bypassed."; E. Hirsch, *op. cit.*, 518 f, had this to say about Baur: "The greatest and perhaps the most controversial theologian . . . there is no other German theological historian who could have had assimilated the results so totally and unconditionally so that there could hardly be anyone who has not learned from him over and over again and who has had no small awareness of his greatness." An appropriate comment on Baur's book is that of G. Fraedrich, *op. cit.*, 194: "No other work of his has produced so many unheard of after-effects, but still has never grown stale"; W. F. Howard, *The Romance of New Testament*, 44, gave a resume of his thought in the following words: "Baur asked the right questions; he gave the wrong answers."

6. E. von Dobschütz (1870-1934), *Der Apostel Paulus*, 2 vol. (Halle: 1926, 1928); A. Deissmann (1866-1937), *Paulus. Eine kultur- und religionsgeschichtliche Skizze*, 2nd ed. (Tübingen: 1925), Eng. tr. *Paul, a Study in Social and Religious History* (1958). One could very well classify these authors as the forerunners of the history of religions. After the end of the nineteenth century, Gunkel and Gressmann made their influence felt. However, their final evaluation on Paul was retained in the minds of some of the liberals. Deissmann's attitude was more personal and more distinct: "His (Paul's) faith, not his dogmatic theology, his morality, not his ethics, his expectation,

not his eschatology — these speak in the epistles, freely scattered here and there in the stammering dialects of theology."

7. A. Deissmann, *Bibelstudien* (Marburg: 1895), p. 251.

8. E. Renan, *Saint Paul* (Paris: no date), pp. 560-570: "The Epistle to the Romans is no more a resume of Christian thought than the sermon on the Mount." Cfr. the excellent article by J. Héring, *De H. J. Holtzmann à Albert Schweitzer*, which is the off-print of the study, *Albert Schweitzer — Ehrfurcht vor dem Leben - Eine Freundesgabe zu seinem 80. Geburtstag* (Berne: 1955).

9. Cfr. W. G. Kümmel, *Das Neue Testament*, p. 310, Eng. tr. *Introd. to the N. T.*, 14th rev. Ed. (Abingdon).

10. W. G. Kümmel, *Das Neue Testament*, pp. 286-309.

11. G. W. Ittel, *Die Hauptgedanken der "religionsgeschichtlichen Schule,"* in *ZRG* 10 (1953), pp. 61-78, which is a resume of his dissertation enentitled *Urchristentum und Fremdenreligionen im Urteil der religionsgeschichtlichen Schule* (Erlangen: 1956), a typewritten copy. Ittel remarked that the term *religionsgeschichtlich* was used in at least three different meanings by the same authors who had referred to the movement: History of a religious movement, comparative religion, and the internal history of religious phenomena. According to his view, no one could hardly call this a school of thought, since it is more a question of terminology.

12. Cfr. W. G. Kümmel, *Das Neue Testament*, pp. 286-309.

13. Concerning R. Reitzenstein, see W. G. Kümmel, *Das Neue Testament*, p. 576; concerning W. Bousset, *ibid.*, p. 561; E. Kamlah, in *RGG*, 2nd ed., 1, 1373-1374; W. Bousset, *Kyrios Christos - Geschichte des Christusglaubens v. d. Anfängen bis auf Irenäus* (Göttingen: 1913, 1921), to which can be added *Jesus der Herr - Nachtr. u. Auseinandersetzungen zu Kyrios Christos* (Göttingen: 1916); for F. Cumont, cfr. B. Rigaux, in *Theologie und Kirche*, 2nd ed., III pp. 107-108.

14. However, it would be erroneous to think that A. Schweitzer did not imitate his predecessors. J. Weiss, *Die Predigt Jesu vom Reiche Gottes* (Göttingen: 1892, 2nd ed., 1900), and A. Loisy, *Jésus et la tradition évangélique* (Paris: 1910), independently and before him, maintained that Jesus had presented the coming of the kingdom as immediate. Loisy explained Paul in terms of the Greek mysteries (*Les mystères païens et le mystère chrétien*, Paris: 1930). Concerning J. Weiss, cfr. K. Prümm, *Johannes Weiss als Darsteller und religionsgeschichtlicher Erklärer der paulinischen Botschaft. Ein Beitrag zur Vorgeschichte der Entmythologisierung*, in *Bib* 40 (1959), pp. 815-836. Schweitzer was different from these two authors in this, namely, that he was more absolutely entrenched in his attitude. See H. A. Babel, *La pensée d'Albert Schweitzer - Sa significantion pour la théologie et la philosophie contemporaines* (Neuchâtel: 1954), pp. 138-139. The three great works of A. Schweitzer in which we are interested are: *Geschichte der Leben-Jesu-Forschung* (Tübingen: 1906, 1913, and its 3rd printing in 1933, photomechanical edition in

1951) English translation, *The Quest for the Historical Jesus* (London: 1954); *Geschichte der paulinischen Forschung von der Reformation bis auf die Gegenwart* (Tübingen: 1911, English translation, *Paul and his Interpreters* (London: 1912), paperback edition, Schocken Books, SB 79 (New York: 1964); *Die Mystik des Apostels Paulus* (Tübingen: 1930), French translation, *La mystique de l'Apôtre Paul* (Paris, 1962), English translation, *The Mysticism of Paul the Apostle* (London: 1931), 2nd ed. (1953).

15. W. Wrede, *Paulus (Religionsgeschichtliche Volksbücher*, I, 5-6, Tübingen: 1904), with reference to A. Schweitzer, *Geschichte der paulinischen Forschung*, p. 132, wrote: "The book does not listen to theology, but does listen to world-literature"; R. Kabisch, *Die Eschatologie des Paulus in ihren Zusammenhangen mit dem Gesamtbegriff des Paulinismus* (Göttingen: 1893); M. Brückner, *Die Entstehung der paulinischen Christologie* (Strassburg: 1903).

16. According to Schweitzer's way of thinking, the eschatological mystique consists in this, that the human being considers the dichotomies of terrestrial-supraterrestrial, temporal-eternal, as no longer existing, and thinks that he exists in the supraterrestrial and eternal, just as he had existed in the terrestrial and the temporal. This is what is meant by "to be in Christ" and to be secure in Him who is of the resurrection. Cfr. *Die Mystik*, pp. 1-3, and the commentary of H. A. Babel, *La Pensée*, pp. 67-69. *Translators' Note*: D. M. Stanley, *Christ's Resurrection in Pauline Soteriology* (Rome: 1961), p. 6, footnotes nn. 27 and 29, stated: "It is important to grasp the meaning Schweitzer gives to the term 'eschatological.' It is applied to the liberation from servitude in the period subsequent to the parousia, but intermediate between that event and the *Endzeit*, i.e. to a Messianic reign of the elect with Christ . . . On Schweitzer's view, eschatology dissolves the natural world in the supernatural, the world of the present in that of the future; and Paul's mysticism asserts the possibility of escape from the present, natural world into the future, supernatural state. Unless, says Schweitzer, we realize that Paul postulated his mysticism because of his concept of the Messianic kingdom, we miss the eschatological quality of Pauline mysticism and fail to understand it. In consequence, Schweitzer's interpretation of Paul rests upon the validity of his exegesis of the texts regarding the Messianic kingdom."

17. H. J. Schoeps, *Paulus*, pp. 1-42, 275-299; W. G. Kümmel, *Das Neue Testament*, V: "Not the entire history of research on the New Testament but . . . the result of the important subsequent or future direction in the question to be asked and the methods." More extensive information is given in the reports of the same author in *TRu*, and in the monographs which are published in *RGG*, 3rd ed.

18. J. Dupont, *Les problèmes du Livre des Actes d'après les travaux récents* (Louvain: 1950); E. Haenchen, *Die Apostelgeschichte (Kritisch-exeget. Kommentar Meyers*, III), 12th ed. (Göttingen: 1959); F. F. Bruce, *The Acts of the Apostles* (London: 1952).

19. R. Bultmann, *Zur Geschichte der Paulus-Forschung,* in *TRu* (new series) 1 (1929), p. 59: "I think . . . that Paul's understanding of world history has no relation whatsoever with the notion that he was a theologian."

20. R. Bultmann, *Ist voraussetzungslose Exegese möglich?* in *TZ* 13 (1957), pp. 409-415, reprinted in *GV* 3 (Tübingen: 1960), pp. 142-150.

21. Cfr. J. I. Parker, *"Fundamentalism" and the Word of God - Some Evangelical Principles* (London: 1958), pp. 75-114, which had three printings in one year.

22. M. Dibelius-W. G. Kümmel, *Paulus* (Sammlung Goschen, 1160, Berlin: 1951) Eng. tr. *Paul* (Westminster: 1953); the first six and a half chapters were completed shortly before the death of Dibelius; these Kümmel revised and added the rest, namely, three and a half chapters.

23. M. Dibelius-W. G. Kümmel, *Paulus,* pp. 141-147. The profound thought of W. G. Kümmel is expressed on page 113: "This then is the common feature of all of Paul's theological thought: he sought to depart from the Hebrew God of history in order to bind the religious life of the Christian family in God's historical redemption in Christ, and to preserve such godliness in a pure mystique or merely in the exemplary work of divine service."

24. J. Munck, *Paulus und die Heilsgeschichte* (*AJ*, XXVI, 1, Copenhagen: 1954), pp. 65-69; in English translation, *Paul and the Salvation of Mankind* (London: 1959).

25. B. Sundkler, *Jésus et les païens* (*AMNSU*, 6, 1937), pp. 1-38, or in *RHPR* 16 (1936), pp. 462-499.

26. W. Manson, *St. Paul's Letter to the Romans and Others,* in *BJRL* 31 (1948), pp. 224-240; cfr. a resume in J. Munck, *Paulus,* pp. 181-194.

27. W. D. Davies, in *NTS* 2 (1955-1956), p. 69; see the reviews of Mgr. L. Cerfaux, in *RHE* 51 (1956), pp. 432-442, of D. Mollat, in *RSR* 45 (1957), pp. 251-257, and of P. Benoit, in *RB* 64 (1957), pp. 683-684.

28. O. Cullmann, *Le caractère eschatologique du devoir missionnaire et de la conscience apostolique de saint Paul - Étude sur le katéchon(on) de 2 Thess.* 2, 6-7, in *RHPR* 13 (1936), pp. 210-245; for a criticism of J. Munck, *Paulus,* see B. Rigaux, *Les Épîtres aux Thessaloniciens* (*Études bibliques,* Paris: 1956), pp. 276-277.

29. At the congress of the *Studiorum Novi Testamenti Societas,* in Norwich, 1959, at which he was the chairman, J. Munck tackled the first problem. In his view, after the year 70, every trace of the primitive judaeo-christianity had disappeared: *Jewish Christianity in Post-Apostolic Times,* in *NTS* 6 (1960-1961), pp. 103-116.

30. Cfr. S. G. F. Brandon, *The Perennial Problem of Paul,* in *HibJ* 58 (1959-1960), pp. 378-386; R. Bultmann, *Ein neues Paulus-Verständnis?* in *TLZ* 84 (1959), pp. 481-486.

31. H. J. Schoeps, *Paulus*, p. 41.

32. H. J. Schoeps wrote some very important works on Ebionism: *Theologie und Geschichte des Judenchristentums* (Tübingen: 1950); *Urgemeinde, Judenchristentum, Gnosis* (Tübingen: 1956). In the last work, Schoeps took up the criticisms which were leveled against his first two works. His book *Paulus* had aroused many authors who otherwise were rather reserved. For him, Paul was incomprehensible; the Apostle did not have the good fortune to encounter his companions as the good counselor who, as Schoeps described it, would have avoided his errors, which had caused antagonism against the Jews. It is a known fact that Schoeps relished forced theses, not only in the field of the history of religions, but also in politics as well; he is an obstinate partisan for the return of the Hohenzollern (cfr. his brochure, *Die Ehre Preussens*, 3rd ed., Stuttgart: 1951).

33 Cfr. the chapter in *Paulus*, pp. 299-314, entitled *Die Gestzeskritik des Apostels als ein innerjüdisches Problem.*

34. H. Windisch, *Urchristentum*, in *TRu* (new series) 5 (1933), p. 187; there is an interesting article by E. Beijer on the work of H. Windisch, which is entitled, *Hans Windisch und seine Bedeutung für die neutestamentliche Wissenschaft*, in *ZNW* 48 (1957), pp. 22-49.

35. C. H. Dodd, *The Parables of the Kingdom*, 2nd ed. (London: 1936); *Idem, The Apostolic Preaching and his Developments* (London: 1936). Cfr. A. Sprunger, *L'eschatologie du N.T. par C. H. Dodd. Essai d'analyse et de critique* (typewritten thesis), the Faculty of Theology in the Canton de Vaud (1958); E. E. Wolfzorn, *Realized Eschatology. An Exposition of Charles H. Dodd's Thesis*, in *ETL* 38 (1962), pp. 44-70.

36. T. Fr. Glasson, *The Second Advent. The Origin of the New Testament Doctrine*, 2nd ed. (London: 1947).

37. J. A. T. Robinson, *Jesus and his Coming. The Emergence of a Doctrine* (London: 1957).

38. J. A. T. Robinson, *The Body - A Study in Pauline Theology* (SBT 5, London: 1952).

39. O. Cullmann, *Christ et le temps* (Paris: 1947), Eng. tr. *Christ and Time* (Westminster: 1964).

40. W. G. Kümmel, *Verheissung und Erfüllung. Untersuchungen zur eschatologischen Verkündigung Jesu (Abhandlungen z. Theol. des A. und N.T.)*, 2nd ed. (Zurich: 1953): a basic work on the eschatology of the New Testament.

41. J. Jeremias, *Die Gleichnisse Jesu*, 2nd ed. (Göttingen: 1952), pp. 36-50, 95-102, Eng. tr. *Parables of Jesus* (Scribner: 1955), pp. 38-52, 93-99.

42. W. G. Kümmel, *op. cit., passim.*

43. H. Schuster, *Die Konsequente Eschatologie in der Interpretation des Neuen Testamentes, kritisch betrachtet*, in *ZNW* 47 (1956), pp. 1-25, a critique of Werner, which we shall take up later.

44. H. A. Babel, *La pensée d'Albert Schweitzer. Sa signification pour la théologie et la philosophie contemporaines* (Neuchâtel: 1954). It is not necessary to make any observations on this book which simply covers the theology and philosophy of A. Schweitzer.

45. M. Werner, *Die Entstehung des christlichen Dogmas, problemgeschichtlich dargestellt* (Berne: 1941, 2nd ed., in 1954) English translation, *Formation of Christian Dogma* (Beacon Press: 1965); *Idem, Der Protestantische Weg des Glaubens* - I. *Der Protestantismus als geschichtliches Problem* (Berne: 1965).

46. F. Buri, *Die Bedeutung der neutestamentlichen Eschatologie für die neuere protestantische Theologie.* (Zurich: 1935); *Idem, Theologie der Existenz* (Berne: 1954), Eng. tr. *Theology of Existence* (Attic).

47. U. Neuenschwander, *Protestantische Dogmatik der Gegenwart und das Problem der biblischen Mythologie* (Berne: 1949); cfr. H. Ott, *Eschatologie. Versuch eines dogmatischen Grundrisses* (Zollikon: 1958), together with the appropriate parallel to this work, A. Brandenburg, *Methode der Eschatologie,* in *Cath* 13 (1959), pp. 70-74.

48. W. Michaelis, *Kennen die Synoptiker eine Verzögerung der Parusie?* (*Synoptische Studien - Festschrift A. Wikenhauser,* Munich: 1953), pp. 107-123: radically opposed to the opinions of Werner.

49. R. Morgenthaler, *Kommendes Reich* (Zurich: 1952).

50. R. Flückiger, *Der Ursprung des christlichen Dogmas - Eine Auseinandersetzung mit. A. Schweitzer und M. Werner* (Zollikon: 1955).

51. Cfr. H. Schuster, *Die konsequente Eschatologie in der Interpretation des Neuen Testaments kritisch betrachtet,* in *ZNW* 47 (1956), pp. 1-25; J. Richter, *Die "konsequente Eschatologie" im Feuer der Kritik,* in *ZRG* 12 (1960), pp. 147-166.

52. Especially cfr. J. Körner, *Eschatologie und Geschichte - Eine Untersuchung des Begriffes des Eschatologischen in der Theologie Rudolf Bultmanns* (*Theologische Forschung,* 13, Hamburg: 1957).

53. E. Grässer, *Das Problem der Parusieverzögerung in den synoptischen Evangelien und in der Apostelgeschichte* (*Beihefte zur ZNW,* 22, Berlin: 1957).

54. O. Cullmann, *Parusieverzögerung und Urchristentum. Der gegenwärtige Stand der Diskussion,* in *TLZ* 83 (1958), pp. 1-12: also cfr. the important work of A. Strobel, *Untersuchungen zum eschatologischen Verzögerungsproblem* (*SupplN.T.,* 2, Leiden-Cologne: 1961).

55. H. J. Schoeps, *Paulus,* pp. 85-126, particularly pp. 119-126.

56. Cfr. K. Stendahl, *Kerygma und Kerygmatisch. Von zweideutigen Ausdrücken der Predigt der Urkirche* . . . in *TLZ* 77 (1952), 715: "Theology also has its own slogans, one of which is 'Eschatology' that can be used in as many meanings as there are colors in the rainbow. (English theological books.) It is similar to the expression "incarnation," with such notions as weapons, everything else can be defended and overcome. Furthermore, in the last instance the term *Kerygma* takes the prize in popularity and applicability"; R. Schnackenburg, *Gottes Herrschaft und Reich. Eine biblische-theo-*

logische Studie (Freiburg: 1959), pp. 49-76, which contains excellent summaries. Eng. tr. *Gods' Rule and Kingdom* (Herder and Herder).

57. It is imperative to refer particularly to the small book of O. Cullmann, *Immortalité de l'âme, ou résurrection des morts?* (Neuchâtel: 1956). Cfr. J. Frisque, Oscar Cullmann. *Une théologie de l'histoire du salut, (Cahiers de l'Actualite Religieuse,* II, Tournai: 1960).

58. K. Elliger, *Studien zum Habakuk-Kommentar vom Toten Meer (Beiträge z. hist. Theologie,* 15, Tübingen: 1953), pp. 191-193, on IQHab, VII, 5-8: "It is rather distressing that, since the *Endzeit* has been prostrated for so long a time and will continue even longer, anyone should have listened to the words of the prophets."

59. G. W. Ittel, *Die Hauptgedanken der "religionsgeschichtlichen Schule,"* pointed out that the study of H. Gunkel, *Zum religionsgeschichtlichen Verständnis des Neuen Testamentes* (Göttingen: 1903), set up the following as the first article of his program: To investigate those influences which were exerted on the essential points and on the terminology of the New Testament, for in his opinion, Christianity was syncretic. Though many protestations were launched against this thesis for a long time (A. B. Ritschl, W. Bousset, J. Weiss), recent authors no longer view it as a new religion, but understand it more as a synthesis of ancient constitutents which had been transformed by a single personality; in fact, if one would exclude a priori the possibility of the supernatural, then the religious question would be nothing more than a computation of historical influences. The set of conclusions therefore would amount to this: 1) the origin of Christianity would not be rooted in a development of Old Testament concepts, but rather in other influences; 2) it is absolutely necessary to treat the question at hand from a purely historical point of view; and 3) the purpose of research is to establish the originality of the fact of Christianity.

The principal areas in which the School of the history of religions has carried on its work are, chiefly, eschatology and apocalypticism; the doctrine of the sacraments; pneumatology; the notions of cult and the presence of mythological elements in Christianity. Cfr. R. Schnackenburg, *La Théologie du Nouveau Testament*, pp. 25-29.

60. G. W. Ittel, *Die Hauptgedanken der "religionsgeschichtlichen Schule,"* p. 76. In place of the doctrine on justification, "the champions of the School of the history of religions would substitute the doctrine on the Spirit as the nucleus of Pauline theology. Such an approach characteristically alive today, and, as the peculiarly latest item in Pauline theology, would appear as a conscious moralization on the doctrine on the spirit."

61. A. Deissmann, *Paulus,* 2nd ed., IX-XI, Eng. tr. *Paul* (1958). A visit to the places and a lecture from the priests who reside there is no trifling matter in any serious efforts to reconstruct the milieu by removing the bookish character which is distinctive of these positions.

62. W. C. van Unnik, *Tarsus of Jeruzalem de Stad van Paulus'Jeugd?* (*Mededelingen der Koninklijke Nederl. Akad. van Wetensch. en Letterkunde,* new series, XVI, 5, Amsterdam: 1952).

63. It is impossible even to give a description of the problem due to the fact that it is much too complex to be treated here, even summarily.

64. H. J. Schoeps, *Paulus,* pp. 16-21.

65. J. Daniélou, *Théologie du judéo-christianisme* (*Bibliothèque de Théologie - Histoire des doctrines chrétiennes avant Nicée,* I, Paris: 1958) Eng. tr. *Theology of Jewish Christianity* (Regnery: 1964). This book does not include a study on the expression of Christianity in terms of the formulas of the Later Judaism from the second century; therefore, we can set it aside. The influences of Tübingen on his theses are easily recognizable.

66. W. D. Davies, *Paul and Rabbinic Judaism. Some Rabbinic Elements in Pauline Theology,* 2nd ed. (London: 1955); and in the same vein, C. G. Montefiore, *Judaism and St. Paul* (London: 1914); H. Windisch, *Paulus und das Judentum* (Stuttgart: 1935), and J. Klausner, who will be cited later; A. Marmorstein, *Paulus und die Rabiner,* in *ZNW* 30 (1931), pp. 271-285.

67. H. J. Schoeps, *Paulus,* pp. 224-230.

68. J. Klausner, *From Jesus to Paul* (London: 1944).

69. According to Schoeps, moreover, the influence of Judaism on Paul did not strike the heart of his message, which was grounded in Hellenism, namely, the divinity of Jesus, the sacraments, and grace.

70. This is the position of R. Bultmann and his followers, including those British authors who have approached the subject with some variation. Cfr. especially the recent authors, C. Schneider, *Geistesgeschichte des antiken Christentums,* 2 vol. (Munich: 1954).

71. There is an indication of some distrust against an interpretation which is too easily and exclusively judaic. Proportionately, the Palestinian world does not seem to have been closed to Hellenism; some authors even find traces of it in Qumran itself.

72. On the subject of gnosticism in the New Testament, see E. Haenchen, *Gnosis und N.T.,* in *RGG* (3rd ed.) II, 1652-1656.

73. H. Schlier, *Die Erlösung der Menschen in urchrist. und griech. Verkündigung,* in *TBl* 7 (1928), pp. 189-197; *Idem, Die Kirche nach dem Briefe an die Epheser* (*Die Zeit der Kirche,* Freiburg: 1956), pp. 159-186; *Idem, Der Brief an die Epheser. Ein Kommentar,* Düsseldorf: 1958); R. M. Wilson, *The Gnostic Problem. A Study between Hellenistic Judaism and the Gnostic Heresy* (London: 1958).

74. R. M. Wilson, *The Gnostic Problem* (London: 1958), pp. 84-85.

75. H. Schlier, *Der Brief an die Epheser,* p. 21.

76. Fr. Mussner, *Christus, das All und die Kirche. Studien zur Theologie des Epheserbriefes* (Trier: 1955).

77. G. Bornkamm, *Das Ende des Gesetzes, 9, Die Häresie des Kolosserbriefes* (*Gesammelte Aufsatze I,* Munich: 1958), pp. 139-156. In

note 139, Bornkamm admits that he does not accept the pauline authenticity of this epistle.

78. E. Käsemann, *Kritische Analyse von Phil.* 2,5-11, in *ZTK* 47 (1950), pp. 313-360; *Idem, Christus, das All und die Kirche - Zur Theologie des Epheserbriefes*, in *TLZ* 81 (1956), pp. 585-590.

79. W. Schmithals, *Die Gnosis in Korinth. Eine Untersuchung zu den Korintherbriefen* (Göttingen: 1956).

80. R. Bultmann, *Das Urchristentum im Rahmen der antiken Religionen*, 2nd ed., (1954) English translation, *Primitive Christianity in Contemporary Setting* (Meridian: 1956); also cfr. E. Haenchen, *Gab es eine vorchristl. Gnosis?* in *ZTK* 49 (1952), pp. 316-349.

81. W. Schmithals, *Die Häretiker in Galatien*, in *ZNW* 47 (1956), pp. 25-67; *Idem, Die Irrlehrer des Philipperbriefes*, in *ZTK* 54 (1957), pp. 297-341.

82. W. Schmithals, *Die Häretiker*, 64, note 123. That F. C. Baur had already claimed that the heretics of the pastoral epistles and of the letter to the Colossians belonged to the gnostic sect is known; cfr. C. Colpe, *Die religionsgeschichtliche Schule. Darstellung und Kritik ihres Bildes vom gnostischen Erlösermythus (Forschungen z. Rel. u. Litt. des N. u. A.T.*, new series, 60, Göttingen: 1961).

83. W. G. Kümmel, *Das Neue Testament*, p. 520.

84. W. G. Kümmel, *Das Neue Testament*, pp. 466-519. Cfr. R. Schnackenburg, *La Théologie du Nouveau Testament*, pp. 11-23.

85. G. Gloege, a monograph on *K. Barth*, in *RGG*, 3rd ed., I, 897: "For the last twenty years, B's theology has conditioned the theological climate. Even the historical disciplines have welcomed the impulse of his thoughts instinctively or reluctantly to some extent." Cfr. H. Fries, *Bultmann, Barth und die katholische Theologie* (Stuttgart: 1955); G. Eichholz, *Der Ansatz Karl Barths in der Hermeneutik - Antwort (Karl Barth zum siebzigsten Geburstag am 10 Mai 1956*, Zollikon: 1957), pp. 52-68; H. Bouillard, *Karl Barth (Théologie*, 39), 3 vol. (Paris: 1957); note the very last phrase in vol. 3, 300: "If theology is to have any *meaning*, it must cease to speak of man from the viewpoint of God; it should concentrate its discussion of man, who is aware of the presence of God."

86. R. Marlé, *Bultmann et l'interprétation du Nouveau Testament* (Paris: 1956); H. Fries, *Bultmann, Barth, und die katholische Theologie* (Stuttgart: 1957).

87. Cfr. the *Epilegomena* of his work *Theologie des Neuen Testamentes*, 3rd ed. (Tübingen: 1958), pp. 585-599 Eng tr. *Theology of the New Testament* (Scribner). In these pages, Bultmann explains very clearly what he understands by a theology of the New Testament. Previously, these pages had been published, with very few differences in the text, in *Aux sources de la tradition chrétienne - Mélanges Maurice Goguel* (Neuchâtel: 1950): *Das Problem des Verhaltnisses von Theologie und Verkündigung im Neuen Testament*, pp. 32-42. The reader of these pages becomes aware of the fact that Bultmann's

viewpoint centers on the man who believes, rather than on an object received as a gift of faith. The New Testament opens up the field towards a new understanding of oneself. He surpasses a purely scientific anthropology by accepting faith as the means of communication and engagement before God. It is impossible to distinguish between the kerygma, that is, the presentation of the message, and the theological propositions of that message, because they are united in the act of "theologizing" ("*theologisant*"), in contact with the divine communications which is expressed in the kerygma and to which man responds by faith. It is in the light of this definition of theology that Bultmann judges those "theologies" that have preceded his own, ever since the research into the *loca probantia* of the seventeenth and eighteenth centuries as, for instance, in the essays of F. C. Baur. To the latter, Bultmann attributed the merit to have wished to explain historically the Christian conscience as the decisive moment when the Age of the Spirit had been inaugurated. However, Baur's position did not persist, neither among the liberals, nor in the School of the history of religions, nor among the conservatives. According to Bultmann, the New Testament, as a document, is both the object of the history of religions and of interpretation. The twofold aspect of Baur's position is easily discernible. With his theory on faith, Bultmann unveiled a very self-conscious Lutheranism; from his views on the nature of interpretation, he is evidently bound up with Hegel and Heidegger. He did not get the idea to go beyond these axioms. For a man who does not accept them, these viewpoints would seem strange, if not contrary to the kerygma itself, which he would understand as a revelation about God as well as about the relations of a God who acts for and with mankind, creating, in the man who believes a supernatural state which is nourished by the sacraments. Such "things" are not merely "thoughts," but "realities." The conscience which belongs to the Church, and the commitment that is imposed on those who believe, are not merely psychological aspects of adaptation to reality. This would render that conscience as perennially relative. If one would deny to theology the possibility of attaining the "real," then he would speak only of "man" but not of "God." In a sense, Bultmann is not a theologian, but an anthropologist. Concerning the influence of Heidegger, cfr. G. W. Ittel, *Der Einfluss der Philosophie Martin Heideggers auf die Theologie Rudolf Bultmanns*, in *Kerygma und Dogma*, 2 (1956), 90 ff. Bultmann added that there must be a unifying factor for those who believe; their life must be the same as the life of the men of the New Testament, in which the act of thinking is nothing more than a form of their activity, which was more profound because they were aware of conscience and of the historical Jesus. Faith gives to man a new understanding of God, of the world, and of himself.

88. E. Lohmeyer, in *TLZ*, 52 (1927), 437-439.

89. On E. Lohmeyer, cfr. E. Esking, *Glaube und Geschichte in der theo-logischen Exegese Ernst Lohmeyers - Zugleich ein Beitrag zur Geschichte der neutestamentlichen Interpretation* (Copenhagen: 1951), pp. 123-242.
90. Cfr. W. G. Kümmel, *Das Neue Testament*, pp. 492-519.
91. C. H. Dodd, *The Parables of the Kingdom* (London: 1935); *Idem, The Interpretation of the Fourth Gospel* (London: 1953); E.C. Hos-kyns and F. N. Davey, *The Riddle of the New Testament* (London: 1931), translated into French as *L'énigme du Nouveau Testament* (Neuchâtel: 1949). One of the most eminent British exegetes and theologians is Vincent Taylor, who represents a strictly conserva-tive line. See especially *The Cross of Christ* (London: 1956), pp. 87-104.
92. J. Knox, *The Man Christ Jesus* (New York: 1941); *Idem, Christ the Lord* (New York: 1945); *Idem, On the Meaning of Christ* (New York: 1947); *Idem, Criticism and Faith* (London: 1953); *Idem, Jesus, Lord and Christ* (New York: 1958); *Idem, The Death of Christ - The Cross in New Testament History and Faith* (London: 1959).
93. Cfr. W. G. Kümmel, *Das Neue Testament*, pp. 247-250, 243-247, 419-423, 442-444.
94. P. Feine, *Theologie des Neuen Testamentes*, 8th ed. (Leipzig: 1951).
95. A. Schlatter centered his thought on the concept of the Creator-God, and in the light of this central concept claimed that profane his-tory was inexplicable without faith: *Theologie des Neuen Testa-mentes* (Gutersloh: 1909-1910); 2nd ed., under the title *Die Theo-logie der Apostel*, 2nd ed. (Stuttgart: 1922).
96. R. A. F. MacKenzie, *The Concept of Biblical Theology*, in *The Catholic Theological Society of America - Proceedings of the Tenth Annual Convention* (New York: 1955).
97. The greatest regret about these works is the frozen systematic treat-ment, which does not correspond with the thought of Paul, but with the design of a highly developed dogmatic theology. M. Meinertz made his defense against such criticisms in *Randglossen zu meiner Theo-logie des N.T.*, in *TQ* 132 (1952), pp. 411, 431; *Idem, Sinn und Bedeutung der neutestamentlichen Theologie*, in *MTZ* 5 (1954), pp. 159-170; cfr. other opinions among Catholic authors: C. Spicq, *L'avènement de la théologie biblique*, in *RSPhTh* 35 (1951), pp. 561-574; W. Hillmann, *Wege zur ntl. Theologie*, in *WW* 14 (1951), pp. 56-67, 200-211; 15 (1952), pp. 15-32, 122-136; V. Warnach, *Gedanken zur ntl. Theologie*, in *GlD* 7 (1952), pp. 65-75; A. Bea, *Der heutige Stand der Bibelwissenschaft*, in *SZ* 153 (1953), pp. 91-104; F. M. Braun, *La théologie biblique*, in *RTh* 61 (1953), pp. 221-253; R. Schnackenburg, *Die Botschaft des N.T.*, in *HSS* (1955), pp. 110-127; H. Schlier, *Über Sinn und Aufgabe einer Theo-logie des Neuen Testaments*, in *BZ* (new series) 1 (1957), pp. 6-23; R. Schnackenburg, *La Théologie du Nouveau Testament*, pp. 11-12 with the Bibliography.

98. J. Bonsirven, *Théologie du Nouveau Testament* (Paris: 1951) English translation, *Theology of the New Testament* (Newman Press: 1963); *Idem, L'évangile de Paul* (Paris: 1948).

99. J. L. McKenzie, *Problems of Hermeneutics in Roman Catholic Exegesis,* in *JBL* 77 (1958), p. 199: "Speaking of the Catholic Church, however, I think the exegete must go beyond the lines so well indicated by Stendahl. The use of the Bible as a mine of proof-texts is dying in Catholic theology, and very few will regret it. But there is no organization of material and elaboration of principles to replace it."

100. This fact has been brought out quite well in the light of R. Schnackenburg, *La Théologie du Nouveau Testament,* pp. 32-34.

101. K. Stendahl, *Implications of Form-Criticism and Tradition-Criticism for Biblical Interpretation,* in *JBL* 77 (1959), pp. 33-38.

Notes to Chapter II

1. The following list includes the principal biographies written by Catholic authors. Of these we shall single out in our text only those works that are more significant. C. Fouard, *Saint Paul,, ses missions* (Paris: 1829; 15th ed., 1925); *Idem, Saint Paul. Ses dernières années* (Paris: 1897; 12th ed., 1925); E. Le Camus, *L'oeuvre des apôtres,* 3 vol. (Paris: 1905); F. X. Poelzl, *Der Weltapostel Paulus* (Ratisbonne: 1905); Th. Coghlan, *St. Paul, his Life, Work and Spirit* (London: 1924); F. Prat, *Saint Paul* (Paris: 1921, 25th ed., 1946); C. C. Martindale, *Saint Paul* (London: 1924); I. Beaufays, Saint Paul (Brussels: 1925; 2nd ed., 1944); É. Baumann, *Saint Paul* (Paris: 1925; 3rd ed., 1928); L. Murillo, *Paulus et Pauli scripta,* I (Rome: 1926); K. Pieper, *Paulus, seine missionarische Personlichkeit und Wirksamkeit,* (Neutest. Abh. 12, Münster: 1926; 2nd-3rd ed., 1929); A. Tricot, *Saint Paul, apôtre des Gentils* (Paris: 1928); A. Steinmann, *Zum Werdengang des Paulus* (Freiburg: 1928); G. Cirioni, *Paolo, apostolo di Gesu Cristo, nella sua vita e nella sua dottrina* (Turin: 1929); E. Hernandez, *S. Pablo, l. La personalidad del gran Apostol* (Granada: 1931); S. Waitz, *Sankt Paulus,* 5 vol. (Innsbruck: 1931-1936); A. Salvini, *S. Paolo apostolo* (Albano: 1933, 2nd ed., 1942); J. Holzner, *Paulus, ein Heldenleben im Dienste Christi* (Freiburg: 1937; 22nd ed., 1949); French translation, *Paul de Tarse* (Paris: 1951) English translation, *Paul of Tarsus* (St. Louis: 1944); C. Lattey, *Paul* (Milwaukee: 1939); J. Pérez De Urbel, *San Pablo, apostol de las gentes* (Madrid: 1940); French translation (Paris: 1958) English translation, *St. Paul, The Apostle of the Gentiles* (Westminster, Maryland: 1956); E. B. Allo, *Paul apôtre de Jesus-Christ* (Paris: 1942); G. Ricciotti, *Paolo apostolo* (Rome: 1946; 2nd ed., 1948); French translation, *Saint Paul, apôtre* (Paris: 1952) English translation, *Paul the Apostle* (Milwaukee: 1953, 1961); J. B. Valvekens, *Paulus, zijn persoonlijkheid, zijn brieven* (Bruges: 1940);

A. Penna, *S. Paolo* (Alba: 1946; 2nd ed., 1951) English translation, *St. Paul the Apostle* (New York: 1961); P. De Ambroggi, *S. Paolo, apostolo delle genti* (Ravigo: 1949); D. Rops, *Saint Paul conquérant du Christ* (Paris: 1951) English translation, *St. Paul: Apostle of Nations* (Chicago: 1953); G. Brillet, *Un chef d'Église, Saint Paul* (Paris: 1956); N. Caserta, *Il Dottore delle Genti* (Rome: 1958); A. Brunot, *Saint Paul et son message* (Paris: 1958).

2. J. Holzner, *Autour de saint Paul* (Paris: 1954).

3. P. Benoit, in *RB* 66 (1959), pp. 442-443.

4. L. M. Dewailly, *"Autour de saint Paul."* Quelques livres récents, in *VSp* 51 (1949), p. 161.

5. The following works have been written by Protestants. Of course, we shall indicate here only those works which are more significant. E. Renan, *Saint Paul* (Paris: no date); H. Hausrath, *Der Apostel Paulus* (Heidelberg: 1862; 2nd ed., 1872); A. Sabatier, *L'Apôtre Paul* (Paris: 1870: 4th ed., 1912); W. J. Conybeare and J. S. Howson, *The Life and Epistles of St. Paul* (London: 1890, 1905); O. Zoeckler, *Paulus, der Apostel Jesus-Christ* (Gutersloh: 1890); W. M. Ramsay, *St. Paul the Traveller and Roman Citizen* (London: 1895; 14th ed., 1920); W. Wrede, *Paulus* (Halle: 1904); C. Clemen *Paulus, sein Leben und Wirken*, 2 vol. (Giessen: 1904); H. Weinel, *Paulus, der Mensch und sein Werk* (Tübingen: 1911; 2nd ed., 1915); E. de Faye, *Saint Paul* (Paris: 1908); 3rd ed., (1928); A. Deissmann, *Paulus. Eine kultur-und religionsgeschichtliche Skizze* (Tübingen: 1911; 2nd ed., 1925) Eng. tr. *Paul: A Study in Social and Religious History* (New York: 1957); E. B. Redlich, *St. Paul and his Companions* (London: 1913); J. Weiss, *Das Urchristentum* (Göttingen: 1917); B. Weiss, *Paulus und seine Gemeinden*, 2nd ed. (Berlin: 1914); D. Smith, *The Life and Letters of St. Paul* (London: 1919); E. Vischer, *Der Apostel Paulus und Paulus und sein Werk*, 2nd ed., Leipzig: 1921); A. Omodeo, *Paolo di Tarso, apostolo delle Genti* Messina: 1922; reprint in 1956); W. Mundle, *Das religiöse Leben des Apostels Paulus* (Leipzig: 1923); R. Bultmann, *Paulus*, in *RGG*, 2nd ed., IV, 119-145; C. I. Wood, *The Life, Letters and Religion of St. Paul* (London: 1925); D. J. Burrel, *Life and Letters of St. Paul* (London: 1925); T. R. Glover, *Paul of Tarsus*, 2nd ed. (London: 1925); A. H. McNeile, *St. Paul his Life, Letters and Christian Doctrine* (Cambridge: 1925); W. L. Knox, *St. Paul and The Church of Jerusalem* (Cambridge: 1925); E. von Dobschütz, *Der Apostel Paulus*, 2 vol. (Halle: 1926-1928); L. Schneller, *Das Leben des Apostels Paulus* (Leipzig: 1926); P. Feine, *Der Apostel Paulus. Das Ringen um das geschichtliche Verständnis des Paulus* (Gutersloh: 1927); F. J. F. Jackson, *The Life of St. Paul* (London: 1927; 2nd ed., 1933); R. Liechtenhan, *Paulus, seine Welt und sein Werk* (Base: 1928); A. R. Witham, *St. Paul* (London: 1929); W. Knox, *St. Paul* (London: 1932); E. P. Santangelo, *Paolo* (Bari: 1933); H. Lietzmann, *Paulus* (Berlin: 1934); A. D. Nock, *St. Paul* (London: 1938); J. A. Findlay,

A Portrait of Paul (London: 1935); J. Klausner, *From Jesus to Paul*, in Hebrew, 2 vol. (Tel Aviv: 1930-1940; English edition, London: 1944); E. Hirsch, *Paulus* (Bremen: 1940); V. Groenbech, *Paulus, Jesus Christi Apostel* (Copenhagen: 1940); W. von Loewenich, *Paulus, sein Leben und sein Werk* (Witten: 1940; 2nd ed., 1949; English translation by C. E. Harris, London: 1960); R. M. Hawkins, *The Recovery of Historical Paul* (New York: 1943); H. J. Schoonfield, *The Jew of Tarsus: An Unorthodox Portrait of Paul* (London: 1946); Paul is the "Nazarean," a Jew who believed that Jesus is the Messiah, but not the Son of God. The Church twisted the Pauline attempt. H. V. Morton, *In the Steps of St. Paul* (London: 1948); M. Dibelius - W. G. Kümmel, *Paulus*, 2nd ed., (Berlin: 1951); O. Linton, *Paulus*, (Svenskt Bibliski Uppsalgsverk, t. II, Gövle: 1952), col. 662-674; J. Knox, *Chapters in a Life of Paul* (London: 1954); O. Moe, *The Apostle Paul* (Minneapolis: 1954); A. N. Williams, *Paul the World's First Missionary* (New York: 1954); W. Fascher, *Paulus*, in *Pauly-Wissowa Realencyklopädie*, Suppl. 8, (1956), pp. 431-456; A. P. Davies, *The First Christian* (New York: 1957); R. S. Kinsey, *With Paul in Greece* (Nashville: 1957); S. Nikolaides, *HO PAULOS* (Athens: 1958); G. Bornkamm, art. *Paulus*, in *RGG*, 3rd ed., (1961), 5, 166-190.

6. E. Haenchen, *Die Apostelgeschichte*, (*Krit. exeg. Komm. H.A.W. Meyers*, 3, 12th ed., Göttingen: 1959).

7. E. Renan, *Saint Paul*, pp. 569-570

Notes to Chapter III

1. This interpretation of Acts is clarified by Ph. H. Menoud, *Le plan des Actes des Apôtres*, in *NTS* 1 (1954-1955), pp. 44-51.

2. Concerning the autobiographical genre, see chapter 6, art. 3.

3. Deference for this twofold perspective is strongly underscored by G. Klein, *Die Zwölf Apostel. Ursprung und Gestalt einer Idee* (Göttingen: 1961).

4. A historical survey of the various opinions can be found in E. Moske, *Die Bekehrung des hl. Paulus. Eine exegetische und kritische Untersuchung* (Munich: 1907), and, above all, in E. Pfaff, *Die Bekehrung des hl. Paulus in der Exegese des 20. Jahrhunderts* (Rome: 1942). For a fairly good restatement of the different problems, cfr. P. Warmoes, *De roeping bij Damascus* (typewritten thesis, Louvain: 1958).

5. E. Stauffer, *Theologie des N.T.*, 4th ed., (Gutersloh: 1948), pp. 238-239, note 53, English translation, *New Testament Theology*, 5th ed. (Macmillan).

6. J. L. Lilly, *The Conversion of St. Paul: The Validity of his Testimony to the Resurrection of Jesus Christ*, in *CBQ* 6 (1944), pp. 180-204.

7. D. M. Stanley, *Paul's Conversion in Acts: Why the Three Accounts*, in *CBQ* 15 (1953), pp. 315-338.

8. E. Hirsch, *Die drei Berichte der Apostelgeschichte über die Bekehrung des Paulus*, in *ZNW* 28 (1929), pp. 305-312.

9. E. von Dobschütz, *Die Berichte über die Bekehrung des Paulus*, in *ZNW* 29 (1930), pp. 144-147. Since the time M. Dibelius proposed his position in *Zur Formgeschichte des N.T.*, in *TRu* new series, 3 (1931), pp. 233-241, and *Aufsätze zur Apostelgeschichte*, 2nd ed., (1953), pp. 136. (note 23) 137-138, 152, the common opinion is that the three accounts do not demand on a plurality of sources: cfr. Grässer, *Die Apostelgeschichte in der Forschung der Gegenwart*, in *TRu*, new series, 26 (1960), pp. 93-167; E. Haenchen, *Tradition und Komposition in der Apostelgeschichte*, in *ZTK* 52 (1953), pp. 210-217; *Idem, Die Apostelgeschichte*, in *Meyers K.*, III, 12th ed., (1959), pp. 274-277, 557-560, 616-621.

10. W. L. Knox, *The Acts of the Apostles* (Cambridge: 1948), pp. 27-28.

11. G. Klein, *Die zwölf Apostel*, pp. 144-145, subjected these texts to a thorough examination. In his opinion, Luke injected into his three accounts those theological themes which were the by-products of his own thoughts, and which characterize his own tendencies (pp. 158-159). The three accounts comprise a large part of the Lucan composition.

12. A. Wikenhauser, *Die Wirkung der Christophanie vor Damaskus auf Paulus und seine Begleiter nach den Berichten der Apostel-geschichte*, in *Bib* 33 (1952), pp. 313-323.

13. *Art. cit.*, together with A. Wikenhauser, *Die Apostelgeschichte* (*Regensburger Bibel*, 5), 3rd ed. (Ratisbonne: 1956). Also cfr. A. Girlanda, *De conversione Pauli in Actibus Apostolorum tripliciter narrata*, in *VD* 39 (1961), pp. 66-81.

14. J. Munck, *La vocation de l'Apôtre Paul* in *ST* 1 (1947), pp. 131-145; *Idem, Paulus und die Heilsgeschichte* (Copenhagen: 1954), pp. 1-27.

15. E. Benz, *Paulus als Visionär. Eine vergleichende Untersuchung der Visionsberichte des Paulus in der Apostelgeschichte und in den paulinischen Briefen* (*Akad. d. Wiss. und d. Lit. in Mainz. Abhandl. d. Geistes- und Sozialw. Klasse*, 1952, 2, Wiesbaden: 1952), pp. 81-121.

16. W. Prentice, *St. Paul's Journey to Damascus*, in *ZNW* 46 (1955), pp. 250-255.

17. J. Weiss, *Das Urchristentum* (Göttingen: 1917), p. 138, Eng. tr. *Earliest Christianity: A.D. 30-150* (Harper Torch bks. 53-54), also (F. C. Grant, 1959).

18. M. Goguel, *La foi à la Résurrection de Jésus dans le christianisme primitif. Étude d'histoire et de psychologie religieuse* (Paris: 1933, p. 424.

19. Cfr. the bibliography in E. Pfaff, *op. cit.*, concerning the question of unconscious preconditioning; cfr. L. Planque, *La conversion de l'apôtre Paul. Étude de psychologie religieuse* (Paris: 1909); G. J. Inglis, *The Problem of St. Paul's Conversion*, in *ExpT* 40 (1928-1929), pp. 227-231.

20. O. Pfleiderer, *Das Urchristentum*, 2nd ed. (Berlin: 1902).

21. M. Goguel, *Origines chrétiennes. Les premières réalisations du christianisme*, in *Histoire générale des Religions*, 3 (Paris: 1952), p. 224.

22. M. Goguel, *La foi à la Résurrection dans le Christianisme primitif* (Paris: 1933), p. 429.

23. J. Weiss, *Paulus und Jesus* (Berlin: 1909), p. 22.

24. K.L. Schmidt, *Der Leib Christi. Eine Untersuchung zum urchristlichen Gemeindegedanken* (Leipzig: 1919); O. Michel, *"Erkennen dem Fleisch nach"* (*2 Kor. 5 16*), in *EvT* 14 (1954), pp. 22-29.

25. F. Büchsel, *Theologie des Neuen Testaments*, 2nd ed. (Gutersloh: 1937).

26. The religionists attributed the origin of the accounts to Jewish and Hellenistic influences; moreover, they rejected every possibility of getting anywhere concerning the historical fact of the conversion, and consequently, of any psychological preparation for the event. Such is the attitude of A. Drews, F. Smend, H. Windisch, W. Wrede, M. Brückner, A. Loisy, and W. Heitmüller; cfr. E. Pfaff, *op.cit.*, pp. 13-16. For further information, cfr. O. Kietzig, *Die Bekehrung des Paulus, religionsgeschichtlich und religionspsychologisch neu untersucht* (*Untersuch z. N.T.*, 22, Leipzig: 1932); W. G. Kümmel, *Römer 7 und die Bekehrung des Paulus* (*Untersuch-z. N.T.*, 17, Leipzig: 1929). In his article, *Die Bekehrung des Paulus als religionsegschichtlichen Problem*, in *ZTK* 56 (1959), pp. 273-293, U. Wilckens took the point of view of the Jewish religion to defend the thesis that Paul's conversion essentially lies within the very context of his own antinomy: Paul was not a Jewish rabbi before he became a Christian; however, his former religious views were so grounded in the apocalyptic that he readily accepted the plan of salvation-history; he realized in Damascus that Jesus marked the end of the Law. One begins to understand how long it took for the religionist problem to have evolved. It was A. Schweitzer who had pinpointed the origin of the movement, namely, that Jewish eschatology was the nucleus of the Christian problem.

27. Those Catholics, who would admit the fact of some positive psychological preparation, resorts to the following factors: Restlessness of conscience or an interior incertitude, the failure of the Law, and the Christian influence. Thus, for example, E. Seipel, F. X. Pölzl, J. Fischer, M. Meinertz, B. Bartmann, A. Steinmann, E. Masure, and J. Holzner. In his biography of Paul, Holzner emphasized the following: 1) the impression which the death of Stephen had on the Apostle; 2) Paul's dissatisfaciton with the Law; and 3) what Paul heard in the preachings concerning the Messiah who had suffered and died. Paul's dissatisfaction with the inability of fulfilling the Law is a point that is also stressed by such authors as V. Rose, E. Moske, F. Prat, P. Dausch, K. Pieper, J. M. Vosté, J. B. Colon, S. Tillmann, and K. Th. Schäfer. Cfr. Pfaff, *op.cit.*, pp. 31-34.

The element of a positive preparation for the conversion is totally rejected by J. Knabenbauer, C. Toussaint, A. Boudou, U. Holzmeister, L. Murillo, P. Teodorico, and E. Kalt. Cfr. Pfaff, *op.cit.*, pp. 35-36; cfr. J. Bonsirven, *L'évangile de Paul* (Paris: 1948), pp. 42-43; J. Huby, *Mystiques paulinien-ne et johannique* (Bruges: 1946), pp. 108-109; J. L. Lilly, *The Conversion of Paul*, p. 201; J. Renié, *Actes des Apôtres* (Paris: 1949), p. 143; H. Schlier, *Der Brief an die Galater* (Göttingen: 1949), p. 24, note 2; A. Wikenhauser, *Einleitung*, p. 251. Similarly, R. Bultmann, *Theologie*, p. 185 Eng. tr. *Theology of the N.T.* (Scribner); E. Haenchen, *Die Apostelgeschichte*, p. 276; Ph. H. Menoud, *Révélation et Tradition. L'influence de la conversion de Paul sur sa théologie*, in *VC* 7 (1953), pp. 2-4; J. Munck, *Paulus und die Heilsgeschichte*, pp. 3,15.

28. Concerning 2 Cor. 5, 16, see H. P. Berlage, *2 Co 5 14-17*, in *TTij* 32 (1898), pp. 343-632; H. F. Perry, *Knowing Christ after the Flesh (2 Co 5 16)*, in *BW* 18 (1901), pp. 284-286; V. Weber, *Wann und wie hat Paulus "Christum nach dem Fleisch" gekannt (2 Kor. 5 16)*, in *BZ* 2 (1904), pp. 178-187; J. Weiss, *Paulus und Jesus* (Berlin: 1909); A. D. Martin, *Knowing Christ "katà sárka,"* in *ExpT* 24 (1912-1913), pp. 334-335; A. M. Pope, *Paul's Previous Meeting with Jesus*, in *Exp*, series 8, 26 (1923), pp. 38-48; R. Reitzenstein, *Die hellenistischen Mysterienreligionen*, 3 (Leipzig: 1927), pp. 375-376; F. C. Porter, *Does Paul Claim to have Known the Historical Jesus?* in *JBL* 47 (1928), pp. 257-275; E. B. Allo, *Excursus XI. - Ce que signifie: ne plus connaître le Christ selon la chair* (V, 16 b), in *Seconde Épître aux Corinthiens* (*Études bibliques*, Paris: 1937), pp. 179-182 (bibliography); R. Bultmann, *Exegetische Probleme des Zweiten Korintherbriefes*, in *SymBUp* 9 (1947), pp. 12-20; J. Dupont, *Gnosis* (Louvain: 1949), pp. 180-186; L. Cerfaux, *Le Christ dans la théologie de saint Paul* (Paris: 1951); O. Michel, *"Erkennen dem Fleisch nach"* (2 *Kor.* 5, 16), in *EvT* 14 (1954), pp. 22-29; S. Lyonnet, *Exegesis Epistulae secundae ad Corinthios* (Rome: 1955-1956); P. Warmoes, *De roeping bij Damascus*, pp. 26-28; J. Cambier, *Connaissance charnelle et et spirituelle du Christ dans 2 Co 5, 16*, in *Littérature et théologie pauliniennes* (*Recherches bibliques*, 5, Paris: 1960), pp. 72-92.

29. Cfr. E. Pfaff, *op.cit.*, pp. 88-91 (bibliography); J. Munck, *Paulus und die Heilsgeschichte*, p. 10 ff, Eng. tr. *Paul and the Salvation of Mankind* (John Knox: 1960).

30. Cfr. J. Munck, *op. cit.*, pp. 11-13, note 21.

31. For a similar interpretation, cfr. R. Bultmann, *Paulus*, in *RGG*, 2nd ed., 4, 1022; J. Dupont, *Les Actes des Apôtres*, in *SBJ* (Paris), 19, 202; E. Haenchen, *Die Apostelgeschichte*, pp. 274-277.

32. On Rom. 7, the basic study is that of W. G. Kümmel, *Römer 7 und die Bekehrung des Paulus* (Leipzig: 1929, bibliography vii-xv); *Idem, Das Bild des Menschen im Neuen Testament* (Zurich: 1948), pp. 20-40. For the best introduction to the problems, cfr. O. Kuss, *Der Römerbrief* (Ratisbonne: 1959), pp. 462-485, particularly the

excursus, *Zur Geschichte der Auslegung von Röm 7, 7-25.* Also, E. de Los Rios, *Peccatum et Lex: Animadversiones in Rom 7, 7-25,* in *VD* 11 (1931), pp. 23-28; R. Bultmann, *Römer 7 und die Anthropologie des Paulus,* in *Imago Dei. Festschr. für G. Krüger* (Giessen: 1932), pp. 53-62; *Idem, Christus, des Gesetzes Ende,* in *BEvT* 1 (1940), pp. 3-27; P. Benoit, *La loi et la Croix d'après saint Paul (Rm VIII, 7 - VIII, 4),* in *RB* 47 (1938), pp. 481-509, reprinted in *Exégèse et Théologie,* II (Paris: 1961), pp. 9-40; A.F.N. Lekkerkerker, *Romeinen 7, een belijdenis der gemeente,* in *NieuTS* 23 (1940), pp. 99-109; A. Rétif, *A propos de l'interprétation du chapitre VII des Romains par saint Augustin,* in *RScR* 33 (1946), pp. 368-371; L. Brun, *Rm 7, 7-25, ennu engang,* in *SEA* 12 (1947), pp. 67-84; D. M. Davies, *Free from the Law, an Exposition to the Seventh Chapter of Romans,* in *Int* 7 (1953), pp. 156-162; C. L. Mitton, *Romans 7 Reconsidered,* in *ExpT* 65 (1953-1954), pp. 78-81, 99-103, 132-135; E. Ellwein, *Das Rätsel von Römer VIII,* in *Kerygma und Dogma* I (1955), pp. 247-268; S. Lyonnet, note, in J. Huby, *Épître aux Romains* (Paris: 1957), pp. 601-604; G. Bornkamm, *Das Ende des Gesetzes,* 2nd ed. (Munich: 1958), pp. 51-69; A. Braun, *Röm 7, 7-25 und des Selbstverständnis der Qumrân-Frommen,* in *ZTK* 56 (1959), pp. 1-18.

33. Such a position has been taken by most exegetes down to the time of Kümmel.

34. F. J. Leenhardt, *Commentaire de l'Épître aux Romains* (Paris-Neuchâtel: 1957), p. 104.

35. O. Kuss, *op.cit.,* pp. 462-485.

36. J. Klausner, *From Jesus to Paul,* p. 326.

37. M. Dibelius and W. G. Kümmel, *Paulus,* p. 40.

38. Cfr. our previous presentation on the *Psychology of Conversion.*

39. E. Hirsch, *Die Auferstehungsgeschichten und der Christliche Glaube* (Tübingen: 1940), pp. 8, 33, contrary to the opinion of P. Althaus, *Die Wahrheit des kirchlichen Osterglaubens. Einspruch gegen Emmanuel Hirsch,* in *Beiträge z. Förderung Christ. Theol.,* 42, 2 (Gutersloh: 1940); W. Michaelis, *Die Erscheinungen des Auferstandenen* (Basell: 1944).

40. W. Prokulski, *The Conversion of St. Paul,* in *CBQ* 19 (1957), pp. 453-473.

41. E. Benz, *Paulus als Visionär,* pp. 95-97; S. M. Gilmour, *Paul and the Primitive Church,* in *JRel* 25 (1945), p. 124. ,

42. Similarly, J. Baruzi resorts to the concept of the mystique in his study, *Création religieuse et pensée contemporaine* I. *La mystique paulinienne et les données autobiographiques des Épîtres* (Paris: 1951), pp. 1-96.

43. J. Dupont, *Gnosis. La connaissance religieuse dans les Épîtres de saint Paul* (Bruges-Paris: 1949), p. 198, note 1.

44. A. Oepke, *Der Brief an die Galater,* in *Theologisches Handkom.,* 9, 2nd ed. (1957), pp. 32-33.

45. W. G. Kümmel, *Röm 7 und die Bekehrung des Paulus*, in *Unters. N.T.*, 17 (Leipzig: 1929).

46. H. G. Wood, *The Conversion of St. Paul. Its Nature, Antecedents and Consequences*, in *NTS* 1 (1954-1955), pp. 276-282.

47. Ch. Guignebert, *La conversion de saint Paul*, in *RH* 63 (1938), pp. 7-23.

48. M. Goguel, *La foi à la résurrection de Jésus dans le christianisme primitif. Étude d'histoire et de psychologie religieuse* (Paris: 1937); *Idem*, *Remarques sur un aspect de la conversion de Paul*, in *JBL* 53 (1934), pp. 257-267.

49. J. Klausner, *From Jesus to Paul* (London: 1946).

50. H. G. Wood, *art. cit.*, p. 276.

51. W. von Loewenich, *Paulus. Sein Leben und sein Werk*, 2nd ed. (Witten: 1949).

52. In the very last moments while our manuscript was already in the press, we became acquainted with the very fine work of Msgr. L. Cerfaux, *La Chrétien dans la théologie paulinienne* (*Lectio divina*, 33, Paris: 1962), wherein all the materials pertinent to this section of our work were subjected to an examination in depth. We were unable to delay publication.

53. G. Klein, *Die zwölf Apostel. Ursprung und Gestalt einer Idee.* (*Forsch. z. Rel. u. Lit. des A. u. N.T.*, new series, 59, Göttingen: 1961), pp. 114-189.

54. By unquestionably accepting that the institution of the twelve apostles does not date back to Jesus, the author betrays his own tendency in being extremely faithful to the thought of his teacher Ph. Vielhauer. The principal point of his demonstration rests on very weak foundations, namely, *verba magistri* ("the words of the master"), which constitute the death-blow to his reasoning. Cfr. B. Rigaux, *Die "Zwölf" in Geschichte und Kerygma*, in *Der historische Jesus und der kerygmatische Christus. Beiträge zum Christusverständnis in Forschung und Verkündigung* (Berlin: 1960), pp. 468-486.

55. E. Lohmeyer, *Grundlagen paulinischer Theologie* (Tübingen: 1929), pp. 201 ff; K. H. Rengstorf, *art. Apóstolos*, in *ThWNT* (1932-1933), pp. 438-443; H. Windisch, *Paulus und Christus. Ein biblisch-religionsgeschichtlicher Vergleich* (*Untersuchungen z. N.T.*, 24, Leipzig: 1934-1937).

56. L. Cerfaux, *Saint Paul et le "Serviteur de Dieu" d'Isaïe*, in *Recueil L. Cerfaux*, 2 (Gembloux: 1954), pp. 439-454.

57. A. Bertrangs, *Damascus en de Bijbel. Topieken voor Sint Paulus' Roeping*, in *SC* 24 (1954), pp. 225-236; *Idem*, *La Vocation des Gentils chez saint Paul, Exégèse et heuristique pauliniennes des citations vétéro-testamentaires*, in *ETL* 30 (1954), pp. 391-415.

58. A. M. Denis, *L'élection et la vocation de Paul, faveurs célestes*, in *RTh* (1957), p. 415.

59. J. Munck, *Paulus und die Heilsgeschichte*, pp. 15-25, who insists less on Is. than on Jer. 1, 8. See also J. Dupont, *Gnosis. La con-*

naissance religieuse dans les épîtres de saint Paul (Louvain: 1949), pp. 239-241.

60. E. Pfaff, *op.cit.*, p. 169.

61. J. Munck, *Paulus und die Heilsgeschichte*, pp. 15-21,

62. L. Cerfaux, *L'antinomie paulinienne de la vie apostolique*, in *RScR* 39-40 (1951-1952), which is reprinted in *Recueil L. Cerfaux*, 2 (Gembloux: 1954), pp. 455-467.

63. E. Stauffer, *Die Theologie des Neuen Testament* (Gutersloh: 1948), Eng. tr. *N.T. Theology*, 5th ed. (Macmillan).

64. H. Schlier, *Der Brief an die Galater* (Göttingen: 1954).

65. L. Cerfaux, *art. cit.*, p. 455.

66. E. Stauffer, *op.cit.*, p. 21.

67. H. Schlier, *op.cit.*, p. 24.

68. E. Barnikol, *Die Christwerdung des Paulus in Galiläe und die Apostelberufung vor Damaskus und im Tempel* (Halle: 1955).

69. A. Oepke, *Der Brief an die Galater*, (*Theologische Handkom.*, 9, 2nd ed., 1957).

70. E. Pfaff, *op.cit.*, pp. 159-161, with its highly pertinent remarks which merit reexamination.

71. E. Benz, *Paulus als Visionär*, p. 101.

72. E. Fascher, *art. Paulus*, in *Pauly-Wissowa*, suppl. 8 (1956), p. 442.

73. A. Fridrichsen, *The Apostle and his Message*, pp. 3, 26.

74. A. Fridrichsen, *op.cit.*, p. 26.

75. A. Bertrangs, *Damascus en de Bijbel*, pp. 228 ff.

76. P. Gächter, *Petrus und seine Zeit* (Innsbruck: 1958), *Schranken im Apostolat des Paulus*, pp. 338-450.

77. *Op.cit.*, p. 411.

78. H. v. Campenhausen, *Der urchristliche Apostelbegriff*, p. 122.

79. *Op.cit.*, p. 411.

80. 1 Thes. 1, 10.

81. Cfr. J. Wagenmann, *Die Stellung des Apostels Paulus neben den Zwölf in den ersten zwei Jahrhunderten* (*Beihefte z. ZNW*, 3, 1926), pp. 3-31; J. Dupont, *Le nom d'Apôtre a-t-il été donné aux Douze par Jésus* (Louvain: 1956); B. Rigaux, *Die "Zwölf in Geschichte und Kerygma*, in *Der historische Jesus und der kerygmatische Christus* (Berlin: 1960), pp. 468-486; L. Cerfaux, *Pour l'histoire du titre Apostolos dans le N.T.*, in *RScR* 48 (1960), pp. 76-92.

82. 1 Thes. 2, 14.

83. U. Wilckens, *Die Bekehrung des Paulus*, p. 274. Relevant to the expression *ophthe* in 1 Cor. 15, 8 ff., he writes: "The expression *ophthe* here connotes the notion of a vision, involving a revelation on the part of God here and now, which is exceptionally unique; such a notion differentiates this unusual experience from the later visions, of which Paul knows how to report, as, for instance, in 2 Cor. 12, 1 ff."

39-43; the same lecture, which was delivered in Rome, was reproduced,

84. Cfr. Card. J. Döpfner, *Paulus und Petrus*, in *BiKi* 16 (1961), pp.

rather faithfully, under the title *Petrus und Paulus. Der heilige Paulus und der römische Primat,* in *TGl* 51 (1961), pp. 180-194; French translation in *La Documentation Catholique,* 28, n. 1350, (1961), pp. 495-506. See also E. Haenchen, *Petrus-Probleme,* in *NTS* 7 (1960-1961), pp. 187-197.

85. P. Gaechter, *Petrus und seine Zeit,* p. 338.

86. H. Dieckmann, S.J., *De Ecclesia,* I (1925), pp. 231-254.

87. T. Zapelena, S.J., *De Ecclesia Christi,* in *Pars Apologetica,* 5th ed. (1950), p. 202.

88. E. B. Allo, in *Vivre et Penser, RB* 50 (1941), pp. 52-53.

89. Ph. H. Menoud, *Revelation and Tradition. The Influence of Paul's Conversion on His Theology,* in *Int* 7 (1953), pp. 131-141; the same article appeared in French as *Révélation et tradition: L'influence de la conversion de Paul sur sa théologie,* in *VC* 7 (1953), pp. 2-10; cfr. A. Verheul, *Apostolat en Verrijzenis. Onderzoek naar de inhoud van het Apostelbegrip in 1 Cor,* in *SC* (1951), pp. 171-184; L. Baeck, *The Faith of Paul,* in *JJS* 3 (1952), pp. 93-110.

90. L. Cerfaux, *La tradition selon saint Paul,* in *VSp* 25 (1953), which was reprinted in *Recueil L. Cerfaux,* 2, pp. 253-263.

91. L. Cerfaux, *Le Christ dans le théologie de saint Paul* (Paris: 1951) Eng. tr. *Christ in the Theology of St. Paul* (Herder and Herder); H. v. Campenhausen, *Der urchristliche Apostelbegriff,* in *ST* 1 (1948), pp. 96-130, 330-331, 365-366; A.M. Denis, *L'investiture de la fonction apostolique par "Apocalypse",* in *RB* 64 (1957), pp. 335-362; H. Schlier, *Der Brief an die Galater,* pp. 142-143, 150-159.

92. W. Michaelis, *Die Erscheinungen des Auferstandenen* (Basel: 1954), pp. 104-109. It is also one of the great accomplishments of J. Munck, *Paulus und die Heilsgeschichte,* to have situated the events of the life of the Apostle again in their proper function and in salvation-history. Cfr. also his study, *Paul, the Apostle and the Twelve,* in *ST* 3 (1949), pp. 96-110. Moreover, cfr. E. Lohse, *Ursprung und Prägung des christlichen Apostolates,* in *TZ* 9 (1953), pp. 259-276.

93. E. M. Kredel, *Der Apostelbegriff in der neueren Exegese. Historisch-kritische Darstellung,* in *ZKT* 78 (1956), pp. 169-193, 237-305, in conjunction with A. Verheul, *De moderne exegese over "apóstolos,"* in *Sacris Erudiri* I (1948), pp. 380-396; G. Linssen, *Het Apostolaat volgens St. Paulus* (Nijmegen: 1952). For more recent studies, cfr. C. K. Barrett, *The Apostles in and after the N.T.,* in *SEA* 21 (1956), pp. 30-44; J. C. Margot, *L'apostolat dans le N.T. et la succession apostolique,* in *VC* 11 (1957), pp. 213-225; M. Ashcraft, *Paul's Understanding of Apostleship,* in *RE* 55 (1958), pp. 400-412; W. Nagel, *Der Begriff des Apostolischen in der christlichen Frühzeit bis zur Kanonsbildung* (Dissertation, Leipzig: 1958); J. Cambier, *Paul, apôtre du Christ et prédicateur de l'Évangile,* in *NRT* 81 (1959), pp. 1009-1028; L. Cerfaux, *Pour l'histoire du titre Apostolos dans le N.T.,* in *RScR* 48 (1960), pp. 76-92.

94. J. L. Leuba, *L'institution et l'evenement* (Neuchatel-Paris: 1950, German translation, 1957) ; G. Klein, *Die Zwolf Apostel.*, p. 9: " 'Spirit' and 'Office' should not be isolated from each other; rather they should be kept together very closely in the concrete historical plan of the theological reflection in a manner so variant according to place and time, so that only then a carefully differentiating interpretation can emerge."

95. J. Hamer, *Une théolgoie du dualisme chrétien*, in NRT (1951), pp. 275-281; R. Aubert, *L'institution et l'événement. A propos de l'oeuvre de M. le Pasteur Leuba*, in ETL 28 (1952), pp. 683-693.

96. L. Cerfaux, *L'unité du corps apostolique dans le N.T., dans l'Église et les églises*, in Recueil L. Cerfaux, 2, pp. 227-237.

97. L. Cerfaux, *L'antinomie paulinienne de la vie apostolique*, in Recueil L. Cerfaux, 2, pp. 455-567.

98. On this point, see Ch. Maurer, *Grund und Grenze apostolischer Freiheit. Exegetisch-theologische zur 1 Kor 4. Antwort*, in Festsch. K. Barth (1956), pp. 630-641, but above all, D. Smolders, *L'audace de l'apôtre selon saint Paul. Le théme de la parrêsia*, in ColMech 43 (1958), pp. 16-21, 117-133.

99. L. Cerfaux, *L'Apôtre en présence de Dieu*, in Recueil L. Cerfaux, 2 pp. 469-481. There is nothing worth retaining of E. Bock, *Paulus, Beiträge zur Geistesgeschichte der Menscheit* (Stuttgart: 1956), which is an interpretation on the basis of the anthroposophic secrets of Rudolf Steiner.

100. M. Sabbe, *Enkele aspecten van het apostolaat bij Paulus*, in ColBG 3 (1957), pp. 507-521.

101. A. M. Denis, *L'investiture de la fonction apostolique par "apocalypse"*, *Gal. 1,16*, in RB 64 (1957), pp. 335-362, 491-515; *Idem, L'élection et la vocation de Paul, faveurs célestes*, in RTh 57 (1957), pp. 405-428; *Idem, La fonction apostolique et la liturgie nouvelle en Esprit. Étude thématique des métaphores pauliniennes du culte nouveau*, in RSPhTh 42 (1958), pp. 401-436; *Idem, L'Apôtre, Paul prophéte "messianique" des Gentils*, in ETL 33 (1957), pp. 245-318.

102. J. Giblet, *Saint Paul, serviteur de Dieu et apôtre de Jésus-Christ*, in VSp 388 (1953), pp. 244-265; J. Cambier, *Paul, apôtre du Christ et prédicateur de l'évangile*, in NRT 81 (1959), pp. 1009-1028.

103. A. Descamps, *L'actualité de l'épître aux Romains*, in Littérature et théologie pauliniennes (Recherches bibliques, V, Bruges: 1960), pp. 12-13.

104. G. Sass, *Zur Bedeutung von "doûlos" bei Paulus*, in ZNW 40 (1941), pp. 24-31; concerning the baptism of Paul cfr. E. Fascher, *Zur Taufe des Paulus*, in TLZ 53 (1955), pp. 643-648.

105. K. Weiss, *Paulus - Priester der Christlichen Kultgemeinde*, in TLZ 52 (1954), pp. 335-364, a study on the priesthood of Paul.

Notes to Chapter IV

1. Recent studies: F. Prat, *La chronologie de l'âge apostolique*, in

RSR 3 (1912), pp. 374-392; *Idem, Chronologie,* in *DBS* 1 (1928), pp. 1287-1291 (with bibliography); D. Plooij, *De Chronologie van het Leven van Paulus* (Leiden: 1918); F. Jackson and K. Lake, *The Beginnings of Christianity,* V (London: 1933), note XXXIV: *The Chronology of Acts,* pp. 445-474; G. Ricciotti, *Paolo Apostolo,* 3rd ed. (Rome: 1940), pp. 145-155 Eng. tr. *Paul the Apostle* (Bruce: 1961); E. Haenchen, *Die Apostelgesechichte (Meyersk.* 2nd ed., Göttingen: 1956), pp. 53-64. Two critical surveys on recent literature are: W. G. Kümmel, *Das Urchristentum,* in *TRu* 17 (1948-1949), pp. 28-32; 18 (1950), pp. 26-29; 22 (1954), p. 207; and J. Dupont, *Les probléms du Livre des Actes* (Louvain: 1950), pp. 51-67.

2. Cfr. J. Dupont, *Les sources du Livre des Actes* (Bruges: 1960) Eng. tr. *Sources of the Acts* (Herder and Herder: 1964).

3. C. J. Cadoux, *A Tentative Synthetic Chronology of the Apostolic Age,* in *JBL* 56 (1937), pp. 177-191, would wish that each passage in Acts where Luke notes the growth of the community Acts 2,47b; 6,7; 9,31; 12,24; 16,35; 19,20; 28,31) may be the mention of one Pentecost, and having made his computation on the basis of six, that there may be six divisions in groups of six between the years 30 and 60. Evidently, such an opinion has quite a bit of fantasy. There is no indication at all that Luke's notations possess a chronological value which were intended for the reader to find. Moreover, Cadoux has completely overlooked the passages in Acts 4,4 and 5,14 where the same indications could have the same meaning.

4. Concerning the inscription, besides those studies cited by F. Prat, see also É. Bourguet, *De rebus Delphicis imperatoriae aetatis capita duo* (Montpellier: 1905); D. Plooij, *De Chronologie,* pp. 27-45; W. Larfeld, *Die delphische Gallionschrift und die paulinische Chronologie,* in *NKZ* 24 (1923), pp. 638-647; A. Deissmann, *Paulus,* 2nd ed. (Tübingen: 1925), pp. 203-225; L. Cantarelli, *Gallio proconsole di Acaiae san Paolo (Rendiconti della R. Accad, Naz. dei Lincei,* Rome: 1923), pp. 157-173; L. Hennequin, *Delphes (Inscription de),* in *DBS* II (1924), 355-373; Th. Schlatter, *Gallio und Paulus in Corinth,* in *NKZ* 26 (1926), pp. 500-513; F. Jackson and K. Lake, *The Beginnings,* V (1935), pp. 464-467; E. Haenchen, *Die Apostelgeschichte;* pp. 58-61; C. K. Barrett, *The New Testament Background: Selected Documents* (London: 1956), pp. 48-49.

5. *CIL,* nn. 2178, 2271, 3883, 4001.

6. *CIL,* VI, n. 1256. H. Dessau, *Inscriptiones latinae selectae* I (Berlin: 1882), 218, 55.

7. Frontinus, *De Aquaeductu Urbis Romae,* I, pp. 13-14, ed. Krohn (Teubner, Leipzig: 1922) pp. 9-10.

8. *CIL,* III, n. 467.

9. *CIL,* III, n. 1977.

10. The twenty-sixth acclamation can be found in G. Cousin and G. Deschamps, *Emplacements des ruines à la ville du Kus en Carie,* in *BCH* 11 (1887), pp. 306-307. We can be assured that this acclama-

tion belonged to the second year of the reign of Claudius, namely, January 25, 52 - January 24, 53 A.D.

11. Compare Acts 9,23 with Acts 9,20; 28,7; contrary to Hennequin, *art. cit.*, p. 370.

12. Acts 20,11.

13. A. Steinman, *Aretas IV, König der Nabatäer* (Freiburg: 1909); D. Plooij, *op.cit.*, p. 5. The date for the beginning of the reign oscillates between the years 8 and 12 B.C. Most authors claim that he died in the year 40 since his reign lasted 48 years. We are reminded, once and for all, that the computation of a reign has its pitfalls as far as precision is concerned because of the fact that there are different systems of computation. Occasionally, the computation of the beginning and end of a reign can be made by beginning with the date for the accession to power itself, which, if it would happen in the course of a year would mark the end of a reign, or if the reign would begin with trouble; thus a forty-eight year period can be reduced to forty-six years. W. Schmauch, in *RGG*, 3rd ed., I, p. 590, dates the death of Aretas to the year 38; J. Héring, *La seconde Épître de saint paul aux Corinthiens* (Neuchâtel: 1958), p. 91 Eng. tr. *Second Epistle of St. Paul to the Corinthians* (Allenson: 1967), prefers the year 39. Since Paul's escape occurred in the year 38 or later, to date the death of Aretas precisely would be of no advantage.

14. L. Cerfaux, in *Introduction à la Bible*, 2. *Le N.T.*, p. 352.

15. J. Dupont, *Les Problèmes*, pp. 53, 56, 63, 65.

16. H. Sahlin, *Der Messias und das Gottesvolk. Studien zur protolukanischen Theologie* (*Acta Seminarii Neotestamentica Upsaliensis*, 12, Uppsala: 1945), pp. 345-373; K. Thieme, *Le plan des "Actes des Apôtres" et la chronologie de son contenu*, in *Div* 26 (1954), pp. 127-133.

17. See K. S. Gapp, *The Universal Famine under Claudius*, in *HTR* 28 (1935), pp. 258-265.

18. Suetonius, *Claudius*, 18: "arctiore autem annona ob assiduas sterilitates detentus": poverty caused by a series of bad harvests. In any case, he is certain that such a setback did not happen only in the year 51 A.D. Of the famine of that year, Tacitus said that it would be alleviated "by the great condescension of the gods and the mildness of the winter months" ("magna deorum benignitate et modestia hiemis"). He then added that Italy was not suffering from drought any more than at other times when it had to supply the distant legions with corn; "we prefer to cultivate Africa and Egypt, whereas the life of the Roman people is abandoned to navies and to dangers" (Tacitus, *Annals*, 43, 4). We could conclude from these texts that the drought spread as far as Africa and Egypt, and since the ordinary granaries of the Empire were there, a lack of grain in Rome could not be explained unless those granaries were low in grain. This is the opinion of Th. Zahn, *Einleitung in d. N.T.*, 3rd ed. (Leip-

zig: 1924), p. 422; D. Plooij, *op.cit.*, p. 19. However, the fact, according to Tacitus, that Rome could be spared with the coming mild winter at which time the ships would sail, indicates that the famine had not reached Egypt and Africa. (E. Haenchen, *Apostelgeschichte,* 55, n. 1).

19. K. S. Gapp gathered indications from the papyri to show that in Egypt in the year 46-47, an exceptionally heavy flood of the Nile had ruined the crops, and the price of corn had more than doubled. *Art. cit.*, pp. 260, 261.

20. Orosius, *Historia contra Paganaos*, VII, 7, a work written in 417-418 A.D.

21. Eusebius, *Chronicle*, ed. R. Helm, *GCS*, VII (Berlin: 1956), p. 181, dated to the year 303 A.D. Orosius and *History*, which are frequently cited, are not authorities of less importance for the certain fixation of the date of the famine. That the famine had spread all the way to Greece was not a fact invented by the *Chronicle*, and hence could pass as an historical datum. The year 48 is equally acceptable, since it does agree with the text of Suetonius. Hence, both Greece and Italy must have suffered from the same droughts.

22. As regards the text of Josephus, we would like to make the following observations. Josephus, *Ant. Jud.*, XX,5,2, is quoted by Dindorf as follows: *epi toutoi de kai ton megan limon kata ten Ioudaian sunebe genesthai,* a reading that is based on manuscripts of the Latin translation and Eusebius (*Hist. Eccl.*, II, 12, 1). On the contrary, Niese, following the tenth-century *Epitome*, reads *epi toutou de k.t.l. . .* (XX, 101) Plooij defends the reading *epi toutois*, because the reading *epi toutou* is the easier reading. In this passage, Josephus speaks of Tiberius Alexander after he was finished with Fadus. If the easier reading would be followed, then the content would be less probable. It could also be added that the *Epitome* frequently corrected the reading of the text. On the hand, Niese counted the instances where the original text was the only good witness, see B. Niese, I, LIX-LXXI. The expression *de* is certainly wrong. Manuscripts *MW* read *phar;* the latin version reads *ergo*. Hudson is responsible for the reading *de*. We also believe that the reading *epi toutois* is the more probable, because there is more evidence for it, and because it is the more difficult reading (*lectic difficilior*). A. M. Tornos is of the same opinion in his study, *La fecha del hambre de Jerusalén aludida por Act 11, 28-30*, in *EstEc* 33 (1959), p. 307. The expression *epi toutois* can be either masculine or neuter in gender. The *Epitome* prefers the masculine gender. J. Jeremias also prefers the masculine, cfr. *Sabbatjahr und neutestamentliche Chronologie*, in *ZNW* 27 (1928), p. 99, n. 4. Schürer, on the other hand, identifies the gender as neuter. We think that the obvious meaning would be in favor of the masculine. E. Haenchen, *Apostelgeschichte*, p. 56, interpreted the expression *epi* in the sense of "and after." According to Josephus, *Ant. Iud.*, XX, 1,2, where the imperial rescript which mentions Fadus is

recorded, it should be noted, as Niese has done, that the word
Ioulious occurs neither in the Greek manuscripts nor in the better
Latin manuscripts, but has been borrowed by Hudson from Latin
manuscripts which are of little value. Hence, to claim that Fadus was
already in charge precisely on June 25th, 45 A.D., is hypothetical. Since the month is not mentioned, the date could be the
Calends of June, that is, May 25th. F. Jackson and K. Lake, *The
Beginnings of Christianity* (London: 1933), V, p. 453, note, however,
that such a date "rests on very slender evidence." Another pertinent
remark would be that the consuls Rufus and Pompeius, who are mentioned in the rescript, did not become Consuls until the year 46 A.D.
Truly, chronology and ancient witnesses never have been a good match.

23. Cfr. A. M. Tornos, *art.cit.*, who thought that the famine occurred in
the year 42-43 A.D. J. Dupont accepted the year 49 as the date,
as also P. Benoit. If the journey, which was taken at the time of
the famine, could be made to coincide with the journey to the Council
of Jerusalem, then this date would be very probable.

24. J. Jeremias, *Sabbatjahr und neutestamentliche Chronologie*, in *ZNW*
27 (1928), pp. 98-103.

25. 1 Mc.2, 29-38; 2 Mc. 6,11.

26. For the chronology of the reign of Agrippa, see Jackson and Lake,
op.cit., pp. 446-452. He was born no later than towards the end of
the year 11 B.C., and began his reign in 37 under Caius, until 41,
and under Claudius for the three years that followed. This chronology is based on Josephus, *Ant.Iud.*, XVIII, 6, 10; 7, 2; XX, 1, 2
concerning the letter of Claudius to the Jews of Alexandria in 45
(H. Idris Bell, *Jews and Christians in Egypt*, London: 1924, pp. 1-37),
and for the numismatic evidence. The latter source of evidence does
pose a particular problem. Two coins of Agrippa bear the date for
the eight year (F. W. Madden, *Coins of the Jews*, London: 1881,
pp. 128-138, which belong to the collection of D. C. Reichhardt),
and one coin which is dated to the ninth year (Echkel, *Doctrina
Numorum Veterum*, vol. VIII, p. 493). Sir Madden never had any
faith in the readings *LH* for the eighth year - and less for the
readings L-*theta* for the 9th year (p. 132). Verification of this point
is impossible. However, it must be admitted that these readings prove
nothing against the chronology of Josephus, for, as Sir Madden has
pointed out very well, the nine-year period could be reduced to seven
by slicing off sections of the years which were computed as entire
years. J. Meyshan (*The Coinage of Agrippa the First*, in *IEJ* 4, 1954,
pp. 186-200) has missed the point of the question completely. The coin
which bears the reading *LE* of Madden and of M. Narkiss, *Coins of
Palestine I*: *Jewish Coins* (Jerusalem: 1936), p. 107 (in Hebrew) is
that of Agrippa II. A. Reifenberg, *Portrait Coins of the Herodian
Kings*, in *NuCir* 43 (London: 1935), p. 7, made a good observation. Moreover, two coins, one of which commemorates the victory of
Claudius over the Britons and the other which celebrates the Olympic

games, bears the inscription *LZ* and *LH*, that is, the dates of the seventh and eighth years of Agrippa I, namely, 42, 43 and 44 A.D. Finally, there are a number of authors who believe that the fifth, seventh, eighth and ninth years should be read, but they are wrong. A misreading of the letter *S*, which occurs in various forms, has led many into error. Such a conclusion is based on the readings of some 2000 coins. E. Schwartz, *Zur Chronologie des Paulus*, in *Nachrichten der Gesellschaft der Wissenschaften zu Göttingen* (1907), p. 265 f., in *Gesammelt Schriften* 5 (1963), pp. 124-169, attempted to prove that the date reads 10-3-44, making allowances for a three-week period before the Passover; but this would contradict the testimony of Acts 12, 4.23. E. Haenchen, *Apostelgeschichte*, pp. 53-55, accepted the position of Schwartz, whose weaknesses have already been exposed by F. Jackson and K. Lake, *op.cit.*, p. 451. There is a mistake in the *Introduction á la Bible*, vol. 2, *N.T.* (Paris: 1959), p. 370, which says that the famine under Claudius could carry us all the way up to the years 49-55 A.D. Nothing in the article of J. Dupont, *Notes sur les Actes der Apôtres*, in *RB* 62 (1955), pp. 52-55, which we have cited, insinuates such a date.

27. The last two verses of chapter 12 are nothing more than a very loose link between what precedes and what follows. They bear the obvious imprint of redactional work. To base on these two verses any attempt at a precise chronology is contrary to all rules of criticism. Cfr. R. W. Funck, *The Enigma of the Famine Visit*, in *JBL* 75 (1956), pp. 130-136.

28. *SBJ, Actes des Apôtres* 12,25. We subscribe to this translation of J. Dupont. However, it supposes that two problems have been resolved. First of all, as against C. Tischendorf, J. Weiss, H. von Soden, H. J. Vogels, E. Jacquier, and A. Merk, the text should read *eis ierousalem*, and not, as according to these authors, *ex ierousalem*, which is attested by *Alexandrinus* 33 syr^h sa bo^ar, the first copyist of Sinaiticus, 1938, 547, 1319, 2127, 1552. In spite of the wealth of manuscript evidence, we prefer, along with B.F. Westcott and F.J.A. Hort, the reading *eis* which is evidenced by *Sinaiticus-Vaticanus* syr^hmq, and the Byzantine tradition; A.C. Clark prefers to retain the reading *apo* on the basis of *Sinaiticus* (first hand?), 1175 D 181 431 1827, and many other Latin minuscles; it appears to be a good attempt at correcting the reading *ex*. The preference of *eis* to *ex* is based on the fact that *eis* is the more difficult reading. J. Dupont, however, has rejected the reading *eis*, (cfr. *Notes*, in *RB* 62, 1955, p. 50), but returns to the reading in *La Mission de Paul "à Jérusalem" (Act XII, 25)*, in *NT* 1 (1956), p. 303. Secondly, there is the problem of the meaning of the phrase. E. Haenchen, *Apostelgeschichte*, p. 57, retained the reading *eis*, but gave it the meaning of *en*, which it does have at times, and it belongs with the expression *plerosantes*. J. Dupont had reason to prefer to translate the preposition *eis* with the French equivalent "en faveur de" ("in behalf of"). Finally, S.

Giet preferred to render the expression *diakonia* of Acts 12,25 in its precise meaning of "collecting," whereas the expression *eis diakonian* in chapter 11 is given the meaning of "for help" (*au secours*), cfr. S. Giet, *Le second voyage de saint Paul à Jérusalem, Actes XI, 27-30; XII, 24-25*, in *RScR* 25 (1951), p. 267. J. Dupont preferred to retain the same meaning in both cases. S. Giet would understand the expression in the very broad sense of "being ready to carry out the apostolic ministry which would even include the various types of charitable works," cfr. *Nouvelle remarques sur les voyages de saint Paul à Jérusalem*, in *RScR* 31 (1957), p. 333.

29. P. Benoit, *La deuxième visite de saint Paul à Jèrusalem*, in *Bib* 40 (1959), pp. 778-792. For the same meaning, cfr. also G. Hoelscher, *Die Hohenpriesterliste bei Josephus und die evangelische Chronologie*, in *Sitzber. d. Heidelb. Akademie*, 1939-1946, 3 Abh., 1940, 17, n. 4; C. J. Cadoux, *art. cit.*, pp. 177-191.

30. P. Benoit, *art. cit.*, p. 779.

31. H. W. Beyer, *Die Apostelgeschichte*, (*Das Neue Test. Deutsch.*), 7th ed. (Göttingen: 1955), p. 78.

32. This is not the opinion of A. M. Tornos, *Kat' ekeinon de ton kairon en Act 12 1, y simultaneidad de Act 12 con Act 11, 27-30*, in *EstEc* 33 (1959), pp. 411-428, for whom Acts 12, 1 must be understood as having a meaning that is intentionally chronological. The voyage of Paul and of Barnabas must be temporarily related to the persecution of Herod. To arrive at this conclusion, the author investigated the Lucan transitions in the Gospel, and concluded that the transition themes were introduced with the use of copulative and adversative conjunctions, and not with expressions which in themselves are temporal. Against J. Dupont, who understood the expression *kat, ekeinon de kairon* as a thematic link (*La mission de Paul à Jérusalem*, in *NT* 1, 1956, p. 283), the author tried to prove that the expression has a temporal meaning because: a) in Greek, the term *kairos* always designates a well defined moment in time; b) of the 22 occurrences of the term in Luke, 20 such occurrences definitely have temporal nuances. However, we think that the study should take into account the first fifteen chapters of Acts, concerning chronology and the meaning of temporal notations. To base one's argument on transition passages limits the scope considerably. Moreover, upon reading the account of Paul's apostolate at Thessalonica, one would be tempted to think that Paul did not stay there more than a few weeks; upon careful examination, on the contrary, the interval of time actually involves many months, cfr. B. Rigaux, *Les Épîtres aux Thessaloniciens* (Paris: 1956), pp. 24-25. But to return to the question of the transition passage, the redactional formula "it was about this time" is still very vague. To what does it refer? It could very well envisage the entire period of activity of Barnabas and Paul at Antioch, or to the time of the prophecy of Agabus when Paul and Barnabas had departed for Jerusalem. The problem is

by far more complicated than one would suspect, since no one would make Barnabas and Paul remain in Jerusalem during the events surrounding the death of Herod. One journey over a long period of time and during the time of very important events could not be passed over in silence from what we know from Gal. 1-2. Moreover, we would return to the *Sachkritik* which offers a more certain field of operation.

33. Cfr. R. Liechtenhan, *Die beiden ersten Besuche des Paulus in Jerusalem*, in *Harnack-Ehrung* (Leipzig: 1921), pp. 51-61.

34. H. Schlier, *Der Brief an die Galater (Kritisch-exeg. Komm. über d. N.T. Meyer, 7 Abt.*, 10th ed., Göttingen: 1949), pp. 66-78. Reviewed by W. G. Kümmel, in *TRu* (new series) 17 (1948), p. 32; D. F. Robinson, *A Note on Acts 11, 27-30*, in *JBL* 63 (1944), pp. 169-172, summarized and reviewed by J. Dupont, *Les problèmes*, pp. 56-60. Robinson identified Gal. 1, 18 ff with Acts 11, 27-30 and the second visit.

35. This old-fashioned suggestion of Grotius is nothing more than a subterfuge.

36. S. Giet, *Les trois premiers voyages de saint Paul à Jérusalem*, in *RSR* 41 (1953), pp. 321-347; *Idem, Nouvelles remargues sur les voyages de saint Paul à Jérusalem*, in *RScR* 31 (1957), pp. 329-342; *Idem, Le second voyage de saint Paul à Jérusalem*, in *RScR* 25 (1951), pp. 265-269, and *Un procédé littéraire d'exposition: l'anticipation chronologique*, in *Rev. des études augustiniennes (Mémorial Bardy*, Paris: 1956), pp. 243-256.

37. J. Dupont, *Notes sur les Actes des Apôtres*, in *RB* 62 (1955), pp. 45-59; *Idem, La mission de Paul à Jérusalem (Actes XII, 25)*, in *NT* 1 (1956), pp. 275-303.

38. W. H. Ramsay A. Loisy, K. Th. Schäfer, A. Steinmann, J. Belser, and recently F. W. Beare, *The Sequence of Events in Acts 9-15 and the Career of Peter*, in *JBL* 62 (1943), pp. 259-306, who really constructs a fantastic chronology.

39. F. Sieffert, Th. Zahn, E. Preuschen, A. Oepke, Ph. Häuser, M. J. Lagrange, P. Bonnard, and many others who based their argument on *epeita* and *palin*. A. Puech, *Histoire de la littérature grecque chrétienne*, I (Paris: 1928), p. 187: "It is the only reasonable meaning that would fit the context." See also, A. v. Harnack, *Chronologische Berechnung des Tages von Damaskus*, in *Sitzungsb. der Königlich Preussischen Ak. d.Wissensch.*, (Berlin: 1912), p. 676.

40. M. Goguel, *Introduction au N.T.*, IV, 1 (Paris: 1925), p. 98. The argument that is advanced by many in favor of computing the fourteen years from the time of the conversion is that Paul was deeply concerned about presenting a number which would make the greatest impression possible. However, such reasoning is nothing more than hypothetical, and there is nothing in the text to prove it. The expression, *epeita* and *palin* otherwise appear to be ample evidence.

41. J. B. Lightfoot, *St. Paul's Epistle to the Galatians* (London: 1902), pp. 123-126; H. Schlier, *Der Brief an die Galater*, p. 76. See also *B. Reicke, Der geschichtliche Hintergrund des Apostelkonzils und der Antiochia Episode. Ga* 2, 1-14, in *Studia Paulina* (Haarlem: 1953), pp. 180-182.

42. M. Dibelius, *Das Apostelkonzil*, in *TLZ* 72 (1947), pp. 193-198, reprinted in *Aufsätze zur Apostelgeschichte* (Göttingen: 1951), pp. 84-90; W. G. Kümmel, *Das Urchristentum*, p. 32. It would be worthwhile also to consult such theses as H. Sahlin, *Der Messias und das Gottesvolk. Studien zur protolukanischen Theologie*, (*Acta Seminarii Neotestamentici Upsaliensis*, 12, Uppsala: 1945); *Idem, Studien zum dritten Kapitel des Lukasevangeliums*, in *Uppsala Universitets Aorsskrift*, 2 (Uppsala: 1949), according to which Acts 11, 17-20 is an interpolation without any historical foundation. Paul was deceitfully involved in the history of the Council, which was held before the time of the first missionary journey, and Gal. 2 relates itself to facts which properly belong to a later period. On the contrary, A. v. Harnack, *Die Apostelgeschichte* (Leipzig: 1908), pp. 134-140, maintained that Acts 11, 19-20 and 12, 25 -15,35 originated from an Antiochian source, and must be understood as two journeys, separated by the first missionary campaign of chapters 13-14.

43. J. Porter, *The "Apostolic Decree" and Pauls' Second Visit to Jerusalem*, in *JTS* 47 (1946), pp. 169-174.

44. Ch. H. Buck, *The Collection for the Saints*, in *HTR* 43 (1950), pp. 1-29.

45. This is the opinion of S. Lyonnet, *Les Épîtres de saint Paul aux Galates, aux Romains*, in *SBJ*, 2nd ed. (Paris: 1959), p. 13. Already in Chrysostom, *Comment. ad Gal.* 2, 1 *ff.*, in *PG*, 61,633. J. Weiss, *Das Urchristentum* (Göttingen: 1947) p. 147 in the footnote; A. Wikenhauser, *Die Apostelgeschichte* 3rd ed., (Ratisbonne: 1956), pp. 136-138 (with some hesitation); G. Ricciotti, *Paolo Apostolo* (Rome: 1946), p. 151 Eng. tr. *Paul the Apostle* (Bruce: 1961); one German author, V. Weber, who was extremely interested in these matters, maintained this thesis even in the year 1912; see also S. Giet, *Les trois premiers voyages de saint Paul*, p. 336.

46. Dom Bernard Orchard split the difference: *Ac XV: A New Solution of the Galatians Problem*, in *BJRL* 28 (1944), pp. 154-174; *Idem, The Problem of Acts and Galatians*, in *CBQ* 7 (1945), pp. 377-397. The learned author distinguished between a first visit according to Gal. 2, 1-2, and a second according to Gal. 2, 6-10. See a refutation of this position in P. Benoit, *La deuxième visite de saint Paul à Jérusalem*, in *Bib* 40 (1959), p. 779, note 3.

47. This is the opinion of W. M. Ramsay, *St. Paul the Traveller and Roman Citizen*, 14th ed., (London: 1920), XXII, XXXI, 116 ff.; V. Weber, *Die Abfassung des Galaterbriefs vor dem Apostelkonzil* (Ratisbonne: 1900), pp. 377 ff.; *Idem, Die antiochenische Kollekte* (Würzburg: 1917); D. Plooij, *op.cit.*, pp. 129-140; F. F. Bruce, *The Acts*

of the Apostles 2nd ed., (London: 1952), pp. 38, 241; F. C. Burkitt, *Christian Beginnings* (London: 1924), pp. 116 ff.; C. W. Emmet, *Beginnings of Christianity,* II, pp. 265 ff., and for the time being, K. Lake, *Earlier Epistles of Paul* (London: 1911), pp. 297 ff.; W. Michaelis, *Einleitung in das Neue Testament,* 2nd ed., (Berne: 1954), p. 135; E. Osty, *Les Épîtres de saint Paul* (Paris: 1945), pp. 146-148; F. Amiot, *Saint Paul, Épître aux Galates, Épîtres aux Thessaloniciens* (*Verbum Salutis,* 14, Paris: 1946), pp. 31-32.

48. W. Manson, *St. Paul in Ephesus: 2. The Problem of the Epistle to the Galatians,* in *BJRL* 24 (1940), pp. 58-80. The system of two conferences is also admitted by S. Giet, *L'assemblée apostolique et le décret de Jérusalem. Qui était Siméon?* in *RSR* 39 (1951), pp. 203-220; the first is recorded in Acts 15, 1-12; the second, with the participation of Simeon Niger, (Acts 13, 11) is related in 15, 13-33.

49. This clashes with the evident fact that Paul encountered an important Christian community in Damascus which was well organized.

50. A. Oepke, *Der Brief des Paulus an die Galater,* (*Theologischer Handkommentar zum N.T.,* 9, Leipzig: 1937); J. B. Lightfoot, *St. Paul's Epistle to the Galatians* (London: 1902), pp. 123-128; O. Bauernfeind, *Die Apostelgeschichte,* 5 (Leipzig: 1939); J. Klausner, *From Jesus to Paul,* English translation by W. F. Stinespring (London: 1946); H. Katzenmayer, *Das sogennante Apostelkonzil von Jerusalem,* in *Internationale kirchliche Zeitschrift,* new series, 31 (1941), pp. 149-157; J. Jeremias, *Untersuchungen zum Quellenproblem der Apostelgeschichte,* in *ZNW* 36 (1937), pp. 205-221. Jeremias dates the Council to the year 49 A.D. and prior to the first missionary journey. Since Paul was in Corinth in the year 51, where did he stay? Jeremias varied his opinion. In *Sabbatjahr und neutestamentliche Chronologie,* in *ZNW* 27 (1928), p. 101, he dated the Council after the first missionary journey. Actually, he tried to demonstrate that the Council was anterior to the first missionary journey by comparing Gal. 1,21 with Acts 15,23. After the letter to the Galatians, during the years which preceded the Council, Paul had visited only Syria and Cilicia, and after Acts 15, 23, at the time of the Council, there were no other Christian communities except at Antioch, in Syria, and in Cilicia, since Christianity had not as yet reached Cyprus and Asia Minor. This opinion had already been defended by J. Jüngst, *Die Quellen der Apg* (Gotha: 1895); in order to set up the chronology, Jüngst did not hesitate to invert the order 15,1-35 and 11, 27-30 and 12,25. According to O. Pfleiderer, *Das Urchristentum,* I, 2nd ed., (Berlin: 1902), the account of the collection in 11, 27-30 and 12,25 is fictitious; rather it is at this point that the Council must have been held.

51. Those authors who upheld this viewpoint are cited in the following two notes. On chapter 15 of the Acts, see the introduction of J. Dupont, *Actes des Apôtres* (*SBJ*), 2nd ed., (Paris: 1958), p. 135.

52. The two accounts in Acts. 11 and Acts. 15 are parallel. The com-

piler did not indicate that the two sources are actually describing the same event: J. Wellhausen, *Noten zur Apostelgeschichte*, in *Nachr. d. Gött. Ges. d. Wiss. Phil. Hist. Kl.*, (1907), pp. 7-9; *Idem*, *Kritische Analyse der Apostelgeschichte* (Berlin: 1914), pp. 21-22, 30; E. Schwartz, *Zur Chronologie des Paulus*, in *Nach. d. Gött. Ges. d. Wiss. Phil. hist. Kl.* (1907), pp. 267 ff.; P. Wendland, *Die urchristlichen Literaturformen*, 3rd ed., (Tübingen: 1912), pp. 317-321; E. Preuschen, *Die Apostelgeschichte* (Tübingen: 1912), pp. 75 f., and 91-93; W. Bousset, *Der Gebrauch des Kyriostitels als Kriterium für die Quellenscheidung in der ersten Hälfte der Apostelgeschichte*, in *ZNW* 15 (1914), pp. 157-162; A. Loisy, *Les Actes des Apôtres* (Paris: 1920), pp. 474 and 509; E. Meyer, *Ursprung und Anfänge des Christentums* (Stuttgart, Berlin: 1923), pp. 165-196; A. Mentz, *Die Zusammenkunft der Apostel in Jerusalem und die Quellen der Apg*, in *ZNW* 18 (1917-1918), pp. 177-195; R. Bultmann, *RGG*, 4 , 2nd ed., (1930), 1023; E. Barnikol, *Die vorchristliche und frühchristliche Zeit des Paulus*; *die drei Jerusalemreisen des Paulus*, in *ZKG*, new series, 12 (1930), p. 91; P.G.S. Hopwood, *The Religious Experience of the Primitive Church* (Edinburgh: 1936), pp. 271-272; F. Jackson and K. Lake, *Beginnings of Christianity*, 5 (1933), pp. 195-204; *Idem, Introduction in the New Testament* (London: 1938), p. 81; G. Hoelscher, *Die Hohenpriesterliste bei Josephus und die evangelische Chronologie*, in *Sitzungsber. der Heid. Akad. d. Wiss. Phil. hist. Kl.* (1939-1940), pp. 3, 25; J. Jeremias, *Untersuchungen zum Quellenproblem des Apostelgeschichte*, in *ZNW* 33 (1937), pp. 213-221; P. Bonnard, *L'Épître de saint Paul aux Galates* (Neuchâtel: 1933), pp. 47-48; L. Cerfaux, *Le chapitre XV du Livre des Actes à la lumière de la littérature ancienne*, in *Recueil. L. Cerfaux* (Gembloux: 1954), pp. 105-124; E. Trocmé, *Le "Livre des Actes" et l'histoire* (Paris: 1957), pp. 157-163; P. Benoit, *La deuxième visite de saint Paul à Jérusalem*, in *Bib* 40 (1959), pp. 778-792, who distinguished between three sources, and roughly follows the line of J. Weiss. See also M. H. Shepherd, *A Venture in the Source Analysis of Acts*, in *Munera Studiosa*, ed. by M. H. Shepherd and S. E. Johnson (Cambridge: 1946), pp. 91-105. In his opinion, Acts 11,28 = Acts 15 = Gal. 2, and the two missionary journeys are really no more than one (13-14 = 16-18). Furthermore, he maintained that there are actually three sources; the Palestinian source has Peter as the central figure; the Hellenistic source is concerned with personalities; and the Lucan source has Paul as the figurehead. The redactor of the collection used these sources and fused them into a superior unit.

53. J. Weiss, *Das Urchristentum* (Göttingen: 1917), pp. 195 ff. Eng. tr. *Earliest Christianity*: *A.D.* 30-150 (Torchbks 53 and 54, Harper) and (Peter Smith: 1959); M. Goguel, *Introduction*, 2 (Paris: 1922), pp. 240 ff.; E. Hirsch, *Petrus und Paulus. Ein Gespräch mit Hans Lietzmann*, in *ZNW* 29 (1930), pp. 64 ff.; H. Waitz, *Das Problem des*

sog. Aposteldekrets und die damit zusammenhängender literarischen und geschichtlichen Probleme des Apostolischen Zeitalters, in *Zeitschr. f. Kirchengeschichte* 55 (1936), pp. 227-263.

54. W. G. Kümmel, *Das Urchristentum,* in *TRu* 17 (1948), p. 30: "The hypothesis of interpolation or collaboration of sources in Acts 15 rests on very weak foundations." *Idem,* in *TRu* 22 (1954), p. 207: "The entire hypothesis is completely indemonstrable and therefore not at all persuasive, and one could very well ask the fruitless question, namely, what benefit such an arbitrary construction should have for historical knowledge."

55. J. Knox, an American, presented his views in *Fourteen Years Later: A Note on the Pauline Chronology,* in *JRel* 16 (1936), pp. 341-349; *Idem, The Pauline Chronology,* in *JBL* 58 (1939), pp. 15-29; *Chapters in a Life of Paul* (New York: 1950), pp. 47-88. His thesis was taken up again by D. W. Riddle, *Paul, Man of Conflict. A Modern Biographical Sketch,* pp. 14-19, 76-79, Appendices I and II; Ch. H. Buck, *The Date of Galatians,* in *JBL* 70 (1951), pp. 113-122; R. W. Funck, *The Enigma of the Famine Visit,* in *JBL* 75 (1956), pp. 130-136.

56. To the contrary, cfr. C. J. Cadoux, *A Tentaive Synthetic Chronology of the Apostolic Age,* in *JBL* 66 (1937), p. 185; G. Ogg, *A New Chronology of St. Paul's Life,* in *ExpT* 64 (1952-1953), pp. 120-123; E. Trocmé, *Le Livre des Actes,* p. 93, n. 1; F. W. Beare, *The Sequence of Events in Acts 9-15 and the Career of Peter,* in *JBL* 52 (1943), pp. 195-306; *Idem, Note on Paul's First two Visits to Jerusalem,* in *JBL* 63 (1944), pp. 407-409; K. Thieme, *Le plan des "Actes des Apôtres" et la chronologie de son contenu,* in *DViv* 26 (1954), pp. 127-133; C. H. Buck, *The Collection for the Saints,* in *AnglTR* 48 (1950), pp. 1-29.

57. Th. Zahn, *Zur Lebensgeschichte des Apostels Paulus,* in *NKZ* 15 (1904), pp. 189-195; *Idem, Einleitung,* 3rd ed., pp. 2,6; W. M. Ramsay, *The Bearing of Recent Discoveries on the Trustworthiness of the New Testament* (London: 1914), pp. 150-172; *Idem, The Family and Religion of L. Sergius Paulus, Proconsul of Cyprus,* in *ExpT* 29 (1917-1918), pp. 324-328; F. Jackson and K. Lake, *op.cit.,* V, pp. 455-459; D. Plooij, *op.cit.,* pp. 21-26; A. Wikenhauser, *Einleitung,* pp. 338-341.

58. L. Palma de Cesnola, *Cyprus, its Ancient Cities, Tombs and Temples* (London: 1877), pp. 424-425, German edition by L. Stern (Jena: 1879).

59. D. G. Hogarth, *Devia Cypria* (London: 1889), p. 114. See the text in D. Plooij, *op.cit.,* p. 23; F. Jackson and K. Lake, *op.cit.,* V, p. 456.

60. J. B. Lightfoot, *Essays on the Work entitled Supernatural Religion* (London: 1899), pp. 291-297.

61. Th. Mommsen, *Die Rechtsverhältnisse des Apostels Paulus,* in *ZNW* 2 (1901), pp. 81 ff.

62. Deductions by W. M. Ramsay, *The Bearing of Recent Discoveries*

(London: 1914), pp. 150 ff., that Sergius Paula, daughter of the Proconsul, became a Christian, as well as his son, C. Caristanius Fronto, a member of an important family in Antioch of Pisidia, are purely conjectural. Unfortunately, they have been accepted by F. F. Bruce, *The Acts of the Apostles*, 2nd ed. (London: 1952), p. 256.

63. *CIL*, VI, 4, 2, 3116 number 31545.

64. Pliny, *Natural History*, I, Cfr. F. Jackson and K. Lake, *op.cit.*, V, p. 428.

65. The western text differs considerably from the Alexandrian text, but it does not shed any additional light on our subject.

66. Suetonius, *Claudius*, 25, 4.

67. Tacitus, *Annals*, XV, 44.

68. Cassius Dio, *Historia Romanorum*, 60, 6, 6.

69. Cassius Dio, *Historia Romanorum*, 57, 18.

70. E. Haenchen, *Die Apostelgeschichte*, p. 58.

71. F. Jackson and K. Lake, *The Beginnings*, V, 6, 459.

72. M. J. Lagrange, *Épître aux Romains* (Paris: 1950), pp. xxi-xxii. cfr. S. Lyonnet, *Quaestiones in Epistolam ad Romanos*, series I (Rome: 1955).

73. O. Holtzmann, *Neutestamentliche Zeitgeschichte* (Freiburg: 1895), p. 127., followed by M. Goguel, *Introduction au Nouveau Testament*, 4, 1, 101, who has pointed out the development of Claudius with regard to the Jews. F. Jackson and K. Lake, *The Beginnings*, V, p. 460, enumerated a series of interventions on the part of the Emperor in the course of the second half of his sojourn, of such a character as to be anti-oriental.

74. Orosius, *Historia contra Paganos*, VII, 6, 15.

75. A. v. Harnack, *Chronologische Berechnung des Tages von Damas kus*, in *Sitzungsberichte der königl. Preussischen Akad. der Wissenschaft*, 2 (1912), pp. 675-676. Cfr. D. Plooij, *op.cit.*, pp. 45-48; A. Wikenhauser, *op.cit.*, pp. 323 ff.; F. Jackson and K. Lake, *Beginnings*, V, pp. 459-460; E. Haenchen, *Die Apostelgeschichte*, pp. 60-64.

76. Cfr. A.v. Harnack, *Geschichte der altchristlichen Literatur*, II, p. 1; *Die Chronologie des Altchristlichen Literatur bis Eusebius*, II (Leipzig: 1897), pp. 239-243; E. Schürer, *Geschichte des jüdischen Volkes*, I, 4th ed. (Leipzig: 1901) pp. 570-571 and Eng. tr. *History of the Jewish People in the Time of Jesus*, I Scribner), pp. 185-186; Th. Zahn, *Einleitung*, 2 (1907), pp. 647-652; D. Plooij, *op.cit.*, pp. 49-72; J. Wellhausen, *Noten zur Apostelgeschichte*, pp. 8-9; E. Meyer, *Ursprung und Anfänge des Christentums*, 3 (1923), pp. 44-48; F. Jackson and K. Lake, *Beginnings*, V (1933), pp. 464-474; E. Haenchen, *Die Apostelgeschichte*, pp. 60-64; M. Goguel, *Introduction au N.T.*, 4, 1 (Paris: 1925), pp. 107-115.

77. D. Petavius, *De doctrina temporum* (Venice: 1757), XI, 11-12, 276; F. X. Patricius, *In Evangelia* (Freiburg: 1852), I, 64-70; *Idem, In Actus* (Rome: 1867), X; V. Weber, *Kritische Geschichte der Exegese des neunten Kapitels des Römerbriefes* (Würzburg: 1899), al-

though he changed his opinion in *Die Abfassung des Galaterbriefs vor dem Apostelkonzil* (Ravensburg: 1900), p. 389; H. Kellner, *Jesus von Nazareth und seine Apostel* (Ratisbonne: 1908), pp. 159-165; O. Holtz- mann, *Neutestamentliche Zeitgeschichte* (1895), pp. 128-145; A.v. Har- nack, *Chronologie des altchristl. Lit.*, I (Leipzig: 1897), pp. 233-238; E. Schwartz, *Zur Chronologie des Paulus* (Göttinger Nachrichten, 1907), pp. 263-291; A. Loisy, *Actes des Apôtres* (Paris: 1920), pp. 868 ff.; F. Jackson and K. Lake, *The Beginnings*, V pp. 445-471; E. Haenchen, *Die Apostelgeschichte*, pp. 60-64.

78. In favor of the year 59: M. W. Ramsay, *A Fixed Date in the Life of St. Paul*, in *Exp* 5, series 3 (1896), pp. 336-345; M. Goguel, *Essai sur la chronologie paulinienne*, in *RHR* 65 (1912), pp. 285-339; *In- troduction*, IV, 1, pp. 307, 387; F. Prat, *La chronologie de l'âge apos- tolique*, in *RSR* 3 (1912), pp. 372-392; D. Plooij, *op.cit.*, p. 174; E. Jacquier, *Actes* (1926), CCLXXXVIII-CCCV.

In favor of the year 60: Th. Zahn, *Einleitung*, 3rd ed., I, p. 315; E. Schürer, *op.cit.*, I, 3rd ed., pp. 577-578. Schürer shows why, in this case, the authority of Eusebius cannot be invoked because Eusebius indulges at this point in a conjecture. A. Brassac. *Une inscription de Delphes et la Chronologie de saint Paul*, in *RB*, new series, 10 (1913), pp. 207-208; E. Schürer, *Zur Chronologie des Lebens Pauli*, pp. 21-42.

In favor of the year 61: C. Clemen, *Paulus*, I (Giessen: 1904), pp. 386-387; E. Meyer, *op.cit.*, pp. 3, 53.

Finally, it should be mentioned that H. H. Wendt, *Apostelgeschichte*, 9th ed. (Göttingen: 1913), has not decided between 59 and 60, where- as H. Lietzmann, in *ZWT* 53 (1911), p. 351, preferred to go back to the years 57-58.

79. Acts 24,27: *Dietías dè plerotheíses élaben diádochon ho Phêlix Pór- kion Phêston*. Petavius, J. Wellhausen, E. Schwartz, K. Lake, and E. Haenchen understood this statement to mean that Felix was re- moved after a ten-year period. Most commentators would realize the expression *dietía* to Paul's stay at Caesarea. E. Haenchen would ad- mit that Luke had intended to say that Paul remained for ten yers, but that his source had attributed the expression *dietia* to Felix. There is no reason to hesitate when one must choose be- tween Luke's interpretation and the literary criticism of Haenchen. To be noted is the fact that the learned commentator has the con- sistent tendency to sacrifice the historical value of Luke. There are no theologians who have the power to dictate dogmas. Cfr. M. Go- guel, *Essai sur la chronologie paulinienne*, p. 329.

80. The *Chronicle* (ed. by A. Schoene, 2 vol., 1866-1875) has been trans- lated from the Armenian by J. Karst, *GCS*, 20 (1911); the translation of Jerome was edited by R. Helm, *GCS*, 24, 34, 2 vol. (1913- 1926); and in one volume, *GCS*, 47 (1956). See the assembled texts in D. Plooij, *op.cit.*, pp. 52-56.

81. Eusebius, *Chronicle*, 5, 215.

82. C. Erbes, *Die Todestage des Ap. Paulus und Petrus und ihre römis-chen Denkmäler*, (*Texte und Unters.*, new series, IV, 1, Leipzig: 1899), pp. 26-27; D. Plooij, *op.cit.*, pp. 57-61.

83. F. Jackson and K. Lake, *Beginnings*, V, pp. 472-473.

84. Cfr. E. Schürer, *Zur Chronologie des Lebens Pauli*, pp. 210-242.

85. This is also the conclusion of E. Haenchen, *op.cit.*, p. 59, n. 1.

86. Tacitus, *Annals*, XII, 54. If one were to take Tacitus literally, — Felix was long since imposed on Judaea — then one could say that Felix had been Procurator in Syria before the year 52. But this would contradict Josephus, who has Tiberius Alexander succeed Felix in the year 52 (*Ant. Iud.*, 20, 103). All speculation concerning the sources of Tacitus and how he used them badly is subjective and fruitless. Cfr. Ed. Meyer, *op.cit.*, p. 48, and E. Haenchen, *op.cit.*, pp. 61-62.

87. E. Haenchen, *op.cit.*, p. 61.

88. Josephus, *Bell.Iud.*, 2, 232-246; *Ant.Iud.*, 20, 118-136.

89. Josephus, *Ant.Iud.*, 20, 182.

90. Tacitus, *Annals*, XIII, 14-15.

91. Suetonius, *Claudius*, 27.

92. Tacitus, *Annals*, XXV, 2: "*biennio*" is the reading of *Mediceus al-ter* "*triennio*," that of *Freinsheim*. H. Goelzer accepts the latter reading in his edition of Tacitus (Paris: 1938), II, p. 324. This would correspond to the birth of Britannicus on February 13th, 41 A.D., and his fourteen years to February 13th, 55 A.D. However, this would not help the calculation, because Nero became Emperor on October 13th, 54 A.D.

93. Suetonius, *Claudius*, 28.

94. Josephus, *Ant.Iud.*, 20, 141; Acts 24,24.

95. Josephus, *Ant.Iud.*, 20, 160-166.

96. Josephus, *Ant. Iud.*, 20, 160-166; *Bell. Iud.*, 2, 254-257.

97. Josephus, *Bell. Iud.*, 13, 261-263; *Ant. Iud.*, 20, 167-172, Cfr. Acts 21, 38.

98. Josephus, *Ant. Iud.*, 20, 266-270; *Bell. Iud.*, 2, 173-178.

99. Josephus, 3. He made the trip to Rome at the age of twenty-seven, and Josephus was born between September 13th, 37 and March 15th, 38 A.D.

100 Josephus, *Bell. Iud.*, 2, 266-270.

101. Tacitus, *Annals*, 12, 54.

102. Cfr. E. Trocmé, *Le "Livre des Actes" et l'histoire* (Paris: 1957), pp. 86-98.

103. *Translator's note*: cfr. T. Corbishley, *The Chronology of New Testa-ment Times*, in *A Catholic Commentary on Holy Scripture* (New York: 1953), sections 676b-d, for the more probable date as 33 A.D. Also George Ogg, *The Chronology of the Public Ministry of Jesus* (Cam-bridge University Press: 1940) has some value. A. van den Born, *Bijbels Woordenboek*, 2nd revised ed. (1954-1957), in English trans-lation by L. Hartman, *Encyclopedic Dictionary of the Bible* (McGraw-

Hill, New York: 1963), "Jesus Christ", especially col. 1148, and bibliography in col. 1156; for the year 30, see W. J. Harrington, *Record of the Fulfillment: The New Testament* (Chicago: 1965), pp. 42-44.

104. *Mishna*, Aboth, V. 21.

105. A. v. Harnack, *Chronologische Berechnung*, pp. 677-682.

106. See J. Ricciotti, *Paolo Apostolo* (Rome: 1946), p. 148.

107. Concerning the question of the sources for this passage, cfr. E. Haenchen, *Die Apostelgeschichte*, pp. 253-258.

108. Cfr. J. Nasrallah, *Souvenirs de saint Paul* (*Les souvenirs chrétiens de Damas*, Harissa: 1954).

109. The items which Luke presents are often inexact: two Sabbaths at Iconium (Acts 14,3); the departure from Lystra the day after the stoning (Acts 14,20); a rather lengthy stay at Antioch (Acts 14, 28); three Sabbaths at Thessalonica (Acts 17, 2); in the last instance, the allusion to the preaching in the Synagogue would be the only event intended.

110. It would be difficult to decide whether that year has any relation to the departure for Jerusalem (Acts 11,30), or to the missionary journey (Acts 13,2-3). For those who would hold that there were two trips to Jerusalem, then the second alternate would have to be chosen.

111. Luke emphasized the prolongation of the sojourn at Iconium (Acts 14, 3); which would agree with the idea that he had intended to indicate a period of many months. Cfr. M. F. Unger, *Pisidian Antioch and Gospel Penetration of the Greek World*, in *BS* 118 (1961), pp. 46-53; *Idem, Archaeology and Paul's Visit to Iconium, Lystra and Derbe, ibid.*, pp. 107-112; *Idem, Archaeology and Paul's Tour of Cyprus, ibid.*, 117 (1960), pp. 229-233.

112. W. A. McDonald, *Archaeology and St. Paul's Journey in Greek Lands*, in *BA* 3 (1940), pp. 18-24; 4 (1941), p. 110; 5 (1942), pp. 36-48; Cfr. M. J. Suggs, *Concerning the Date of Paul's Macedonian Ministry*, in *NT* 4 (1960), pp. 60-68.

113. See above, "Gallio at Corinth."

114. M. M. Parvis, *Archaeology and St. Paul's Journey in Greek Lands, IV Ephesus*, in *BA* 8 (1945), pp. 61-73; F. V. Filson, *Ephesus and the New Testament, ibid.*, pp. 73-80.

115. S. Nikolaides, *Paul en Macédoine orientale*, in *Paulus-Hellas Oikumene. An Ecumenical Symposium* (Athens: 1951), pp. 146-160; A. Donkers, *Paulus' sporen in Griekenland*, in *Hermeneus* 23 (Zwolle: 1951), pp. 48-51; H. Metzger, *Les routes de saint Paul dans l'Orient chrétien* (Neuchâtel: 1954); O. Broneels, *Studies in the Topography of Corinth at the Time of St. Paul*, in *Archaiologike Ephemeris* (1937), pp. 125 ff.

116. C. Sant, *La data del naufragio de S. Paulo*, in *Lucerna* 2 (Malta: 1955), pp. 45-49, 52 f.

117. M. Miguens, *Pablo prisionero*, in *FrLA* 8 (1957-1958), pp. 5-112.

Concerning Paul's trial, cfr. F. R. M. Hitchcock, *The Trials of St. Paul and Apollonius*, in *Herm* 75 (1950), pp. 24-34; *Idem, On what Charge was St. Paul Beheaded, ibid.*, 77 (1951), pp. 25-36.

118. L. P. Pherigo, *Paul's Life after the Close of Acts*, in *JBL* 69 (1951), pp. 276-284; V. Capocci, *Sulla tradizione del martirio di S. Paolo alle Acque Salvie*, in *SBN* 8 (1953), pp. 11-19; E. Kirschbaum, *Die Gräber der Apostelfürsten* (Freiburg: 1957); cfr. H. Schade, *Die Gräber der Apostelfürsten*, in *SZ* 162 (1958), pp. 223-227.

Notes to Chapter V

1. Concerning the authenticity of 1-2 Thes., cfr. B. Rigaux, *Les Épîtres aux Thessaloniciens*, pp. 112-152, with bibliography; D. Guthrie, *The New Testament Introduction*, in *The Pauline Epistles* (London: 1961), pp. 182-190.

2. W. Wrede, *Die Echtheit des 2 Thessalonicherbriefs untersucht*, (*Texte und Unters.*, new series 9,2, Leipzig: 1903).

3. A. Wikenhauser, *Einleitung in das N.T.*, 3rd ed. (Freiburg: 1959), pp. 263-264, Eng. tr. *N.T. Introd.*

4. R. Bultmann, *Theologie des N.T.* (Tübingen: 1953), p. 476, Eng. tr. *Theology of the N.T.* (Scribner), H. J. Schoeps, *Paulus*, p. 44, Eng. tr. *Paul*.

5. Cfr. Ch. Masson, *Les deux Épîtres de saint Paul aux Thessaloniciens* (Neuchâtel: 1957).

6. See my review of Ch. Masson, in *RB* 65 (1958), pp. 275-277.

7. H. Braun (*Zur nachpaulinischen Herkunft des zweiten Thessalonicherbriefs*, in *ZNW* 44, 1952-1953, pp. 152-156) did not offer anything new. He simply took up again those theological considerations which concluded to a different viewpoint between the two letters; G. Bornkamm, art. *Paulus*, in *RGG*, 3rd ed., V, p. 167, rejected the second letter to the Thessalonians together with the other deutero-Pauline compositions; A. Strobel, *Untersuchungen zum eschatologischen Verzögerungsproblem*, in *SupplNT* 2 (Leiden-Cologne: 1961), pp. 110-116, defended the authenticity of 2 Thes.

8. E. Percy, *Die Probleme der Kol. - und Ephes.-Briefe* (Lund: 1946). See also J. Schmid, *Der Epheserbrief des Apostels Paulus. Seine Adresse, Sprache und literarische Beziehungen untersucht*, in *BST* 22, 3-4 (Freiburg: 1928), and P. Benoit, art. *Paul. Épître aux Colossiens*, in *DBS* 36 (1961), pp. 157-170 (bibliography).

9. P. Wendland, *Die urchristlichen Literaturformen*, 2nd-3rd ed., (Tübingen: 1912), pp. 363-364.

10. R. Bultmann, *ThWNT*, II, p. 529, in Eng. tr.

11. R. Reitzenstein, *Nachrichten von der Gesellschaft der Wissenschaften zu Göttingen*, in *Phil.-hist. Klasse* (1916), p. 393.

12. E. Käsemann, *Leib und Leib Christi* (Tübingen: 1933), p. 138, note 2. In his work, *Eine urchristliche Taufliturgie* in *Festschrift R. Bultmann* (Stuttgart: 1949), pp. 133-148, the author hoped to

discover in Col. 1, 15-20 a pre-Christian hymn in honor of the gnostic redeemer.

13. G. Bornkamm, *Die Häresie des Kolosserbriefes*, in *TLZ* 73 (1948), pp. 11-20, as compared with *Das Ende des Gesetzes*, in *Paulus-studien, Gesammelte Aufsätze*, I (Munich: 1958), p. 139, note 1. He admits that its source is the "Pauline School."

14. Ch. Masson, *L'Épître de saint Paul aux Colossiens* (Neuchâtel: 1950), p. 86 — the remainder and development of an early letter by Paul to the Colossians by the author of the letter to the Ephesians.

15. P. N. Harrison, *Onesimus and Philemon*, in *AnglTR* 32, p. 268-294; 1, 15-25 and 4,8-20-23 are the only passages on which there is disagreement, together with the problem of dating Paul's imprisonment.

16. J. Schoeps, *Paulus*, p. 44.

17. E. Percy, *Die Probleme*, p. 6.

18. C.F.D. Moule, *The Epistles of Paul the Apostle to the Colossians and to Philemon* (*Cambridge Greek Testament Commentary*, Cambridge: 1957), p. 13.

19. E. R. Goodenhough, *Paul and Onesimus*, in *HTR* 22 (1929), pp. 181ff.

20. H.J. Holtzmann, *Kritik der Epheser und Kolosserbriefe* (Leipzig: 1872).

21. F. Hitzig, *Zur Kritik paulinischer Briefe* (Leipzig: 1870); H. von Soden, in *Jahrbücher für protestantische Theologie*, II (1885), pp. 320 ff., 497 ff., 672 ff (he reduced the number of interpolations).

22. W. Bieder, *Die Kolossische Irrlehre und die Kirche von heute*, in *ThS* 33 (Zollikon-Zurich: 1952); J. Knox, in *TZ* 8 (1952), pp. 137-143.

23. H. Chadwick, "*All Things to all Men*" (1Cor. 9,22), in *NTS* 1 (1954-1955), pp. 261-295; cfr. P. Benoit, *Corps, tête et plérôme dans les épîtres de la Captivité*, in *RB* 63 (1956), pp. 5-54, reprint in *Exégèse et Théologie* 2, pp. 107-153. For the same interpretation, see F. F. Bruce, *Commentary on the Epistle to the Colossians* (London: 1957), pp. 170-173.

24. F. C. Synge, *Philippians and Colossians* (*The Torch Bible*, London: 1951), pp. 51-57.

25. J. Coutts, *The Relationship of Ephesians and Colossians*, in *NTS* 4 (1957-1958), pp. 201-207.

26. D. Guthrie, *New Testament Introduction*, in *The Pauline Epistles*, pp. 99-128, gave a good presentation of the pros and cons for the authenticity of the letter to the Ephesians. He concluded in favor of a vigorous defense of the authenticity. His method of argumentation was often directed against the opinion which supposes a forger who operated at the end of the first century. In one note on p. 128, he examined the hypothesis concerning the *amanuensis*, who supposedly had composed the letter to the Ephesians, and noted the following difficulties: 1) the disciple would have had access only with great difficulty to all Pauline epistles with which the letter to the Ephesians would have had contact; 2) his work would not have reflected the same kind of literary relation with the letter to

the Colossians — certainly, the literary relationship would have been much more confined; 3) with great difficulty he would have enlarged the moral passages as they occur in Ephesians; 4) such an hypothesis does not take into account the references which the author makes to himself in the letter; 5) it would be difficult to find a reason why the Apostle would have adopted such an outmoded method. We would like to make the further observation that D. Guthrie's note used a method of reasoning which could be criticized by those who would rally for unauthenticity: 1) we do not know to which letters the disciple would have had access. We do know that the letter to the Ephesians, more than any other letter, contains numerous parallels as far as eight authentic letters are concerned; 2) why could he not have actually depended on the letter to the Colossians to a great extent? Such would depend on his choice of a literary form. If an explanation is necessary, then it must be done in terms of dependence; 3) If Paul had commissioned a disciple, we would have no idea concerning the terms of the commission. He could have allowed the disciple to speak as he himself had done in his letter to the Colossians. What is striking is that in those sections in which he does speak of himself, the author depends heavily on the contents of the letter to the Colossians; 4) if it would have been a question of limiting the freedom of choosing a form other than that of the other epistles, then the disciple could have done just as good a job as Paul himself. Without keeping in mind what was said in Col. 3, 7-8, just how could the author have resumed the same vocabulary to compose the lengthy encomium concerning Tychicus (Eph.6, 21-22)? Cfr. the excellent explanation of P. Benoit, art., *Paul, Éphésiens (Épître aux)*, in *DBS* 36 (1961), pp. 195-211.

27. H. J. Holtzmann, *op.cit.*, together with G.H.A. Ewald, K. Holsten, A. Hilgenfeld, K. Weizsäcker, A. Klöpper, W. Wrede, J. Weiss, W. Bousset, E. Norden, P. Wendland, R. Reitzenstein, H. von Soden, H. Weinel, J. Moffat, *An Introduction to the Literature of the New Testament*, 3rd ed. (Edinburgh: 1918), pp. 373-395.

28. M. Goguel, *Esquiss d'une solution noubelle du problème de l'épître aux Éphésiens*, in *RHR* 111 (1935), pp. 254-284; 112 (1936), pp. 73-94; E. J. Goodspeed, *The Meaning of Ephesians* (Chicago: 1933); *Idem, The Key to Ephesians* (Chicago: 1956); *Idem, Ephesians and the First Edition of Paul*, in *JBL* 70 (1951), pp. 285-291, and in his book *Paul* (Philadelphia: 1947). C. L. Mitton, *The Epistle to the Ephesians. Its Authorship, Origin and Purpose* (Oxford: 1951); Ch. Masson, *L'Épître de saint Paul aux Éphésiens* (Neuchâtel: 1953).

29. The hypothesis of Goodspeed has had its antecedents. C. Weizsäcker, *Das apostolische Zeitalter des christlichen Kirche*, 3rd ed. (Tübingen: 1902), pp. 541 ff., had claimed to see in Col. and Eph. a reaction against the Johannine literature and in favor of Paul, who was being threatened by the growing authority of Peter. J. Weiss, *Das Urchristentum* (1917), p. 534, Eng. tr. proposed that the author of the

Ephesians was the person who had compiled the entire collection of Pauline literature. Goodspeed simply revived both ideas.

30. W. L. Knox, *St. Paul and the Church of the Gentiles* (Cambridge: 1939); *Idem, Philemon among the Letters of Paul* (Chicago: 1935).

31. E. Renan, *L'Antéchrist* (Paris: 1873), p. 91; E. Meyer, *Ursprung und Anfänge des Christentums*, III (1923), p. 482, note 1; M. Goguel, *Introduction au N.T.*, IV, 2 (1926), pp. 472-475; M. Albertz, *Botschaft des N.T.*, I, 2 (1952), p. 167.

32. C. L. Mitton, *The Epistle to the Ephesians. Its Authorship, Origin and Purpose* (Oxford: 1951); (cfr. Fr. Lo Bue, *Protestantesimo*, 8, 1953, pp. 64-101); *Idem, The Authorship of the Epistle to the Ephesians (Important Hypothesis reconsidered, 7)*, in *ExpT* 67 (1955), pp. 195-198; as well as *The Relationship between 1 Pet and Ephes.*, in *JTS*, new series 1 (1950), pp. 65-73.

33. D. E. Nineham, in F.L. Cross, *Studies in Ephesians* (London: 1956), pp. 21-35; J. N. Sanders, *ibid.*, pp. 9-20.

34. J. Schmid, *Der Eph. des Apostles Paulus* (Freiburg: 1928); E. Percy, *Zu den Problemen der Kolosser- und Epheserbriefes*, in *ZNW* 43 (1950), pp. 178-194; a response to a review of his work by E. Käsemann, in *Gnomon* 21 (1949), pp. 242-247.

35. Those who recognized its authenticity are: J. B. Lightfoot, B. F. Westcott, F. A. Hort, T. K. Abbott, J. A. Robinson, W. Sanday, A. C. Headlam, E. F. Scott, E. Reuss, A. Sabatier, B. Weiss, T. Zahn, E. Haupt, G. Wohlenberg, A. Deissmann, W. Michaelis, J. de Zwaan, E. K. Simpson (*Commentary on the Epistle to the Ephesians*, London: 1957), and D. Guthrie.

36. H. Schlier, *Der Brief an die Ephesier* (Düsseldorf: 1957). It is precisely on the basis of Percy's obvious mistake (*Die Probleme*, pp. 4-6) that H. Schlier, *Christus und die Kirche im Epheserbrief*, in *Beitr. z. hist. Theol.*, 6 (Tübingen: 1930), had denied the authenticity of Ephesians.

37. J. Schille, *Liturgisches Gut in Ephes.* (Diss., Göttingen: 1953); *Idem, Der Autor des Epheserbriefes* in *TLZ* 82 (1957), pp. 325-334.

38. H. J. Cadbury, *The Dilemma of Ephesians*, in *NTS* 5 (1958-1959), pp. 91-102.

39. A. v. Harnack, G. Heinrici, H. Windisch, A. Jülicher, M. Dibelius, A. S. Peake, B. W. Bacon, A. H. McNeile, *An Introduction to the Study of the New Testament*, 2nd ed. (Oxford: 1953), pp. 185-187.

40. W. Ochel, *Die Annahme einer Bearbeitung des Kol. im Eph.* (Marburg: 1934).

41. J. Coutts, *The Relationship of Eph. and Col.*, in *NTS* 4 (1957-1958), pp. 201-207. Likewise, *Eph 1, 3-14 and Peter 1, 3-12*, in *NTS* 3, pp. 115-127. To some extent it was the thesis of Holtzmann which Masson had simply brought up to date.

42. Cfr. P. Benoit, *art. cit.*, pp. 107-220.

43. To have recourse to a disciple from the Pauline circle is nothing new. See already W. Bousset, *Kyrios Christos. Geschichte des Christus-*

glaubens von den Anfängen des Christentums bis Irenaeus (Göttingen: 1913), pp. 351-353; W. L. Knox, *St. Paul and the Church of the Gentiles* (1939), pp. 184-185; G.F. Hall, in *JBL* 69 (1950), p. 81. See the criticism of H. Schlier, *Der Brief an die Epheser*, p. 25: "How can such a disciple be described? On the one hand, he had to be of such a type as to have reproduced not only the ideas of his master, but also to have penetrated deeply into these concepts and into the language of Paul, so as to have been able to develop these ideas as an independent agent with an intelligibility that would have been proper to him alone. Rather, would not such a man have been a second Paul, a Paul after Paul? Would he not have been precisely an incorporation into a developing Paulinism? However, on the other hand, could he not have been a plagiarizer and a compiler without a personality of his own, in the modern sense of the term? It is probable that he would not have been that type of disciple, since Paul had never encountered one like that." Msgr. L. Cerfaux had the same idea: "The hypothesis of the nom-de-plume was welcomed in order to create a veritable intellectual counterpart of the Apostle." Cfr. L. Cerfaux, *En faveur de l'authenticité des épîtres de la captivité. Homogénéité doctrinale entre Éphésiens et les grandes Épîtres*, in *Littérature et Théologie paulinienne* (*Recherches Bibliques*, V, Bruges: 1959), p. 61. This study reflected the clever manipulations of a counsel in court. Should he accept all of the facts, particularly the literary evidence? But it is much more convenient to examine only such evidence so that the case for authenticity would be immediately accepted.

44. P. Benoit, *L'horizon paulinien de l'épître aux Éphésiens*, in *RB* 46 (1937), pp. 342-361, 505-525; *Idem*, in *SBJ, Les Épîtres de saint Paul aux Éphésiens*, 2nd ed. (Paris: 1959), pp. 81-82; *Idem*, a review of H. Schlier's *Der Brief an die Epheser*, in *RB* 67 (1960), pp. 138-139.

45. From the title of the complements, here are the parallel passages as listed by P. Benoit, *art.cit.*, pp. 207-208: Eph.5,22-6,9 = Col.3,18-4,1: the directives, counsels, and expressions are the same; Eph.6,18-22 = Col.4,2-8; Eph. 4,2-3 + 4,32-5,2 = Col.3,12-14; Eph.4,16 = Col.2,19; Eph.4,22-24 = Col.3,9-10; Eph.4,31 = Col.3,8; Eph.5,6 = Col. 8,6; Eph. 5, 15f. = Col.4,5; Eph.5,19f. = Col.3,16f.; all of these passages pertain to the moral section of the letter. In the doctrinal section, which forms the first part of the letter, the following parallels exist: Eph.1,4 = Col.3,12 + 1,22; Eph. 1,6f. = Col.1,13f.; Eph.1,10 = Col. 1,16:20; Eph.1,13 = Col.1,5; Eph.1,15f. = Col.1,9 + 3-4; Eph. 1,19f. = Col.2,12; Eph.1,21 = Col.1,16; Eph. 1, 22b-23 = Col.1,18-19; Eph. 2,5f. = Col.2,12f.; Eph.2,11 = Col.2,11; Eph.2,12 = Col.1,21:27; Eph. 2,14-16 = Col.1,20-22; Eph.2,15 = Col.2,14; Eph.3,1-13 = Col.1,23c-29; Eph.3,17 = Col.1,23 + 2,7; Eph.3,19 = Col.2,9-10. In certain instances, one could say that Col depends on Eph: Col.1,18 = Eph.1,22f.; Col. 2,19 = Eph.4,16. Benoit investigated the particular instance of Col.

1,24-29 = Eph.3,1-13, wherein he discovered expert work but some-what artificial." Moreover, he insisted on the warped meanings of the term *oikonomía*: in Col.1,25, it signifies "divine management," but in Eph.3,2, "divine disposition"; similarly with Eph.3,5 and Col. 1,26. He concluded (p. 210): "It would be impossible to attribute to Paul himself the belabored imitations which have been disclosed by analyses together with the accompanying consequences. Such work would rather have been placed into the hands of some zealous disciple." See E. J. Goodspeed, *The Key to Ephesians* (Chicago: 1956).

46. H. Schlier, *op.cit.*, pp. 22-28; L. Cerfaux, *Introduction à la Bible, II* (Paris: 1959), pp. 506-507; *Idem, En faveur de l'authenticité des épîtres de la captivité. Homogénéité doctrinale entre Éphésiens et les grandes Épîtres*, in *Littérature et Théologie paulinienne (Recherches bibliques, V, Bruges)*, pp. 60-71.

47. Note on the date and the place of composition of the Captivity Epistles. The problem would not arise at all if one would admit the Pauline authenticity of the epistles, or at least the direct influence of Paul on the disciple who would have drafted the letter, for example, the letter to the Ephesians. Furthermore, the problem of the place of composition is related to that of the date. The letter to the Philippians need not be involved with the letters to Philemon, Colossians, and Ephesians. Concerning the date for Philippians, see especially: W. Michaelis, *Die Datierung des Phil.* (Gutersloh: 1933); O. Linton, *Zur Situation des Phil.*, in *Arbeiten und Mitteilungen aus dem nt. Seminar zu Uppsala*, IV (1936), pp. 9-21; W. Manson, *St. Paul in Ephesus: The Date of the Epistle to the Philippians*, in *BJRL* 23 (1939), pp. 182-200; Cfr. W. Michaelis, *War Paulus in Ephesus gefangen?* in *Deutsches Pfarrerblatt* 43 (1939), pp. 649-650; D. Guthrie, *op.cit.*, pp. 145-154.

Three places have been proposed:

1. *ROME*: place of composition for the four epistles and the Roman captivity as the period of time: E. Percy, *Die Probleme* (1946); C. H. Dodd, *The Message of the Epistles: Ephesians*, in *ExpT* 45 (1933-1934), pp. 60-66. The most probing study was that of J. Schmid, *Zeit und Ort der paulinischen Gefangenschaftsbriefen* (1931); D. Guthrie, *op.cit.*, pp. 153-154. Some are hesitant as for as Philippians is concerned: M. Dibelius, *Handbuch Lietzmann*, 2nd ed. (1927) — Rome or Ephesus. A. Wikenhauser does not seem to be very certain (*Einleitung*, p. 312, Eng. tr. N.T. Introd.). C.F.D. Moule, *The Epistles*, pp. 21-25, prefers Rome as the place of composition for Col and Phlm.

2. *CAESAREA*: This opinion, which in its own time was favorably accepted, has quickly lost ground. It was launched by D. Schulz in 1829 and had been revived by H. A.W. Meyer, A. Hilgenfeld, P. Pfleiderer, Fr. Spitta, E. Haupt, and B. Weiss; above all, M. Goguel, *Introduction*, IV, 1 (1926), pp. 69ff.; *Idem, Le livre et la date de la composition de l'épître aux Philippiens*, in *RHR* (1912), pp. 330-

342; P. Feine, *Die Abfassung des Philipperbriefes in Ephesus*, in *Beitr. g. f. christl. Theol.*, 20-24 (Gutersloh: 1915), pp. 94-95; E. Lohmeyer, *Der Brief an die Philipper* (*Meyers Komment.*, IX), 11th ed. (Göttingen: 1956).

3. *EPHESUS*: That all of the Captivity Epistles were composed at the time of the captivity at Ephesus deserves serious examination. See A. Deissmann, *Licht vom Osten*, 4th ed. (1923), p. 201, note 6; *Idem, Zur ephesenischen Gefangenschaft des Apostels Paulus*, in *Anatolian Studies W.M. Ramsay* (1929), pp. 121-127; *Idem, Paulus*, 2nd ed. (1926), pp. 13ff., 192, 288; W. Michaelis, *Einleitung*, p. 199; *Idem, Die Gefangenschaft des Paulus in Ephesus und das Itinerar des Timotheus* (Gutersloh: 1925); *Idem, Pastoralen und paulinischen Gefangenschaftsbriefen* (Gutersloh: 1930); H. Lisco, *Vincula Sanctorum* (Berlin: 1900), and *Roma pelegrina* (Berlin: 1901); M. Albertz, *Über die Abfassung des Phil. zu Ephesus*, in *Theol. Stud. und Krit.* 83 (1910), pp. 551 ff.; G.S. Duncan, *St. Paul's Ephesian Ministry. A Reconstruction with Special Reference to the Ephesian Origin of the Emprisonment Epistles* (London: 1929); *Idem, Were Paul's Emprisonment Epistles Written from Ephesus?* in *ExpT* 67 (1955-1956), pp. 163-166; *Idem, Paul's Ministry in Asia. The Last Phase Acts* 19-22, in *NTS* 3 (1956-1957), pp. 211-218; 5 (1958-1959), pp. 43-45. Likewise, P. N. Harrison, J. Héring, and Ch. Masson accepted Ephesus as the place of origin for both Phlm and Col.

4. *ROME* for Phlm, Col, and Eph; *EPHESUS* for Phil. This is the thesis of K. Lake, *Introduction to the N.T.*, p. 139, and of F.F. Bruce, in his commentary on the Acts, of J.H. Michael and P. Bonnard for Phil in their respective commentaries as found in W. Manson, *The Date of Phil.*, pp. 182-200. For the Catholic authors, cfr. P. Gächter, *Summa Introductionis in N.T.* (Innsbruck: 1938), pp. 204-206, and P. Benoit, *Les Épîtres de saint Paul aux Philippiens*, in *SBJ*, 3rd ed. (Paris: 1939), pp. 11-13.

Wikenhauser claimed that it is impossible to decide, which we think is a rather pessimistic point of view. First of all, Paul does not seem to have visited the community since its foundation; this would exclude Rome as the place of composition (Phil.1,26-30; 2,12; 4,.15-16). Secondly, Paul was captured because of the Gospel (Phil.1,7:12-13:1, 30; cfr. Acts 16,20-21), which could be conveniently placed at Ephesus, but not in Rome, since Paul was arrested in Jerusalem under the pretense of a profanation of the Temple. Thirdly, the distance between Philippi and Ephesus would allow for a number of journeys, as Phil.2,25-29 supposes. Fourthly, Paul announced an imminent visit, which would agree with his journey to the Philippians (Acts 19, 21-22; 20,1 and 1 Cor.4, 17; 16,5:10; 2 Cor.2,12-13; 7,5). See the various reasons given by A.H. McNeile, *An Introduction*, pp. 182-183. We believe that the letter to the Philippians was more probably composed at Ephesus in the year 54-55 A.D.

48. At first, consult the commentary of P.C. Spicq, *Les Épîtres Pastorales* (*Études Bibliques*, Paris: 1947), where all former studies are carefully presented. The author took up the question in his article, *Pastorales* (*Épîtres*), in *DBS* 36 (1961), pp. 1-73, together with ample bibliography. P. Spicq is a more qualified and convinced advocate for total authenticity of the Pastoral Letters. Then see A. Médebielle, *Les Épîtres à Tim. et à Tite*, in *DTC* XV, 1, col. 1036-1121; P. De Ambroggi, *Questioni sulle origini delle epistole pastorali a Tim. et a Tito*, in *ScuolC* 79 (1951), pp. 409-434.

49. B. M. Metzger, *A. Reconsideration of Certain Arguments against the Pauline Authorship of the Pastoral Epistles*, in *ExpT* 70 (1958-1959), pp. 91-94.

50. R. Falconer, *The Pastoral Epistles* (Oxford: 1937).

51. P.N. Harrison, *The Problems of the Pastoral Epistles* (Oxford: 1921); *Idem, The Pastoral Epistles and Duncan's Ephesian Theory*, in *NTS* 2 (1956-1957), pp. 250-261; *Idem, The Authorship of the Pastoral Epistles* (*Important Hypotheses Reconsidered* III), in *ExpT* 67 (1955), pp. 77-81; W. Schmithals, art. *Pastoralbriefe*, in *RGG* 3rd, ed., V, pp. 144-148, claimed that the unauthenticity had been assured.

Harrison's book restated certain points: F.R. Montgomery Hitchcock, *Test for the Pastorals*, in *JTS* 30 (1928-1929), pp. 272-279; *Idem, Philo and the Pastorals*, in *Hermathena* 56 (1940), pp. 113-135; W. Michaelis, *Pastoralbriefe und Wortstatistik*, in *ZNW* 28 (1929), pp. 69-76; cfr. also F. Torm, *Ueber die Sprache in den Pastoralbriefen*, in *ZNW* 18 (1917), pp. 225-243; D. Guthrie, *New Testament Introduction*, p. 124, note 3; F.J. Badcock, *The Pauline Epistles and the Epistle to the Hebrews in their Historical Setting* (London: 1937), pp. 115-133; B.M. Metzger, *A Reconsideration of Certain Arguments against the Pauline Authorship of the Pastoral Epistles*, in *ExpT* 70 (1958), pp. 91-94.

52. Ch. Maurer, *Eine Textvariante klärt die Entstehung der Past.*, in *TZ* 3 (1947), pp. 321-337.

53. H. von Campenhausen, *Polycarp von Smyrna und die Past.*, in *Sitzungsber.* (Heidelberg: 1951), p. 2.

54. M. Dibelius and H. Conzelmann (*Comment. de Lietzmann*), 13th ed. (Tübingen: 1955)

55. W. Michaelis, *Pastoralbriefe und Worstatistik*, in *ZNW* 28 (1929), pp. 69 ff. See also *Einleitung*, 2nd ed., pp. 238-259, a very important contribution.

56. O. Michel, *Grundfragen der Pastor.*, in *Festschrift Th. Wurm* (Stuttgart: 1948), pp. 83-99.

57. B.S. Easton, *The Pastoral Epistles* (New York: 1947); J. Behm, *Einleitung*, pp. 206-210; J. Jeremias, in *NTD*, 6th ed. (1955); D. Guthrie, *The Pastoral Epsiles and the Mind of Paul* (London: 1956); *Idem, The Pastoral Epistles*, (*Tyndale New Testament Commentary*, London: 1958); the same author took up the question at great lengths in *New Testament Introduction*, pp. 198-237;

E.K. Simpson, *The Authenticity and Authorship of the Pastoral Epistles,* in*EvQ* 12 (1940), pp. 289-311.

58. H.A. Sanders, *A Third-Century Papyrus Codex of the Epistles of Paul* (Ann Arbor: 1935), p. 11.

59. M. Goguel, *Introduction,* IV, 2, p. 530.

60. R. Bultmann, art. *Paulus,* in *RGG,* 2nd ed., pp. 491-492.

61. H.A. Sanders, *op.cit.*

62. G. Udny Yule, *The Statistical Study of Vocabulary* (Cambridge: 1943).

63. K. Grayson and G. Herdan, *The Authorship of the Pastorals in the Light of Statistical Linguistics,* in *NTS* 6 (1959-1960), pp. 1-14; F. Torm, *Ueber die Sprache in den Pastoralbriefen,* in *ZNW* 18 (1917-1918), pp. 225-243.

64. W. Michaelis, *Pastoralbriefe und Wortstatistik,* in *ZNW* 28 (1929), pp. 69-76. Concerning the insufficiency of the use of statistics, see B.M. Metzger, *A Reconsideration of Certain Arguments against the Pauline Authorship of the Pastoral Epistles,* in *ExpT* 70 (1958-1959), pp. 91-94; W.C. Wake, *The Authenticity of the Pauline Epistles. A Contribution from Statistical Analysis,* in *HibJ* 47 (1948), pp. 50-55. We would also mention W. Nauck, *Die Herkunft des Verfassers der Pastoralbriefe* (diss. Göttingen: 1950).

65. L. Cerfaux, *Introduction à la Bible,* p. 529. Recourse to the existence of a secretary has taken many forms. H.J. Holtzmann, *Die Pastoralbriefe, kritisch und exegetisch bearbeitet* (Leipzig: 1880), pp. 92 ff.; J.D. James, *The Genuineness and Authorship of the Pastoral Epistles* (London: 1906), pp. 154 ff.; E.F. Scott, *The Pauline Epistles* (London: 1960), pp. 329-371. These three authors spoke of a collaboration with Luke, but J. Moffat, *Introduction,* p. 414, has refuted such a theory. F. J. Badcock, *The Pauline Epistles and the Epistle to the Hebrews in their Historical Setting* (London: 1937); A. Nairne, *The Faith of the New Testament* (London: 1920), pp. 60-61; J.A. Eschlimann, *La Rédaction des Épîtres Pauliniennes,* in *RB* 53 (1946), pp. 185-196, claimed that the secretary was much more than just an *amanuensis.* O. Roller, *Das Formular der paulinischen Briefe* (Stuttgart: 1933), pp. 20-21, exposed a thesis according to which it was impossible for Paul to have dictated the Pastoral Letters. As he saw it, such a theory could have no foundation since Paul, as a prisoner, would not have enjoyed the liberty necessary to do the writing himself, and therefore, dictation would have been the only way. J. Jeremias, *op.cit.,* pp. 5-8, followed Roller's suggestion and identified the secretary as Tychicus. C. Spicq, *Les Épîtres Pastorales,* CXIX, did not follow this opinion, and W. Michaelis, *Einleitung,* pp. 241-244, rejected the idea of having any recourse to a secretary.

66. K.G. Eckart, *Der Zweite echte Brief des Apostels Paulus an die Thessalonicher,* in *ZTK* 58 (1961), pp. 30-44, after having rejected the idea of the authenticity of 2 Thes without any hesitation at all and

without giving reasons for his opinion, divided the first letter to the Thessalonians into two separate letters: Letter A = 1,1-2,12; 2,17-3,4; 3,11-13; Letter B = 3,6-10; 4,13-5,11; 4,9-10a and 5, 23-26:28; but when he declared in order to prove his thesis that the expression *eudokésamen* in 3,1 must be the present tense (!), one would wonder how he could be seriously complimented for making a contribution? Whatever else he might have said would have been jeopardized.

67. See A. Feuillet, art., *Paul, Corinthiens (Les Épîtres aux)*, in *DBS* 39 (1961), pp. 170-195.

68. P. Cleary, *The Epistles to the Corinthians*, in *CBQ* 12 (1950), pp. 10-13.

69. W. Schmithals, *Die Gnosis in Korinth, Eine Untersuchung zu den Korintherbriefen* (Göttingen: 1955). Cfr. W. Michaelis, in *TZ* 14 (1958), pp. 321-326.

70. In M. Goguel (*Introduction au N.T.*, 4,2, *Les Épîtres Pauliniennes*, Paris: 1926, pp. 86-88, in the note), there are presented the positions of these different authors. The following is Goguel's position: Letter A = 2 Cor.6,14-7,1; 1 Cor. 6,12-20; 10,1-22; Letter B = 1 Cor. 5,1-6,11; 7,1-8,13; 10,23-14,40; 15,1-58 (?); 16,1-9,12; Letter C = 1 Cor. 1,10-4,21; 9,1-27; 16,10-11; Letter D = 2 Cor. 10,1-13,10; Letter E = 2 Cor. 1,1-6,13; 7,2-8,24; Letter F = 2 Cor. 9,1-15; what remains is either doubtful or indeterminable.

R. Bultmann, *Exegetische Probleme des 2 Kor.*, in *SymBUp* 9 (1947), p. 14, note 16 proposed the following: Letter A = 2,14-7,4 without 6,14-7,1; 10-13 is an intermediate letter; Letter B = 1,1-2,13; 7,5-16, was written after the return of Titus; chapters 8 and 9 could not have been composed as a literary unit.

E. Dinkler, art., *Korintherbriefe*, in *RGG*, 3rd ed., 4 (1960), in conjunction with the suggestions of R. Bultmann, proposed the following: Letter A = 6,12-20; 9,24-27; 10,1-22; 11,2-34; 12-14; Letter B = 1, 1-6,11; 7,1-9,23; 10,23-11,1; 15,16. As for 2 Cor = Letter C = 2,14-7,4; 9; 10-13,10; Letter D 1,1-2,13; 7,5-16; 8 ; 2 Cor. 6,14-7,1 is not Pauline. Dinkler rejected the system of Schmithals.

71. J. Héring, *La premiere épître de saint Paul aux Corinthiens* (Neuchâtel: 1949), p. 11. The author depended on J. Weiss, *Urchristentum*, and M. Goguel. His intention was to avoid bringing into the picture "any editorial work to an over extensive degree and consequently sufficiently hypothetical." He also distinguished between two letters in 1 Cor: Letter A = 1,8; 10,23-11,1; 16,1-4:10-14; Letter B = 9; 10, 1-22; 11-15, and the rest of chapter 16. Chapter 13 is a digression. J. Héring devoted some judicious pages to the problem on the unity of the second letter in *La seconde épître de saint Paul aux Corinthiens* (Neuchâtel: 1958), pp. 11-13.

72. A. Wikenhauser, *Einleitung*, pp. 283-284 Eng. tr. *N.T. Introd.* J.T. Dean, *St. Paul and Corinth* (London: 1947), pp. 40 ff., saw four let-

ters in 2 Cor. See the presentation of the system in D. Guthrie, *New Testament Introduction*, p. 63.

73. See A. Schlatter, *Paulus der Bote Jesu. Eine Deutung der Briefe an die Korinther* (Stuttgart: 1934); N.A. Dahl, *Das Volk Gottes* (Oslo: 1941), pp. 221,324, note 43; C.L. Mitton, *The Formation of the Pauline Corpus of Letters* (London: 1955), p. 26, thought that 2,14-7,4 formed a separate unit.

74. H. Windisch, *Commentaire*, (*Meyers Kom.*, 6), 9th ed. (1924).

75. É. Osty, *Les Épîtres de saint Paul aux Corinthiens*, in *SBJ* 3rd ed. (1959), pp. 81-85.

76. A. Hausrath, *Der Vierkapitelbrief des Paulus an die Korinther* (Heidelberg: 1870).

77. M. Krenkel, *Beiträge zur Aufhellung der Geschichte und der Briefe des Apostels Paulus* (Brunswick: 1890); followed by Ch. Bruston, H. Windisch, A. Jülicher and E. Fascher, *Einleitung* (1931), p. 99; see the commentary of H. Windisch and É. Osty, *op.cit.*, pp. 83-84. The "Four-Chapter Hypothesis" was revived and strongly defended by G. Bornkamm, *Die Vorgeschichte des sogenannten Zweiten Korintherbriefes*, in *Sitzungsber. d. Heidelberger Akad. d. Wissensch. Phil-hist. Rl.* (Heidelberg: 1961), pp. 13-21. We could not have acquired a knowledge of the contents of this study at the time we were correcting the proof-sheets for our volume. We can only indicate the conclusions of the author. His analysis is similar to a "disconcerting" tableau. The letter in its present state is the actual work of a compiler. The basis for this letter is a letter of reconciliation which brings to an end the quarrels of Paul with the Church at Corinth. Then, to this letter he joined fragments of earlier letters: 2,4-7,4 concerning the nature of the apostolic function and the four chapters (10-13) which originated from a letter that he "wrote with tears." The eighth chapter could be joined to this in which occurs a letter of recommendation for Titus and his six companions, which was destined actually for the churches in Achaia. Finally, 6,14-7,1 is not the work of Paul. Noteworthy is the author's vibrant reaction against Schmithals. The originality of the study consists less in a new literary division than in a reconstruction of events whose meaning is kept in abeyance by the divisions which are proposed.

78. See also R.V.G. Tasker, *The Unity of 2 Corinthians*, in *ExpT* 47 (1935-1936), pp. 55-58. W.B. Sedgwick, *The Authorship of the Pastorals*, in *ExpT* 30 (1918-1919), pp. 230-231, has shown that there is a greater difference in the stylistic development in Plato than in the first letters of Paul and the Pastoral Letters.

79. F.W. Beare, *Epistle to the Philippians* (London: 1959), p. 5, admits that 3,2-4,1 is an interpolation.

80. P. Benoit, *Épître aux Philippians*, p. 19. This is also the opinion in P. Bonnard, *L'épître de saint Paul aux Philippiens* (Neuchatel: 1950), p. 9; B.D. Rahtjen, *The Three Letters of Paul to the Philippians*, in *NTS* 6 (1959), pp. 167-173; a critique by B.S. Mackay,

Further Thoughts on Philippians, in NTS 7 (1960-1961), pp. 161-170. In a comeback, W. Schmithals, *Zur Abfassung und ältesten Sammlung des paulinischen Hauptbriefe, in ZNW* 51 (1960), pp. 225-245, condensed his views on the question in the following manner:

Cor A = 2 Cor. 6,14-7,1; 1 Cor. 9,24-10,22; 6,12-20; 11,2-34; 15; 16, 13-24.

Cor B = 1 Cor. 1,1-6,11; 7,1 - 9,23; 10, 23-11,1; 2-1-14,40; 16,1-12.

Cor C = 2 Cor. 2,14 - 6,13; 7, 2-4.

Cor D = 2 Cor. 10,1 - 13,13.

Cor E = 2 Cor. 9,1-15.

Cor F = 2 Cor. 1,1-2,13; 7,5-8,24.

Gal

Phil A = Phil. 4,10-23.

Phil B = Phil. 1,1-3,1! 4,4-7.

Phil C = Phil. 3,2-4,3; 4,8-9.

Rom = Rom. 1-15.

Rom,Eph = Rom. 16,12.

1 Thes

2 Thes. 1-2 Thes (which he supposes are authentic) were written during the third voyage (p. 232).

The Letters are then set up in the following sequence: Gal; Phil A; Phil B; Cor A; Cor B; Cor C; 1 Thes; 2 Thes; Cor D! Phil C; Cor E! Cor F; Rom; Rom-Eph (p. 235).

The correspondence to Corinth continued for eight months; three or four months after that, the letter to the Romans appeared; two or three months before the Corinthian dossier, Phil A and B had been written whereas Gal and Phil A would have been existing a year before that time. See also J. Müller and Bardorff, *Zur Frage der literarischen Einheit des Philipperbriefes, in Wissenschaftliche Zeitschrift* 7 (Jena: 1957-1958), pp. 591-604 (we were not able to consult this last article).

81. A. Wikenhauser, *Einleitung*, pp. 292-293 Eng. tr. *N.T. Introd.;* But also S. Lyonnet, *Les Épîtres de saint Paul aux Galates et aux Romains, in SBJ* 2nd ed. (Paris: 1959), pp. 47-51; to be always consulted are: R. Schumacher, *Die beiden letzten Kapitel des Röm.* (*Neutest. Abh.,* 14,4), 1929; J. Huby and S. Lyonnet, *Épîtres aux Romains* (Paris: 1957), pp. 513-520; the notes of O. Michel, in his commentary on Romans, are not relevant; a better explanation in more recent times on the question of Rom 16 is that of T.M. Taylor, in *JBL* 67 (1948), pp. 281-295.

82. Cfr. P. Feine, *Die Abfassung des Phil in Ephesus, mit einer Anlage über Röm. 16, 3-20 als Epheserbrief, in Beitr. z. Förd. Theol.,* 20, 4 (Gutersloh: 1916), pp. 121 ff.; A. Deissmann, *Licht vom Osten,* 4th ed. (Tübingen: 1932), pp. 372-377, expressed the hypothesis that Paul had retained copies of his letters. The copy which Paul kept did not have chapter 16.

83. W. Michaelis, *Einleitung*, pp. 162-163.

84. J. Dupont, *Pour l'histoire de la doxologie finale de l'épître aux Romains*, in *KB* 58 (1948), pp. 3-22; *Idem, móno sopho theo, Rom. 16,27*, in *ETL* 22 (1946), pp. 362-375; W. Kamlah, *Traditionsgeschichtliche Untersuchungen zur Schlussdoxologie des Römerbriefs* (Diss., Tübingen: 1955) (not examined).

85. F. Müller, *Zwei Marginalien im Brief des Paulus an die Römer*, in *ZNW* 40 (1941), pp. 249-254.

86. R. Bultmann, *Glossen im Röm.*, in *TLZ* 72 (1947), pp. 197-202.

87. H. Sahlin, *Einige Textemendationen zum Röm*, in *TZ* 9 (1953), pp. 92-100. Note: It was not possible for us to delay the printing press to cover the information on an important problem which has arisen in the last few years concerning the structure of the letter to the Romans. W. Leonard, *Theme and Composition of the Epistle to the Romans*, in *AusCR* 25 (1948), pp. 8-14; A. Feuillet, *Le plan salvifique de Dieu d'après l'épître aux Romains*, in *RB* 57 (1950), pp. 333-387, 489-529; S. Lyonnet, *Note sur le plan de l'épître aux Romains*, in *RSR* 39-40 (1951-1952), pp. 301-316; K. Prümm, *Zur Struktur des Römerbriefes. Begriffsreihen als Einheitsband*, in *ZKT* 72 (1950), pp. 333-349; J. Kürzinger, *Die Grundgedanken des Römerbriefes*, in *BiKi*, fasc. 4 (1953), pp. 3-11; E. Ortiques, *La Composition de l'épître aux Romains (I-VIII)*, in *VC* 8 (1954), pp. 52-81; J. Dupont, *Le problème de la structure littéraire de l'épître aux Romains*, in *RB* 62 (1955), pp. 365-397; Suitbertus a S. Johanne a Cruce, *De structura idearum in Ep. ad Romanos*, in *VD* 34 (1956), pp. 68-87. See also J. Jeremias, *Zur Gedankenführung in den paulinischen Briefen*, in *SP* (1953), pp. 146-154.

88. T.M. Taylor, *The Place of Origin of Romans*, in *JBL* 67 (1948), pp. 281-295, suggested Philippi as the place of composition, at the time when Paul preparing for his trip to Jerusalem for the Passover of the year 58 A.D., whereas G.S. Duncan, *Important Hypotheses Reconsidered. VI. Were Paul's imprisonment Epistles written from Ephesus?* in *ExpT* 68 (1955-1956), p. 165, claimed that the letter was written during the time of Paul's stay at Ephesus. Likewise, *St. Paul's Ephesian Ministry* (London: 1929).

Notes to Chapter VI

1. O. Kuss, *Der Römerbrief übersetzt und erklärt*, 1-2 (Ratisbonne: 1957, 1959).

2. R. Asting, *Die Verkündigung des Wortes im Urchristentum* (Stuttgart: 1932).

3. M. Dibelius, *Zur Formgeschichte des Neuen Testaments (ausserhalb der Evangelien)*, in *TRu*, new series, 3 (1931), pp. 207-242. Besides these studies, see some recent and older works which would help the exegete to begin work in the field of literary criticism, e.g. F.G. Heinrici, *Der literarische Charakter der neutestamentliche Schriften* (Leipzig: 1908); P. Wendland, *Die Urchristliche Literaturformen*

(*Handb. z. N.T.*, Tübingen: 1912); U. von Wilamowitz-Moellendorf, *Die griechische Literatur des Altertums*, in *Die Kultur der Gegenwart*, I, 8, 3rd ed. (Berlin: 1912); E. Norden, *Agnostos Theos. Untersuchung zu Formengeschichte religiöser Rede* (Leipzig: 1913); Idem, *Die Antike Kunstprosa*, 3rd ed. (Berlin: 1918); R.M. Pope, *Studies in the Language of St. Paul* (London: 1939); J.A. Eschlimann, *La rédaction des Épîtres pauliniennes d'après une comparaison avec les lettres profanes de son temps*, in *RB* 63 (1946), pp. 185-196; J. Jeremias, *Zur Gedankenführung in der Paulinischen Briefen*, in *Studia Paulina* (Harlem: 1953), pp. 146-154; S. Lyonnet, *L'étude du milieu littéraire et l'exégese du N.T.*, in *Bib* 35 (1954), pp. 480-502; 36 (1955), pp. 202-212; G. Karlsson, *Formelhaftes in Paulusbriefen*, in *Era* 54 (1956), pp. 138-141. The problem concerning the very understanding of Paul was posed by M. Magnusson, *Der Begriff "Verstehen" in exegetischem Zusammenhang unter besonderer Berücksichtigung der Paulinischen Schriften. 1. Allgemeine Probleme des exegetischen Verständnisses* (*Studia Theologica Lundensia*, 8, Lund: 1955).

4. A Descamps, *L'actualité de l'épître aux Romains*, in *Littérature et théologie pauliniennes* (*Recherches bibliques*, V, Bruges: 1960), p. 15.

5. R. Lafoscade, *De Epistulis imperatorum magistratorumque romanorum quas graece scriptas lapides papyrive servaverunt* (Lille: 1902); O. Gerhardt, *Studien zur Geschichte des griechischen Briefes. I. Die Anfangsformel* (Tübingen: 1903); A. Deissmann, *Licht vom Osten. Das N.T. und die neuentdecken Texte der hellenistisch-römischen Welt*, 4th ed. (Tübingen: 1923); J.A. Exler, *The Form of the Ancient Letters. A. Study of Greek Epistolography* (Westminster: 1923), pp. 24-60; F. Ziemann, *De Epistularum graecarum formulis solemnibus quaestiones selectae* (Halle: 1911); J. Sykutris, *Epistolographie*, in *Pauly-Wissowa RE*, suppl. 5 (1931), pp. 186-220; E.C. Malte, *Certain Papyrological Elements in the Letters of St. Paul* (Pittsburg: 1946); S. del Páramo, *Las formulas protocolarias en las cartas del N.T.*, in *EstBib* 10 (1951), pp. 333-335; A.M. Perry, *Epistolary Form in Paul*, in *CQ* 26 (1944), pp. 48-53; R.L. Archer, *The Epistolary Form in the N.T.*, in *ExpT* 68 (1951-1952), pp. 296-298; R. Gyllenberg, *De inledande häsningsformler i de paulinska breven*, in *SEA* 16 (1951), pp. 21-31; O. Roller, *Das Formular der paulinischen Briefe Ein Beitrag zur Lehre vom antiken Briefe* (Stuttgart: 1953); W. F. Frijns, *De briefvorm in het N.T.*, in *HL* 9 (1956), pp. 53-56; G. Karlsson, *Formelhaftes in Paulusbriefen*, in Era 54 (1956), pp. 138-141; S. Lyonnet, *De arts litteras exarandi apud antiquos*, in *VD* 34 (1956), pp. 3-11. Collections of private letters, cfr. G. Milligan, *Selections from Greek Papyri* (Cambridge: 1910); St. Witkowski, *Epistulae privatae graecae quae in papyris aetatis Lagidarum servantur*, 2nd ed. (Leipzig: 1911); B. Olsson, *Papyrusbriefe aus der frühesten Römerzeit* (Uppsala: 1925).

6. H. Koskenniemi, *Studien zur Idee und Phraseologie des griechischen Briefes bis* 400 *n. Christus* (*Annales Acad. Sc. Fenn,* Helsinki: 1956).

7. W. Michaelis, *Einleitung in das N.T.,* pp. 250-254; E. Percy, *Die Probleme der Kolosser-und Epheserbriefe,* pp. 10-14; S. Lyonnet, *art. cit.,* pp. 5-10, inspected the arguments on which Roller based his computations of the dates for the composition of the letters; E. Stange, *Diktierpausen in den Paulus-briefen,* in *ZNW* 18 (1917), pp. 109-117, thought that Paul dictated 1 Thes in two hours and Rom in eleven hours.

8. J.A. Eschlimann believed that Paul did not dictate but simply allowed his secretaries to take care of the editing (*art.cit.,* pp. 185-196).

9. E. Lohmeyer, *Probleme paulinischer Theologie.* I. *Briefliche Grussüberschriften,* in *ZNW* 26 (1927), pp. 158-159; G. Friedrich, *Lohmeyer's These über das paulinische Briefpräskript beleuchtet,* in *TLZ* 81 (1956), pp. 343-346; cfr. *ZNW* 46 (1955), pp. 272 ff.

10. cfr. Phlm. 19.

11. See A. Deissmann, *Licht vom Osten,* p. 137.

12. A good study on thanksgivings is that of P. Schubert, *Form and Function of the Pauline Thanksgivings,* (*Beih. ZNW,* 20: 1939); see his conclusions concerning the structural forms of thanksgivings, pp. 34-39; similarly, *Form and Function of the Pauline Letters,* in *JRel* 19 (1939), pp. 366-377.

13. See the discussion and proof in B. Rigaux, *Les Épîtres aux Thessaloniciens,* pp. 357-359.

14. G. Misch, *Geschichte der Autobiographie, Das Altertum* 1-2 (Berne: 1949, 1950).

15. Cfr. above, chapter III, no. 2, "Psychology of Conversion", concerning Rom. 7,7-25.

16. Cfr. above, chapter I, art. 3.

17. B. Rigaux, *Le vocabulaire paulinien antérieur à la Première Épître aux Thessaloniciens,* in *Sacra Pagina* (Gembloux: 1954), p. 2.

18. Cfr. B. Rigaux, *Les Épîtres aux Thessaloniciens,* pp. 170-183; O. Cullmann, *Las Premières Confessions de Foi chrétienne* (Paris: 1943); E. Stauffer, *Die Theologie,* pp. 219-231.

19. See the cautions suggested by J. Barr, *The Semantics of Biblical Language* (Oxford: 1961), especially chapter 6: "Some Principles of Kittel's Theological Dictionary," pp. 206-262.

20. B. Rigaux, *Les Épîtres aux Thessaloniciens,* pp. 389-397.

21. The best study is that of E. Earle Ellis, *Paul's Use of the Old Testament* (Edinburgh: 1957), which we follow in our own presentation and to which we refer the reader for further detail. The study is well documented and clear. Towards the end of the book are appendices relevent to citations in Paul. Other references are: H. St. J. Thackeray, *The Relation of St. Paul to Contemporary Jewish Thought* (London: 1910); W. Dittmar, *Vetus Testamentum in Novo* (Göttingen: 1903) is always useful; H. Monnet, *Les citations de 'A.T. dans*

les épîtres de saint Paul (Lausanne: 1874); H. Vollmer, *Die alt-testamentlichen Citate bei Paulus* (Freiburg: 1896); T. Haering, *Das Alte Testament im Neuen*, in *ZNW* 17 (1916), pp. 213-227; A. von Harnack, *Das Alte Testament in den paulinischen Briefen in den paulinischen Gemeinden*, in *Sitzungsber. der Preuss, Ak. d. Wiss.* (Berlin: 1928), pp. 124-141; A. F. Puukko, *Paulus und das Judentum*, in *SOr* 2 (Helinski: 1928); O. Michel, *Paulus und seine Bibel* (Gutersloh: 1929) is a principal work; L. Vénard, *Citations de l'A.T. dans le N.T.*, in *DBS* 2 (1934), pp. 23-51; R. Chasles, *L'A.T. dans le N.T.* (Paris: 1937); H.K. Moulton, *Scriptures Quotations in the Pastoral Epistles*, in *ExpT* 54 (1937-1938), p. 94; J. Bonsirven, *Exégèse rabbinique et exégèse paulinienne* (Paris: 1939); C.J. Costello, *The O.T. in St. Paul's Epistles*, in *CBQ* 4 (1942), pp. 141-145; B.F.C. Atkinson, *The Textual Background of the Use of the Old Testament by the New*, in *VictI* 79 (1947), pp. 39-70; B.M. Metzinger, *Gedanken zum Paulinischen Schriftbeweis*, in *Miscellanea A. Miller* (Rome: 1951), pp. 366-371; W. Manson, *The Old Testament in the Teaching of Jesus*, in *BJRL* 34 (1952), pp. 312-333; C. Smits, *Oud-Testamentische Citaten in het Nieuwe Testament*, in *ColFrN* VIII, 1-3, 3 vol.'s (Hertogenbosch: 1952-1957); R.V.G. Tasker, *The Old Testament in the N.T.* (London: 1954).

22. Cfr. P.E. Kahle, *The Cairo Geniza* (London: 1947), also A. Sperber, *N.T. and Septuagint*, in *JBL* 59 (193-289; *Idem, The N.T. and the Septuagint* (Tarbiz,6 : 1934), pp. 1-29; B.J. Roberts, *The Old Testament and Versions* (Cardiff: 1951), pp. 101-109; P. Katz, *Das Problem des Urtextes der Septuaginta*, in*TZ* 5 (1949), pp. 15-24; F.M. Cross, *The Manuscripts of the Dead Sea Scrolls*, in *BA* 17 (1954), p. 221; D. Barthélemy, *Redécouverte d'un chaînon manquant de l'histoire de la Septante*, in *RB* 60 (1953), pp. 18-29.

23. Cfr. B.B. Warfield, *Revelation and Inspiration* (New York: 1927).

24. B.M. Metzger, *The Formular Introducing Quotations of Scripture in the N.T. and Mishnah*, in *JBL* 70 (1951), pp. 297-307.

25. E. Lohmeyer, *Grundlagen der Paulinischer Theologie* (Tübingen: 1928); H. Windisch, *Paulus und das Judentum*. As against: Michel, *Paulus und seine Bibel*, pp. 130-131.

26. Cfr. J. Bonsirven, *Exégèse rabbinque et exégèse paulinienne* (Paris: 1939); R.T. Herford, *Christianity in the Talmud and Midrash* (London: 1903); G. Aicher, *Das Alte Testament in der Mischna* (Freiburg: 1906); M. Mielziner, *Introduction to the the Talmud* (New York: 1925); G.F. Moore, *Judaism*, 3 vol. 2nd ed. (Cambridge, Mass.: 1927); J.J. Collins, *Rabbinic Exegesi sand Pauline Exegesis*, in *CBQ* 3 (1941), pp. 15-26, 145-158; R. Le Déaut, *Traditions targumiques dans le Corpus Paulinien?* (*He* 11,4 *and* 12,24; *Gal* 4, 29-30; *2 Cor* 3,16), in *Bib* 42 (1961), pp. 28-48.

27. Cfr. B.J. Roberts, *The Dead Sea Scrolls and the Old Testament Scriptures* (Manchester: 1953); J.P. Hyatt, *The View of Man in the*

Qumran Hodayot, in *NTS* 2 (1955-1956), pp. 256-284; S.E. Johnson, *Paul and the Manual of Discipline*, in *HTR* 48 (1955), pp. 157-165; A. Dietzel, *Beten im Geist. Ein religionsgeschichtliche Parallele aus den Hodayoth zum paulinischer Gebet im Geist*, in *TZ* 13 (1957), pp. 12-32; H.J. Cadbury, *A Qumran Parallel to Paul* (1 *Co* 11,10), in *HTR* 51 (1958), pp. 1-2. Concerning the entire group of texts, cfr. W.D. Davies, *St. Paul and Rabbinic Judaism*, 2nd ed. (Cambridge: 1955) 3rd ed. (London: 1958); A. Vis, *Messianic Psalm Quotations in the New Testament* (Amsterdam: 1939).

28. A.W. Argyle, *Parallels Between the Pauline Epistles and Q*, in *ExpT* 60 (1949), pp. 318-320; *Idem, St. Paul and the Mission of the Seventy*, in *JTS*, new Series, 1 (1950), p. 63.

29. L. Goppelt, *Typos. Die typologische Deutung des A.T. ih Neuen* (Gutersloh: 1939); W.H. Lampe, *Typological Exegesis*, in *Th* 16 (1953), p. 202; S. Amsler, *La typologie de l'A.T. chez saint Paul*, in *RTP* 37 (1949), pp. 113-128.

30. Cfr J. Weiss, *Beiträge zur paulinischen Rhetorik* (Göttingen: 1917), pp. 174-181; J. Nélis, *Les antithèses littéraires dans les épîtres de saint Paul*, in *NRT* 70 (1948), pp. 360-387.

31. O. Kuss, *Der Römerbrief*, pp. 131-154.

32. W. Kamlah, *Buchstabe und Geist, Die Bedeutung dieser Antithese für die alttestamentliche Exegese des Apostles Paulus*, in *EvT* 14 (1954), pp. 276-282.

33. B. Schneider, *The Meaning of Paul's Antithesis "The Letter and the Spirit,"* in *CBQ* 15 (1953), pp. 163-207.

34. L. Cerfaux, *Le Christ dans la Théologie de saint Paul* (Paris: 1951), pp. 189-208, Eng. tr. *Christ in the Theology of Saint Paul* (Herder and Herder).

35. E. Schweizer, *Rm 1,3s. und der Gegensatz von Fleisch und Geist vor und bein Paulus*, in *EvT* 15 (1955), pp. 563-571; D. Flusser, *The Dead Sea Sect and Pre-Pauline Christianity. 9. Flesh and Spirit*, in *ScrH* (1958), pp. 252-267.

36. J. Jeremias, *Chaismus in der Paulusbriefen*, in *ZNW* 49 (1958), pp. 139-156.

37. V. Heylen, *Les métaphores et les métonymies dans les épîtres pauliniennes*, in *ETL* 8 (1935), pp. 253-290.

38. B. Rigaux, *Les Épîtres aux Thessaloniciens*, pp. 89-90. Cfr. E. von Dobschütz, *Zwei- und dreigliedrige Formeln. Ein Beitrag zur Vorgeschichte der Trinitätsformel*, in *JBL* (1931), pp. 117-147; *Idem, Paarung und Dreiung in der evangelischer Ueberlieferung*, in *Festsch. G. Heinrici* (Leipzig: 1914), pp. 92-100.

39. R. Volkmann, *Die Rhetorik der Grieken und Römer in systematischer Uebersicht*, 2nd ed. (Leipzig: 1885); J. Weiss, *Beiträge zur paulinischen Rhetorik* (Göttingen: 1897); W. Kroll, art. *Rhetorik*, in *Pauly-Wissowa RE*, suppl. 7 (1940), col. 1128-1135; A.M. Vitti, *L'eloquenza di S. Paolo nelle sue lettere*, in *Bib* 21 (1940), pp.

413-425; W.A. Jemrich, *Rhetorical Style in the N.T., Romans and Hebrews* (Diss. Washington: 1946) ; E.B. Allo, *Le défaut d'éloquence et le style oral de saint Paul*, in *RSPhTh* 23 (1934), pp. 29-39; L.V. Garland, *The Sequence of Thought in the Pauline Epistles*, in *Th* 33 (1936), pp. 228-238; A. Brunot, *Le génre littéraire*, pp. 200-201.

40. S. Lyonnet, *Quaestiones in epistolam ad Romanos*, I (Rome: 1959), pp. 52-62.

41. R. Bultmann, *Der Stil der paulinischen Predigt und die kynische-stöische Diatribe* (Göttingen: 1910), p. 73; A. van Geytenbeck, *Musonius Rufus en de Griekse diatribe* (Brussels: 1948) ; H. Thyen, *Der Stil der Jüdisch-Hellenistischen Homilie* (Göttingen: 1955).

42. Grammars analyze such phenomena. Cfr. F. Blass and A. Debrunner, *Grammatik des neutestamentlichen Griechisch, 9th ed.* (Göttingen: 1954), pp. 478-496.

43. B. Rigaux, *Les Épîtres aux Thessaloniciens*, p. 92.

44. L. Nieder, *Die Motive der religiös-sittlichen Paränese in den Paulinischen Gemeindebriefen. Ein Beitrag zur paulinischen Ethik* (*Münchener Theologische Studien, Historische Abteilung*, I, Munich: 1956).

45. R. Bultmann, *Der Stil der Paulinischen Predight und die kynisch-stöische Diatribe* (Göttingen: 1910). See also: C. Schmich, *De arte rhetorica in Musenii diatribis conspicua* (Freiburg: 1902) ; H. Oltramare, *Les Origines de la diatribe romaine* (Geneva: 1926) ; J. Konopasek, *Les "questions rhétoriques" dans le N.T.*, in *RHPR* 12 (1932), pp. 47-66, 141-161; R.M. Pope, *The Greek Style of St .Paul*, in *ExpT* 49 (1937-1938), pp. 534-535.

46. Due to a lack of specialized studies, cfr. Th. Boman, *Das Hebräische Denken im Vergleich mit dem Griechischen* (Göttingen: 1952) ; L. Köhler, *Der Hebräische Mensch. Eine Skizze* (Tübingen: 1953) ; C. Tresmontant, *Essai sur la pensée hébraïque* (Paris: 1953) Eng. tr. *Study of Hebrew Thought* (Desclee: 1960) ; E.E. Flack, *The Apostle Paul and the Old Testament*, in *LQ* 53 (1923), pp. 330-356.

47. R. Schnackenburg, *Die Johannesbriefe,* (*Herders Theol. Kommentar z. N.T.*, Freiburg: 1953), *Zur Vorgeschichte des "Antichrist"* - *Erwartung*, pp. 127-132; J. Chaine, *Les Épîtres Catholiques* (*Études Bibliques*, Paris: 1939), p. 168.

48. L.G. Champion, *Benedictions and Doxologies in the Epistles of Paul* (Diss. Heidelberg: 1934) ; A. Stuiber, *Doxologie*, in *Reallexikon für Antike und Christentum* (1959), pp. 210-226; J.A. Jungmann, art. *Doxologie*, in *LTK*, 2nd ed. (1959), p. 534.

49. B. Rigaux, *Les Épîtres aux Thessaloniciens*, pp. 259-280.

50. Cfr. A. Campbell, *Ephesians in the Light of Form Criticism*, in *ExpT* 63 (1951-1952), pp. 273-276.

51. See N.A. Dahl, *Anamnesis. Mémoire et Commémoration dans le Christianisme primitif*, in *ST* 21 (1947), p. 82, note 1; E. Schweizer, *Erniedrung und Erhöhung bei Jesus und seinen Nachflogern* (Zurick:

1955), pp. 51-52, note 221; H. Conzelmann distinguishes between confessions in prose as Col.1,13-14, in chant form, as Col.1,15-20, and reserves the term, hymn, for such type compositions as the psalms. Cfr. E. Schweizer, *Erniederung*, note 221.

52. F.R.M. Hitchcock, *The Structure of Paul's Hymn of Love*, in *ExpT* 34 (1923), pp. 488-492.

53. Cfr. H. Riesenfeld, *Étude bibliographique sur la notion biblique d' AGAPE*, in *Coniectanea Neotestamentica*, 5 (1941), completed by his study, *Note bibliographique sur 1 Co XIII*, in *Nuntius Sodalicii neotestamentici Upsaliensis*, 6 (1952), pp. 47-48. Actually, no other introduction can surpass the study of C. Spicq, *Agapé dans le Nouveau Testament*, 2 (Paris: 1959), pp. 53-120, Eng. tr. *Agape in the N.T.* (Herder: 1963), Nevertheless, we would single out the following: G. von Rad, *Die Vorgeschichte der Gattung von 1 Co 13*, 4-7, in *Beitr. z. hist. Theol.*, 16. *Festschr. A. Alt* (Tübingen: 1953), pp. 154-168; A. Barr, *Love in the Church, A Study of 1 Co 13*, in *ScotJT* 3 (1950), pp. 416-425; J. Brennan, *The Exegesis of 1 Co 13*, in *ITQ* 21 (1954), pp. 270-278.

54. Spicq, *Op.cit.*, p. 59.

55. A von Harnack, *Das hohe Lied des Apostels Paulus von der Liebe*, in *Sitz. Ber. der Akad. d. Wiss.* (Berlin: 1911), I, pp. 132-163.

56. E. Hoffmann, *Zu 1 Co XIII und Col III, 14* (*Coniectanea Neotestamentica*, 3, 1938), pp. 28-31.

57. G. Rudberg, *Zu 1 Cor XIII, ibidem*, p. 32.

58. N.W. de Witt, *1 Kor XIII. Eine christlich-stoïsche Diatribe*, in *TSK* 94 (1922), pp. 55-95; W. Jaeger, *Tyrtaios. Über die wahre Arete*, in *Sitzungsb. d. Akd. d. Wissensch.* (Berlin: 1932), pp. 537-568.

59. Cfr. Spicq, *op.cit.*, pp. 62-63.

*** *Translator's Note*: R.H. Charles, *The Apocrypha and Pseudepigrapha of the Old Testament in English*, vol. II, *Pseudepigrapha* (Oxford: 1966 reprint), pp. 326, 357.

60. G. von Rad, *Die Vorgeschichte der Gattung von 1 Kor XIII*, 4-7, in *Geschichte und Altes Testament, Festschrift A. Alt* (Tübingen: 1953), pp. 153-168.

61. E. Lohmeyer, *Kyrios Jesus*, in *Sitzungsb. der Heidelberger Akad. Phil.-Hist. Klasse* 18 (1927-1928), *Eine Untersuchung zu Phil. 2, 5-11*. Before this study, there was the work of M. Guignebert, *Exégèse de Phil. 2*, in *RHPR* 3 (1923), pp. 512-533.

62. P. Benoit, *Aux Philippiens*, 3rd ed. (1959), p. 26.

63. P. Bonnard, *L'Épître de saint Paul aux Philippiens* (Neuchâtel: 1950).

64. Dibelius, *An die Philipper*, 3rd ed. (1937).

65. W. Michaelis, *Einleitung*, pp. 203-204.

66. L. Cerfaux, *L'hymn au Christ-Serviteur de Dieu*, in *Miscell. historic.*, *A. de Meyer* (1946), I, pp. 117-130 = *Mélanges Cerfaux*, II, pp. 425-437.

67. J. Jeremias, *Zur Gedankenführung in den Paulinischen Briefen*, in

Studia Paulina (Haarlem: 1953) pp. 152-154, which is followed by O. Michel, *Zur Exegese von Phil.2,5-11, Theologie als Glaubenwagnis*, in Festsch. K. Heim, (1954), pp. 759f. Jeremias is not acquainted with the article of Cerfaux.

68. W.K.L. Clarke, in *New Testament Studies*, pp. 146 f., which is cited by J.M. Furness, in *ExpT* 70 (1958), pp. 240-243.

69. P. Bonnard, *L'Épître de saint Paul aux Philippiens* (Neuchâtel: 1950), pp. 47-49.

70. O. Cullmann, *Les premiéres confessions chrétiennes* (Paris: 1943), pp. 47-48.

71. E. Barnikol, *Die marcionitische Ursprung des Mythossatzes Phil. II, 6-7* (Kiel: 1932).

72. J. Héring, *Kyrios Anthropos*, in *RHPR* 16 (1936), pp. 196-209; *Idem*, *Le Royaume de Dieu et sa venue*, 2nd ed. (Neuchâtel: 1959), pp. 159-170.

73. E. Stauffer, *Theologie des N.T.* (Gutersloh: 1948), pp. 97-98.

74. V. Taylor, *The Person of Christ in New Testament Teaching* (London: 1958), p. 63.

75. J.M. Furness, *The Authorship of Philippians, II, 6-11*, in *Expt* 70 (1958), pp. 240-243.

76. R.P. Martin, *An Early Christian Confession: Philippians II, 5-11 in Recent Interpretation* (London: 1960).

77. L. Cerfaux, *Le Christ dans le théologie de saint Paul* (Paris: 1951), pp. 298-301, Eng. tr. *Christ in the Theology of Saint Paul* (Herder and Herder), P. Benoit also dealt with the passage as a hymn, fasc. *SBJ*, 2nd ed., pp. 57-58.

78. E. Lohmeyer, in *Meyerskommentar*, 9th ed. (1954), which is a flimsy revision of the 8th ed. (1930).

79. J. Weiss, *Christus. Die Anfänge des Dogmas* (1909), pp. 45-46; A. Deissmann, *Paulus*, 2nd ed., p. 75, Eng. tr. *Paul*.

80. E. Norden, *Agnostos Theos*, 2nd ed. (Leipzig: 1913).

81. M. Dibelius, *Handbuch de Lietzmann*, 3rd ed. by H. Greeven, Dibelius personally re-examined Col.

82. E. Stauffer, *Theologie*, p. 225, Eng. tr. *N.T. Theology*.

83. E. Percy, *Die Probleme*, p. 40.

84. J. Héring, *Le Royaume de Dieu*, p. 165, note 1.

85. Ch. Masson, *Commentaire de N.T., Aux Colossiens*, p. 185.

86. E. Käsemann, *Eine urchristliche Taufliturgie*, pp. 133-148, in *Festschrift R. Bultmann* (Stuttgart: 1949); reprinted in *Exegetische Versuche und Besinnungen*, I (Göttingen: 1960), pp. 34-51.

87. G. Bornkamm, *Das Bekenntnis in Hebräerbrief*, in *TBl* (1942), p. 63. The ideas of G. Bornkamm have been extensively developed by K.G. Eckart, *Exegetische Beobachtungen zu Kol 1, 9-20*, in *TV* 7 (1959-1960), pp. 87-106. Cfr. *TLZ* (1960), pp. 468-469, a review of a dissertation written by H. Hegermann.

88. E. Schweizer, *Die Kirche als Leib Christi in den paulinischen Antilegomena*, in *TLZ* 86 (1961), pp. 241-256.

89. N.A. Dahl, *Anamnesis*, p. 86.

90. W. Bieder, *Die Kolossische Irlehre und die Kirche von Heute*, in *ThS* (Zollikon: 1952), p. 52, note 93; G. Schille, *Liturgisches Gut*, 61, and Maurer, *Die Begründung der Herrschaft Christi über die Mächte nach Kolosser 1, 15-20*, *Wort und Dienst*, in *Jahrbuch der theologischen Schule Bethel*, new series, 4 (1955), p p. 74-93 admitted the nature of the passage as a hymn, without lingering on proof, similarly, G. Harder, *Paulus und das Gebet* (1936), pp. 47-51; G. Delling, *Das Gottesdienst im N.T.* (1952), pp. 57, 87.

91. J. M. Robinson, *A Formal Analysis of Col 1, 15-20*, in *JBL* 76 (1957), pp. 87-106.

92. Ch. Masson, *Éphésiens* (Neuchâtel: 1953), p. 48.

93. E. Norden, *Agnostos Theos*, p. 253, note 1.

94. Ch. Masson, *op. cit.*, p. 149.

95. E. Lohmeyer, *Das Proomium des Epheserbriefes*, in *TBl* 5 (1926), pp. 120-125; cfr. *ibidem*, pp. 233-234, a response to A. Debrunner, *Grundsätzliches über Kolometrie im N.T.*, *ibid.*, pp. 231-233; Th. Innitzer, *Der "Hymnus" im Epheserbrief (1, 3-14)*, in *ZKT* 28 (1904), pp. 612-621. N.A. Dahl, *Adresse und Proömium des Epheserbriefes*, in *TZ* 7 (1951), pp. 241-264.

96. J. Knabenbauer, *Commentarius . . . ad Ephesios* (Paris: 1912).

97. F. Prat, *La Théologie de saint Paul* (Paris: 1925), 2, pp. 126-133, 152-155.

98. H. Coppieters, *La doxologie de la lettre aux Ephésiens* in *RB*, new series (1906), pp. 74-106.

99. J. M. Bover, *Doxologiae epistulae ad Ephesios logica partitio*, in *Bib* 2 (1921), pp. 458-460.

100. M. Dibelius, *Handbuch de Lietzmann*.

101. W. Ochel, *Die Annahme eines Bearbeitung des Kolosserbriefes im Epheser Brief* (Marburg: 1934), pp. 18-32.

102. Ch. Maurer, *Der Hymnus von Eph 1 als Schlüssel zum ganzen Brief*, in *EvT* 11 (1951-1952), pp. 151-172.

103. Ch. Masson, *Éphésiens*, p. 149.

104. P. Benoit, *Aux Éphésiens*, 3rd ed., pp. 86-88.

105. H. Schlier, *Der Brief an die Epheser*, pp. 38-42.

106. Cited by Schlier, *op. cit.*, pp. 40-41, note 4.

107. N.A. Dahl, *Adresse*, pp. 241-264.

108. H. Schlier, *op. cit.*, p. 41.

109. H. Schlier, *op. cit.*, p. 38.

110. Ch. Masson, *op. cit.*, p. 152, note 4: "Only by trying over and over again in studying this genre can we hope to reach the goal." The author admitted that these are only conjectures.

111. A. Vögtle, *Die Tugend und Lasterkataloge exegetisch, religions-und formgeschichtlich untersucht*, (*Neutestamentliche Abhandlungen*, 16, 4-5, Munster: 1936).

112. K. Weidinger, *Die Haustafeln. Ein Stück urchristliche Paränese*, (*Untersuchungen z. N.T.*, 14, Leipzig: 1928), and M. J. Lagrange,

Le catalogue des vices dans l'Épître aux Romains (1, 28-31), in *RB*, new series, 8 (1911), pp. 534-549.

113. S. Wibbing, *Die Tugend- und Lasterkataloge im Neuen Testament und ihre Traditionsgeschichte unter besonderer Berücksichtigung der Qumran-Texte, (Beihefte zur ZNW*, 25, Berlin: 1959, with bibliography); W. Schrage, *Zur formalethischen Deutung der Paulinischen Paränese*, in *ZEvE* 4 (1960), pp. 207-233. C. J. Bjerkelund, *Stilen i de paulinske formaningssetninger*, in *NTT* 61 (1960), pp. 193-217.

114. A. Seeberg, *Der Katechismus der Urchristenheit* (Leipzig: 1908); Ph. Carrington, *The Primitive Christian Catechism* (Oxford: 1940); E. G. Selwyn, *The First Epistle of St. Peter* (London: 1952); E. Lohse, *Paränese und Kerygma im 1 Petrusbrief*, in *ZNW* 45 (1954), pp. 68-89.

115. Cfr. J. Barr, *The Semantics of Biblical Language* (Oxford: 1961).

Notes to Chapter VII

1. C. Spicq, *L'épître aux Hébreux (Études bibliques*, 2 vol. Paris: 1952); *Idem*, art. *Paul, Épître aux Hébreux*, in *DBS* 36 (1961), pp. 226-256 (to be continued).

2. O. Michel, *Über einige neuere Beiträge zur Exegese des Hebräerbriefes*, in *TGl* 42 (1967), pp. 186-204. The commentary of Michel is volume XIII of the collection, 1st ed. (1957). Besides, the commentary of F. C. Grant (New York: 1957) could be cited.

3. C. Spicq, *op. cit.*, I, pp. 379-411, which would complete the bibliography cited in his article.

4. A. M. Vitti, *Le bellezze stilistische della lettera agli Ebrei*, in *Bib* 17 (1936), pp. 137-166; *Idem, L'eloquenza de S. Paolo nelle sue Lettere*, in *Bib* 21 (1940), pp. 413-425; *Idem, Ultimi studi sulla lettera agli Ebrei*, in *Bib* 22 (1941), pp. 412-432; A. Médibielle, *L'épître aux Hébreux* (Paris: 1938): the structure, themes, arguments, advice, and exhortations by Paul; W. Leonard, *The Authorship of the Epistle to the Hebrews* (London: 1939). See J. Renié, *Manuel d'Écriture Sainte* (Paris: 1938), 6, p. 471; H. Simon and J. Prado, *Praelectiones biblicae (NT*, II, Turin: 1942), pp. 391-392.

5. J. Bonsirven, *Saint Paul, Épître aux Hébreux* (Paris: 1943); *Idem, Theologie du Nouveau Testament* (Paris: 1941), p. 217.

6. O. Kuss, *Der Brief an die Hebräer (Reg. Bibel*, Ratisbonne: 1953).

7. C. Spicq, *L'Épître aux Hébreux*, pp. 195-196.

8. A. Wikenhauser, *Einleitung*, pp. 333-334, Eng. tr. *N.T. Introd.*, pp.

9. J. Cambier, *Introduction à la Bible*, 2, pp. 552-553.

10. In C. Spicq, *op. cit.*, I, pp. 197-219, there are lists of authors and their works, which propose one or the other of these names.

11. Among the Protestants: E. Riggenbach, *Der Brief an die Hebräer* (Leipzig: 1922), xl-xli; K. Bornhäuser, *Empfänger und Verfasser des Briefes an die Hebräer* (Gutersloh: 1932), pp. 75-80; H. Strathmann, *Der Brief an die Hebräer (NTD*, 6th ed., Göttingen: 1953). Among

the Catholics: F. Prat, *Théologie de saint Paul*, 9th ed. (Paris: 1920), I, p. 427; A. Merk, art. *Hebräerbrief*, in *LTK*, 1st ed., 4, p. 586; K. Pieper, *Verfasser und Empfänger des Hebräerbriefes*, in *Neutestamentliche Untersuchungen* (Paderborn: 1939), pp. 46-65.

12. Martin Luther in his commentary on *Hebrews* (1522); Fr. Bleek, *Der Brief an die Hebräer* (Berlin: 1828-1840), 3 vols.; Th. Zahn, *Einleitung*, pp. 154-155; H. Appel, *Der Hebräerbrief, ein Schreiben des Apollos an judenchristen der Korintischen Gemeinde* (Leipzig: 1918); R. Ch. Lenski, *The Interpretation of the Epistle to the Hebrews* (Columbus, Ohio: 1946); J. Belser, *Einleitung in das Neue Testament*, 2nd ed. (Freiburg: 1905), pp. 576-577; I. Rohr, *Der Hebräerbrief* (Bonn: 1932), p. 10; W. Manson, *The Problem of the Epistle to the Hebrews*, in *BJRL* (1949), pp. 1-17; P. Ketter, *Hebräerbrief* (Freiburg: 1950), pp. 3-4; G. P. Lewis, *Study Notes on the N.T.* (London: 1949); C. Spicq, *op. cit.*, pp. 209-219: "Apollos would definitely fit the circumstances given by the epistle better than any other name" (p. 217); Fr. Lo Bue, *The Historical Background of the Epistle to the Hebrews*, in *JBL* (1956), pp. 52-57; G. Pérez, *Autenticidad y canonicidad de la Carta a los Hebreos*, in *CB* 13 (1956), pp. 216-226.

13. Cfr. C. Spicq, *op. cit.*, pp. 145-168.

14. Cfr. C. Spicq, *op. cit.*, pp. 145-155.

15. H. von Soden, *Der Brief an die Hebräer* (Freiburg: 1893), pp. 18-19; G. Milligan, *The Theology of the Epistle to the Hebrews* (Edinburgh: 1924); I. Nikel, *Der Hebräerbrief* (Münster: 1914); J. Behm, *Der gegenwärtige Stand der Frage nach dem Verfasser des Hebräerbriefes*, in *Festsch. des Friedrich-Franz-Gymnasiums* (1919), pp. 75-97; H. Windisch, *Der Hebräerbrief*, 2nd ed. (Tübingen: 1931), pp. 124-126; O. Michel, *Der Brief an die Hebräer* (*Meyerskommentar*, 10th ed., Göttingen: 1957), pp. 9-11; M. Meinertz, *Einleitung*, pp. 144-145; J. Schneider, *Der Hebräerbrief, übersetz und ausgelegt* (Leipzig: 1938); W. Michaelis, *Einleitung*, pp. 271-73; E. F. Scott, *The Epistle to the Hebrews* (Edinburgh: 1922), p. 8; E. Mangenot, art. *Hébreux* (*Épître aux*), in *DTC* 6 B, col. 2092; L. Pirot, art. *Hébreux*, in *DBS* 3, col. 1440; A. Oepke, *Das Neue Gottesvolk* (Gutersloh: 1950).

16. See especially C. Spicq, *op. cit.*, pp. 211-219, and *art. cit.*, pp. 248-249, where the author gives nine arguments.

17. Internal criticism can gives nothing more than indications to the effect that Apollos would be the most suitable candidate for authorship. Besides, identification of the author is not very important since we know very little about him from other sources and since we have no other composition of this author. The problem of canonicity is not determined by solutions to the question of authorship.

18. E. J. Goodspeed, *First Clement Called Forth by Hebrews*, in *JBL* (1911), pp. 157-160; *Idem, The Problem of Hebrews*, in *JBR* 22 (1954), p. 322.

19. See the list in C. Spicq, *op. cit.*, p. 253, note 3.

20. H. Strathmann, *Der Brief an die Hebräer* (Göttingen: 1937), p. 65; W. Michaelis, *Einleitung*, p. 273 (shortly after the year 80 A.D.); F. V. Filson, *The Epistle to the Hebrews*, in *JBR* 22 (1954), pp. 20-26; V. Taylor, *The Atonement in N.T. Teaching*, 2nd ed. (1946), p. 101.

21. Cfr. the authors cited by C. Spicq, *op. cit.*, p. 253, note 2, p. 254, notes 4 and 5; cfr. W. Manson, *The Epistles to the Hebrews* (1951). For Spicq, it is highly probable that it should be worded "before the harvest time in 70, when the Temple and the Holy City were destroyed"; *art. cit.*, p. 255, and "at the beginning of the Jewish War in 68" (p. 256).

22. Cfr. C. E. Carlston, *Eschatology and Repentance in the Epistle to the Hebrews*, in *JBL* 48 (1959), pp. 296-302.

23. Cfr. C. Spicq, *art. cit.*, pp. 226-230.

24. H. Thyen, *Der Stil der jüdisch-hellenistischen Homelie* (Göttingen: 1955), pp. 8-17.

25. H. von Soden, *Der Hebräerbrief*, in *Jahrbücher für protestantische Theologie* (1884), pp. 485-493, 627-656.

26. See C. Spicq, *op. cit.*, p. 223, note 1, the principal authors who favor the addressees as ethnically Christian; cfr. A. M. Dubarle, *Rédacteur et destinataires de l'Épître aux Hébreux*, in *RB* (1939), pp. 521-528, and F. J. Schierse, *Verheissung und Heilsvollendung. Zur theologischen Grundfrage des Hebräerbriefes* (Munich: 1955), p. 3.

27. A. M. Dubarle, *art. cit.*, pp. 521-528.

28. W. Manson, *The Epistle to the Hebrews* (1951).

29. The names of those authors who claim that the letter was written to Romans, in C. Spicq, *op. cit.*, p. 232, note 2. Concerning the nature of the domestic assembly, *ibidem*, p. 224, note 2. Cfr. F. V. Filson, *The Significance of the Early House Churches*, in *JBL* (1939), pp. 105-112.

30. Cfr. C. Spicq, *op. cit.*, p. 239, note 1, for the names of those who hold this opinion.

31. Since St. John Chrysostom and St. Ephrem. The opinion was widely prevalent. Cfr. C. Spicq, *op. cit.*, p. 239, note 1.

32. Cfr. art. 1 of this chapter to see the response of these two authors to the question of authorship of the epistle.

33. E. Riggenbach, *Der Brief an die Hebräer* (*Kommen. z. N.T. Zahn*, 14, Leipzig: 1922), xlvi-xlvii.

34. F. Lo Bue, *The Historical Background of the Epistle to the Hebrews*, in *JBL* 75 (1956), pp. 52-57; H. Appel, *Der Hebräerbrief* (Leipzig: 1918).

35. Cfr. C. Spicq, *op. cit.*, pp. 234-238.

36. This is not the only instance in which the author reverts to a Pentateuchal text which was not in accord with contemporary usage. See S. Lach, *Les ordonnances du culte israélite dans la Lettre aux Hébreux*, in *SP* 2 (1959), pp. 390-403; Heb. 7, 27; 9, 4b, and our

text 9, 4a. The author goes back to the ideal times of Moses, a device common to the monks at Qumran.

37. F. V. Filson, *art. cit.*

38. K. Pieper, *Verfasser und Empfänger des Hebräerbriefes* (Paderborn: 1939).

39. C. Spicq, *op. cit.*, pp. 226-231; *art. cit.*, pp. 251-253. Cfr. J. V. Brown, *The Authorship and Circumstances of "Hebrews" Again*, in *BS* 80 (1923), pp. 505-538; K. Bornhäuser, *Empfänger und Verfasser des Briefes an die Hebräer* (Gutersloh: 1932); M. E. Clarkson, *The Antecedents of the High-Priest Theme in Hebrew*, in *AnglTR* (1947), pp. 89-95; P. Ketter, *Hebräerbrief* (Freiburg: 1950).

40. And this is the reason why I do not accept the attempt of Yigael Yadin, *The Dead Sea Scrolls and the Epistle to the Hebrews*, in *ScrH* 4 (1957), pp. 36-55, to identify the addresses of the epistle to the Hebrews as a group of the members of the community at Qumran who became Christians, a theory which he claimed would clarify the contents of the letter.

41. A. Deissmann, *Licht vom Osten* 4th ed., (Tübingen: 1923), p. 207.

42. O. Michel, *Der Brief an die Hebräer.*

43. F. J. Schierse, *Verheissung und Vollendung*, pp. 206-207: "the first liturgical homily"; O. Kuss, *Zur Deutung des Hebräerbriefes*, in *TR* 53 (1957), pp. 247-254.

44. H. Windisch, *Der Hebräerbrief* (*Handbuch z. N.T.*, Tübingen: 2nd ed.: 1931), pp. 122 f.: H. Strathmann, *Der Brief an die Hebräer* (*NTD*, 4th ed., 9, Göttingen: 1947); G. Schille, *Katechese und Taufliturgie. Erwägungen zu Hb II 9*, in *ZNW* 51 (1960), pp. 112-131.

45. C. Spicq, *L'authenticité du ch. XIII de l'Épître aux Hébreux*, (*ConNT*, 11, 1947), pp. 226-236.

46. Cfr. the lengthy chapter concerning the language and the literary characteristics of Hebrews in C. Spicq, *op. cit.*, pp. 351-378.

47. O. Michel, *Der Brief an die Hebräer*, pp. 6-7; H. Windisch, *Der Hebräerbrief*; E. Käsemann, *Das Wandernde Gottesvolk. Eine Untersuchung zum Hebräerbrief* (Göttingen: 1959).

48. "Formerly it was customary to distinguish between the dogmatic section and, from 10, 19 the moral section in the letter to the Romans; now for all practical purposes such a distinction is universally recognized as unfeasible." F. J. Schierse, *op. cit.*, p. 196. Cfr. W. Hillmann, *Das Wort der Mahnung. Einführung in die Grundgedanken des Hebräerbriefes*, in *BL* 1 (1960), pp. 17-27.

49. F. Bleek, *Der Brief an die Hebraer*, 3 vol. (Berlin: 1828-1840); *Idem, Der Hebräerbrief erklärt* (Ebberfeld: 1868), a work published after his death; J. Moffatt, *The Epistle to the Hebrews* (Edinburgh: 1924); W. Michaelis, *Einleitung*, pp. 65-266.

50. O. Holtzmann, *Das Neue Testament* (Giessen: 1926); H. Windisch, *Der Hebräerbrief*, 2nd ed. (1932).

51. E. Riggenbach, *Der Brief an die Hebräer*, 2nd-3rd ed. (Erlangen: 1922).

52. G. Hollmann, *Der Hebräerbrief* (*Die Schriften des N.T. neu übersetzt und für die Gegenwart erklärt von J. Weiss*, Göttingen: 1908), vol. 2, pp. 443-502.

53. O. Michel, *Der Brief an die Hebräer*, 10th ed. (1957).

54. H. Strathmann, *Der Brief an die Hebräer* (1947).

55. F. J. Schierse, *Verheissung und Heilsvollendung*, pp. 196-209.

56. L. Vaganay, *Le plan de l'Épître aux Hébreux*, in *Mémorial Lagrange* (Paris: 1940), pp. 269-277.

57. C. Spicq, *Le plan de l'Épître aux Hébreux, op. cit.*, pp. 27-38.

58. A. Vanhoye, *La structure centrale de l'épître aux Hébreux* (*He.* 8, 1 - 9, 28), in *RSR* 47 (1959), pp. 44-60. A. Vanhoye made a complete study of the literary structure of the epistle to the Hebrews in the first volume of *Studia Neotestamentica*.

59. A. Descamps, *La structure de l'épître aux Hébreux*, in *RDT* 9 (1954), pp. 251-258, 333-338.

60. P. Gillis, *De Brief aan de Hebreeën, 1, 1-10, 18. Studie van het plan en literaire ontleding*, a type-written thesis (Louvain: 1959).

61. R. Gyllenberg, *Die Komposition des Hebräerbriefs*, in *SEA* 22-23 (1957-1958), pp. 137-147.

62. We cannot expand on these topics here since they pertain more to the theology of the letter.

63. C. Spicq, *op.cit.*, pp. 109-138; *art. cit.*, pp. 241-244.

64. Cfr. B . Rigaux, *Révélation des Mystéres et perfection à Qumrân et dans le Nouveau Testament*, in *NTS* 4 (1957-1958), pp. 237-262ffi A. Wikgren, *Patterns of Perfection in the Epistle to the Hebrews*, in *NTS* 6 (1959-1960), pp. 159-167.

65. Cfr. C. Spicq, *op.cit.*, pp. 334-336.

66. Cfr. G. Wüttke, *Melkisedeq, der Priesterkönig von Salem* (Giessen: 1927) ; V. Burch, *The Epistle to the Hebrews. Its Sources and Message* (London: 1936) ; J. van den Ploeg, *L'exégèse de l'Ancien Testament dans l'épître aux Hébreux*, in *RB* (1947), pp. 187-228, an excellent study; P. Katz, *The Quotations from Deuteronomy in Hebrews*, in *ZNW* 49 (1958), pp. 217-223; G.B. Caird, *The Exegetical Method of the Epistle to the Hebrews*, in *CanJT* 5 (1959), pp. 44-51; F.C. Synge, *Hebrews and the Scriptures* (London: 1959) ; S. Kistemacher, *The Psalm Citations in the Epistle to the Hebrews*, a thesis (Amsterdam: 1961) ; J. Coppens, *Les affinités qumrâniennes de l'Épître aux Hébreux*, in *NRT* 84 (1962), pp. 128-141, 257-282. The author gives the structure of the epistle on pp. 136-139.

67. The author who championed the idea concerning the influence of Philo on the letter to the Hebrews was C. Spicq, *Apollos est un disciple de Philon, op.cit.*, pp. 47, 49, 70, and 89. Cfr. J. Cambier, *Eschatologie ou hellénisme dans l'épître aux Hébreux* (Louvain: 1949), with bibliography; C.K. Barrett, *The Eschatology of the Epistle to the Hebrews*, in *The Background of the N.T. and its*

Eschatology in Honour of C.H. Dodd (1956), pp. 363-393; C.
Spicq, *L'Épître aux Hébreux, Apollos, Jean-Baptiste, les hellénistes et
Qumrân,* in *RevQ* 1 (1959), pp. 365-390.
68. E. Käsemann, *Das wandernde Gottesvolk,* p. 156.
69. H. Jonas, *Gnosis und spätantiker Geist (Forsch. zur Rel. u. Lit. des
A. u. N.T.,* 51). 1. *Die mythologische Gnosis,* 2nd ed. (Göttingen:
1954) ; 2. *Von der Mythologie zur mystischen Philosophie* (Göttingen: 1954).
70. F.J. Schierse, *Verheissung und Heilsvollendung,* pp. 9-11, 196.

Notes to the Epilogue

1. The German version of the present volume by Rigaux has appeared under the title, *Paulus und seine Briefe. Der Stand der Forschung (Biblische Handbibliothek,* 2, Munich: 1964). E. Earle Ellis offers a good
synthesis of present positions in *Paul and his Recent Interpreters*
(Grand Rapids, Michigan: 1961), of which only the first chapter on
pp. 11-34 is relevant to the title of the book. The Pauline epistles are
explained in popular form by J. Cantinat, *Les épîtres de saint Paul
expliquées* (Paris: 1960), and in F.W. Beare, *St. Paul and his
Letters* (London: 1962). A similar work is that of R.H. Fuller, *The
New Testament in Current Studies* (New York-London: 1962-1963),
whose chapter on *Pauline Studies,* pp. 68-83 is worthwhile. To follow
the bulletins on biblical theology by A. Viard would be profitable,
in *RSPhTh* 45 (1961), pp. 284-313; 46 (1962), pp. 254-282; 47 (1963),
pp. 221-246; by F. Dreyfus in the same review, 48 (1964), pp.
316-341. It is hardly necessary to single out the current bibliography
in *Bib, NTA, ETL, ZNW,* together with the latest volume of *Internationale Zeitschriftenschau für Bibelwissenschaft und Grenzgebiete* 13
(1966-1967). There is moreover the *Index to Periodical Literature on
the Apostle Paul (New Testament Tools and Studies,* I, Grand Rapids,
Michigan: 1960), which is useful, but could hardly be considered an
exhaustive treatment, since the collator had overlooked some important
items. Cfr. A. Feuillet, *L'hymne christologique de l'Épître aux Philippiens (II,* 6-11), in *RB* 72 (1960), p. 352, n.2; J.A. Fitzmyer, in
TS 21 (1960), pp. 643-644; G.S. Glanzmann and J.A. Fitzmeyer, *An
Introductory Bibliography for the Study of Scripture* (Westminster,
Maryland: 1961), p. 126-127. Finally, there is the classic study of W.
G. Kümmel, *Einleitung in das Neue Testament,* 13th ed. (Heidelberg:
1964).

2. B. Rigaux, *Vocabulaire chrétien antérieur á la première épître aux
Thessaloniciens,* in *Sacra Pagina* 2 (Paris-Gembloux: 1959), pp.
380-389; Cfr. P.E. Langevin, *Le Seigneur Jésus selon un texte pré-
paulinien, I Th.* 1,9-10, in *Sciences Ecclésiastiques* 14 (1965), pp.
163-282, 423-512.

3. G. Braumann, *Vorpaulinische Christliche Taufverkündigung bei Paulus
(Beiträge zur Wissenschaft von A. u. N.T.* 5/2, Stuttgart: 1961).

4. W. Kramer, *Christus. Kyrios. Gottessohn. Untersuchungen zu Gebrauch der christologischen Bezeichnungen bei Paulus und in den vorpaul. Gemeinden (Abhandlungen zur Theologie des A. u. N.T.* 44, Zurich-Stuttgart: 1963). St. Paul is the point of reference for the titulature of Jesus. Besides the works already referred to, see B.M.F. van Iersel, *Der Sohn in den synoptischen Jesusworten (SupplNT* 3, Leiden: 1961); F. Hahn, *Christologische Hoheitstitel. Ihre Geschichte im frühen Christentum (Forschungen zur Rel. u. Lit. des A. u. N.T.* 83, Göttingen: 1963). Cfr. the critical reviews of Ph. Vielhauer, *Die Frage der christologischen Hoheitstitel*, in *TLZ* 90 (1965), pp. 569-588; P. E. Langevin, *La seigneurie de Jésus dans quelques textes prépauliniens du N.T.* (Dissert. Pont. Gregorianae, Rome: 1964), cfr. H.L. Jungman, *Pistis. A Study of its Presuppositions and its Meaning in Pauline Use (Acta Regia Soc. Hum. Litt. Lundensis* 64, Lund: 1964). *Translator's Note*: cfr. also J. Jeremias, *Artikelloses Christos. Zur Ursprache von I Cor* 15: 3*b*-5, in *ZNW* 57 (1966), pp. 211-215, in its original form, goes back to a primitive semitic text, against Ph. Vielhauer and H. Conzelmann. P. Fannon, *Paul and Tradition in the Primitive Church*, in *Scrip* 16 (1964), pp. 47-56.

5. B. Rigaux, *Réflexions sur l'historicité de Jésus dans le message paulinien*, in *S. P. Congressus* 1961 (Rome: 1963), pp. 373-382; W. Schmithals, *Paulus und der historischer Jesus*, in *ZNW* 53 (1962), pp. 145-160; also *Paulus und Jakobus* (Göttingen: 1963).

6. E. Jüngel, *Paulus und Jesus. Eine Untersuchung zur Präzisierung der Frage nach dem Ursprung der Christologie (Hermeneutische Untersuchungen zur Theologie* 2, 2nd ed. Tübingen: 1964). Cfr. the reviews of H. Gollwitzer, in *EvT* 25 (1965), pp. 11-24; J.M. Robinson, *The New Hermeneutic at Work*, in *Int* 18 (1964), pp. 346-359; J. Blank, *Rückehr zum Mythus?* in *Una Sancta* 18 (1963), pp. 167-173.

7. W.G. Kümmel, *Jesus und Paulus* (Presidential Address at the Nothingham Meeting of SNTS, September: 1963), in *Heilsgeschehen und Geschichte. Gesammelte Aufsätze*, 1933-1964 (Marburg: 1965), pp. 439-456 (cfr. also *NTS* 10, 1963-1964, pp. 163-181), a reprobation of the theses of E. Stauffer, contained principally in *Jesus, Paulus, und Wir* (Berne: 1961), where Stauffer claims that Paul stands irreducibly in opposition to the spirit of Jesus.

8. E. Earle Ellis, *op.cit.*, p. 34: "Pauline redemption is not a 'spiritual' deliverance culminating in the escape of the 'soul' at death (Dodd); it is a physical redemption culminating in the deliverance of the whole man at the parousia (Cullman). It is to be understood not in terms of a Greek dualism but in the framework of the Old Testament-Jewish view of man as a unified being and as one who lives not only as an individual but in 'corporate solidarities'. The future that has become present in the Resurrection of Jesus Christ is a future which the Christian realizes now only corporately, as the 'Body of Christ'. However, at the parousia faith shall become sight, 'away' shall become 'at home', and the solidarities of the new age shall become individually

actualized in all their glory. This is the living hope of Paul's heart and in it one finds the meaning of his theology." W.G. Kümmel perceives very well that eschatology constitutes the central factor of contemporary discussions: "The insight gained from the latest discussions is that we must clarify above all else three problems in efforts to understand Pauline theology so as to obtain a correlation between Pauline theology and the preaching and person of Jesus: a) the nature of Pauline eschatology; b) where Paul stands in the context of religious history; and c) the meaning of the traditional Jesus and of the person of Jesus in Paul's mind." *Op.cit.*, pp. 447-448. Similar ideas are offered by E. Käsemann, *Anfänge christlicher Theologie*, in *Exegetische Versuche und Besinnungen* 2 (Göttingen: 1964), p. 104.

9. O. Koch, *Die eschatologische Frage, ihre Entwicklung und ihr gegenwärtiger Stand. Versuch einer knappen Uebersicht*, in *BZ* 6 (1962), pp. 112-120; J.A. Sint, *Parusie-Erwartung und Parusie-Verzörgerung im paulinischen Briefcorpus*, in *ZKT* 86 (1964), pp. 47-79. Also see B. Vawter, *And He Shall Come Again With Glory, Paul and Christian Apocalyptic*, in *Analecta Biblica* 17-18 (1963), pp. 143-150. *Translator's Note*: Cfr. also R. Schnackenburg, *Leben auf Hoffnung hin. Christliche Existenz nach Röm* 8, in *BiLit* 39 (1966), with bibliography. H. W. Boers, *Apocalyptic Eschatology in I Corinthians* 15. *An Essay in Contemporary Interpretation*, in *Int* 21 (1967), pp. 50-65, reviewed by the author himself in *NTA* 11 (1967), p. 340, n. 1126; U. Gerber, *Röm. viii* 18*ff. als exegetisches Problem der Dogmatik*, in *NT* 8 (1966), pp. 58-81; C.H. Pinnock, *The Structure of Pauline Eschatology*, in *EvQ* 37 (1965), pp. 9-20.

10. H. Conzelmann, art. *Eschatologie. Im Urchristentum*, in *RGG* 2 (1958), pp. 665-672; P. Pringent, art. *Ende*, in *Biblisch-Historisches Handwörterbuch* 1 (1962), pp. 407-409.

11. See H.I. Marrou, *Le métier d'historien*, in *L'Histoire et ses méthodes* (Paris: 1961), pp. 1467-1540.

12 The statement of K. Stendahl is always apropos, *Kerygma und kerygmatisch. Von zweideutigen Ausdrücken der Predigt der Urkirche*, in *TLZ* 77 (1952), p. 715: "Theology has its own shibboleth. The term 'eschatology' is but one that could have as many different meanings as there are colors in the rainbow." These words have greater basis in reality than one would be tempted to think.

13. It would be impossible to list those monographs and studies covering detailed aspects of Pauline assertions that have been published. We can only designate currents of thought in present-day interpretations.

14. It is hardly to the point to recall the famous statement of R. Bultmann: "Eschatology is the mother of theology," which has its echo in E. Käsemann, *Die Anfänge christlicher Theologie*, in *Exegetische Versuche und Besunnungen* 2 (Göttingen: 1964), p. 104, in the following words: "The principle motif (of the New Testament) was the expectation of the Epiphany of the Son of Man who was coming in

order to be enthroned; without this theme, out of which sprang the Easter-experience and in which is rooted the Easter-faith, one may well wonder just what would become of Christian theology." Cfr. also H. Gollwitzer, in *EvT* 25 (1965), p. 23.

15. H.P. Owen, *Eschatology and Ethics in the New Testament*, in *ScotJT* 15 (1962), pp. 374-378; Cfr. C.H. Pinnock, *The Structure of Pauline Eschatology*, in *EvQ* 37 (1965), pp. 9-20.

16. W. Sachs, *Schweitzers Böcher zur Paulus-Forschung*, in *A. Schweitzer. Sein Denken und Weg* (Tübingen: 1962), pp. 178-183; G. Marchall, *Alberts Schweitzers Paulusdeutung, ibid.*, pp. 172-177; J.H. Burtness, *Eschatology and Ethics in the Pauline Epistles. A Study of Six Current Interpretations* (Diss. Princeton Theol. Sem.: 1958, a work which I have not examined); W.G. Kümmel, *Futurische und präsentische Eschatologie im ältesten Urchristentum*, in *NTS* 5 (1958-1959), pp. 351-363, reprinted in *Heilsgeschehen und Geschichte* (Marburg: 1965), pp. 351-363, and the English version in *Futuristic and Realized Eschatology in the Earliest Stages of Christianity*, in *JRel* 43 (1963), pp. 303-312.

17. We may just as well include E. Stauffer (*Agnostos Christos Joh. 2,24 und die Eschatologie des vierten Evangeliums*, in *The Background of the N.T. and its Eschatology . . . in Honor of C.H. Dodd*, Cambridge: 1956, pp. 281-299); *idem, Jesus. Gestalt und Geschichte* (Berne: 1957), pp. 11, 117; and J. Jeremias (*Die Gleichnisse Jesu*, 6th ed. Göttingen: 1962). Both adhere to this type of exegesis, although they have not studied Paul in this light. On the contrary, some catholics are still influenced by the views of Dodd. As they see it, there is a "rejudaisation" by the redactors of the synoptics and by Paul of the thought of Jesus. It is in the gospel of St. John in which they admittedly find pure eschatology uniquely presented. See also W. Grundmann, *Ueberlieferung und Eigenaussage im eschatologischen Denken des Paulus*, in *NTS* 8 (1961-1962), pp. 17-31; S.S. Smalley, *The Delay of the Parousia*, in *JBS* 83 (1964), pp. 41-54.

18. O. Cullmann, *Heil als Geschichte. Heilsgeschichtliche Existenz im N.T.* (Tübingen: 1965), well focused on the problems together with abundant bibliography. Cfr. L. Malevez, *Les dimensions de l'histoire du salut*, in*NRT* 86 (1964), pp. 561-578; F. Sciuto, *L' "histoire du salut" selon O. Cullman. Observations au point de vue historique*, in *Orpheus* 11 (Catania: 1964), pp. 43-62. For a similar idea on *Heilsgeschichte*, see H. Conzelmann, *Fragen an Gerhard von Rad*, in *EvT* 24 (1964), pp. 113-125; G. Klein, *Individualgeschichte und Weltgeschichte bei Paulus, ibid.*, pp. 126-163; Von Rad's response, *ibid.*, pp. 388-394. As for the first two, it is not a question of continuity between the Old and the New Testaments. Rather than a fulfillment, there is a complete break (*Abbruch*). *Translator's Note*: Cfr. also L. Goppelt, *Paulus und die Heilsgeschichte: Schlussfolgerungen aus Röm. IV und I Kor. x. 1-13*, in *NTS* 13 (1966), pp. 31-42. Typological hermeneutical principle to express Paul's concept of salvation-history.

19. As, for example, in the works of J. Körner, *Eschatologie und Geschichte* (1957), and E. Grässer, *Das Problem* (1957); also F. Hohmeier, *Das Schriftverständnis in der Theologie Rudolf Bultmanns* (*Arbeiten zur Geschichte und Theologie des Luthertums* 13, Berlin-Hamburg: 1964). The work of A. Malet, *Mythos et Logos. Le pensée de Rudolph Bultmann* (Geneva: 1962), has nothing of importance to offer on the question. A worthwhile appreciation of the work of Bultmann can be found in J.L. McKenzie, *Rudolf Bultmann. A Catholic Survey*, in *Month* 32 (1964), pp. 51-62. A less detailed presentation in G. Hasenhuetti, *Der Glaubensvollzug. Eine Begegnung mit Rudolf Bultmann aus katholischen Glaubensverständnis* (*Koinonia* I, Essen: 1963). For a critical presentation, cfr. J. Körner, *Katholisches Votum zur existentialen Interpretation*, in *TRu* 30 (1964), pp. 316-355; H.J. Forstmann, *The Interpretation of Scripture. IV. Bultmann's Conception and Use of Scripture*, in *Int* 17 (1963), pp. 450-465.

20. R. Bultmann most recently expressed his ideas in an article written in response to E. Käsemann: *Ist die Apokalyptik die Mutter der christlicher Theologie? Eine Auseinandersetzung mit Käsemann*, in *Apophoreta. Festschrift Ernst Haenchen* (Berlin: 1964), pp. 54-69. Cfr. Käsemann, *Die Anfänge christlicher Theologie*, in *Exegetische Versuche und Besinnungen 2* (Göttingen: 1964), cited above in footnote n. 14, and *Zum Thema der urchristlichen Apokalyptik*, in *ZTK* 59 (1962), pp. 257-284, reprinted in *Exegetische Versuche und Besinnungen 2* (Göttingen: 1964), pp. 105-131. Concerning the Post-Bultmannians, cfr. R.E. Brown, *After Bultmann, What? An Introduction to the Post-Bultmanians*, in *CBQ* 26 (1964), pp. 1-30; E. Fuchs, *Ueber die Aufgabe einer christlichen Theologie. Zum Aufsatz E. Käsemann über "Die Anfänge christlicher Theologie,"* in *ZTK* 58 (1961), pp. 246-267. Finally, there is the interesting observation made by G. Bornkamm, *Die Theologie Rudolfs Bultmanns in der neueren Diskussion. Zum Problem der Entmythologisierung und Hermeneutik*, in *TRu* 29 (1963), pp. 33-141, together with the bibliography of E. Brandenburger, pp. 33-46.

21. J.M. Robinson-J.B. Cobb, Jr. (ed.), *The New Hermeneutic: New Frontiers in Theology. Discussion among Continental and American Theologians* (New York: 1964), p. 2.

22. N.A. Dahl, *Eschatologie und Geschichte im Lichte der Qumrantexte*, in *Zeit und Geschichte. Dankesgabe an Rudolf Bultmann zum 80. Geburtstag* (Tübingen: 1964), pp. 3-18.

23. G. Delling, *Das Zeitverständnis des Neuen Testaments* (Gutersloh: 1960); O. Cullmann, *Heil als Geschichte*, pp. 10-46, a masterly drawn tableau of opinions and positions (with bibliography).

24. R. Bultmann, *Ist die Apokalyptik die Mutter der christlicher Theologie?*, cfr. above in note 20. Note that Bultmann refers *Apokalyptik* to biblical statements that pertain to future eschatology. *Translator's Note*: Also P. Stuhlmacher, *Erwägungen zum ontologischen Charakter der kaine ktisis bei Paulus*, in *EvT* 27 (1967), pp. 1-35.

25. J. Moltmann, *Theologie der Hoffnung. Untersuchungen zur Begründung und zu den Konsequenten einer christlichen Eschatologie (Beiträge zur evangelischen Theologie. Theologische Abhandlungen,* Bd. 38, Munich: 1966); C.K. Barrett, *From first Adam to Last. A Study in Pauline Theology* (London: 1962), especially the last chapter, *The Man to Come,* pp. 92-119; F.F. Bruce, *Promise and Fulfilment in Paul's Presentation of Jesus,* in *Festschrift S.H. Hooke* (Edinburgh: 1963), pp. 36-50.

26. N.G. Hamilton, *The Holy Spirit and Eschatology in Paul* (Edinburgh: 1957); R. Koch, *L'aspect eschatologique de l'Esprit du Seigneur d'après St Paul,* in *SP Congressus* 1961, I (Rome: 1963), pp. 131-141.

27. Recently, M. Bouttier, *En Christ. Étude d'exégèse et de théologie pauliniennes* (Paris: 1962), pp. 116-122. Formerly, F. Neugbauer, *In Christus. Untersuchungen zum paulinischen Glaubensverständnis* (Göttingen: 1961); P. Valotton, *Le Christ et la foi* (Geneva: 1960).

28. M. Rissi, *Die Taufe für die Toten. Ein Beitrag zur paulinischen Tauflehre (Abhandl. z. Theol. d. A.u. N.T.,* 42, Zurich-Stuttgart: 1962); J. Coppens, *L'Eucharistie, sacrement et sacrifice de la Nouvelle Alliance, fondement de l'Église,* in *Aux Origines de l'Église* (*Recherches Bibliques* 7, Paris-Bruges: 1965), pp. 125-158 (bibliography); N. Fueglister, *Die Heilsbedeutung des Pascha* (*Studien z. A. u. N.T.,* 8, Munich: 1963); R. Schnackenburg, *Baptism in the Thought of St. Paul,* rev. ed., transl. by G.R. Beasley-Murray (New York: 1964); B. Larsson, *Christus als Vorbild. Eine Untersuchung zu paulin. Tauf- und Eikontexten* (Uppsala: 1962).

29. Ch. Maurer, *Paulus als Apostel der Völker,* in *EvT* 19 (1959), pp. 28-40; F. Hahn, *Das Verständnis der Mission im N.T.* (*Wissenschaftliche Monographien z. A. u. N.T.,* 13, Neukirchen: 1963), pp. 80-94 126-134; G. Delling, *Römer 13 1-7 innerhalb der Briefe des N.T.* (Berlin: 1962).

30. W. Schrage, *Die konkreten Einzelgebote in der paulinischen Paränese* (Gutersloh: 1961). Cfr. R. Voelke, *Christ und Welt nach dem Neuen Testament* (Würzburg: 1961), pp. 138-154; E. Kamlah, *Die Form der katalogischen Paränese im N.T.* (*Wissenschaftl. Unters. z. N.T.,* 7, Tübingen: 1964).

31. H. Greeven, *Kirche und Parusie Christi,* in *Der Dogma* 10 (1964), pp. 113-135, a very important work.

32. S. Sandmel, *Parallelomania,* in *JBL* 81 (1962), pp. 1-13; J. Barr, *The Semantics of Biblical Language* (Oxford: 1961); *idem, Biblical Words for Time* (*Studies in Biblical Theology* 33, London: 1962).

33. L. Goppelt, *Apokalyptik und Typologie bei Paulus,* in *TLZ* 89 (1964), pp. 321-344; nature of the problem, a critique, and the author's own solution. Cfr. D.B. Bronson, *Paul and Apocalyptic Judaism,* in *JBL* 83 (1964), pp. 287-292. *Translator's Note*: L. Stefaniak, *Tworzywo projeciowe i literackie doktryny sw. Pawla Apostola* (*Idearum thesaurus et formae litterariae doctrinae S. Pauli*), in *RuchBL* 18 (1965), pp. 152-161, demonstrates that a deep faith in Jesus Christ as the Son

of God and a profound knowledge of the Old Testament and contemporary Jewish literature were the two important formative influences in Paul's intellectual development.

34. The literature is most abundant: H. Braun, *Qumran und das Neue Testament. Ein Bericht über 10 Jahre Forschung, 1950-1959,* in *TRu* 29 (1963), pp. 142-176, 189-260; 30 (1964), pp. 1-38, 89-137. See above all the masterful presentation of H. Braun, *Qumran und das Neue Testament,* 2 vol. (Tübingen: 1966), particularly the chapter on Paul, vol. 2, pp. 165-180. Cfr. H.H. Rowley, *The Qumran Sect and Christian Origins,* in *BJRL* 44 (1961-1962), pp. 119-156 (with bibliography); M. Black, *The Scrolls and Christian Origins. Studies in the Jewish Backgrounds of the N.T.* (Edinburgh: 1961). Of special interest is O. Betz, *Offenbarung und Schriftforschung in der Qumransekte* (Tübingen: 1960); H.W. Huppenbauer, *Zur Eschatologie der Damaskusschrift,* in *RevQ* 4 (1964), pp. 567-573; *Translator's Note*: R.E. Osborne, *Did Paul go to Qumran?* in *CanJT* 10 (1964), pp. 15-24; C. Daniel, *Une mention paulinienne des Esséniens de Qumran,* in *RevQ* 5 (1966), pp. 553-567 - 2 Cor 2.17 contains an allusion to the Essences; H. Chadwick, *St. Paul and Philo of Alexandria,* in *BJRL* 48 (1966), pp. 286-307, stated that Paul and Philo apparently have both drawn on a common stock of Hellenistic Jewish tradition; J.E. Wood, *Pauline Studies and the Dead Sea Scrolls,* in *ExpT* 78 n. 10 (July: 1967), pp. 308-311.

35. W. Schmithals, *Paulus und die Gnostiker. Untersuchungen zu den kleinen Paulusbriefen* (*Theologische Forschung* 35, Hamburg-Bergstedt: 1965); D. Georgi, *Die Gegner des Paulus im 2 Korintherbrief. Studien zur religiösen Propaganda in der Spätantike* (*Wissenschaftl. Monograph. z. A. u. N.T.,* 11, Neukirche: 1964). Cfr. also J.N. Sevenster, *Paul and Seneca* (*SupplNT,* 4, Leiden: 1961), pp. 219-240. The *religionsgeschichte* question is subjected to detailed investigation in the monograph of G. Wagner, *Das religionsgeschichtliche Problem von Röm 6 1-11* (*Abhandl. z. Theol. des A. u. N.T.,* 39, Zurich-Stuttgart: 1962). The entire question concerns the relations of Paul with the mysteries which he took up. The conclusion is that Paul moved in a world other than that of the mysteries.

36. R. Mc L. Wilson, *The Gnostic Problem. A Study of the Relations between Hellenistic Judaism and the Gnostic Heresy* (London: 1958). Since then, the bibliography has continued to grow particularly in the influence of the gnostic writings of Nag Hammâdi. The Apostle has not become very involved in such investigations. Indirectly, however, he could be easily included in the overall movement to rather remote origins. Concerning the question of Paul's relation with the pagan mysteries, there is the excellent work of G. Wagner, *Die religionsgeschichtliche Problem von Römer 6 1-11* (*Abhandl. z. Theol. des A. u. N.T.,* 39, Zürick-Stuttgart: 1962), with bibliography on pp. 307-326.

37. L. Cerfaux, *Le Chrétien dans la théologie paulinienne* (*Lectio divina,*

33, Paris: 1959). We might also single out two works of M. Bouttier, *En Christ. Études d'exégèse et de théologie pauliniennes (Études d'histoire et de philosophie religieuses,* Paris: 1962); *idem, La condition chrétienne selon S. Paul (Nouv. série théol.,* 16, Geneva: 1964); L. Cerfaux, *Le Christ dans la théologie de saint Paul,* 2nd ed. (Paris: 1954); *idem, La théologie de l'Église suivant saint Paul (Unam sanctam,* 54, Paris: 1948). *Translator's Note:* These last two works are in English translation as *The Church in the Theology of Saint Paul* (New York: 1959), and *Christ in the Theology of St. Paul* (New York: 1958). There is also the publication of *Recueil L. Cerfaux,* vol. 3 (Gembloux).

38. D.E.H. Whiteley, *The Theology of St. Paul* (Oxford: 1964), who has published important articles on Pauline doctrine. I would like to point out that the first chapter of the book does not intend nor can it present more than the broad lines of general orientation. A synthetic presentation of the Pauline message can be offered only in relation to scientific exigencies and to the problematic of unresolved questions, taking into account the means of information together with the various avenues of approach available, and as for the rest, to write.

39. G. Delling, *Die Botschaft des Paulus* (Berlin: 1965).

40. For more recent bibliographies, cfr. E. Fascher, *Paulus,* in *Sokrates und Christus. Beiträge zur Religionsgeschichte* (1959), pp. 245-308; N.I. Louvaris, *Eisagwgn eis tâs perì Pauloû spoudás,* 2nd ed. (Athens: 1960); F.C. Grant, *The Historical Paul,* in *Early Christian Origins* (London: 1961), pp. 48-59; J. Cambier, art. *Paul,* in DBS 7 (1962), pp. 279-387; J. Cantinat, *Vie de S. Paul apôtre* (Paris: 1964); R.G. Leavell, *The Apostle Paul. Christ's Supreme Trophy* (Grand Rapids: 1963); R.N. Longenecker, *Paul, Apostle of Liberty* (New York: 1964), cfr. *CBQ* 27 (1965), pp. 170-171; H. Ridderbos, *Paulus. Ontwerp van zijn theologie* (Kampen: 1966), a very important work; Ph. Seidenstieker, *Paulus, der verfolgter Apostel Jesu Christ* (Stuttgart: 1965).

41. L. Cerfaux, *La vocation de S. Paul,* in *Euntes Docete* 14 (1961), pp. 3-35; W. Pesch, *Die Bekehrung des Apostels Paulus nach dem Zeugnis seiner Briefe,* in *BiKi* 16 (1961), pp. 36-38; F.W. Maier, *Paulus als Kirchengründer und kirchlicher Organizator* (Würzburg: 1961); O. Haas, *Berufung und Sendung Pauli,* in *Zeitschrift für Mission Wissenschaft* 46 (1962), pp. 81-92; E. Klostermann, *Noch einmal über Paulus zum Apostelamt,* in *Wissenschaftl. Zeitschr. der Martin Luther Universität in Halle* 13 (1964), pp. 149-150.

42. G. Strecker, *Die sogenannte zweite Jerusalemreise des Paulus (Act. 11 27-30),* in *ZNW* 53 (1962), pp. 67-77.

43. F. Hahn, *Das Verständnis der Mission im Neuen Testament (Wissensch. Monogr. z. A. u. N.T.,* 13, Neukirchen: 1963), pp. 74-79, repeated in a study by D. Georgi, *Die Geschichte der Kollekte des Paulus für Jerusalem* (Heidelberg: 1965).

44. Bo Reicke, *Neutestamentliche Zeitgeschichte. Die biblische Welt 50 v. - 100 n. C. (Sammlung Topelmann,* 2nd series, 2, Berlin: 1965),

pp. 161-167. Cfr. S.D. Toussaint, *The Chronological Problem of Gal. 2 1-10*, in *BS* 120 (1963), pp. 334-340.

45. V. Mancebo, *Gal. II, 1-10 y Act. XV. Estado actual de la cuestion*, in *EstBib* 22 (1963), pp. 315-350.

46. H. Conzelmann, *Die Apostelgeschichte (Handb. z. N.T.*, 7, Tübingen: 1963).

47. A. Penna, *Le due pregione romane di S. Paolo*, in *Rivista Biblica* 9 (1961), pp. 193-208, a worthwhile expose of the entire question; V.J. Brondegaard, *Paulus i Rom*, in *Cath* 20 (1963), pp. 103-109; D. Squillaci, *L'Apostolo delle Genti. Saggi in ricordo del XIX Centenario della venuta a Roma e del suo passagio lungo le costi di Catania* (Catania: 1962); D. Lorenzo de Lorenzi, *Przybycie św. Pawla do Rzymu (La venue de Paul à Roma)*, in *Studia biblijne i archeologicze* (1963), pp. 49-69 (cfr. *Intern. Zeitschr. f. Bibelwiss, u. Grenzgebiete* 11, 1964-1965, no. 700); *San Pablo en España. Commemoracion del XIX centenario de sua venida*, 2nd ed. Tarragona: 1963); J. Leal, *Planes de S. Pablo sobre España* in *CB* 20 (1963), pp. 222-225; A.C. Vega, *La venida de S. Pablo a España y los Varones Apostolicos*, in *Bol. Real. Acad. de la Hist.* 154 (1964), pp. 7-78; S. del Paramo, *S. Pablo en España*, in *Sal Terrae* 51 (1963), pp. 257-268; See also P.E. Davies, *The Macedonian Scene of Paul's Journey*, in *BA* 26 (1963), pp. 91-106; G. Ogg, *Derbe*, in *NTS* 9 (1962-1963), pp. 367-370; F.F. Bruce, *St. Paul in Rome*, in *BJRL* 46 (1964), pp. 326-345; *Translator's Note*: W. Gnutek, *Pawel z Tarsu, Apostol Jezusa Chrystusa i pisarz natchniony (Paulus Tarsensis, Christi Jesu Apostolus et hagiographus)*, in *RuchBL* 18 (1965), pp. 142-151.

48. Concerning new methods of literary criticism with the use of the computer, see B.M. Ahern, *Who Wrote the Pauline Epistles?* in *The Bible Today* 1 (1964), pp. 54-60; R. Schippers, *Paul and the Computer*, in *Christianity Today* 9 (1964), pp. 223-225; cfr. W.G. Kümmel, *Das literarische und geschichtliche Problem des ersten Thessalonicherbriefes (Neutestamentica et Patristica. Freundesgabe O. Cullmann, SupplNT* 6, Leiden: 1962), pp. 213-227, also in *Heilsgeschehen und Geschichet. Gesammelte Aufsätze 1933-1964,* (Marburg: 1964), pp. 406-416. *Translator's Note*: concerning the question of authenticity and computer-criticism, cfr. the criticism of A.Q. Morton and J. McLeman, *Christianity in the Computer Age* (New York: Evanston, Ill., Harper & Row: 1955), by H.K. McArthur, *Computer Criticism*, in *ExpT* 76 (1965), pp. 367-370; the review of Morton and McLeman, by J.W. Ellison in *JBL* 84 (1965), pp. 190-191; Morton's reply to McArthur in *ExpT* 77 (1966), pp. 116-120, reviewed by G.W. Mac Rae, in *NTA* 10, n. 3 (1966), p. 358, n. 980.

49. S. Sandmel, *A Jewish Understanding of the New Testament* (New York: 1960), p. 83; cfr. W.G. Kümmel, *art. cit.*, pp. 411-412.

50. K. Thieme, *Die Struktur des ersten Thesslonicher-Briefes*, in *Abraham unser Vater. Festschrift für O. Michel (Arbeiten zur Geschichte des Spätjudentums und Christentums* 5, Leiden-Köln: 1963), pp. 450-458.

51. W. Schmithals, *Die Thessalonicherbriefe als Briefkompositionen*, in *Zeit und Geschichte. Festschr. R. Bultmann* (Tübingen: 1964), pp. 295-315.

52. W. Marxsen, *Einleitung in das Neue Testament* 2nd ed. (Gutersloh: 1964), pp. 43-44. The contrary opinion in R.M. Grant, *A Historical Introduction to the New Testament* (London: 1963), pp. 176-179, and J.L. Price, *Interpreting the New Testament* (New York: 1961), pp. 361-369.

53. L.M. Dewailly, *La jeune église de Thessalonique* (*Lectio divina* 37, Paris: 1963); *Translator's Note*: R. Gregson, *A Solution to the Problems of the Thessalonian Epistles*, in *EvT* 38 (1966), pp. 76-80, proposed that the present sequence of the two letters should be inverted because the eschatology of 1 Thes is more mature, much more complete, and its joyfully assured tone would be a fitting sequel to the anxiety of 2 Thes.

54. P. Neuenzeit, *Das Herrenmahl* (*Studien zum A. u. N.T.*, 1, Munich: 1960), pp. 23-25. Also the critical review of R. Mc L. Wilson, in *ScotJT* 15 (1962), pp. 324-327.

55. A.M.G. Stephenson, *Partition Theories on 2 Corinthians* (*Stud. Ev. II. Texte und Unters. 87*, Berlin: 1964), pp. 639-646.

56. J.C. Hurd, Jr., *The Origin of 1 Corinthians* (London: 1965). *Translator's Note*: reviewed by W.G. Kümmel in *TLZ* 91 (1966), pp. 505-508; also by L.W. Barnard, *1 Corinthians*, in *ChQR* 166 (1965), pp. 516-517, who appreciated the insights, but did not accept the main argument. K. Prümm, *Zur neutestamentlichen Gnosis-Problematik. Gnostischer Hintergrund und Lehreinschlag in den beiden Eingangskapiteln von I Kor?*, in *ZKT* 87 (1965), pp. 399-442; 88 (1966), pp. 1-50, rejected any Gnostic connections where biblical thought as an explanatory background is nearer at hand - in criticism of U. Wilcken's insistence on gnostic influences in *Weisheit und Torheit* (1959); J.N. Sanders, *First Corinthians 13. Its Interpretation Since the First World War*, in *Int* 20 (1966), pp. 159-187.

57. D. Georgi, *Die Gegner des Paulus im 2 Korintherbrief. Studien zur religiösen Propaganda in der Spätantike* (*Wissenschaftliche Monographien z. A. u. N.T.*, 11, Neukirchen: 1964); *Translator's Note*: see also W.H. Bates, *The Integrity of II Corinthians*, in *NTS* 12 (1965), pp. 56-69; recapitulation by G.W. Mac Rae in *NTA* 10, n.2 (1966), pp. 217-218, n. 607: 2 Cor. 10-13 can be explained by analogy with Gal. 5-6; J. Harrison, *St. Paul's Letters to the Corinthians*, in *ExpT* 77 (1966), pp. 285-286, stated that 1 Cor.1, 1-4,21 and 2 Cor.10,1-13, 14 together might well form one complete letter because of the same strands of thought.

58. G. Friedrich, *Gegner des Paulus im Korintherbrief*, in *Abraham unser Vater. Festschrift für O. Michel* (Leiden-Cologne: 1963), pp. 181-215. Cfr. C.K. Barrett, *Cephas and Corinth, ibid.*, pp. 1-12, claims that Peter had been to Corinth. Moreover, he was not Paul's opponent, but rather the judeo-Christians - for an analogous situation, see Gal. 2, 12.

59. R.G. Hoerler, *Galatians 2 1-10 and the Acts of the Apostles*, in *ConTM* 31 (1960), pp. 482-491; C.E. Faw, *The Anomaly of Galatians*, in *Biblical Research* 4 (1960), pp. 25-38; H.L. Ramsey, *The Place of Galatians in the Career of Paul* (Ph.D. Thesis, Columbia University, 1960; Ann Arbor, Michigan, University Microfilms Inc.: 1961). *Translator's Note*: V. Mancebo, *Gal. II*, 1-10 *y Act. XV. Estado actual de la cuestion*, in *EstBib* 22 (1963), pp. 315-350.

60. R.C.M. Ruys, *De Struktuur van de Brief aan de Romeinen. Een stilistische, vormhistorische en thematische analyse van Rom 1 16 - 3 23* (Utrecht-Nijmwegen: 1964), with excellent bibliography on pp. xxxxii. *Translator's Note*: cfr. observations which argue that Rom. 13, 1-7 is an interpolation by J. Kallas, *Romans xiii*. 1-7: *An Interpolation*, in *NTS* 11 (1965), pp. 365-374, summarized by G.W. Mac Rae in *NTA* 10, n. 2 (1966), p. 216, n. 600; H.W. Bartsch, *Die historische Situation des Römerbriefes*, in *ComV* 8 (1965), pp. 199-208, argues that Romans is not a theoretical doctrinal letter of introduction, but one that was occasioned by a split between Jews and Gentiles within Roman Christianity; B. Noack, *Current and Backwater in the Epistle to the Romans*, in *ST* 19 (1965), pp. 155-166, argues that the main current of Paul's argument is to be found in 1,1-17; 3-9-20: 27-31; chapter 4; and chapters 9-11. Therefore, chapters 9-11 are not an independent literary unit inserted as some kind of parenthesis.

61. A. Feuillet, *Le plan salvifique de Dieu d'après l'épître aux Romains. Essai sur la structure littéraire de l'épître et sa signification théologique*, in *RB* 57 (1950), pp. 336-387, 489-529; S. Lyonnet, *Note sur le plan de l'épître aux Romains*, in *RSR* 39-40 (1951-1952), pp. 301-316; J. Dupont, *Le problème de la structure littéraire de l'épître aux Romains*, in *RB* 62 (1955), pp. 365-397; Suitbertus a S. Joanne a Cruce, *De structura idearum in ep. ad Romanos*, in *VD* 34 (1956), pp. 68-87; X. Leon-Dufour, *Juif et Gentil dans l'Épître aux Romains*, in *SP. Congressus* 1961 (*Analecta Biblica* 17, Rome: 1963), pp. 309-315; idem, *Situation litteraire de Rom. V*, in *RSR* 51 (1963), pp. 83-95; A. Descamps, *La structure de Rom. 1-11*, in *SP. Congressus* 1961 (*Analecta Biblica* 17, Rome: 1963), pp. 3-14. Among the Protestants, see E. Ortigues, *La composition de l'épître aux Romains (I-VIII)*, in *VC* 8 (1954), pp. 52-81; F.F. Bruce, *St. Paul in Rome*, in *BJRL* 46 (1963-1964), pp. 326gg; K.H. Rengstorf, *Paulus und die römische Christenheit*, in *Studia Evangelica II* (*Texte und Unters.*, 87, Berlin: 1964), pp. 447-464; A. Roosen, *Le genre littéraire de l'Épître aux Romains, ibid.*, pp. 465-471; R. Grayston, *"Not Ashamed of the Gospel". Rom. 1 16a and the Structure of the Epistle, ibid.*, pp. 574-583; J. Kinoshita, *Romans - Two Writings Combined. A New Interpretation of the Body of Romans*, in *NT* 7 (1965), pp. 258-277, a very simple solution. Cfr. A.F.N. Lekkerkerker, *De Brief van Paulus aan de Romeinen, I* (*1 1 a 8 39*) (Nijkerk: 1962). For an example of a thorough examination of chiasmus, cfr. K. Grobel, *A Chiastic Retribution-Formula in Romans 2*, in *Zeit und Geschichte. Danksgabe an R. Bultmann* (Tubingen: 1964), pp. 255-261.

62. W.G. Kümmel, *Einleitung*, pp. 227-229. *Translator's Note*: as a separate composition and earlier than 1 Cor, see J.R. Richards, *Romans and I Corinthians: Their Chronological Relationship and Comparative Dates*, in *NTS* 13 (1966), pp. 14-30.

63. J. Müller-Bardorff, *Zur Frage der literarischen Einheit des Philipperbriefes*, in *Wiss. Zeitschr. der Friedrich-Schiller-Universität, Gesellschaft- und Sprachwissenschaftl. Reihe* 4 (Jena: 1957-1958), pp. 591-604; G. Bornkamm, *Der Philipperbrief als paulinische Briefsammlung*, in *Neotestamentica et Patristica. Festschr. O. Cullmann* (Leiden: 1962), pp. 192-202; also G. Delling, in *RGG* 5 (1961), pp. 333ff; H. Koester, *The Purpose of the Polemic of a Pauline Fragment (Phil III)*, in *NTS* 8 (1961-1962), pp. 317-332. *Translator's Note*: T.E. Pollard, *The Integrity of Philippians*, in *NTS* 13 (1966), pp. 57-66, follows the lead of M. Jones and P. Bonnard on the theological integrity of the letter which extends through chapter 3 in a triple parallelism, plus two other arguments he develops himself: 1) combination of illusions to Is. 53 and 45 which underlies both the hymn of chapter 2 and also 3-9-10; 2) six notable verbal relationships between chapter 3 and the rest of the letter. Concerning Phil.4,12 where Paul uses the language of the mysteries, cfr. D. O'Callaghan, *Christianity and the Mystery Cults*, in *ITQ* 32 (1965), pp. 241-245, where it is stated that primitive Christianity borrowed the term "mystery" from the LXX, and not from these cults.

64. Cfr. D. Georgi, *Der vorpaulinische Hymnus Phil 2 6-11*, in *Zeit und Geschichte. Dankesgabe an R. Bultmann* (Tübingen: 1964), pp. 263-293; J. Jeremias, *Zu Phil 2 7*, in *NT* 4 (1963), pp. 182-188; G. Strecker, *Redaktion und Tradition des Christushymnus Phil.2:6-11*, in *ZNW* 55 (1964), pp. 63-78, *Translator's Note*: also in *TLZ* 89 1964), pp. 521-522, in summary form; A. Feuillet, *L'hymne christologique de l'Épître aux Philippiens (ii, 6-11)*, in *RB* 72 (1965), pp. 352-380, 481-507, together with J. Coppens, *Les affinités littéraires de l'hymne christologique Phil., II, 6-11*, in *ETL* 42 (1966), pp. 238-241.

65. V. Furnish, *The Place and Purpose of Philippians III*, in *NTS* 10 1963-1964), pp. 80-88; A.F.J. Klijn, *Paul's Opponents in Philippians III*, in *NT* 7 (1965), pp. 278-284.

66. P. Benoit, *Paul. Épître aux Colossiens*, in *DBS* 7,36 (1961), pp. 157-170; G. Bornkamm, *Die Hoffnung im Kolosserbrief - zugleich ein Beitrag zur Echtheit des Briefes*, in *Studien zum N.T. u. z. Patristik . . . E. Klostermann (Texte u. Untersuchungen* 77, Berlin: 1961), pp. 56-64. The hymn in Col.1,15-20 still holds the attention of the critics; of particular interest are G. Schille, *Frühcrdistliche Hymnen* (Berlin: 1962); Schattermann, *Studien zum neutestamentlichen Prosahymnus* (Munich: 1965). Specifically on Col.1,15-20: E. Bammel, *Versuch zu Col 1 15-20*, in *ZNW* 52 (1961), pp. 88-95; P. Ellingworth, *Colossians 1 15-20 and its Context*, in *ExpT* 73 (1962), pp. 252-253; K.G. Eckart, *Urchristliche Tauf - und Ordinationsliturgie (Kol 1 9-20; Act 26 18)*, in *TV* 8 (1961-1962), pp. 23-37; H. Hegermann, *Die Vorstellung vom*

Schöpfungsmittler im hellenistischer Judentum und Urchristentum (*Texte und Unters*. 82, Berlin: 1961), pp. 88-110; H.G. Gabathuler, *Jesus Christus, Haupt der Kirche, Haupt der Welt. Der Christushymnus Colosser 1 15-20 in der theologischer Forschung der letzten 130 Jahre* (Zurich: 1965). *Translator's Note*: cfr. also F.F. Bruce, *St. Paul in Rome. 3. The Epistle to the Colossians*, in *BJRL* 48 (1966), pp. 268-285, above other items, claimed that the Colossian heresy shows the influence, not particularly of Qumran, but of nonconformist Judaism; E. Yamauchi, *Qumran and Colosse*, in *BS* 121 (1964), pp. 141-152, concluded that the Colossian heresy reflects a stage of doctrinal evolution subsequent to Jewish Heterodoxy and prior to the development of later gnosticism, since some features of Colossians are quite dissimilar to Qumran's views, while others have greater affinities with the gnostics at Chenoboskion; E.P. Sanders, *Literary Dependence in Colossians*, in *JBL* 85 (1966), pp. 28-45, leaves Ephesians out of the discussion to check Colossians against the genuine Pauline letters on the basis of literary dependence; cfr. review of J.R. Michaels, in *NTA* 10, n. 3 (1966), pp. 369-370, n. 1019.

67. P. Benoit, *Rapports littéraires entre les épîtres aux Col. et aux Ephésiens*, in *Festschrift J. Schmid* (Regensburg: 1963), pp. 11-22.

68. P. Benoit, *Ephésiens (Épître aux)*, in *DBS* 7,36 (1961), pp. 195-211; P.N. Harrison, *The Author of Ephesians*, in *Studia Evangelica 2 (Texte u. Unters*. 87, Berlin: 1964), pp. 595-604. For the hymn, cfr. S. Lyonnet, *La bénédiction de Eph 1 5-14 et son arrière-plan judaique*, in *Mémorial A. Gelin* (Le Puy: 1961), pp. 341-352. *Translator's Note*: L. Foster, *The Earliest Collection of Paul's Epistles*, in *BETS* 10 (1967), pp. 44-55 nominates Luke as the earliest collector who published 10 (omitting the Pastorals) as a third volume to the Gospel and the Acts; G. Schille, *Frühchristliche Hymnen* (Berlin: 1965), provided precision in the isolating of the particular genre; a summary in *NTA* 10, n.2 (1966), p. 287; J.N. Sanders, *Hymnic Elements in Ephesians 1-3* in *ZNW* 56 (1965), pp. 214-232, reviewed by himself in *NTA* 10, n.3 (1966), p. 367, n. 1010.

69. W.G. Kümmel, *Einleitung*, pp. 267-278. The linguistic method as the criterion for authenticity has been studied by M.P. Brown, *The Authentic Writings of Ignatius. A Study of Linguistic Criteria* (1963).

70. E. Earle Ellis, *Paul and His Recent Interpreters*, pp. 49-57; J. Jeremias, *Zur Datierung der Pastoralbriefe*, in *ZNW* 52 (1961), pp. 101-104; C. Spicq, *Pastorals (Épîtres)*, in *DBS* 7,36 (1961), pp. 1-73; J. Jeremias and H. Strathmann, *Die Briefe an Timotheus und Titus. Der Brief an die Hebräer*, 8th ed. (N.T. Deutsch, 9, Göttingen: 1963). A similar opinion in J. Mc Ray, *The Authorship of the Pastoral Epistles*, in *RQ* 7 (1963), pp. 2-18; J. Schmid, art. *Pastoralbriefe*, in *LTK* 8 (1963), pp. 155-158; also J. Kohl, *Verfasser und Entstehungzeit der Pastoralbriefe im Lichte der neueren Kritik* (Wien: 1964).

71. C.K. Barrett, *The Pastoral Epistles (New Clarendon Bible*, London-New York: 1962), pp. 4-12; J. Müller-Bardorff, *Zur Exegese von 1*

Tim 5 3-16, in Gott und die Götter. Festgabe für L. Fascher (Berlin: 1958), pp. 113ff.; W. Schmithals, art. *Pastoralbriefe*, in *RGG* 3rd ed., 5 (1961), 144 ff.; K. Wegenast, *Das Verständnis der Tradition bei Paulus und in den Deuteropaulinen* (*Wissenschaftl. Monographien z. A. u. N.T.*, 8, Neukirchen: 1962), pp. 132ff.; J.A. Allan, *The "in Christ" Formula in the Pastoral Epistles*, in *NTS* 10 (1963-1964), pp. 115-121.

72. C.F.D. Moule, *The Problem of the Pastoral Epistles. A Reappraisal*, in *BJRL* 47 (1965), pp. 430-452. The hypothesis of an *amanuensis* is also admitted by J. Jeremias. Moule had already proposed this solution in *The Birth of the New Testament* (*Black's New Testament Commentaries*, London: 1961), pp. 220-221.

73. P.N. Harrison, (London: 1964).

74. L. Cerfaux, *L'itinéraire spirituel de saint Paul* (*Lire le Bible* 4, Paris: 1966), pp. 185-186. *Translator's Note*: English translation, *The Spiritual Journey of Saint Paul* (New York: 1968), p. 211. The analysis of 1 Clement by K. Beyschlag, *Clemens Romanus und der Frühkatholizismus. Untersuchungen zu 1 Clemens 1-7*, (*Beiträge zur historischen Theologie* 35, Tübingen: 1966) interestingly concludes that Roman traditions other than those in the New Testament were current very early in the Church. For further information on the Pastorals, cfr. J.N.D. Kelly, *The Pastoral Epistles. I Timothy. II Timothy. Titus* (*Harper's New Testament Commentaries*, New York: 1964), reviewed with praise by J. Schmid in *BZ* 11 (1967), pp. 145-146, defends Pauline authenticity, particularly by rejecting the fragment hypothesis, but according to J.J. Collins in *NTA* 11, n.3 (1967), p. 343, n. 1136r, the defense does not seem to give sufficient weight to the counter arguments; J.W. Roberts, *The Genuineness of the Pastorals: Some Recent Aspects of the Question*, in *RQ* 8 (1965), pp. 104-110, which contrasts the major points of J.N.D. Kelly with C.K. Barrett, *The Pastoral Epistles* in the New English Bible (London: 1963), who denied Pauline authorship.

75. J.N. Sanders, *The Transition from Opening Epistolary Thanksgiving to Body in the Letters of the Pauline Corpus*, in *JBL* 81 (1962), pp. 348-365.

76. W.G. Kümmel, *Einleitung*, pp. 175-179; W. Marxsen, *Einleitung*, pp. 26-31.

77. R. Le Déaut, *Traditions targuminques dans le Corpus paulinien?* in *Bib* 42 (1961), pp. 28-48; P. Grelot, *Études néotestamentaires et sources haggadiques*, in *Bib* 42 (1961), pp. 455-459; M. Gertner, *Midrashim in the New Testament*, in *Journal of Semitic Studies* 7 (1962), pp. 267-292. Also J.A. Fitzmyer, *A Feature of Qumran Angelology and the Angels of 1 Co 11 10*, in *NTS* 4 (1957-1958), pp. 48-58; *idem, Qumran and the Interpolated Paragraph in 1 Cor 6 14 - 7 1*, in *CBQ* 23 (1961), pp. 271-280. H.M. Gale, *The Use of Analogy in the Letters of Paul* (Philadelphia: 1964); L. Goppelt, *Apokalyptik und Theologie bei Paulus*, in *TLZ* 89 (1964); D.B. Bronson, *Paul and Apocalyptic Judaism*, in *JBL* 83 (1964), pp. 287-292.

78. W. Schrage, *Die konkreten Einzelgebote in der paulinischen Paränese. Ein Beitrag zur neutestamentlichen Ethik* (Gutersloh: 1961).

79. E. Kamlah, *Die Form der katalogischen Paränese im Neuen Testament* (*Wissenschaftl. Untersuch. z. N.T.* 7, Tübingen: 1964).

80. V.H. Neufeld, *The Eearliest Christian Confessions* (*New Testament Tools and Studies* 5, Leiden: 1963). *Translator's Note*: cfr. the reviews of O.C. Edwards in *JRel* 45 (1965), pp. 55-56, and J.J. Collins in *NTA* 9 (1964-1965), p. 414, n.1161r. H. Conzelmann, *Zur Analyse der Bekenntnisformel I. Kor. 15, 3-5*, in *EvT* 25 (1965), pp. 1-11, in English translation, *On the Analysis of the Confessional Formula in I Corinthians 15:3-5*, in *Int* 20 (1966), pp. 15-25.

81. E. Grässer, *Der Hebräerbrief 1938-1963*, in *TRu*, new series 30 (1964), pp. 138-230. *Translator's Note*: praised by C.F.D. Moule in *JTS* 17 (1966), pp. 147-150, but indicated that some questions were unanswered; also O. Michel, in *TLZ* 91 (1966), pp. 35-36 with reservations; A. Vanhoye, in *Bib* 47 (1966), pp. 139-141, criticized particularly the manipulation of the expression *pistis*.

82. *Translator's Note*: H. Chadwick, *St. Paul and Philo of Alexandria*, in *BJRL* 48 (1966), pp. 286-307, states that Hebrews seems to depend directly on Philo.

83. *Translator's Note*: H. Mulder, *Barnabas en de Gemeente te Jeruzalem*, in *HomBib* 24 (1965), pp. 198-200, proposed that the hypothesis of Barnabas' authorship of Hebrews helps to explain both form and content; also *De schrijver van de Brief aan de Hebreeën*, in *HomBib* 24 (1965), pp. 110-114; K.J. Thomas, *The Old Testament Citations in Hebrews*, in *NTS* 11 (1965), pp. 303-325, indicated that the LXX used in Hebrews is a primitive text rather than an "edited" one; stylistic unity in Heb.9,15-18 to unity of outlook, in J. Sweetnam, *A Suggested Interpretation of Hebrews 9,15-18*, in *CBQ* 27 (1965), pp. 373-390. W. Hillmann, O.F.M., *Der Brief an die Hebräer*, ed. J. Hillmann, *Die Welt der Bibel, Kleinkommentare zur Heiligen Schrift* (Düsseldorf: 1965). A discussion on some style forms as, 1) terms of necessity and logical conclusions; 2) rhetorical questions; and comparisons by W.C. Linss, *Logical Terminology in the Epistle to the Hebrews*, in *ConTM* 37 (1966), pp. 365-369. H. Montefiore, *The Epistle to the Hebrews* (*Harper's New Testament Commentaries*, New York-Evanston, Ill.: 1965) suggested in his introduction that Apollos may have written Hebrews as a letter to Corinth some time between 52 and 54 A.D., and that it should be read against the historical setting of 1 Cor - heavily criticized by G. Johnston, in *JBL* 85 (1966), pp. 96-98, and S. Mac L. Gilmour in *CanJT* 12 (1966), pp. 220-221. M.C. Tenney, *A New Approach to the Book of Hebrews*, in *BS* 123 (1966), pp. 230-236, held that the composition seems to belong to a period of social and religious confusion during which Christians were compelled to reorient themselves at a time midway between the beginning of the Church with Judaism and the final separation from it. F.F. Bruce, *The Epistle to the Hebrews. The English Text with Introduction, Ex-*

position and Notes, (*The New International Commentary on the New Testament*, Grand Rapids, Michigan: 1964), surveys recent research on the much disputed matters of the addressees, date and authorship together with a lengthy bibliography.

84. Cfr. F.C. Synge, *Hebrews and the Scriptures* (London: 1959); L. Vaganay, *Le plan de l'épître aux Hébreux* (*Hb 8 1 - 9 28*), in *Mémorial Lagrange* (Paris: 1940), pp. 269-277; R. Gyllenberg, *Die Komposition des Hebräerbriefes*, in *SEA* 22/23 (1957-1958), pp. 137-147.

85. A. Vanhoye, *La structure littéraire de l'Épître aux Hébreux* (*Studia Neotestamentica* 1, Bruges: 1963); *idem, Structure littéraire et thèmes bibliques de l'Épître aux Hébreux*, in *SP Congressus* 1961, 2 (Rome: 1963), English translation in 1964; *idem, Les indices de structure littéraire de l'Épître aux Hébreux*, in *Studia Evangelica* 2 (1964), pp. 493-505.

86. E. Grässer, *Der Glaube im Hebräerbrief* (*Marburger Theol. Stud.2*, Marburg: 1965), with bibliography on pp. 221-237. Compare D.M. Stine, *The Finality of the Christian Faith. A Study of the Unfolding of the Argument of the Epistle to the Hebrews* (dissertation, Princeton: 1964). Of all studies on Hebrews, the question that has attracted most attention is the relation of the letter to the Old Testament: cfr. W.L. Duliere, *Les Chérubins du troisième Temple à Antioche*, together with its complement, *Antioche et la lettre aux Hébreux. Essai de datation de la lettre aux Hébreux*, in *ZRG* 13 (1961), pp. 216-279; C. Spicq, *Paul. Épître aux Hébreux*, in *DBS* 7 (1961), pp. 226-279; F.F. Bruce, "*To the Hebrews*" or "*To the Essences*", in *NTS* 9 (1962-1963), pp. 217-232; M. Barth, *The Old Testament in Hebrews. An Essay in Biblical Hermeneutics*, in *Festschrift O.A. Piper* (New York: 1962), pp. 53-78, 263-273; C. Smits, *Oud-testamentlische citaten in het N.T. Deel IV. De Brief aan de Hebreeën. Het O.T. in het Nieuwe. Algemeene Beschouwingen*, in *ColFrN* 8/4 ('s Hertogenbosch: 1963), pp. 551-744; B.P.W.S. Hunt, *The "Epistle to the Hebrews": An Anti-Judaic Treatise*, in *Studia Evangelica* 2 (1964), pp. 408-410; S. Kistemaker, *The Psalm Citations in the Epistle to the Hebrews* (Amsterdam: 1961); J. de Vuyst, *Oud en Nieuw Verbond in de brief aan de Hebreeën* (Diss. Hoogeschool v.d.Geref.Kerken in Nederland, Kampen: 1964).

87. John Bligh, *Chiastic Analysis of the Epistle to the Hebrews* (Oxon, England: 1966).

88. cfr. *CBQ* (1967), p. 134.

INDEX OF AUTHORS

262